Silent Spring at 50

THE FALSE CRISES OF RACHEL CARSON

Silent Spring at 50

Edited by Roger Meiners, Pierre Desrochers, and Andrew Morriss

CATO INSTITUTE
WASHINGTON, D.C.

Library of Congress Cataloging-in-Publication Data

Silent spring at 50 / edited By Roger Meiners, Pierre Desrochers, and Andrew Morriss.
  p. cm.
  Includes bibliographical references and index.
  ISBN 978-1-937184-99-5 (hardback : alk. paper)
  1. Carson, Rachel, 1907-1964. Silent spring. 2. Pesticides--Environmental aspects.
3. Pesticides--Toxicology. 4. Pesticides and wildlife. 5. Insect pests--Biological
control. I. Meiners, Roger E. II. Desrochers, Pierre, 1969- III. Morriss, Andrew P.,
1960-

QH545.P4C386 2012
363.738'4—dc23   2012026669

Cover design by Jon Meyers.

Printed in the United States of America.

CATO INSTITUTE
1000 Massachusetts Ave., N.W.
Washington, D.C. 20001
www.cato.org

Contents

1. *Silent Spring* at 50

Roger Meiners, Pierre Desrochers, and Andrew Morriss

Rachel Carson's *Silent Spring*, the book widely credited with launching the modern environmental movement, turned 50 in 2012. The book sparked controversy at its inception. It was serialized in the *New Yorker* a few months before the launch of its first 40,000-copy run, and that was soon followed by an order for 150,000 copies by the Book-of-the-Month Club. Some praised its clear writing on technical topics and calls for major changes in how the world used man-made chemicals. Others attacked it as misrepresenting science.

Because of its profound impact on American popular culture, *Silent Spring* quickly became more than just a book. President John F. Kennedy commented positively on it and asked his Science Advisory Committee to examine issues it raised. CBS produced a favorable special program, "The *Silent Spring* of Rachel Carson," in 1963. That attention helped lead to creation of a Senate subcommittee before which Carson testified. Her death from cancer in 1964 further enhanced her mystique and that of her book. Today, *Silent Spring* remains an important document in our intellectual, environmental, and political histories. Its 50th anniversary is a fitting time to reassess its legacy.

Silent Spring and Rachel Carson are much remembered in 2012, and rightly so. The runaway best-seller captured something quite important about America in 1962, and its author is hailed as one of the great nonfiction writers of our time. Indeed, *Silent Spring* has now achieved something of an iconic status that generally shields it from sustained critical inquiries. This book attempts to fill this void by looking at the legacy of *Silent Spring* from a variety of viewpoints. We asked the authors who contributed chapters to this volume to assess *Silent Spring* with the benefit of 50 years' distance. Our objectives as editors were to put the book into the context of its time, evaluate how the science it was built upon has held up, and examine the policy consequences of its core ideas. Some conclusions reached by our contributing authors might surprise those who have not recently read *Silent Spring* or who know of it only from its general reputation.

Part I of the book has three chapters that put *Silent Spring* into its historical context. Environmental activist, author, English professor, and property developer Wallace Kaufman relates *Silent Spring* to the larger intellectual story of Carson's life in Chapter 2. He asks why this book caught America by storm, but similar books published at the time did not. Kaufman uses his own environmental awakening to connect Carson's prior books on the sea with *Silent Spring* and makes informed guesses as to her unequalled capacity to reach ordinary Americans. He also shows how *Silent Spring* differed from Carson's celebration of the natural world in her earlier writings through the "despair, anger, and urgency" that emanates from most of its pages. Moreover, Kaufman explores Carson's long interest in the subject of pesticides, contradicting the widely held belief that she came to the subject only in the late 1950s.

In Chapter 3, Pierre Desrochers and Hiroko Shimizu put Carson into the context of a long tradition of authors who warned against human hubris in environmental matters. *Silent Spring* was an environmental blockbuster in its day, but it was not alone. Consumer activists, along with advocates of organic farming and population control, had long been concerned by the threats to human health posed by synthetic chemicals and the environmental impact of a rapidly growing population. Other books echoed many of the same themes as Carson; some sold well, but others did not. Understanding how these ideas were already a significant part of the marketplace of ideas helps us see why Carson's more fluid prose was able to capture the public's attention. Their analysis suggests *Silent Spring* was less ground-breaking than it is now typically thought to have been, and they identify Carson's most important contribution as her ability to reach out to a broad audience rather than the originality of her ideas.

Economist Robert Nelson then situates *Silent Spring* in the contest between environmentalism and economics to define America's "civic religion." The book emerged at a time when the "gospel" of progress and efficiency had long been dominant. Tracing this "economic religion" back to the Progressive Era's faith that greater material progress could transform the world into "heaven on earth," Nelson puts Carson's views into the context of the growing movement in the 1950s that sought to reject this as "heresy." Carson helped focus attention on the dangers inherent in man's efforts to dominate nature by using popular science to reframe a traditional Protestant message of mankind in a fallen world. Her role in this larger struggle helps explain both the book's remarkable staying power with the public and some problems for it caused by later scientific advances.

Part II of this volume provides a different set of perspectives on *Silent Spring*: how does it relate to the science and politics of the time in which it was written? In Chapter 5, Desrochers and Shimizu return to consider the evidence then available on a key issue. The central metaphor of *Silent Spring*—a town where "no birds sang"— rested on the impact of synthetic pesticide use on bird populations. But were bird populations in imminent danger of collapsing in the early 1960s? Carson was intimately involved with the Audubon Society, so she had to know of its bird count data. Yet, as the authors show, she ignored information that directly contradicted her claims about birds being decimated by pesticides.

In Chapter 6, Roger Meiners notes that a major reason for the book's impact on the public was the frightening vision it portrayed of increases in cancers from man-made chemical exposure. He finds that Carson neglected to make key statistical adjustments for population age and tobacco use. After making the proper statistical and logical adjustments, he notes the rise in cancer rates that so alarmed *Silent Spring*'s readers disappears. Despite her reputation as a careful writer widely praised for building her arguments on science and facts, Carson's bestseller contained significant errors and sins of omission.

In Chapter 7, conservation biologist Nathan Gregory examines Carson's view of nature. Like her contemporaries, she focused on the importance of "the balance of nature." Her concerns about maintaining this balance led her to argue in favor of greater use of biological controls and against excessive pesticide use. Since *Silent Spring*'s publication, conservation biology—a discipline still in its formative stage in Carson's day—has made great strides in understanding the interrelationships within ecosystems. Today, as Gregory illustrates with examples drawn from his own work in Kenya, there is a more complex view of the resilience of nature and the process of change, with greater concern for the impact of the introduction of invasive species as measures for biological control. Because it is based on a now obsolete scientific perspective, *Silent Spring* should no longer be used as a guide by policymakers concerned with the management of ecosystems.

Perhaps Rachel Carson's greatest sin of omission in *Silent Spring* was that she focused almost entirely on pesticide use in agriculture and essentially ignored pesticides' public health role, particularly that of DDT in controlling malaria and other diseases transmitted by insects. This gap is all the more puzzling because DDT's popularity in the 1950s stemmed from its use in public health campaigns during World War II—which many soldiers personally witnessed. Saving many lives and greatly reducing human misery was the reason Dr. Paul Müller received the Nobel Prize in Physiology or Medicine in 1948 for his role in the discovery of DDT's insecticidal properties. In Chapter 8, Donald Roberts and Richard Tren, who have devoted decades to malaria control, review the evidence about DDT's use for public health purposes—including significant benefits for the poor in the South in the United States—that was known at the time Carson wrote and explore the legacy of its fall from grace.

In Chapter 9, Roger Meiners and Andrew Morriss examine how *Silent Spring*'s concern over agricultural pesticide use fit into the larger political struggle in the 1950s to control the regulation of U.S. food production. *Silent Spring* appeared at the end of a period of rapid transformation of American agriculture by the spread of mechanical and chemical substitutes for labor which radically transformed the American diet. The spread of processed food meant that consumers' growing distance from food production fed into concerns over food safety. At the same time as agriculture was dramatically changing, the U.S. Department of Agriculture was struggling to resist efforts by the Food and Drug Administration to play a larger role in regulating food production. Focusing on early 1950s congressional hearings, Meiners and Morriss show how that struggle influenced *Silent Spring*'s impact.

Part III turns to examining *Silent Spring*'s legacy in the policy arena. In Chapter 10, law professor Jonathan Adler explains how Carson's arguments set in motion two important chains of events that resulted in increased federalization of pesticide regulation. First, amendments to the federal pesticide statute in 1964 incorporated Carson's concern with impacts on nontarget species, setting the stage for the battle to cancel DDT's registration in the early 1970s. Second, Carson's impact on public opinion led to an increase in state regulatory efforts with respect to pesticides, giving pesticide manufacturers an incentive to preempt such efforts by moving regulation to the federal level. Far from being a victory for pesticide control advocates, the one-size-fits-all federal regulation undercut active efforts at the state level that provided important information about chemical use that differed from the Washington orthodoxy.

In Chapter 11, Larry Katzenstein, a professional science writer and editor like Rachel Carson, discusses her role in popularizing what would later be termed the "precautionary principle." Cast as being based on sound science and profoundly commonsensical (innovators must "prove" that no harm can come from anything new), the precautionary principle has actually retarded the adoption of innovations that, while not perfect, were arguably less damageable alternatives than previous imperfect practices. Katzenstein relates episodes of advances that have been rejected because of superstition about something new. Such attitudes have costly consequences for human well-being and the environment in general.

In the last chapter, law professor and geneticist Gary Marchant expands on this theme by examining how the "you can never be too safe" stance of Carson and many of her contemporaries came to permeate the American legislative agenda of the 1960s and 1970s. By translating a simplistic risk paradigm about environmental toxicity into ineffective, inefficient, and often impossible standards, Marchant argues, the individuals who shared Carson's fundamentally flawed vision in effect stalled real progress. Now transformed into the "precautionary principle," this approach to risk may be the most enduring legacy of *Silent Spring*.

The chapters in this book suggest that the legacy of the book is mixed. It is a key historical document that must be read to understand the evolution of environmentalism. Carson intended to shock the public out of its ignorant complacency about the state of the environment. At the very end of her book she says that "Stone Age" and "Neanderthal . . . science has armed itself with the most modern and terrible weapons." The result has been that our turning these chemical weapons "against the insects . . . has also turned them against the earth."[1]

She accomplished that goal and our world is different than if she had not written when she did or as well as she did. But as a number of the authors in this volume note, *Silent Spring* was as much a product of its time and larger intellectual forces as it was an influence on later developments. Perhaps we cannot imagine the crowds at Earth Day in 1970 or Richard Nixon creating the Environmental Protection Agency without Rachel Carson, but we also cannot imagine *Silent Spring* without the role of the more problematic authors described by Desrochers and Shimizu, the struggle between environmental and economic "civic religions" described by Nelson, or the credibility Carson had earned from her writings on the oceans, as described by Kaufman.

The legacies of *Silent Spring* are mixed at best. Carson influenced American views of the environment in beneficial ways, but—as Desrochers, Shimizu, and Meiners show—some of her major arguments rested on what can only be described as deliberate ignorance. Moreover, she entrenched in the popular imagination views of the "balance of nature" that have now been superseded. She helped end massive, federally subsidized spraying in agriculture and silviculture, but—as Roberts and Tren describe—the human suffering that resulted from the ban on DDT for public health uses is staggering. Finally, *Silent Spring* was not an isolated event, but part of a larger drama created by the changes in American agriculture and food production described by Meiners and Morriss.

Silent Spring also played an important role in shaping subsequent public policy approaches to environmental issues. The book helped federalize environmental issues as Adler discusses, entrenched the ideas that became the precautionary principle in the public imagination, as Marchant explains, and changed how science writers conceived of their role, as Katzenstein illustrates.

Carson never asked for the saint-like status she now holds. She sought to change public policy—the rules by which we live—in a particular direction. To a great extent she did. We need to look clearly at *Silent Spring* as part of our national conversation about the environment rather than treat it as a holy text by a secular saint. The Environmental Protection Agency hosts the annual "Rachel Carson Sense of Wonder Contest."[2] The book is still widely used, in whole or in part, in environmental education and treated as a work of science. Like much conventional wisdom from many decades past, however, it is sadly out of date for educational purposes. Much of what was presented as certainty then was slanted; today we know much of it is simply wrong.

2. The Lady Who Started All This

Wallace Kaufman

"I knew a very wise man . . . [who] believed if a man were permitted to make all the ballads, he need not care who should make the laws of a nation. And we find that most of the ancient legislators thought they could not well reform the manners of any city without the help of a lyric, and sometimes of a dramatic poet."

Andrew Fletcher, Scottish 17th century politician[1]

On May 15, 1963, the diminutive and semi-reclusive science writer Rachel Carson sat alone behind a dozen microphones at a long table facing the famous Senator Abraham Ribicoff flanked by his full committee. The subject of the special hearing was the dangers of chemical pesticides to humans and wildlife. Carson read from the pages of her prepared testimony word for word, in a near monotone, slowly, without a single gesture. The senators listened attentively from their raised platform. Neither her carefully read text nor her cautiously worded answers moved the standing-room-only crowd to shows of approval or disapproval. The woman the senators heard and the bestselling writer who had brought them and all the major news outlets to that room were the same person but two distinct personas. No one watching that testimony in person or later on Fox Movie Tone News[2] could imagine her leading millions of activists in a political crusade. Yet, in less than 10 years, she would become for all time, "the mother of the environmental movement."

Carson was that most uncommon writer who could make science interesting to common people without losing the approval of the scientists who provided her material. In the early 1950s, common people included my blue collar family, whose only bookshelf was inside the upper part of a cheap writing desk. Except for a Bible and three or four *Reader's Digest* books, the shelf was empty. One of the *Digest* books abridged was Rachel Carson's first best seller published in 1951—*The Sea around Us*. Maybe it got onto our shelf because my mother had been an avid swimmer since childhood. And maybe I opened it because I spent every possible minute by, in, or on the water swimming, fishing, and clamming. But non-swimmers and residents of inland America also bought *Reader's Digest* books by the millions, including *The Sea around Us*.

How Rachel Carson became the mother of environmentalism and how I became an environmental activist reveals something important about the environmental movement. On that premise, I ask the reader to indulge me if I use myself as part of the evidence in this chapter. I do it not because I put myself on the same level with Rachel Carson, just the opposite. My movement from a blue-collar family's preoccupation with buying a refrigerator, a stove, and a washing machine— one by one and each on installments—to becoming the leader of three statewide environmental groups is typical of how Carson's influence worked on enough individuals to prepare a political movement.

Come on In, the Water's Wonderful

Maybe my parents bought *The Sea around Us* because, like many Americans, they found the new writing about oceans and ocean voyages filled a need in their lives. It is not a mere fluke that Carson satisfied such needs and won public confidence and applause by writing about the oceans and sea life. Consider the place of the sea in the human psyche. A public fascination with the literature of oceans and ocean travel is as old as literature itself. Over 2000 years ago, the Greeks (or a bard named Homer) embedded in Western popular literature and the vocabularies and cultural touchstones of European languages one of the world's all-time favorite stories, the voyages of Ulysses in *The Odyssey*. In the late 16th and early 17th centuries, ocean travel stories by Daniel Defoe and Richard Hakluyt found large audiences across Europe. Combining the mystical pull of the oceans with art had also made underwater adventure the proven stuff of commercial best sellers. Europeans eagerly devoured the 1697 narrative, *A New Voyage Round the World*, by the English buccaneer and naturalist William Dampier. In 1869, Jules Verne's science fiction novel, *Twenty Thousand Leagues under the Sea*, took millions of readers below the surface into strange new worlds.

Herman Melville captures the root of our fascination with the sea in the first paragraphs of *Moby Dick*: "Let the most absent-minded of men be plunged in his deepest reveries—stand that man on his legs, set his feet a-going, and he will infallibly lead you to water, if water there be in all that region. . . . Surely all this is not without meaning. And still deeper the meaning of that story of Narcissus, who because he could not grasp the tormenting, mild image he saw in the fountain, plunged into it and was drowned. But that same image, we ourselves see in all rivers and oceans. It is the image of the ungraspable phantom of life; and this is the key to it all."[3]

Rachel Carson's first chapter of *The Sea around Us* contains a similar speculation. After bringing a rapid and lyrical summary of earth's history to the evolution of humans, she writes, "Eventually man, too, found his way back to the sea. Standing on its shores, he must have looked but upon it with wonder and curiosity, compounded with an unconscious recognition of his lineage."[4] In many ways, and in a much more easily read form, Carson elaborates Walt Whitman's vision in his well-known poem, "Out of the Cradle Endlessly Rocking." Whitman says that in a transcendental boyhood experience of the sea, "My own songs, awaked from that hour."[5] In that mystical moment, he understood the sea or its voice as being both a cradle and a grave.

In a recent meditation on the prestigious Man Booker Prize for fiction, the novelist Chris Cleave noted how often the prize had been given to narratives in which the ocean is the main setting and often a character in its own right. "This strange power of the sea to give insight is why the Booker, like the great novelists of an earlier epoch, returns time and again to the ocean." Writers like Melville and Conrad, he says, "put to sea in order to prove something about dry land: to survey its limits, to discover more of it, to claim more of life. . . . In these days when the world is all discovered and few of us believe that we will imminently be colonizing outer space, the sea fulfills a new office. It has become the symbol, rather than the enabling medium, of our yearning for the undiscovered. For the strange, for the beautiful, for the outlandish, we now cast our eyes towards the waves."[6]

Rachel Carson had begun to write about the ocean before she ever saw it. In her freshman year at the Pennsylvania College for Women in Pittsburgh, she wrote a term paper in the form of a short story called, "The Master of the Ship's Light." The content of the story, which takes place on the New England coast and on the ocean, was nourished by her avid reading about the sea. Her English instructor commented, "Your style is so good because you have made what might be a relatively technical subject very intelligible to the reader."[7] This talent would be the key to Carson's success and influence for the rest of her life.

Rachel Carson herself had a kind of Whitmanesque revelation and beginning as a writer in the summer of 1929. She graduated from college in June, and in July she left home to begin work as a "beginning investigator" at the prestigious Marine Biological Laboratory in Woods Hole, Massachusetts. Her designated research was a continuation of work she had begun in college—investigating the cranial nerves of turtles. That work, however, interested her much less than the international scientific magazines in the library there, the dissections of marine animals, the long talks with other students and senior scientists, walking along the shore inspecting sea life, and walking the beaches at night listening to the ocean and breathing the sea air. A roommate and friend from college understood that Carson was undergoing a mystical as well as professional transformation.[8] At Woods Hole, she found both the science and the artistic vision that prepared her to become the author of *The Sea around Us*, but first she needed practice and then the right moment in history. Her practice began after her father's death when she had to drop out of the PhD program at Johns Hopkins University to support her mother and sister. She still thought of herself as a scientist, however. When she set up her personnel file at the Johns Hopkins Bureau of Appointments, she listed her profession as "scientific research."[9]

The late 1950s and first years of the 1960s saw a revival of popular ocean documentary. In 1947, Ferdinand Lane published *Mysterious Sea*. Although he wrote clearly, he made up for somewhat plodding prose by reinforcing the mystery with quotations from well-known poets. His first chapter on the origin of oceans begins, "The origin of the oceans is obscure." Carson also began with a chapter on the origin of the oceans and the first sentence, "Beginnings are apt to be shadowy." Carson went on to write a much more popular book than Lane's. She dedicated her book to William Beebe, who had become famous when he and the inventor of the bathysphere, Otis Barton, made record deep descents. Beebe wrote about it for

National Geographic in a 1931 article, "A Round Trip to Davy Jones's Locker."[10] In 1934, the two men reported from more than 3,000 feet down. Ten years later, when Beebe edited *The Book of Naturalists*, its final chapter was an essay by a government science writer named Rachel Carson. They became friends, and he nominated her for the Eugene Saxton Memorial Fellowship that financed the last year of her writing for *The Sea around Us*.

Beebe's book, *Half Mile Down*, came out in 1951, the same year as Carson's. Beebe's book sold well for its suspense and adventure. Carson's book sold much better even though she dove beneath the surface of the sea only once, a 1950 event in Florida where she kept her hold on a boat's ladder while wearing an 84-pound helmet. The other best seller that created the new hunger for ocean books was Thor Heyerdahl's 1951 account of floating across the Pacific on a balsa raft, *Kon Tiki*. He and comrades made the journey to demonstrate the possibility that natives of South America might have been the first humans in Polynesia. I remember how that great adventure awed me not with the migration theory but with the vastness of the ocean and the endless drama of life and death played out on its surface and beneath. Carson admired Heyerdahl and sent him chapters of *The Sea around Us* to read. He returned them with great praise.

Like Defoe, Dampier, Melville, and Verne of earlier centuries, writers who "went to sea" in books during the late 1940s and early 1950s benefitted from readers who sought an alternative or an escape from the worlds they lived in. In the early 1950s, Americans, having survived the misery of the Great Depression and then the uncertainty and horrors of World War II, were ready for art and entertainment that made them feel that the world was wondrous and wide with opportunity for both the mind and the spirit. The American psyche still felt its greatest achievements were physical and its destiny was best fulfilled by discovery. This was both the product of the frontier experience and the reason we still needed a frontier. Space was not yet a possible frontier, a fact I regretted deeply because I was already building little rockets. To my dismay, serious scientists said the physics of energy in fuel and the mass of a rocket made reaching beyond our atmosphere and gravity impossible. So, like the rest of America, I felt the last frontier for physical exploration lay in the depths of the oceans. Rachel Carson understood that the ocean was her chance to become America's frontier guide, but not as a scientist.

Science, in fact, had been the briefest of detours in her life, though a passionate and useful detour. From her first published story at age 10 in *St. Nicholas Magazine* for children, she had thought of herself as a writer. Her detour into hands-on science had begun when she changed majors in college from English to biology. But when she took a position as a biologist with the U.S. Bureau of Fish and Wildlife Services in the Commerce Department, her job there was as a writer, summarizing, then popularizing the work of scientists in the lab and in the field.

In 1945, when she tried to leave government service and applied for a job at *Reader's Digest*, she described herself to its owner DeWitt Wallace as a scientist first. "Probably the most important single point to bring to the attention of the *Digest* is the fact that I am that comparatively rare phenomenon, a scientist who is also a writer."[11] When she told Quincy Howe, a senior editor at Simon and Schuster, why she wanted the *Digest* job, she confirmed that she now saw herself as a public guide to nature and science. "I feel very strongly that the reporting of the progress of science is going to assume even greater importance in the months and years to come. We are all aware that startling developments have come, or are on the way, that cannot be talked about at the present time. When the necessary restrictions are lifted some very important stories will be told to the American public, and undoubtedly the *Digest* will take the lead in presenting them."[12] She also seemed to sense Americans' readiness to welcome wonders and the miraculous after years of economic depression and war. The miraculous could be natural or technological. From her wartime writing, she knew that technology had given humankind new powers to explore and understand nature.

Science writer would continue to be her profession despite holding jobs whose title included "biologist." Her first government assignment came in 1935 when Elmer Higgins, a division chief at the U.S. Bureau of Fisheries, asked her to take over the production of a public radio series, "Romance under the Waters." Several other government workers had had a go at it with poor results. Carson took on the short-term assignment and made the series a success. A relieved Higgins asked her to write an introduction to a government brochure on marine life. In April 1936, she handed Higgins the 11-page essay "World of Waters." Carson remembered that he said, "I don't think it will do. Better try again. But send this one to *The Atlantic*."[13] A year later, she did send the essay to *The Atlantic* with this opening paragraph: "The charting of the white wastes of Antarctica is accomplished; the conquest of Mount Everest has passed into history. But although the flags of explorers have waved on the highest peaks of the world and floated on the frozen rims of the continents, a vast unknown remains, the world of waters. Even from those who have spent their lives in patient questioning, the sea knows how to guard its secrets well. To most it is, in very truth, a *'mare incognita'*."[14] She did not have to say the obvious—that herewith she would be the reader's guide to the sea, the last frontier. Nor did she realize at the time that successful American frontier guides become national heroes.

The Atlantic bought the article, and Carson, for the first time, used her full name. She had previously agreed with her colleagues at Fisheries that readers would be more comfortable with R. L. Carson because they could and probably would assume the writer was a man. After all, guides to a frontier, not to mention almost all famous and trusted scientists, were men. The venerable *Atlantic* had always been a trend-setter that endowed the new writers it published with standing in the literary community. Rachel Carson soon found new friends and supporters. Although she would labor in the relative obscurity of government bureaucracy for another 14 years before she became a household name, the future was hers to lose. Both financially and professionally, she was determined not to lose it. The path from her four-page article, retitled "Undersea," to *The Sea around Us* was straight and without detours or lapses. Like her much loved mother, once she had decided on a course, she would not be deterred. She went back to Johns Hopkins to update her employment dossier. Now she listed herself as a part-time "feature writer of scientific subjects" working in the U.S. Bureau of Fisheries "educational division."[15]

One of her first new friends after "Undersea" appeared in *The Atlantic* was the prolific historian and best-selling author Dr. Hendrik Willem van Loon. He wrote her an enthusiastic letter saying, "Maybe Jules Verne and his *20,000 Leagues under the Sea* started me 60 years ago, but I have always wanted to read something about that mysterious world and suddenly . . . In the *Atlantic*, most appropriately . . . I found your article which shows that you are the woman . . . [who can help me.]"[16] No one can say if these were his own words or a paraphrase of what *Atlantic* editor Ed Weeks wrote in the Contributors' Column about

Carson: "Ever since Jules Verne's imagination went twenty thousand leagues deep, people have wondered what it would be like to walk on the ocean's floor. Rachel Carson has a clear and accurate idea."[17] Both men implicitly recognized and accepted the role that Carson would play later on the public stage—a trusted guide to science and nature.

Van Loon pushed her in that direction by suggesting she go on to do a book about the sea. So did van Loon's friend Quincy Howe at Simon and Schuster. A book contract offered her badly needed funds. More important, she had already become sure that she needed to be free from her assigned government writing.

In her first commercial articles, Carson learned how to take her readers vicariously into the ocean frontier—a frontier she knew from one brief and shallow dive clinging to a boat's ladder. Nevertheless, like writers in earlier centuries who wrote without personal experience, from Pliny the Elder to the fictitious Sir John Mandeville (*The Travels of Sir John Mandeville*), she became the most famous guide of her time. Unlike Mandeville and Pliny, however, she could and did apply rigorous standards to the evidence she used, and unlike them, she did not claim to have been where she had not been. However, she used the same technique they used—guiding the reader in narrative form, observing as if with her own eyes—or the readers.' Beginning with "Undersea" in *The Atlantic*, she continued steadily to build public faith in her as America's trusted guide to nature and science.

Her first book, *Under the Sea-Wind*, published in November 1941, did report her own observations, and her recognition of the big ideas she could draw from her subject by becoming the reader's guide to life and death. "To stand at the edge of the sea, to sense the ebb and the flow of the tides, to feel the breath of a mist moving over a great salt marsh, to watch the flight of shorebirds that have swept up and down the surf lines of the continents for untold thousands of years, to see the running of the old eels and the young shed to the sea, is to have knowledge of things that are as nearly eternal as any earthly life can be."[18]

The month after the book's publication, the Japanese bombed Pearl Harbor, and America's attention turned to war. Despite good reviews, including one by William Beebe in the very important *Saturday Review*, the first year sales amounted to 1,348 copies, and her total royalties until the book went out of print in 1946 came to $689.17.[19] She had hoped for much more. "The world received the event with superb indifference," she told an audience of journalists years later. "The reviewers were kind, but the rush to the book store that is the author's dream never materialized."[20] She would have to wait 10 years until *The Sea around Us* brought the fame and money she hoped for.

Contrary to popular images of the generation before mine and the label "Silent Generation" applied to my generation, in the late-1940s and 1950s (and I'm speaking in broad generalities), ferment and creativity were far more characteristic than preoccupation with survival or silent apathy. World War II had restored both American confidence and the economy. Victory and peace liberated scientists and engineers and writers to apply their talents wherever they could find support. The profits from wartime employment and production, followed by a "peace dividend" boost to the economy, also provided the economic cornerstones for a new creativity, not to mention growth in consumption that included a new book-buying public fueled in part by the hundreds of thousands of veterans going to college on the G.I. Bill. The accompanying Cold War, with communism and the threat of nuclear annihilation, only added to the appeal of books and technology that took us into nature's wonders, especially the oceans. Carson's time had come, and her timing was perfect.

On June 2, 1951, the *New Yorker* began its serialized version of Carson's second book, *The Sea around Us*. On July 1, *the New York Times* ran a front page review written by *Time Magazine*'s science editor Jonathan Norton Leonard, "—And His Wonders in the Deep; A Scientist Draws an Intimate Portrait of the Winding Sea and Its Churning Life." Although Carson was a scientist by training but not by practice, Leonard began his review validating Carson as both scientist and poet. "When poets write about the sea their errors annoy scientists. When scientists write about the sea their bleak and technical jargon paralyzes poets. Yet neither scientists nor poets should object to 'The Sea around Us.'" Oxford University Press (an infrequent source of best sellers but a prestige imprint) published the book on July 2.

The clichés about publishing success began to sound— phenomenal, meteoric, explosive. Three weeks later, *The Sea around Us* was all around America, becoming number five on the *New York Times* "Best Seller List." Oxford had issued a fifth printing by the end of August, bringing sales to 60,000. By the end of the year, the Book-of-the-Month Club had sold 167,181 copies. Sales increased to 200,000 the next year as *Reader's Digest* Books brought it to homes like mine.[21] the *New York Times*, which carried it on the best seller list for a year and a half and as number one for 32 weeks, called it the outstanding book of 1951.

Carson sold the film rights, and the documentary began playing in theaters in 1953. Carson didn't like it, but the public did. So did the critics who gave it an Oscar for best documentary. Her legacy had begun to take on its own life. Among other things, her writing, her background, and the way the media presented her work set the pattern and the methods for winning public approval and translating science into the emotions that are the necessary precursors and fuel for a social movement. Had she lived, she might have found the way the environmental movement deployed her reputation, her methods, and even the substance of her books as unacceptable as the sentimentalized film.

She did not know then or in the remaining 11 years of her life that soon many people would call her "the mother of the environmental movement." Nor did I know that I would become an environmental activist and president of three statewide environmental groups. I was 13 and Carson was 45. Like most serious writers, she wrote with the intent of changing people's lives. Looking back, I see that my own path illustrates how Carson came to have such a deep impact on American thinking and political action. Maybe most 13-year-olds want to change their own lives, as I certainly did, but I had also begun to think I could change the world. More important, I thought the world needed changing. So did many adults who had lived through the Great Depression and World War II. Among them were millions of families like mine that by the 1950s had moved out of cities into suburbs and small towns and had begun to take vacations. In their new homes and with their new leisure and turning their backs on the squalor of the Depression and the destruction of war, they began to appreciate nature.

Carson had always appreciated the natural world, but with the end of the war she experienced some of the same release as other Americans. She continued to work for government until her fame and fortune were fully established in 1952. But as soon as the war ended she rapidly increased the number of popular articles she wrote for newspapers and magazines. She became active in the Wilderness Society and in 1948 joined the national board of the Audubon Society. She found her network of friends outside government rapidly expanding. Writers she had once respected, now respected her. *Time Magazine's* Leonard was right when he predicted, "neither scientists nor poets should object to 'The Sea around Us.'" She made many new friends among scientists who became valuable sources of information. She was part of the new creativity. America was ready for her, and she was ready to feed its new interests and needs.

Infection as Inspiration

When I took from my family's single bookshelf the *Reader's Digest* version of *The Sea around Us* and began reading, I was immediately infected with Carson's curiosity and her reverence for natural wonders—both things and processes. I began to understand our local beach and the long finger-like Hempstead Harbor not as a playground and a tub full of fish and clams, but as part of the far greater sea. Occasionally, a reminder of that larger life arrived in our harbor—a pod of porpoises would come in on a high tide or a storm would wash up the two-foot-wide monk fish with its head spanning mouth, its needle teeth, and the "antennae" rising from the back of its head. I felt privileged to see the proof of what people in Ohio and Montana could only read about. Nevertheless, the sales of Carson's book and its reviews prove that those inlanders too enjoyed Carson's guided tour of the seas. They were like ball fans hearing a radio announcer; I was in the front row seats. For all of us, Carson made the sea into *our* sea.

The soaring acclaim and honors bestowed on *The Sea around Us* led to the re-publication of *Under the Sea-Wind* in 1952. It became a Book-of-the-Month Club alternate selection. All of part I was published by *Life* magazine, which millions of Americans read and which lingered in barber shops and beauty parlors across America. In April, *Under the Sea-Wind* reached number 10 on the *New York Times* best seller list while *The Sea around* Us had just the week before relinquished number one to a political exposé and held at number two. In 1955, the *New Yorker* serialized Carson's third book, *The Edge of the Sea*. It soon appeared as number eight on the *New York Times* best seller list. It rose to number three in December, then held that position for five months. At the top of the list was Anne Morrow Lindbergh's *Gift from the Sea*, and, as if to underscore why these two books were selling so well, the number two slot for some weeks listed the Rev. Dr. Norman Vincent Peale's *The Power of Positive Thinking*.

The Edge of the Sea did not enjoy the intense praise and popularity of her earlier books, but it received enough to make any author proud. Again, reviewers cited her scientific expertise and her lyrical writing. The *New York Times* daily reviewer, Charles Poore, noted the quality that gave Carson an entrée into ordinary homes across America. He described the writing as "profoundly learned yet unencumbered with the numbing jargon of the squid and seaweed set."[22]

Carson had acquired those assets of literary success—fame, money, respect, and thus power—which she could have used to found a movement. Those assets came not from her scientific achievement but from her artistic achievement. Instead, as soon as her fame spread in 1951, she chose to stay in the role where she would be most effective. She turned down innumerable speaking offers so she could continue writing. She understood that her real power, not to mention her pleasure, came from writing. She was not a good speaker. She was comfortable with colleagues, not crowds. She chose to talk to the world through the largely safe and one-way form of writing. The world was listening.

She knew she had power, even if she did not think about what forms it might take. She was thinking, however, about the dream of all writers—changing people's lives and behavior. For her that meant fighting the destruction of the natural world she loved. Environmental protection, no less political activism, was not a central theme in her ocean books, but the destructive powers of humankind were always on her mind. In *The Sea around Us*, she writes of the destruction of resources on the continents but presents the sea as unconquerable. This is in keeping with the subtle way in which the book changes its readers' thinking. Throughout the book, she presents the seas and oceans as immense, powerful, ancient, enduring, and mysterious realms, while humankind is short-lived, frail, and ignorant by comparison. *The Sea around Us* opens by putting humankind in its place, so to speak.

> And yet he has returned to his mother sea only on her own terms. He cannot control or change the ocean as, in his brief tenancy of earth, he has subdued and plundered the continents. In the artificial world of his cities and towns, he often forgets the true nature of his planet and the long vistas of its history, in which the existence of the race of men has occupied a mere moment of time. The sense of all these things comes to him most clearly in the course of a long ocean

voyage, when he watches day after day the receding rim of the horizon, ridged and furrowed by waves; when at night he becomes aware of the earth's rotation as the stars pass overhead; or when, alone in this world of water and sky, he feels the loneliness of his earth in space. And then, as never on land, he knows the truth that his world is a water world, a planet dominated by its covering mantle of ocean, in which the continents are but transient intrusions of land above the surface of the all encircling sea.[23]

Maybe this was her way of putting in perspective the immense powers unleashed in World War II, but from there it was only a short step to the position that would soon be held by many environmentalists—that humanity is a mistake and a plague on nature.

Carson spoke much more explicitly to a select audience than to her anonymous audience of readers. In 1952, she accepted the John Burroughs Medal and told her audience:

Mankind has gone very far into an artificial world of his own creation. He has sought to insulate himself, in his cities of steel and concrete, from the realities of earth and water and the growing seed. Intoxicated with a sense of his own power, he seems to be going farther and farther into more experiments for the destruction of himself and his world.[24]

This is still not the gloom and doom that would characterize the beginning of the environmental movement with its wholesale contempt for human achievement and its predictions that nature would respond with plagues and disasters of Biblical proportions. Carson the careful science writer says, "he *seems* to be going farther and farther" toward destruction. She followed that warning immediately with hope. Writers like her had a critical role to play in changing the civilized world's behavior.

There is certainly no single remedy for this condition and I am offering no panacea. But it seems reasonable to believe— and I do believe—that the more clearly we can focus our attention on the wonders and realities of the universe about us, the less taste we shall have for the destruction of our race. Wonder and humility are wholesome emotions, and they do not exist side by side with a lust for destruction.[25]

Her exceptional ability to "focus our attention on the wonders and realities of the universe" also infected us with her perspective and to various degrees with her commitment to preserving the natural environment. That achievement demonstrates the folly of considering art as little more than entertainment and diversion. In fact, *entertainment* should not be considered a pejorative. Literature of any quality aims to entertain, and the essence of *entertain* is the same today as in its Latin roots—to hold (*tenere*) among (*inter*). Art in all its forms, but particularly writing and film, has been a vital bridge between new thinking and a change in public attitudes. Every effective movement has recognized the practical necessity of using art to win converts, to motivate members, and to prevent, diminish, or demonize opposition or other new ideas. This fact has been widely recognized by all governments that seek to censor art, and also by those who use art as propaganda.

Carson's scientific training and her ability to absorb and transform highly technical data into scenes and stories that appeal to the senses fulfills Leo Tolstoy's requirement that, "The highest limit of the artist's relation to his subject will be such as evokes in the soul of all men an impression of reality—the reality not so much of what exists, as of what goes on in the soul of the artist." Tolstoy also says, "This impression of reality is produced by truth only, and therefore the highest relation of an author to his subject is sincerity."[26] Carson affirmed this view when she accepted the National Book Award for Nonfiction in 1952. "If there is poetry in my book about the sea, it is not because I deliberately put it there, but because no one could write truthfully about the sea and leave out the poetry."[27]

Rachel Carson's deep imprint on American thinking validates Tolstoy's ultimate test of art—can a story be understood and admired by common people and infect them with the artist's own feelings?[28] "Artistic (and also scientific) creation is such mental activity as bring dimly perceived feelings (or thoughts) to such a degree of clearness that these feelings (or thoughts) are transmitted to other people."[29]

And isn't Tolstoy describing the way art prepares its audience to accept and join a movement when he writes that the effect of true art on its audience is

> that the recipient of a truly artistic impression is so united to the artist that he feels as if the work were his own and not someone else's—as if what it expresses were just what he

had long been wishing to express. A real work of art destroys in the consciousness of the recipient the separation between himself and the artist, and not that alone, but also between himself and all whose minds received this work of art. *In this freeing of our personality from its separation and isolation, in this uniting of it with others, lies the chief characteristic and the great attractive force of art.*[30] [Emphasis added.]

Even if Carson's academic degrees had been in literature and she had spent all her time writing, she practiced her art so well that the public would have believed her word as good as any scientist's. Carson, however, had the added benefit of two degrees in science and a job in a branch of government where good scientists did work in both field and lab. Carson's job description usually included "biologist," and the media often called her a scientist. For most of the audience, that word meant someone actively engaged in methodical laboratory or field research. This understanding, along with the public trust and affection she had already won, made her the ideal guide to the subject of her last and most influential book, *Silent Spring,* published in 1962.[31] This is her passionate, desperate, and angry attack on the pesticide industry. She believed she now had ironclad proof that their chemicals validated the warning she had given in 1952 at the Burroughs Medal award ceremony—"Intoxicated with a sense of his own power, [man] seems to be going farther and farther into more experiments for the destruction of himself and his world." In *Silent Spring,* however, she includes no "seems," no doubt.

The writing of *Silent Spring* had been a race against sure death— environmental death and Rachel Louise Carson's own death. In 1946, doctors had removed a small cyst from one breast, and in 1950 a surgeon removed a walnut-sized tumor that he said was nonmalignant. To most friends, Carson minimized any worries, but in a letter to nature writer Edwin Way Teale, she wrote, "This time I'm not going to sit back for seven years before starting another [book]! I seem now to have, as writers should, a sense of urgency and passing time—and so much to say!"[32] Many observers have tried to explain the pessimism and aggressiveness of *Silent Spring* by the fact that Carson was dying from cancer. In fact, Carson had started work on the book in 1958, and only in the spring of 1960 did doctors remove several tumors and perform a radical mastectomy. Even then, the surgeon told her that he could not confirm malignancy, only

21

"a condition bordering on malignancy."[33] Almost to the very end, she continued to hope for a return to good health.

She had every chance to blame her own cancer on chemicals, but she did not do it even when she wrote her chapters tying chemical exposure to cancer. Good nature writers know that nature kills, and they accept this fact even if their followers do not. A great irony of the environmental movement and its narrow focus on the evils of human technology and economy is that its two most inspiring writers were killed in their prime by forces of nature—Henry David Thoreau by tuberculosis and Rachel Carson by cancer. And both writers sought to cure themselves with the powers of modern technology. Thoreau was glad to take the railroad to what he hoped would be the restorative airs of the wide open plains of Minnesota. Carson, often described as a scientist and whose writing inspired the "precautionary principle," embraced treatment with the hoax drug Krebiozen. She also submitted hopefully to the most toxic of all human technologies—radiation. (Later in this book, Larry Katzenstein makes the case that Carson established the precautionary principle as a mainstay of modern environmentalism.)

Carson's health continued to deteriorate as she wrote, but her confidence in humankind and its handling of chemicals had begun to deteriorate long before *Silent Spring*, and even before the publication of *The Sea around Us* in 1952. In 1945, while she was still working for the government and just beginning to publish in newspapers and magazines, she had begun editing reports on DDT in the marine environment. Experts in Carson's own department engaged in vigorous discussion, and Carson thought the public should know about the dark side of DDT. She proposed an article to *Reader's Digest*, writing,

> [P]ractically at my back door here in Maryland, an experiment of more than ordinary interest and importance is going on. We have all heard a lot about what DDT will soon do for us by wiping out insect pests. The experiments at Patuxent have been planned to show what other effects DDT may have when it is applied to wide areas: what will happen to insects that are beneficial or even . . . central; how it may affect waterfowl, or birds that depend on insect food; whether it may upset the whole delicate balance of nature if unwisely used.[34]

Reader's Digest turned down her proposal, but her interest in the subject continued. Suspicion turned to dismay, and dismay became despair, and despair erupted into the anger of *Silent Spring*.

I leave the judgment of her evidence and conclusions to other writers in this volume; but this writer believes Carson was too professional to let her own health troubles bias her writing, and her interest in the subject had been too sustained for that charge to stick. That is not to deny she had a passionate personal interest in how and when she chose to write about a subject. Outside of her government-assigned work, all of her writing choices were intensely personal. Although she paid careful attention to financial opportunity, even after *The Sea around Us* assured her fortune, she was never a writer for hire or a hired gun. In her three ocean books, she had written about what she loved. Science explained why the subjects were worthy of her love and attention, while her artistic writing infected readers with her emotions, or at least a degree of them. When the topic of pesticide toxicity was first proposed to her, she thought she was not qualified to write about it—or at least that others were more qualified to do so. Then she accepted a proposal to collaborate on the subject with a science writer from *Newsweek*. Soon she decided that no one else could do it, and collaboration might require compromise. She chose to write *Silent Spring* not because she loved the subject but because she felt she had to defend the natural world she loved.

When her mother died as she began writing in 1958, Carson described her in a letter to a friend. The description of the woman who had been with her all her life could easily have been a self-description: "Her love of life and of all living things was her outstanding quality, of which everyone speaks. More than anyone else I know, she embodied Albert Schweitzer's 'reverence for life.' And while gentle and compassionate, she could fight fiercely against anything she believed wrong, as in our present crusade! Knowing how she felt about that will help me return to it soon, and carry it through to completion."[35]

She took on the task of writing *Silent Spring* even against the earnest pleas of her friend Dorothy Freeman, who felt the book would be an unfortunate and dark departure from the ocean books and their own idyllic forays into the natural world.[36] Freeman was the human friend Carson loved most dearly and intimately. (How dearly and how intimately is unknown, irrelevant, and out of bounds.) Her first and longest love was nature. "The beauty of the world I was trying to save has always been uppermost in my mind—that, and anger at the senseless, brutish things that were being done. I have felt bound by a solemn obligation to do what I could—if I didn't at least try I could never again be happy in nature."[37]

Her decision to write *Silent Spring*, her intensity, and the selection of facts to create a lawyer-like adversarial argument was a very personal choice. It was William Shawn, the famous editor of the *New Yorker*, who encouraged her to take an adversarial rather than scientific approach, who encouraged her not to worry about maintaining the appearance of a disinterested scientist. He was offering her both a fat fee and a very large audience for a book-length series condemning the use of pesticides. His words demonstrate a serious flaw in logic and why *Silent Spring* is so different from Carson's earlier books: "After all there are some things one doesn't have to be objective and unbiased about—one doesn't condone murder!" This is classic polarization—if you're not for us, you're against us. Clearly, objectivity and the open mind of scientific inquiry do not condone or condemn. This liberation from scientific objectivity delighted Carson. In the same letter reporting Shawn's offer, she says, "Best of all, I can (indeed he wants me to) present it strictly from my own point of view, pulling no punches."[38]

With this beginning on *Silent Spring*, Carson had ceased to be either a scientist or a science writer and had become an environmentalist. She was able to use all her powers as a writer to infect an audience and guarantee the book's emotional impact: she set herself up as the advocate of the earth against humankind.

The original title was actually stated like a court case, *Man against the Earth*. (Since she was of that era when all writers used *man* to mean all of humankind, let's not read into the title an attack on the exclusively male hierarchy of business and government that produced and promoted the heavy use of pesticides.) At her agent's urging, she later dropped the adversarial title and used the title of a chapter on birds; that title might have been suggested by lines from the poet Keats which appear as one of two quotations on the page after the dedication.

> The sedge is wither'd from the lake,
> And no birds sing.

The other two quotations displayed prominently before Chapter 1 convey other versions of the modern environmentalist perspective.

She dedicated the book to Albert Schweitzer with his own words: "Man has lost the capacity to foresee and to forestall. He will end by destroying the earth."

On the next page, below Keats, she quoted the well-known *New Yorker* editor E. B. White. "I am pessimistic about the human race because it is too ingenious for its own good. Our approach to nature is to beat it into submission. We would stand a better chance of survival if we accommodated ourselves to this planet and viewed it appreciatively instead of skeptically and dictatorially."

If Carson had begun her writer's crusade against pesticides in 1945, she might never have developed the credibility and public power she achieved before *Silent Spring*. She would have immediately drawn fire from the chemical industry, from agricultural interests, and even from government agencies that were promoting the heavy use of DDT and other chemicals. Personally, she would have weathered such attacks, as she did after *Silent Spring* even when her health was fragile. If the controversy had come at the beginning of her career, it would have polarized opinion about her credibility and objectivity. The credibility she built during her career by using scientific discoveries to offer readers beauty and inspire wonder contributed enormously to the impact of *Silent Spring*. In fact, another major publisher, Alfred Knopf, brought out Murray Bookchin's condemnation of chemical toxicity in food and the natural world six months before *Silent Spring*, but *Our Synthetic Environment* went almost unnoticed. Knopf even tried to avoid associating its book's argument with Bookchin's radical reputation by publishing it under the pseudonym Lewis Herber. (Later chapters in this volume by Desrochers and Shimizu and by Meiners and Morriss show in considerable detail how earlier writers had already attacked the chemical and pesticide industries.)

Silent Spring's success was immediate and on a scale even Carson, the author of two previous best sellers, had not expected. In July of 1962, the *New Yorker* began running the book in several installments, but what made Carson happier was word that the Book-of-the-Month Club had made *Silent Spring* its choice for October. "The BOM will carry it to farms and hamlets all over the country that don't know what a bookstore looks like—much less the *New Yorker*." It's worth noting that the *New Yorker* launched a pre-emptive editorial against expected criticism. The editors assured readers that although Carson would be "accused of alarmism" or "lack of objectivity," she was not an extremist who wanted to ban all chemical pesticides. In the second chapter of her book, really one of two short introductions, she concludes, "It is not my contention that chemical insecticides must never be used."[39] That was the truth, and when Carson testified before Ribicoff's Senate committee, she stated very carefully that she understood the value of pesticides and that the problem was misuse and over-use.[40] However, she did not use her great gift of communication to relate even a single story of what values pesticides had, nor did she mention a single benefit.

The Mother and the Movement

Although another eight years would pass before the environmental movement would become a decisive political power on Earth Day 1970, the reactions to the *New Yorker* segments helped formulate the nascent movement's message—that large, selfish, and greedy corporations had bought the virtue of government officials and Congress so they could profit from poisoning helpless people and the natural world they depended on. And this disaster was the inevitable result of human arrogance and its lost awe and appreciation of the natural world. Carson even suggests we should apprehend the culprits and punish them.

> Who has made the decision that sets in motion these chains of poisonings, this ever-widening wave of death that spreads out, like ripples when a pebble is dropped into a still pond? Who has placed in one pan of the scales the leaves that might have been eaten by the beetles and in the other the pitiful heaps of many-hued feathers, the lifeless remains of the birds that fell before the unselective bludgeon of insecticidal poisons? Who has decided—who has the *right* to decide—for the countless legions of people who were not consulted that the supreme value is a world without insects, even though it be also a sterile world ungraced by the curving wing of a bird in flight? The decision is that of the authoritarian temporarily entrusted with power; he has made it during a moment of inattention by millions to whom beauty and the ordered world of nature still have a meaning that is deep and imperative.[41]

This passage is nothing short of a call to arms and a demand to mete out justice. It has the shape of a legal argument about rights and guilt. Carson was a lifelong bird watcher, and this passage comes at the end of Chapter 8, "And No Birds Sing." Carson uses the demise of bird populations as a warning of what will happen to other species, including humans. She concludes with this argument that would have moved any jury to quick and severe judgment. The environmental movement, of course, would make legal action one of its most constant and effective weapons. Consider other ways in which *Silent Spring* models the methods of the new environmentalism.

The condemnation of authority and large corporations and, by extension, the free market system and capitalism appealed to many young people from the radical student movements, to anarchist groups, and to socialists. Their movements were losing steam, and the environmental movement had much broader appeal to average Americans who now cared more about nature than about economic and political theory.

Carson's occasional comments affirming that the world could not sustain its standard of living without synthetic chemicals are meek, mild, and rare compared to page after page of text and chapter titles laden with emotional words and metaphors. They provide a catalog of language and ideas that become staple fare in the environmental movement. Chapters include "Elixirs of Death," "Needless Havoc," "Rivers of Death," and "Indiscriminately from the Skies." She relates how enough parathion is sprayed in California alone to "provide a lethal dose for five to ten times the whole world's population," and that we are saved from "extinction by this means" only because the chemical decomposes rapidly.[42] Our rivers and lakes, she writes "have become almost universally contaminated with insecticides."[43]

Carson also engages in demonization. "Under the philosophy that now seems to guide our destinies, nothing must get in the way of the man with the spray gun. The incidental victims of his crusade against insects count as nothing. . . ."[44] She portrays Americans as helpless victims of ruthless poisoners: "As matters stand now, we are in little better position than the guests of the Borgias."[45] She sets up black and white alternatives and warns that readers are in danger of dire personal consequences: "Confusion, delusions, loss of memory, mania—a heavy price to pay for the temporary destruction of the few insects, but a price that will continue to be exacted as long as we insist upon using chemicals that strike directly at the nervous system."[46]

She portrays humankind at a life-and-death fork in the path of history: "We stand now where two roads diverge." But unlike the roads in Robert Frost's familiar poem, they are not equally fair. The road we have long been traveling is deceptively easy, a smooth superhighway on which we progress with great speed, but at its end lies disaster. The other fork of the road—the one less traveled—offers our last, our only chance to reach a destination that assures the preservation of the earth.[47]

Carson, who once expressed great disapproval of the way filmmakers had turned *The Sea around Us* into kitsch, approved every bit of *Silent Spring*. That includes the sentimentalized line drawings of animals where even the bugs are cute. In fact, she wrote to Dorothy Freeman, "I consider my contributions to scientific fact far less important than my attempts to awaken an emotional response to the world of nature."[48] This too would become a staple of environmental art, especially in fund raising appeals.

She concludes *Silent Spring* with ridicule: "The 'control of nature' is a phrase conceived in arrogance, born of the Neanderthal age of biology and philosophy, when it was supposed that nature exists for the convenience of man. The concepts and practices of applied entomology for the most part date from that stone age of science."[49]

Carson should not be judged by what others have done with her work any more than boxers should be blamed for gang violence. In *Silent Spring*, Carson exercises her usual skillful technique of melding concrete detail and dramatic stories and the appeal to the senses. The science she selects, she reports carefully and clearly. The ensuing controversy, which others in this volume will explore at length, concerns her omissions, analysis, and conclusions.

I write as one of the many ordinary Americans who came to admire and respect Rachel Carson's science writing, and who sat as a member of the national jury listening to her argument in *Silent Spring*. We understood that her argument was telling us what we should do. Consciously or not, we also learned from her how we should do it. In her despair and anger and urgency, she took her familiar approach to the wonders of nature and added to it all the rhetorical devices and misanthropic perspectives that would be repeated and elaborated on endlessly by the gloom-and-doom core of the new environmental movement.

The Disruptive Vision

In technology and economics, we often hear about "disruptors" that change the way we live or do business—fire, agriculture, steam power, the internal combustion engine, the transistor, the computer, the Internet. Writing subtly in her ocean books and with anger and polemic in *Silent Spring*, Rachel Carson popularized a disruptive vision of how nature works and of human responsibility and morality.

When I returned to America from graduate work at Oxford two years after the publication of *Silent Spring*, I took a temporary position in a Long Island middle school teaching English to classes of seventh graders from affluent middle-class families. Almost immediately, the school psychologist invited me to help conduct a special seminar for "gifted but opinionated" freshmen. They were students, he and the principal believed, who needed some thought-provoking reading and discussion. In other words, we intended to be disruptive. Our text would be the most disruptive book of the time—*Silent Spring*.

I was glad to have a reason to read and talk about a new book by Rachel Carson. Like many university students of my generation, I thought the world needed disruption and that possibly our entire free-market system was doomed because it was free. Besides, I had just returned from living in a country where a still powerful class system discriminated against people from my walk of life. I now had degrees from Duke University and Oxford, and I was ready to rumble. At still-segregated Duke, I had participated in civil rights demonstrations and experimented with peyote (then legal) to unlock what Aldous Huxley called "the doors of perception" because I was ready and felt I should be "shaken out of the ruts of ordinary perception."[50] At Oxford, the British class system had hit me like a smack in the face, and if I had been given to sloganeering, I would have joined the meetings and demonstrations shouting "down with the establishment." And here was Carson attacking the establishment.

I also wanted to get away from Long Island and the city influence, so the next year I accepted an offer to teach at the University of North Carolina at Chapel Hill. I immediately found a country rental and soon bought an ancient house and five acres far enough into the countryside that professionals from the universities and the growing Research Triangle Park had not yet penetrated. I was allowed to teach one special freshman seminar and chose the theme "man and nature" to guide the reading and writing. I also became a

29

charter member of the newly formed Conservation Council of North Carolina. I would go on to become the president of the council and also president of the Conservation Foundation of North Carolina and the North Carolina Land Trustees of America. Like many young college-educated Americans in the years between *Silent Spring* and the first Earth Day, I was looking for ways to do what Rachel Carson had demanded and what the new movement demanded—change the way America treated its environment.

The years between the publication of *Silent Spring* and the environmental movement's official birth on the first Earth Day had all the richness and rapid development of pregnancy. Was *Silent Spring* really such a powerful force? It was for me, and I have had much more famous company. When Al Gore was vice president, he posted on the White House website a special tribute to Rachel Carson. "For me personally, *Silent Spring* had a profound impact. It was one of the books we read at home at my mother's insistence and then discussed around the dinner table. My sister and I didn't like every book that made it to that table, but our conversations about *Silent Spring* are a happy and vivid memory. Indeed, Rachel Carson was one of the reasons I became so conscious of the environment and involved with environmental issues."[51]

The leaders of movements know what the best fiction writers know—there are only three great stories: betrayal, love, and death. To engage a reader's attention or the attention of possible recruits to a movement, leaders must engage the audience in outrage against betrayal and in saving the thing they love from imminent death. In her ocean books, Carson taught them how to convince their recruits and followers to love nature. In *Silent Spring*, she gave a virtuoso demonstration of how to identify its betrayers, convict them, and offer the rest of civilization the hope of salvation.

We should not forget that Carson offered many alternatives to the practices she condemned, and she ended *Silent Spring* with a chapter of alternatives to pesticides. The environmental movement, of course, has expanded the supposed alternatives manifold times, usually accompanied by the claim that what is good for the environment is good for the economy. Often environmentalists turn this into a self-evident truth by pointing out the common linguistic roots of economy and ecology in the Greek *oikos*—house or household. Thus, by way of definition, what is good for nature is good for the economy. If a claimed economic benefit harms the environment, then some accounting is missing, external costs ignored, and the claim is false. In the same vein, as creationists arguing against evolution, belief dictates facts.

Would Carson approve? Give the dead the benefit of the doubt. She might have favored the hypothesis, but she would have recognized that embracing such dogma draws a distinct line between environmentalism and science. She does come very close to endorsing the idea even if she might not have approved of it as dogma. "If we have been slow to develop the general concepts of ecology and conservation, we have been even more tardy in recognizing the facts of the ecology and conservation of man himself. We may hope that this will be the next major phase in the development of biology. Here and there awareness is growing that man, far from being the overlord of all creation, is himself part of nature, subject to the same cosmic forces that control all other life. *Man's future welfare and probably even his survival depend upon his learning to live in harmony, rather than in combat, with these forces.*"[52] [Emphasis added.]

The way her followers took her insistence on alternatives and made it into dogma demonstrates that her contribution to the environmental movement was not a respect for science but nourishment of a faith. We see something like this in the way creationists use gaps in the geological record of evolution to support the divine creation of species. (Robert Nelson explores the religious nature of environmentalism later in this volume.)

I was among those who liked the idea that what was good for nature was also good for the economy and vice versa. First, I tried an organic vegetable farm pledged to selling produce at or below the price in the local supermarket. I always sold out, but since I was earning less than $1 an hour for my labor, what was good for the environment was not good for my economy. I next organized investors to buy rural land on which I wrote covenants to protect trees, endangered species, wild animals, and important habitat. One success led to another, and now more than 2,000 acres of land in North Carolina's Research Triangle area are protected while yielding a profit. What I learned from these two experiments, of course, was what I hope Carson might have concluded from a study of her alternatives to pesticides—that economic benefits are the best way to ensure environmental benefits. The fact is, my two lessons were bound to separate me from both Carson and the environmental movement. I suspect that by failing to distinguish between greed and profits, and equating profit with environmental destruction, she established a bias she could not have overcome. It is certainly a bias that came to dominate the environmental movement.

In the movement's frequent disregard for testing alternatives in reality, perhaps it demonstrates a subconscious faith that, given any challenge, human ingenuity will triumph. But this is unacknowledged at best, and at worst it postulates an environmentalist heaven reached only after modern society has died. The dominant vision of the movement mirrors Carson's anger and despair and transforms it into doom and gloom. Between *Silent Spring* and the first Earth Day in 1970, the future leaders and thinkers of the movement issued a number of influential doom-and-gloom predictions, articles, and books.

Ballantine Books, credited with inventing the paperback, began publishing cheap books sponsored by David Brower and his revitalized Sierra Club. Several were large-format books with high-quality color photos. The title of the first book was Thoreau's famous statement that would become a shibboleth of environmentalist philosophy; it fits neatly with the dogma that what is good for nature is good for the economy: *In Wildness Is the Preservation of the World*. Its text was a series of quotations from Thoreau, and the pictures were pleasant nature photographs, not a human face, form, or object among them. Brower's clever strategy mirrored Carson's success in her ocean books—win with wonder. The books were popular with many people who had not yet thought about environmental problems, much less joined the Sierra Club. One of Ballantine's new authors was Dr. Paul Ehrlich, a Stanford University specialist in butterfly species who, in April 1967, had given a lecture on what he considered the disaster of population growth. Brower and Ballantine convinced Ehrlich and his wife Anne to write *The Population Bomb*. (For unknown reasons, the publisher and Paul Ehrlich decided his wife Anne should not be listed as an author.) The book began, "The battle to feed all of humanity is over. In the 1970s hundreds of millions of people will starve to death in spite of any crash programs embarked upon now. At this late date nothing can prevent a substantial increase in the world death rate."[53]

One of Ehrlich's heroes, biologist Raymond Dasmann, sounded the call for more government power in planning in his prophetic 1965 book, *The Destruction of California*. Supreme Court Justice

William O. Douglas wrote *Wilderness Bill of Rights,* in which he proposed that animals, plants, and natural objects should have legal rights just as humans do. Landscape architect Ian McHarg proposed a new kind of planning in *Design with Nature.* McHarg's book had many innovative ideas, but it also contributed to dogmatic, oppressive, and expensive regulations administered by an elite bureaucracy of converts with degrees from new schools of urban planning.

Every movement has three human components. The *followers* are the muscle, the *leaders* are the strategists and tacticians, and the *writers and thinkers* are the inspiration for both. Carson was the principle writer and visionary for those who would become activists. Her intellectual DNA continues in most variations of the movement from The Nature Conservancy to Greenpeace.

Social and political movements are not created by reason, logic, philosophy, or science any more than a human being is created by meat and vegetables. Movements grow from the experience of a people as crystals emerge from a super-saturated solution. Unlike the writers and thinkers, the founders of most social and political movements that change a country or the world are usually highly visible figures in the movement's first days. (They may write as well as speak, but they seldom write at Thoreau's or Carson's level.)

For the environmental movement that would dominate the environmental conscience of America from 1970 until now, the prime movers enjoyed being on the public stage and leading organizations. Dennis Hayes and Sen. Gaylord Nelson organized the first Earth Day in 1970 and drew almost 20 million Americans to a single day's events across the country. They were modeled on the highly political "teach-ins" of the student movement and the anti-Vietnam protests. David Brower brought the old and quiet Sierra Club into the political arena, multiplying its membership manifold times and sacrificing its tax-exempt status. Stewart Brand toured the country promoting his *Whole Earth Catalog* full of environmentally friendly ideas and products. Ron Cobb, a cartoonist whose work often appeared in the *Whole Earth Catalog,* drew the Ecology Flag, and poet Gary Snyder published his popular *Declaration of Interdependence.* The 95-cent, 367-page paperback *The Environmental Handbook,* edited by Garrett de Bell and published for Friends of the Earth by Ballantine Books, went to three printings in 1970 alone.

Last, and close to least, on Earth Day 1970, there I was in Princeton, New Jersey, delivering a talk as part of the local celebration. I had written only one article on the intellectual roots of environmental thinking. But I had been an organic farmer, and I had already begun to organize investors to buy rural land for experimental homesteads and protect them with covenants that limited tree cutting and prohibited the use of chlorinated hydrocarbons like chlordane that Carson had tied to cancer. Because I was also an assistant professor of English, the Woodrow Wilson Foundation of Princeton had selected me to tour nonacademic small towns of America presenting a multimedia show about man and the environment. None of us might have been movers of that first Earth Day except for Rachel Carson.

Ecologist Dr. Carl Safina, president of The Blue Ocean Institute, wrote a foreword to the 2003 commemorative edition of *The Sea around Us*. Instead of dwelling on Carson's scientific credentials, he recognizes her much more important influence as the mother and muse of the environmental movement. "Her very name evokes the beatific luminosity of the canonized." Safina also notes, "The Rachel Carson we think of is the author of *Silent Spring*, birth mother of modern environmentalism, messenger of a story that rocked the world. The real Rachel Carson never met her. . . . She didn't live long enough to become acquainted with the Carson we know, that towering figure whose light illuminated our sense of the world forever."[54]

The reverse is also true—the Rachel Carson beatified by the environmental movement is not the real Rachel Carson. Sainthood is an inspirational story, not careful biography.

A new way of thinking about a scientist's (or science writer's) influence has recently appeared on the Internet. In collaboration with Google, a team led by French psychologist Jean-Baptiste Michel and Harvard mathematician Erez Lieberman Aiden has created a method of analyzing data from 15 million books with trillions of words digitalized by Google. Entering a person's name for a given period of years produces a graph showing how often that name (or a phrase) appears in each of the included years. The plots you'll see are the frequency of those names and phrases in the pages of all books published each year between the dates you choose.[55] In Figure 2.1, Rachel Carson's name ranks below only Henry David Thoreau and

---

Figure 2.1
Frequency of Published Names of Environmentalists
(1940–2008)

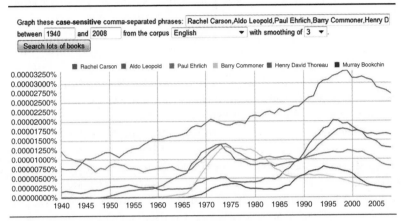

Graph these case-sensitive comma-separated phrases: Rachel Carson,Aldo Leopold,Paul Ehrlich,Barry Commoner,Henry D
between 1940 and 2008 from the corpus English ▼ with smoothing of 3 ▼ .
Search lots of books

■ Rachel Carson ■ Aldo Leopold ■ Paul Ehrlich ▨ Barry Commoner ■ Henry David Thoreau ■ Murray Bookchin

Source: Google Labs, Books Ngram Viewer.

above scientists who were environmental writers—Aldo Leopold, Barry Commoner, Murray Bookchin, and Paul Ehrlich.[56]

Carson is clearly still a powerful force. It's also interesting that the only writer mentioned more often in the years of her own career is the very quotable curmudgeon of the mid-19th century, Henry David Thoreau.

Carson was neither a profound nor an original thinker, as Pierre Desrochers and Hiroko Shimizu will show in Chapter 3. Rachel Carson, however, would have been a good writer in any century, and she happened to be the right kind of writer at a time when America was ripening for change and ready for her material and talent. The environmental movement would certainly have crystallized without her. She was not its founder or its lifeblood, but first an inspiration and then, with *Silent Spring,* a catalyst that set off reactions waiting to happen—and she imparted to them a special character.

The channel of Carson's influence—arousing the emotions and awareness of the general public through a work of art—is almost a reincarnation of another powerful American writer's success. Exactly 100 years before publication of *The Sea around Us*, in 1851, another woman writer who had lived in Ohio published the first installment of the book that drew more than a million readers and energized the Abolitionist Movement. The writer was Harriet Beecher Stowe and her book, *Uncle Tom's Cabin*. *Uncle Tom's Cabin* became a theater drama, and Carson's book became a film.

On December 2, 1862, when Harriet Beecher Stowe visited Abraham Lincoln in the White House, he is supposed to have greeted her with the words, "So you are the little woman who started all this?"[57] When Abraham Ribicoff welcomed Rachel Carson to his Senate hearing on pesticides in the environment, he began, "Miss Carson, you are the lady who started all this."

Ribicoff was unaware that by placing Carson at the center of the legislative deliberation he was proving a claim made by the English poet Percy Bysshe Shelley (1792–1822). Shelley, using the words *poetry* and *poets* to mean most literary work, said that such writers become our interpreters of mysteries and prophets, "the mirrors of the gigantic shadows which futurity casts upon the present; the words which express what they understand not; the trumpets which sing to battle, and feel not what they inspire; the influence which is moved not, but moves. Poets are the unacknowledged legislators of the world."[58]

3. The Intellectual Groundwaters of *Silent Spring*: Rethinking Rachel Carson's Place in the History of American Environmental Thought

Pierre Desrochers and Hiroko Shimizu

The publication of *Silent Spring* is often credited with singlehandedly launching the modern American environmental movement and serving as a crucial stepping stone for the recognition later bestowed upon the work of Paul Ehrlich,[1] Garrett Hardin,[2] Barry Commoner,[3] Roderick Nash,[4] Ernst F. Schumacher,[5] and the Club of Rome.[6] Historian of environmental thought J. E. de Steiguer describes Rachel Carson's contribution as more than "a simple warning" about the dangers of indiscriminate synthetic chemical use, because its "immediate and lasting impression on the public" was her denunciation of "traditional human attitudes toward the environment." Once a large audience got the message through her writings, "the issue would not vanish from view."[7] Historian Steven Stoll observes that *Silent Spring* differed from earlier Malthusian and conservationist offerings because "it told readers that their own choices and decisions mattered in the larger world; that chemicals like DDT did not discriminate, but were, in fact, *biocides* with the potential to destroy all forms of life; and that the companies that manufactured DDT cared nothing about the health of the people who used it."[8] Carson, he tells us, ultimately "stunned the nation with the simple revelation that consumption in industrial society could erode the very fabric of life."[9] Marxist sociologists John Bellamy Foster and Brett Clark[10] similarly suggest that "Carson's attack on synthetic pesticides is not her most notable achievement," but rather that "her wider, ecological critique challenging the whole nature of our society" is.

Despite their pervasiveness, the claims made on behalf of *Silent Spring*'s intellectual originality—as distinguished from its political significance—are somewhat puzzling. True, Carson synthesized an impressive amount of information and created an original piece of work. Yet, her core arguments had been presented countless times to popular audiences. For instance, fears of pesticides—including previous "natural" arsenic-, copper-, and lead-based products— had long been raised by writers, activists, bureaucrats, and politicians. Prominent popular outlets opened their pages to critical assessments of the human health and environmental impact of the synthetic products denounced in *Silent Spring* (mainly DDT, but also other chlorinated hydrocarbons and organophosphates) even before the end of World War II. Many portions of Carson's "other road" of pest management had long been well-trodden, and their significant shortcomings—from the always uncertain impact on nontarget species of "biological" and other control methods[11] to failures to solve specific problems—had provided strong incentives to develop pesticides in the first place. Nature writing with strong environmentalist overtones was also well represented in the post–World War II era by the likes of Marjory Stoneman Douglas[12] in *The Everglades: River of Grass* and Aldo Leopold in *A Sand County Almanac*,[13] to say nothing of Carson's[14] own best sellers on ocean environments. The creation of many influential American environmental organizations whose stated aim was to protect nature against human actions—for example, the Sierra Club (1892), the National Audubon Society (1905), the Conservation Foundation (1947, later incorporated into the World Wildlife Fund), and the Nature Conservancy (1951)—also predated *Silent Spring*. Last but certainly not least, the ideological core of modern environmentalism can be traced back to ideas that had been around for centuries and in some cases millennia.[15]

In the diplomatic words of the political scientist Charles T. Rubin, "the precise nature of [Carson's] contribution is not easy to pin down."[16] Our main argument in the remainder of this chapter is that, far from breaking new ground, Rachel Carson's core message in *Silent Spring* was very much in line with the content of previous best-selling books and articles published in widely circulated magazines and newspapers. Our first section demonstrates how, far from being a lone voice warning an unsuspecting public about the environmental and health impact of "dangerous chemicals," Carson was actually the heir to a well-established tradition whose most important American manifesto had been Arthur Kallett and Frederick J. Schlink's 1933 *100,000,000 Guinea Pigs: Dangers in Everyday Foods, Drugs, and Cosmetics*.[17] Next, we highlight briefly how specific concerns about the potential environmental pitfalls of DDT had been voiced publicly from the mid-1940s onward in outlets ranging from *The Atlantic Monthly* and *Harper's* to the *Saturday Evening Post* and *Reader's Digest*, to say nothing of prominent newspapers. We then illustrate that the remaining foundations of modern environmentalism highlighted by Carson had long been firmly implanted in the American popular intellectual landscape. Our main piece of evidence in this respect is the previous, biggest environmentalist best seller of all time, William Vogt's 1948 *Road to Survival*.[18] Our reflective conclusion offers a few thoughts as to why and how Rachel Carson came to occupy the place she is now given in the pantheon of modern environmental thinkers.

Popular Fears of "Chemical Products" and Pesticides before *Silent Spring*

The English writer Douglas Adams observed that technology that existed when humans are born seems normal; anything developed before people turn 35 is exciting; and whatever is developed after that age is treated with suspicion.[19] Hostility to novelty, however, has probably always been most powerful whenever food, human health, and the "natural" order of things are concerned. Fears about the detrimental impact of synthetic (or human-made) agricultural inputs are as old as these technologies. For instance, the backlash against synthetic fertilizers began as soon as ammonia synthesis from the atmosphere became cost-efficient early in the 20th century. One of its most significant opponents was the Austrian spiritualist and organic-farming theorist Rudolf Steiner (1861–1925). Harking back to a 19th century perspective known as "vitalism," according to which life arises from and depends upon unique "life forces" apart from the purely chemical/physical realm, Steiner argued that synthetic nitrogen fertilizers were "dead" and therefore lacking in this respect. The result, he inferred, was "dead" food and poorer health among the people who ate it. This claim became an article of faith among organic growers and remains surprisingly widespread despite overwhelming scientific evidence to the contrary.[20] Technophobia was even more pronounced in the case of pesticides because they are, by definition, poisonous substances whose reckless use can have severe health consequences. The key claim made by activists and best-selling authors has always been that greedy corporations, careless public officials, and agricultural producers *deliberately* showered *lethal doses* on an unsuspecting public. As we will now illustrate, this concern long predates the development of synthetic pesticides.

Fears of Organic Pesticides[21]

Fears associated with pesticide use became especially significant after the large-scale introduction of arsenic-based substances in the second half of the 19th century.[22] A contributor to an agricultural publication asserted in 1891 that "hundreds of tons of a most virulent mineral poison in the hands of hundreds of thousands of people, to be freely used in fields, orchards and gardens all over [North America]" presented a "danger worthy of serious thought."[23] Other critics claimed that "potatoes would absorb the poison to such an extent that the tubers would carry poisonous doses, so that after each meal it would be necessary to take an antidote."[24] Reports of dead livestock soon followed, although, according to James Whorton, "all the deaths had been due to gross negligence on the part of the animals' owners."[25] In the end, the development of less damageable forms of arsenic-based insecticides (most notably lead arsenate that supplanted so-called Paris Green and London Purple), the absence of effective alternatives, and the recognition that their benefits far exceeded potential problems insured that their use was never banned.

Popular fears stemming from the use of highly toxic substances in food and other products destined for human consumption were periodically revived by best-selling authors. Perhaps the most successful example of the genre before *Silent Spring* was Arthur Kallett and Frederick J. Schlink's *100,000,000 Guinea Pigs: Dangers in Everyday Foods, Drugs, and Cosmetics* (the number in the title referred to the size of the U.S. population upon its publication in 1933).[26] Although rarely discussed today outside of scholarly histories of the consumer protection movement and remote corners of the health and wellness blogosphere, the book remained at the top of the best sellers lists for a couple of years and had gone through 32 printings by 1937.[27] Kallett and Schlink were engineers by training but radical social reformers by vocation who conveyed their misgivings about the market system, corporations, and the profit motive through, among other things, the creation of Consumers' Research (Schlink) and the more radical Consumers Union (Kallett). Indeed, the background material for their book had "been assembled by Consumers' Research through its long continued study of the complex technical literature on consumers' goods, and through contacts with professional and scientific experts among its subscribers and consultants."[28] Their main concern was to counteract "self-serving business men and politicians in [their attempt to break] down the regulatory system."[29]

Kallet and Schlink's targets were much more numerous than Carson's. Their main assertion was that the "food and drug industries have been systematically bombarding us with falsehoods about the purity, healthfulness, and safety of their products, while they have been making profits by experimenting on us with poisons, irritants, harmful chemical preservatives, and dangerous drugs."[30] Like *Silent Spring* three decades later, Kallett and Schlink's real stroke of genius was to develop a powerful and lasting new imagery, that of consumers as "guinea pigs" and "unwitting test animals in a gigantic experiment with poisons, conducted by the food, drug, and cosmetic manufacturers."[31] On the specific subject of pesticides, they observed that "willing or not," because of the lead arsenate sprayed liberally on fruits and some vegetables, American consumers in the 1930s were "eating arsenic, and there [was] good reason to believe that it may be doing [them] serious, perhaps irreparable injury."[32] Worse yet, "[g]overnment officials have even suppressed important information on the arsenic hazard, and have resisted in every way the opening up of the question to discussion in the interest of public safety."[33] This secrecy was even more outrageous considering that lead, the other residue of lead arsenate spray, was "certainly far more dangerous" because it was a "cumulative poison" stored in the body that "may become dangerous to the point of disaster when enough of the metal has collected."[34]

Not surprisingly, Kallet and Schlink's success launched a few sequels and a wave of imitators whose evocative titles ranged from *Eat, Drink and Be Wary*[35] to *American Chamber of Horrors: The Truth about Food and Drugs*.[36] Interestingly, the latter book was written by the chief information officer of the U.S. Food and Drug Administration. She dedicated it "to that gallant group of women who have been holding the front-line trenches in the consumers' war for pure food, drugs and cosmetics."[37] Lamb denounced "irresponsible persons who look upon consumer protection as a private racket to be exploited by the same sort of exaggeration and misrepresentation the patent medicine vendors so often employ," and who described consumer activists as Washington-based fanatics who "want to burn down the house to get rid of a few rats in the attic."[38] To the contrary, even the most sensible industry representatives were, because of their position, "not trying to further any legislation proposed in the interests of consumers."[39] Although more balanced than Kallett and Schlink in her discussion of "poisonous metallic sprays," Lamb devoted a chapter to the "spray-residue crisis."[40] She observed that much of the furor over the issue could be traced back to the (seemingly fortuitous) discoveries of dangerously high levels of pesticide residues on nonlocal fruits sold in regions where their lower prices were hurting the business of local producers, such as in the case of California fruits in Massachusetts or American apples in the United Kingdom. Not surprisingly, in all such cases local officials had diligently blocked the importation of nonlocal goods in the name of public health protection.[41]

Another argument raised by Lamb echoed earlier concerns that *"legally safe"* (italics in the original) toxicity levels in individual products were not an acceptable guide for public policy. Thus, cases of cancers "of certain arsenical origins"[42] could be traced back to the ingestion of pears, apples, cabbages, cauliflowers, and celery that contained very minute amounts of arsenic (typically less than $1/100$ grain per pound) because in the aggregate (and especially with the addition of products such as shellfish that naturally contained much higher concentrations) their consumption amounted to nothing short of "a steady intake of poison which might be more than your system could tolerate." Such warnings, however, were perhaps superfluous, inasmuch as the "mere mention of arsenic to the average person is enough to conjure up a vision of death."[43]

"Guinea pig muckraking," as this literary genre often came to be known, quickly generated much political interest and eventually culminated in the expansion and strengthening of the Food and Drug Administration and its regulatory apparatus.[44] The fact that

Americans became increasingly numerous and enjoyed longer life spans in the following decades did not prevent John Grant Fuller, a writer who specialized in the study of extra-terrestrial life and the supernatural, from publishing a sequel 40 years later. As could be expected, the core thesis of *200,000,000 Guinea Pigs: New Dangers in Everyday Foods, Drugs and Cosmetics* was that the situation was now logarithmically worse than in the 1930s and that "time bombs" were "ticking away in several dark corners."[45]

The obvious parallels between Carson's best seller and the guinea pig books were not lost on some early *Silent Spring* reviewers. None was as trenchant as the science writer (and past failed collaborator of Carson in the writing of her future best seller) Edwin Diamond, who observed that "*Silent Spring* might just as easily have been called *190,000,000 Guinea Pigs* [for in it] I met again the old victims of my childhood dressed in more graceful prose."[46] Once more, the villains turned out to be "the same tired stereotypes" of greedy businessmen, bought-and-paid-for mad scientists, and government regulators. Anyone who dared to challenge the crusade conducted on behalf of the hapless public was obviously on "Monsanto's or Shell's payroll." Like earlier chemical muckrakers, however, Carson couldn't explain "why an industrialist or a scientist, no matter how grasping, would poison our food and water—the same food and water he himself eats and drinks."[47]

Despite finding faults with virtually every synthetic chemical used in products ranging from toothpaste and bread to cosmetics, the original guinea pig muckrakers couldn't busy themselves with products that were not economically significant at the time, the most prominent being DDT which, although first synthesized in 1874, was only produced on a significant scale for its insecticidal properties at the beginning of the 1940s.[48] Widespread concerns about the new substance, however, immediately followed its introduction, as will now be illustrated.

Popular Fears of DDT[49]

Perhaps the most unfortunate consequence of the alleged "pathbreaking" status of *Silent Spring* is the now widespread perception that no serious scientific inquiries into or popular discussions of the potentially negative environmental impact of DDT came before its publication. Actually, significant tests (at least by the standards of the time and keeping in mind the war context) on the product were begun as soon as it came to be considered a viable alternative to other substances, which by then were severely rationed and in great demand because of increasing fighting in tropical areas.[50] The ubiquity of DDT use by the end of World War II[51] then ensured that the topic would be given broad coverage in the popular press. For instance, in a piece published in early 1945 in the *Saturday Evening Post*, the first magazine ever to sell more than 1,000,000 copies per issue, U.S. Brigadier General James Stevens Simmons observed that "reports of the amazing uses of DDT are passed over for yarns telling of its destructiveness which sound like newly created versions of the *Arabian Nights*. These incredible rumours picture DDT as a substance which may bring complete ruin to both the animal and the vegetable kingdoms." Thus "a serious scientific report that DDT has killed millions of malaria mosquito larvae in Gatun Lake may be overshadowed by a fantastic story claiming the particles of the chemical, transported by the trade winds, have annihilated all the blue butterflies in the Isthmus of Darien."[52] Simmons was not blind to possible problems and fully realized that "such a powerful insecticide may be a double-edged sword, and that its unintelligent use might eliminate certain valuable insects essential to agriculture and horticulture. Even more important, it might conceivably disturb vital balances in the animal and plant kingdoms, and thus upset various fundamental biological cycles."[53] He then assured his readers that significant research efforts had been launched in this regard. As an anonymous author of a *Time* magazine piece would also remind his readers a few years later, when DDT "was first offered to the general public in 1945, the U.S. Army and Public Health Service warned that the wonder insecticide had better be used cautiously. No one knew much about DDT's long-range effect on human beings or on the balance of nature." Besides, no one ever "stepped forward to deny that careless use of DDT is dangerous."[54]

Perhaps the most comprehensive early popular piece on the topic was penned by the great British entomologist Vincent Brian Wigglesworth in the December 1945 issue of *The Atlantic Monthly*.[55] Titled "DDT and the Balance of Nature," the article's subtitle stated the author's intent in no uncertain terms: "Will man's extensive use of DDT upset the balance of nature in our forests, fields, and streams?" Wigglesworth's piece was far from alarmist.[56] It described numerous trials being conducted from the United States to West Africa and India and raised some then unanswered questions. The "Wiggler" (as he was known to his friends) then added that what remained to be seen was whether the methods used were "feasible economically and desirable biologically" and that if DDT was a big step forward in insectide research and applications, it was certainly not the last word.[57] He then turned his attention to the effect that DDT might have on the balance of nature, by which he meant the "complex assemblage of interacting organisms," including insects beneficial to humans, to which the compound might turn out to be much like a "blunderbuss discharging shot in a manner so haphazard that friend and foe alike are killed."[58]

The British entomologist had no reservation against its use in houses as most people deemed all indoor insects undesirable. In this context, DDT "confer[red] nothing but benefits," which he also believed true in the case of "the insects which live on the bodies of man and animals."[59] When used against mosquitoes through either spraying it on water or through aerial spraying of forests, however, its use was more problematic as "it may have far-reaching effects which it is impossible at present to predict," such as removing or poisoning important food sources for birds and fishes, attacking beneficial insects such as pollinating honey bees[60] and others that kept damaging insect populations under control. In time, like other insecticides before it, it might also result in the development of insects with innate resistance to it. Wigglesworth then added that "chemicals which upset the balance of nature have been known before DDT," and DDT was "merely the latest and one of the most violent" in this respect.[61] What was needed was a better understanding of the ecology of insect pests, which would then allow a more timely planting of crops and better crop rotations to minimize damage. Despite advances in the use of "so-called cultural or naturalistic methods of controls," the need for insecticides would remain. The development and use of "insecticides which discriminate between friend and foe" could be made more efficient through a better understanding of their targets, for in the end an "insecticide which kills 50 percent of the pest insect and none of its predators or parasites may be far more valuable than one which kills 95 percent but at the same time eliminates its natural enemies."[62]

Figure 3.1
Government Pamphlet on DDT, 1946

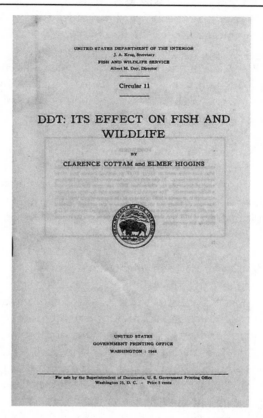

UNITED STATES DEPARTMENT OF THE INTERIOR
J. A. Krug, Secretary
FISH AND WILDLIFE SERVICE
Albert M. Day, Director

Circular 11

**DDT: ITS EFFECT ON FISH AND
WILDLIFE**

BY

CLARENCE COTTAM and ELMER HIGGINS

UNITED STATES
GOVERNMENT PRINTING OFFICE
WASHINGTON : 1946

For sale by the Superintendent of Documents, U. S. Government Printing Office
Washington 25, D. C. - Price 5 cents

Like all significant technological advances, DDT had its early scientific supporters and detractors. Perhaps the most significant in the latter case were U.S. Fish and Wildlife Service researchers, most prominently its senior biologist (and soon to be assistant director), Clarence Cottam, who observed in a widely circulated pamphlet (see Figure 3.1) that from "the beginning of its wartime use, the potency of DDT has been the cause of both enthusiasm and grave concern. Some have come to consider it a cure-all for pest insects; others are alarmed because of its potential harm."[63] Interestingly, Cottam had been one of the two most prominent critics of marshland drainage for mosquito control in the previous decade, the other being the National Association of Audubon Societies' William Vogt, whose later work will be discussed in the following section. Cottam's main argument in that case was that unrestricted drainage "removes the water that wildfowl like and fish must have," a procedure that upsets "the whole biological balance."[64] He had also taken "early leadership in pointing to the detrimental effect of environmental pollution by insecticides and pesticides"[65] and was not only Carson's colleague when she joined the federal bureaucracy but also arguably her most important mentor on the subjects of pesticides and land conservation. Interestingly, Carson edited his early reports on the topic—along with those of other Fish and Wildlife Service scientists on DDT use—and Cottam would later play a crucial role in helping her write *Silent Spring*. Carson also occasionally interacted socially with both Cottam and Vogt through her active involvement in the D.C. branch of the Audubon Society.[66]

The New Republic quickly echoed Cottam's concerns in an article titled "Dynamite in DDT" by John Kenneth Terres,[67] a former field biologist of the Soil Conservation Service who later became perhaps the most important popular American bird writer.[68] Like other commentators, Terres reported a test conducted the previous year in a Pennsylvania forest afflicted by a gypsy-moth caterpillar outbreak in which aerial spraying of deliberately high doses of DDT had lead the sun to rise the next morning "on a forest of great silence—the silence of total death." Indeed, "not a bird call broke the ominous quiet" as thousands of them "had been sacrificed to a practical experiment to see how much DDT birds could withstand."[69] He further observed that removing "the birds and helpful insects from large areas of the earth" might result in a "great famine" and that "DDT's greatest defect for use out-of-doors is its nonselective killing power," which might be "likened to firing a broadside at a throng of people in which we have both enemies and friends." While DDT was the perfect indoors insecticide, when "used out-of-doors it is the most dangerous insecticide ever devised by man" because it failed to harm many "destructive pests" while hurting beneficial ones.[70] Ample evidence also showed that, as with some other insecticidal compounds, "some destructive insects develop an immunity to certain insecticides" after years of spraying; DDT might move up the food chain if "dairy cattle are allowed to graze on areas sprayed or dusted" with it; and its use might eventually have to be reduced "to a much finer selectivity if it is to spare many wild creatures which we not only seek for recreation but depend on for existence."[71]

Two years later, a series of articles on "DDT and You" was published by the journalist-activist Albert Deutsch in the *New York Post* in which he claimed that a mysterious ailment "Virus X" had risen to epidemic proportions in the Los Angeles area that could be traced back to the "indiscriminate use of the chemical" and that DDT was also getting into foodstuffs and milk products in dangerous amounts. Critics of this exposé admitted the problematic nature of the widespread use of DDT in dairy barns, on milk cows, and on the fodder destined for their consumption—but then quickly added that the practice had already been banned even though no dangerously contaminated milk samples had ever been found. Besides, the so-called mysterious diseases already existed before DDT use began.[72]

Interestingly, in the wake of her editing work on DDT research at the Fish and Wildlife Service, Carson pitched an article on the subject to the editors of *Reader's Digest* in 1945, to no avail. A decade and a half later the magazine did publish a highly critical piece on the aerial spraying of DDT. By then Carson was widely known, and the article probably reflected the content of a lengthy letter she had sent the magazine upon learning a staff reporter was researching a story on the practice.[73] Titled "Backfire in the War against Insects," the article was replete with vivid descriptions of wildlife kills and told readers in no uncertain terms that there was "mounting evidence that massive aerial spraying of pesticides may do more harm than good." While the "costs of the[se] campaigns in money, destruction of wildlife and possible harm to human health are not adequately known," their need was both "hotly challenged and hotly defended."[74]

Another contribution to the topic hit the bookshelves a few months before the publication of *Silent Spring*. In 1962, authored by the radical social theorist Murray Bookchin[75] under the pen name of Lewis Herber, *Our Synthetic Environment* was a direct throwback to the guinea pig literature—indeed, it relied heavily on Consumers' Research staff work—but added new environmental concerns.[76] As could be expected, Bookchin discussed new products and compounds developed since the 1930s, including DDT. Because modern societies had become increasingly dependent on synthetic products and modern (mono) agricultural practices, he wrote, a point had been reached "where the natural supports for life . . . [were] rapidly dwindling" as modern man was "undoing the work of organic evolution, replacing a complex environment with a simpler one" and "disassembling the biotic pyramid that ha[d] supported human life for countless millennia."[77] He had previously written a lengthy essay on "The Problems of Chemicals in Food." In that 1952 piece, building on recent scientific controversies, he suggested that DDT was probably causing an "epidemic of nervous and physical disorders" and that the "use of chemicals in food has, in fact, become so extensive and reckless that mass poisoning is now a real danger to the American population" while "instances of acute toxic effects have already approached the point of national disasters."

An additional source of Bookchin's claims and speculations was the zoologist Robert Rudd, who published two influential articles on pesticides in *The Nation* in 1959.[78] Rudd wrote this material as he was working on a lengthy yet reasonably accessible study on the topic that became *Pesticides and the Living Landscape.*[79] The book was originally scheduled to be published before *Silent Spring* but got bogged down in controversy during its review process. Be that as it may, Rudd's work played a crucial role in shaping Carson's thinking as they corresponded and became personal friends in 1958. Rudd had begun his outreach efforts at the suggestion of officers of the Conservation Foundation who had asked him to produce "a general study of the influence of pesticides in nature."[80] The first foundation officer thanked by Rudd in his acknowledgements was the organization's co-founder and first president (from 1948 to 1961), Fairfield Osborn.[81] In his 1948 best seller, *Our Plundered Planet,* Osborn observed that while DDT might seem a "cure-all," some initial experiments had shown it to be "withering to bird life as a result of birds eating the insects that have been impregnated with the chemical." In addition, the careless use of this substance could result in the destruction of "fishes, frogs and toads, all of which live on insects."[82] Carson acknowledged in *Silent Spring* that she was vastly indebted to "a host of people, many of them unknown to me personally," who "first spoke against the reckless and irresponsible poisoning of the world that man shares with all other creatures, and who are even now fighting the thousands of small battles that in the end will bring victory for sanity and common sense in our accommodation to the world that surrounds us."[83]

Contrary to now widespread beliefs as to the originality of her writings on pesticides, Carson's contribution on the topic can legitimately be characterized as vintage technophobic muckraking in quality literary clothing. While she acknowledged an "insect problem" and opposed a complete ban on synthetic pesticides, the implication of her book title and her "fable for tomorrow" left little room to the imagination of her readers. Besides, she further argued that, because they were "man-made," synthetic insecticides "differ sharply from the simpler insecticides of prewar days [that] were derived from naturally occurring minerals and plant products" and, because of their "enormous biological potency," they had "immense power not merely to poison but to enter into the most vital processes of the body and change them in sinister and often deadly ways."[84] She not only raised old and contentious allegations that arsenic-based insecticides had caused "sickness and death among horses, cows, goats, pigs, deer, fishes, and bees" but went one step further and stated in no uncertain terms that "modern insecticides are still more deadly."[85]

If Carson's arguments on pesticides were hardly groundbreaking, even by popular book and article standards, the same can also be said of her broader ecological vision, as will now be reviewed through a brief discussion of the biggest environmental best seller of all time before the publication of *Silent Spring*.

Laying the Foundations of Modern Environmentalism: William Vogt's 1948 *Road to Survival*

Pessimistic stances on overpopulation and growth-induced depletion of soils, minerals, and biomass resources, along with the core insights behind such concepts as ecological balance and steady-state economics, are probably as old as civilization and were discussed in various forms by ancient thinkers such as Confucius, Plato, and Aristotle, among others.[86] Such concerns were also pervasive in advanced economies in the decades preceding the publication of *Silent Spring*. To give but two illustrations, the American engineer Frederick Winslow Taylor began his 1911 *Principles of Scientific Management* by stating that his contemporaries could "see our forests vanishing, our water-powers going to waste, our soil being carried by floods into the sea; and the end of our coal and our iron is in sight."[87] Widespread fears about the impact of land mismanagement, irremediable top soil losses, and potential ecological collapse were reflected in abundant literature on erosion that was synthesized in G. V. Jacks and R. O. Whyte's 1939 *The Rape of the Earth: A World Survey of Soil Erosion*.[88] This line of thinking reached an even larger audience in the post–World War II era with the publication in 1948 of William Vogt's *Road to Survival* and Fairfield Osborn's *Our Plundered Planet*. As historian Samuel P. Hays observed 10 years later, these books shifted the dominant American intellectual atmosphere "from optimism to a guarded pessimism" where people thought "less of possibilities and more of limits" and "less in terms of human betterment, and more in terms of human survival."[89] The result was a growing acceptance that "technology was not enough; resources were not unlimited [and] the pressure of population itself must be reduced." Because Vogt's book was the biggest environmental best seller in history before *Silent Spring*, we turn to its content to put Carson's alleged originality in broader perspective.

Vogt's *Road to Survival*—translated into nine languages and also published in a condensed version by *Reader's Digest* in 1949 (soon itself translated into 11 languages)—reached an estimated 20 to 30 million individuals.[90] Indeed, the great French demographer Alfred Sauvy,[91] a man not known for exaggerated claims, compared its impact to that of Malthus.[92] Soon after its publication, the book was added to the list of mandatory readings in several American institutions of higher education. In time, it influenced notable individuals such as Paul Ehrlich and Al Gore. Despite its prominence, discussions of Vogt's best seller are now limited to a few academic contributions.[93] As David Cameron Duffy observed, William Vogt would turn out to be "one of those frustrating people who influenced people and events but never received the credit his contributions merit. He left several books, institutions, ideas, and numerous friends, but little in the way of fame."[94]

Born in 1902 in Minneola, New York, Vogt was a descendant of New Amsterdam's first Episcopal rector. Influenced at an early age by the nature writings of Ernest Thompson Seton, he trained in literature and languages but also became an avid birdwatcher and a self-described ecologist. In time, he became curator of the Jones Beach State Bird Sanctuary (Long Island, New York), editor of *Bird-Lore* magazine, and field naturalist and lecturer for the Audubon Society. The latter position gave him the opportunity to travel extensively in the United States and to specialize in water conservation and bird populations. He became America's leading opponent of marshland drainage for mosquito control in the 1930s.[95] Following internal conflicts that forced him to leave Audubon,[96] Vogt became an adviser to the Peruvian state-owned guano company and eventually returned from South America with a newfound interest in overpopulation, resource scarcity, and agricultural land degradation. He further developed his expertise on these issues as head of the conservation section of the Pan American Union (later the Organization of American States), where he coordinated surveys of the agricultural potential and environmental state of Latin American countries. These experiences, along with his reading of the environmental and eugenics literatures of his time, eventually came together in the *Road to Survival*. Interestingly, while the book gained him much recognition, it also probably cost him his day job, as his open advocacy of birth control did not sit well with the political and religious authorities of Latin American countries.[97] He later served as National Director of the Planned Parenthood Federation from 1951 to 1962 and then as Secretary of the Conservation Foundation and representative of the International Union for the Conservation of Nature and Natural Resources to the United Nations, positions he occupied until almost his last days in 1968.[98]

In *Road to Survival,* Vogt did not mince words as to the scope and interconnectedness of the environmental crises of his time. "By exploitation of the world's resources on a purely extractive basis," he wrote, humans "had postponed the meeting at the ecological judgement seat." The "handwriting on the wall of five continents," however, was now telling them unequivocally that "the Day of Judgment is at hand."[99] All people were in this together, as they now formed "an earth-company, and the lot of the Indiana farmer can no longer be isolated from that of the Bantu" because environmental degradation half a world away ultimately affected the living standards of citizens everywhere.[100] In this context, dominant ideas that evolved 20 centuries ago, while "magnificent in their days," had now become "millstones about [human] necks" and were nothing short of "idiotic in an over peopled, atomic age, with much of the world a shambles."[101]

Like many environmentalists before and since, Vogt's basic thesis ultimately rested on the finiteness of available resources coupled with humanity's drastic disturbance of the "living web."[102] He observed that "as the varied soils depend on many interacting factors, so does the form that the life upon them takes. The interrelationships of these factors are dynamic, not static. A system of stresses and strains is set up, and an ecological equilibrium is reached over long periods of time. In any area, plants and animals themselves influence the total environment and thus the equilibrium."[103] While men everywhere disturbed these equilibriums in various ways, he opined, the cessation of their activities would, in time, allow ecosystems to recover, although obviously the "time required for return of the climax will depend on the severity and extent of disturbance, in relation to local conditions."[104] He added, "the earth is not made of rubber; it cannot be stretched; the human race, every nation, is limited in the number of acres it possesses. And as the number of human beings *increases*, the relative amount of productive earth *decreases*, by that amount."[105] Indeed, if history had taught the conservationist anything, it was that ecological collapse inexorably followed so-called "civilizational progress" for, with rare exceptions, man had "taken the bounty of the earth and made little or no return" through overgrazing and overcropping.[106] This self-destructive tendency, which had already spelled the doom of many civilizations, was once again repeating itself, but this time on a magnified scale. True, he argued, warnings similar to his had been made before, but the only reason the theories of the "clear-sighted English clergyman" Dr. Malthus[107] had failed to materialize was that Europeans had been awash in "the bounty from the New World cornucopia"[108] and had increasingly come to depend on imports from distant lands from Africa to Australia and Latin America. Unbeknown to most people, however, sugar production "was wearing out the soil in the West Indies," and coffee was "ripping down hillsides from Guatemala to Brazil."[109] Other imports were obtained at the cost of "gullies in Georgia, dongas in South Africa, barrancas in El Salvador, floods in Missouri, [and] dust storms in the Tasman Sea."[110]

In this context, Vogt saw drastic population control as the only effective solution. He thus chastised the authors of a Food and Agricultural Organization report on the prospects of post–WW II Greece because it didn't contain any "suggestion that a positive effort be made to reduce the breeding of the Greeks," a stance that "would disqualify a wildlife manager in our most backward states!"[111]

Rich countries like the United States should absolutely refrain from subsidizing "the unchecked spawning" of the inhabitants of poor countries such as India and China until they had adopted a "rational population policy."[112] Vogt followed his core ideas to their logical ends when he wrote that "one of the greatest national assets" of poor economies was their high death rates;[113] that the introduction of new cultivars was also destructive in the long run, for even corn had probably caused more misery than another potent contribution of the New World, syphilis;[114] that pests such as tsetse flies and malaria-carrying mosquitoes[115] were truly "blessings in disguise" as well as the "protector of important resources,"[116] and that indeed measures to alleviate human suffering, such as the "flank attack on the tsetse fly with DDT[117] or some other insecticide" carried out by "ecologically ignorant sanitarians, entomologists, and medical men"[118] were in the end worse than doing nothing. Anticipating later writings on the "lifeboat ethics" and the "economics of spaceship earth,"[119] Vogt failed to see "any kindness in keeping people from dying of malaria so that they could die more slowly of starvation."[120] The modern medical profession, he added, was setting the stage for a disaster of epic proportions by continuing to believe that it had "a duty to keep alive as many people as possible" because, "through medical care and improved sanitation," it would end up being responsible "for more millions living more years in increasing misery."[121]

Like most environmentalist theoreticians, Vogt professed an overt dislike of urbanization and of advances in production technologies. The case against cities was straightforward. Their growth and the "extension of highways" shrank the amount of land available for farming and thereby reduced its "potential carrying capacity."[122] Despite short-term benefits, he added, past innovations such as fire, the axe, the plough, and firearms had ultimately resulted in "despoiled forests, erosion, wildlife extermination, overgrazing, and the dropping of water tables" and the consequent reduction of productivity in "some of the most fertile and productive regions of the earth" to levels almost comparable to those observed in "the Gobi or the tundras in Siberia."[123] Recent agricultural technologies were similarly "of dubious value to the land," as they were "more purely extractive than older methods," brought lower quality land under cultivation; were too dependent on rapidly dwindling petroleum reserves; and triggered a drift away from rural to urban areas, thereby reducing "the effectiveness of the self-contained rural population as an economic shock absorber" during future recessions.[124] Even so, Vogt considered the farmer "far more useful, productive, able and hard-working a member of our society than the vast majority of businessmen."[125]

Vogt's contempt for technological advances and urbanization were matched by his disdain for "the methods of free competition and the application of the profit motive" because people operating under "so-called economic laws" generally disregarded "the physical and biological laws" governing the land itself. "Profits are loss" he stated. Indeed, the fact that humans assumed that "what has been good for industry must necessarily be good for the land" would likely turn out to be "one of the most expensive mistakes in history."[126] Vogt's dislike of free markets stemmed in part from his abhorrence of popular consumerism and the environmental impact of its attendant "gadgetry," such as the destruction of the world's forest required for the production of "pulp-paper ordure of 'love' stories, crime tales, and 'comics' and the building of large hydroelectric dams for the sake of "unessential electrical knickknacks" and industries. Besides, these vulgar pleasures also meant that the United States exhibited "one of the highest insanity rates in the world."[127] The problem, as he saw it, was largely the impossibility of assigning "a cash value to the heart's lift at the flash of a scarlet tanager, the outpoured song of the solitaire, the towering of white ibises over the Everglades, or even the homely chattering of the dooryard wren."[128] Unfortunately, when touched by colonization, native populations exhibited much the same tendency to show off newfound wealth, which often took the form of new cattle acquisitions that resulted in the destruction of natural capital such as "pasturage, fertility, and available water resources."[129]

Vogt's dislike of economic development also stemmed from his observation of the destructive practices of the American stockmen and sheepherders who "deteriorate and destroy the grasses, expedite erosion, and contribute to flood peaks," of the "cut-out-and-get-out lumberman," of the "wheat grower who recklessly sets the trigger for a new dust-bowl explosion," of the "hunter or trapper who takes more than his share of *surplus* animals," and of "the farmer who exhausts his soil and fails to utilize soil-stabilization methods."[130] Of course, he added, "renewable resources" were only truly so when "managed on a sustainable-yield basis, with the crop restricted to replacement capacity." Unfortunately, Americans had been living on their "resource capital" since 1607.[131] "Get rich quick" schemes had also fostered among his compatriots a "waster's psychology" that would have "appalled [their] frugal forebears" and was regarded as "lunacy—even criminal lunacy—by people in other parts of the world."[132]

Vogt's take on the environmental impact of the profit motive typically equated free markets with profits at any costs and by any means, including government subsidies, government-granted privileges, and environmentally destructive public initiatives that trampled private parties' property rights. He did nonetheless allude to the impact of social institutions on resource stewardship when he acknowledged that "because sharecroppers and other farm tenants do not have a long-range stake in the land, their tendency—a reflection of our industrial philosophy—is to make as large a profit as possible and to spend on the land as little as possible."[133] Although he did observe that turning tenancy into ownership would improve the land's prospects in some circumstances,[134] he couldn't refrain from observing that in "other areas, such a change might well tend to have the opposite effect."[135] A case in point was Zapatista's Mexico, where land reform had empowered less educated individuals who were reluctant to change their farming methods. Vogt also described cases later labelled as tragedies of the commons, rent seeking, and perverse subsidies.[136] Cases of the former included mismanaged underground water supplies and commercial fisheries whose practitioners, "assuming the pirate's prerogative to take whatever he can get, have reduced the populations of several important fishes to a point where it is no longer economically possible to take them."[137] Illustrations of the latter circumstances ranged from subsidies to sheep producers who were overgrazing and degrading the land[138] to incentives to build on flood plains that turned out to be "national liabilities" when the unavoidable water outbursts periodically occurred.[139] In the end, he left little doubt in the minds of his readers that professional public land managers freed from political pressures would achieve better results than less-educated and competent private owners.[140]

Vogt's remedies were fairly straightforward, if not always spelled out in much detail. Although "economic, political, educational, and other measures" were indispensable, they would succeed only if "population control and conservation [were] included." Indeed, economic and political prescriptions that ignored "the ecological" dimension might force "the human race deeper into the mire."[141] In turn, ecological health depended on two factors. First, renewable resources must be used to produce as much wealth as possible on a sustained-yield basis, but not more. Second, human demands must be adjusted to "natural" supply, either through lowered living standards or population control and reduction. Since most people would not accept the former, he argued, the need for population cuts was unavoidable.[142]

Although now largely forgotten, Vogt's best seller was undoubtedly crucial in shaping the intellectual content of modern environmentalism. Indeed, as the journalist Alston Chase[143] observed, "for the next three decades, every argument, every concept, every recommendation made in *The Road to Survival* would become integral to the conventional wisdom of the post-Hiroshima generation of educated Americans." That statement remains true to this day if one excludes high levels of concern about both synthetic pesticides and human-induced climate change, issues which Vogt didn't address save a few comments on the impact of agriculture on microclimates and their disastrous consequences (for instance, he linked grasshopper outbreaks to "man's disturbance of microclimates through his destruction of vegetation"[144]). As can be expected, however, anthropogenic influences on the climate have been a concern since before the 18th century, and are perhaps as old as agriculture itself.[145]

An objective assessment of both Carson's and her friend Vogt's best sellers can only result in a verdict of greater originality and scope for the former. An interesting footnote to this consideration is Vogt's reviews of both *Silent Spring* and Bookchin's *Our Synthetic Environment* in a 1963 issue of the periodical *Natural History*. In the piece titled "On Man the Destroyer," he surmised that "*Silent Spring* could do for the control of chemical pollution of our environment what Upton Sinclair's *The Jungle* did for the Pure Food and Drug Act of 1906."[146] A self-described "admirer of Miss Carson and her writings" who thought that, "on the whole," her facts and interpretations were "substantially correct," he considered *Silent Spring*'s most important message to be "that man is still as much a part of nature as, more than a century ago, Darwin showed him to be," and that its theme was "man's mismanagement of his environment." On the other hand, Carson did not quite achieve "an ecological approach" by viewing the problems she raised "as a dynamic structure of dependent variables in which our economy is embedded."[147]

Vogt's statements are a far cry from the notion that Carson was breaking any new ground. He also pointed out a number of flaws and shortcomings in her presentation. For example, she quoted the work of Dr. Joseph Hickey on "heavy robin mortality—86 to 88 percent—as a result of spraying" without telling her readers that, in another paper, the same researcher had observed that "when such killing is concentrated and large populations of birds live outside the sprayed areas, they will repopulate empty habitats once the toxicants disappear, sometimes in a matter of weeks," a fact that was also true in the case of trout food populations after spruce budworm spraying in Maine.[148] Another issue was that "her reports on the effect of new chemicals on cell physiology, with possible genetic and carcinogenic results, are fascinating and hair-raising—as well as speculative and supposititious."[149] Finally, her suggested alternatives to synthetic pesticide spraying struck him as "not, on the whole, practices that would be feasible until after years, or even decades, of experimentation and adjustment."[150] "Certainly," he added, "without chemical aids our vaunted farm-production-per-man-hour would drop sharply, and it is dubious whether we could maintain production-per-acre at anything like current levels."[151] Interestingly, Vogt later told Carson's editor that his review of the book could not be entirely positive because he had been contacted by officials of the World Health Organization who feared that *Silent Spring* might undermine their anti-malarial campaign,[152] a claim that is somewhat surprising in light of his previous statements on the issue.

Conclusion

Rachel Carson's impact on the environmentalist movement and the broader culture was significant. The standard claims made on behalf of the intellectual originality of her most famous book, however, are more difficult to sustain. Although not the most outgoing individual, Carson's position in the federal bureaucracy, her involvement with the Audubon Society, and her later fame as a popular writer made her very much a part of the environmentalist circles of her time. She also had affinities for and friendships with individuals who were steeped in intellectual traditions, from the New England transcendentalists to the organic farming movement, which shaped her outlook on life.[153] *Silent Spring* was therefore not the work of an isolated and pioneering mind that swam alone against an overwhelming intellectual current but rather of someone who belonged to a broader network of like-minded writers, scientists, and activists that was much more significant than is now generally recognized. As one prominent critic put it, the book would naturally appeal to "the organic gardeners, the anti-fluoride leaguers, the worshipers of 'natural foods,' those who cling to the philosophy of a vital principal, and pseudo-scientists and faddists."[154] As such, the book is probably better thought of as the most successful post–World War II installment of a perspective that had been rather fully developed in previous popular best sellers than as the watershed monument it is typically made out to be. Assuming we are right in our assessment, what explains its now iconic status and the fact that other environmental best sellers of the post-war era are now virtually forgotten? We can think of a few possible explanations.

The first is that Carson's original popularity can essentially be attributed to old-fashioned "chemical muckraking" and long-standing popular fears of pesticides of all kinds, but especially synthetic ones because they are produced by industrial corporate chemical processes rather than by biological organisms or geological processes. Although governmental policy regarding some of these substances might have been reckless and misguided, we doubt that a vast majority of people never harbored any doubts as to their potential side-effects until *Silent Spring* came along. Far from being a canary in a coal mine or a chemical factory, Carson actually delivered, in the words of science writer Edwin Diamond,[155] "just what the public wanted to hear"—in essence, distrust of mad scientists who played God and meddled with nature, large corporations who put profit ahead of people, and governmental lackeys who were only too happy to cover up incriminating evidence. Had she produced a more balanced account rather than claims of gross corporate negligence, life extinctions, widespread cancers, and cellular mutations, *Silent Spring*'s popular impact might have been negligible.

Other factors also undoubtedly played in Carson's favor. She was already a well-known and respected popular author and also a sincere woman with a science degree willing to take on the profit-seeking establishment. Her advocacy of an "other road" of working closer with "Nature" rather than against it came in the wake of a few dramatic technological developments and events, from nuclear testing and the cranberry scare of 1959 to the thalidomide fiasco and the mass spraying of insecticides on a reluctant citizenry. Carson also wrote for a rapidly growing urban population that was reaping the benefits of decades of public health interventions and whose practical knowledge of modern agricultural practices and epidemic diseases was superficial. Unlike most previous environmental writers and activists, she did not come from or could not be directly associated with the aristocracy, the moneyed elite, or even hunting clubs and associations, not to mention intellectual traditions such as eugenics, racial ideologies, or the radical left. Carson was in the business of saving lives from a toxic menace rather than making sure that lives deemed not worth living were not lived in the first place, thus making her more palatable to broader audiences later. Finally, she often spoke of present and future menaces in somewhat vague terms, without naming specific products. As such, she could not be ridiculed for her failed apocalyptic predictions soon after the publication of her book. These factors, along with the timing of her publication at the beginning of a decade of major social unrest, are probably the true reasons why a somewhat reclusive nature writer became a popular icon rather than another now largely forgotten technophobic muckraker and neo-Malthusian essayist.

4. *Silent Spring* as Secular Religion

Robert H. Nelson

Rachel Carson and I had some common formative experiences. I spent 18 years at the U.S. Department of the Interior from 1975 to 1993, one year longer than the 17 years that she was there from 1935 to 1952. Admittedly, Carson was trained as a biologist, while I am trained as an economist. She worked for the Fish and Wildlife Service, while I worked in the Office of Policy Analysis, the principle policy office serving the Office of the Secretary of the Interior.[1] Still, whatever the differences in professional backgrounds and outlooks, my Interior years, like Carson's, did much to shape my future thinking and writing.

My Interior job gave me the opportunity to observe many environmental policy debates first hand. The clashes between environmentalists and their opponents (many of them economists), I increasingly concluded, amounted to a new form of religious warfare, fortunately in this case without violence. As an economist, I initially felt unprepared to address this subject, which clearly involved matters well beyond my professional training. My first published writing on this subject thus was long delayed, until three years before I left the Interior Department, a 1990 article—"Unoriginal Sin: The Judeo-Christian Roots of Ecotheology"—that described environmentalism as a new form of religion.[2] In 1991, I applied a similar lens to the thinking of the economics profession in a book, *Reaching for Heaven on Earth: The Theological Meaning of Economics*.[3] Many subsequent articles, chapters, and books have followed on these matters.[4]

Environmentalism and economics, as I discovered over the years, fall within the overall category of a "secular religion." A secular religion is a real religion. It is nevertheless "secular" in the sense that it may not mention a god in the hereafter at all, or it may minimize the role of any such god. Despite this difference, secular religions compete with traditional religions in that they both provide an overarching framework of meaning in the world. As Paul Tillich famously put it, a religion can be defined as a belief system that seeks to answer the "ultimate concerns" of human existence.[5] Like the Bible for Christians and the Tanakh for Jews, western secular religions typically provide an account of the true meaning of history.[6] There is a beginning, a middle shaped by a god or other causal force that determines the course of history, and in many cases a final glorious ending. In the secular religions of western civilization, also reflecting the influence of Judaism and Christianity, the final ending typically resolves a fierce conflict between good and evil that has been waged throughout history.

In the 20th century, secular religions exerted as much if not more influence on the course of history as Judaism, Christianity, and other traditional religions. National Socialism in Germany and Marxism were particularly important religions of a secular kind. Recognition of the underlying religious character of both of these movements grew steadily over the course of the century. Today, it is almost a truism; no account of the history of National Socialism or Marxism would be complete without some mention of their religious character. In a recent review of a book about French resistance and collaboration with the Germans during World War II, for example, Ian Buruma writes of a subsequent French collaborator who "was invited in 1937 to attend the Nazi rally in Nuremberg, and came back so impressed with all the drum beating, flag-waving, goose-stepping Hitler worship that he compared the event to the Eucharist. Perhaps you had to be a French reactionary to see the body of Christ in the Führer"—but all too many people seemingly did (or something like it).[7]

Igal Halfin is an Israeli historian who explained in 2000, on the basis of extensive archival research, how life in revolutionary Russia in the 1920s was everywhere a reflection of "messianic aspirations," as found in the teachings of Marxist religion that "shaped the identity of the Soviet citizen." Marxism was, moreover, significantly derived from biblical sources, even if few Marxists recognized it. As Halfin reports, "Marxists would doubtless have renounced notions such as good, evil, messiah, and salvation as baseless religious superstitions that had nothing to do with the revolutionary experience. Yet, these concepts, translated into a secular key, continued to animate Communist discourse" in Russia for at least two decades after the

1917 revolution.[8] As described by Halfin, the parallels have become easy to see today:

> The Marxist concept of universal History was essentially inspired by the Judeo-Christian bracketing of historical time between the Fall of Adam and the Apocalypse. The Original Expropriation, at the beginning of time, represented a rupture in the timeless primitive Communism, which inaugurated History and set humanity on a course of self-alienation. The universal Revolution, an abrupt and absolute event, was to return humanity to itself in a fiery cataclysm. . . . Imbuing time with a historical teleology that gave meaning to events, Marxist eschatology described history as moral progression from the darkness of class society to the light of Communism.[9]

As this chapter will explore, Rachel Carson's 1962 book *Silent Spring* is also a statement of secular religion, if obviously well removed from gospels such as National Socialism or Marxism that preached violence in society as the natural path of history.[10] The large historical influence of *Silent Spring* in the United States reflects its role as an important work in the development of environmental religion in this country.[11] The progressive "gospel of efficiency" was the dominant religious influence on public affairs for the larger part of the 20th century. Environmental religion, a faith more skeptical of the ability of economic progress to save the world, emerged to challenge economic religion in the last decades of the 20th century.[12] *Silent Spring* helped set the stage for this rise of environmental faith in American life.[13]

To fully understand Rachel Carson and the historical significance of *Silent Spring*, some background is necessary on the developments in American—mainly secular—religious history in which *Silent Spring* played a significant part.[14]

Sin and Redemption

The story of America as a nation is a religious story. Mainstream Protestantism has declined sharply in recent decades in the United States, but the big speeches of our political leaders still routinely echo the Protestant history of the nation. The message is one of sin and redemption. We have committed many past wrongs, but the time has now come to repent and reform. As Americans in particular, we are called to a higher standard, because this nation, as the early Puritans in Massachusetts said, is a "city upon a hill" to shine a beacon to all mankind. This idea of America as a beacon for the world was partially secularized after the American Revolution to become a new model of economic progress, liberty, and democracy. Each new president is required to repeat this message on suitable public occasions, if in ways that reflect the specific economic and other circumstances of that president.

In his 2011 State of the Union address, for example, President Obama not only offered an agenda of specific policy proposals but also the latest updating of the American national faith. This was an opportunity for him to transcend traditional political differences, a bi-partisan stance politically useful in the wake of the 2010 elections. America is a nation uniquely created, Obama said in the address, on "common hopes and a common creed."[15] This mission is what "sets us apart as a nation" from other nations around the world. As a nation of immigrants, we are a place where "every race and faith and point of view can be found," binding us together as "one people"—a message of particular poignancy coming from the first black president of the United States. America must be "not just a place on a map, but the light to the world." John Winthrop could not have said it much better.

Owing to many large failings of our government and business leaders, who put indifference or greed above the national interest, we have recently suffered the worst economic downturn since the Great Depression. We fell into sin once again. But now, the president said, we are renouncing our recent wayward past; instead, "we are poised for progress." If we can address the many "challenges that have been decades in the making," the products of our past failures as a nation, our success is assured. But it will not be easy. We must be committed to remaking ourselves. As President Obama said, "Sustaining the American dream has never been about standing pat. It has required each generation to sacrifice, and struggle, and meet the demands of a new age." God offers no guarantees.

One of our greatest sins has been the corruption of our national politics by private interests and the forces of greed more broadly. We have lost all fiscal discipline. Deficits have ballooned, "the legacy," Obama said, of out-of-control "deficit spending that began almost a decade ago." Again, a new national spirit of sacrifice will be required.

The president proposed to freeze domestic spending for five years which "will require painful cuts" for many Americans.

We have also sinned against the environment. Here again, new sacrifices will be required. "By 2035, 80 percent of America's electricity will come from clean energy sources." But here as well, America can reform its ways: we can meet the challenge. "We're telling America's scientists and engineers that if they assemble teams of the best minds in their fields, and focus on the hardest problems in clean energy, we'll fund the Apollo projects of our time."

There are many other such passages in the 2011 State of the Union address. The same messages have been heard over and over again in American political life, ever since the Puritans settled in Massachusetts almost 400 years ago.[16] The specific context of today is of course new: new examples, new policy questions, new implementation proposals. But we are hearing again the religious story of America—we have sinned, we will be called to account, we must reform our ways—but God will bless us in the end, if we now heed his commands.[17] We are the chosen people.

Unlike many of our previous presidents, President Obama barely mentioned God by name (only once in the closing obligatory line, "God bless you, and may God bless the United States of America"). But his speech was characteristic of secular religion in the United States: it was Christian and in this case Protestant through and through. That is the way it has been with much of the most important religions in America (and Europe) in the modern era. Political and economic thinking is no less religious than in earlier times, but the most important forms of religion are now implicit and at least partially disguised.[18] That was true of *Silent Spring*. Indeed, in a different context and with different examples, the book preached many of the same traditional American themes of sin and redemption that President Obama repeated in his State of the Union address.

Environmental Repentance and Reform

While superficially a work of popular science, *Silent Spring* was ultimately a religious treatise. It called on Americans to reform their ways, to renounce their false worship of the dominant secular religion of progress of 20th-century America.[19] That goes a long way toward explaining its large impact; it was seeking to renew American religion, rejecting the Progressive-Era obsessions with expertise and economic growth, returning to an older and truer American religion of an old-fashioned Protestant—and specifically Calvinist—kind. (Carson was brought up in the Presbyterian Church, the Scottish branch of Calvinism). Calvin had warned against the ever-present temptation to worship false idols, as Americans had done in the 20th century with their single-minded pursuit of heaven on earth along a path of ever-continuing economic progress.

In criticizing the use of DDT, Carson quoted approvingly the concerns expressed by a prominent ecologist: "In the name of progress, are we to become victims of our own diabolical means of insect control?"[20] Carson herself wrote of government policies for federal lands in the West: "In the name of progress, the land management agencies have set about to satisfy the insatiable demands of the cattlemen for more grazing land." In a "program of sage eradication," covering large parts of the arid western rangelands, many "millions of acres of sagebrush lands are sprayed each year." Tractors also pulled large chains that ripped the sagebrush from the land. Although Carson did not mention it, federal livestock grazing fees were a pittance, meaning that the government funds for the grazing program were in large part a subsidy to the western livestock industry.[21] Carson was explicitly concerned, however, that the government subsidies had yielded the result that "the whole closely knit fabric of life has been ripped apart" over significant parts of the American West. It meant that "the antelope and the [sage] grouse will disappear along with the sage" itself.[22] Instead of actual progress, federal government rangeland policies pursued in the name of progress had amounted to a large-scale economic and ecological retrogression.

And DDT use for insect control and sagebrush spraying were just two examples. Carson wrote that all of American society had "long been traveling . . . [along] a smooth superhighway on which we progress with great speed, but at the end lies disaster."[23] It was admittedly not such a novel message as it might have appeared. America had once again fallen into sin. The temptations of modern economic progress had encouraged Americans to believe that, using the latest tools of economics and science, they could "play God" with the world for their own human benefit. In the end, progressive religion preached, there would be human salvation by economic means. But as Carson argued (mostly implicitly), only the true God in heaven can remake the world. Fallen human beings, who must work through gravely flawed political systems, will only destroy themselves if they try.[24]

Carson, like many a Protestant preacher before her, called for a new era of repentance and reform.[25] Modern technological hubris and arrogance had to be replaced by a new humility in the human relationship with the natural world. Human beings should not think they could be the new gods. In this and other significant respects, late 20th century environmentalism was in fact a secular religion of "Calvinism minus God."[26] Not only Carson but also John Muir, David Brower, Edward Abbey, and Dave Foreman—indeed a remarkable number of influential figures of American environmental history—were brought up in the Presbyterian Church. Like many other modern thinkers, Carson's ideas were actually shaped by an older religious heritage, even though she may have believed she had left that heritage behind. As environmental historian Mark Stoll observes, "the moral urgency that animates the environmental movement is also a direct legacy of Calvinism and Puritanism. . . . The activist wing of environmentalism traces its roots through the Puritans directly to God's holy self-appointed instruments, the committed Calvinists."[27]

Economic Religion

Marxism is a clear example of an economic religion. The beginning of economic history is found in the arrival of civilization and surplus economic production; the resulting class struggle for scarce material outputs creates human alienation; the rise of religion and other human ideas is merely a false superstructure of illusion—a false consciousness—that reflects the deeper economic workings of the class struggle; and the end of history is the culminating economic apocalypse among warring capitalist and proletarian classes, assuredly leading to a new heaven on earth. The laws of economics for Marx are the new god. Marxism might thus be seen as a great Christian heresy, a main reason it swept across the world in the early-and mid-20th century with all the force of a religious revolution.[28] Marxism offered a Christian understanding of history in the guise of a valid science, thus proving attractive to large numbers of people who had grown up in Christianity but had however mistakenly—rejected it as adults.

In the United States, economic religion is often blended with ideas of America as a chosen nation where democracy and economic progress will be perfected together, thus creating a political and economic model for the world.[29] One might see this mixing of political and economic ideals in alternative lights: as a religion of economic progress in which American democracy is the chosen setting for the perfection of the economic system (and the world), or as a religion of America itself in which rapid economic progress is one key element which happens to play a central, indeed indispensable, role in perfecting the American project.

In the 20th century in the United States, the progressive "gospel of efficiency" was the leading economic religion.[30] It took shape in the Progressive Era, typically dated from 1890 to 1920. Progressives preached the scientific management of society, guided by the apparatus of the central state. Only at the federal level could the leading professional experts of the nation be gathered together to coordinate the material and other perfections of American society. Applying science to political and economic affairs would produce wondrous results in all such areas to match the astonishing material gains already being seen in American industry in the late 19th century.

This Americanized and more democratic version of ideas can be traced back to the scientific positivism of the early French socialists such as Claude Henri de Saint-Simon and Auguste Comte. American intellectual historians Frank and Fritzie Manuel described Comte as the new "High Priest of Humanity" in a new "positivist religion." As objective science increasingly shaped all domains of society, a new perfection of the world meant "a total loss of personality" would replace the old selfish individualism and "man [would merge] in the perfect transcendent unity of Humanity." The lineage was again Christian, but in this case it departed in important ways from the Puritan heritage. Indeed, it owed more to the Roman Catholic tradition.

According to the Manuels, French positivism, and American progressivism to the extent that it followed in that faith, reflected a religious historical past that "ran from the priests of fetishism, through the Catholic Church, to the high sacerdotal authority of the new religion."[31] Thomas Huxley considered Comte's vision of the scientific perfection of society, in essence, a new "Catholicism, minus Christianity."[32] A new priestly hierarchy, the scientists and other technical experts of America, would replace the priesthood of old of the Catholic Church. Washington, D.C., would become the new headquarters of the progressive state church, the American Rome. Progressive faith was the religion, as it developed over the course of the 20th century, of the American welfare and regulatory state.

Admittedly, American progressivism also drew much of its strength from the secularization of the social gospel movement in late 19th-century Protestant Christianity. But this was no longer the Protestantism of Martin Luther, John Calvin, or the 18th-century Jonathan Edwards in New England. By traditional Calvinist standards, the social gospel was yet another economic heresy—a religion not of God but about economic progress in this world as the true path to the salvation of the world. The leading early American economist, Richard Ely, also a leading figure in the social gospel movement of the late 19th century, preached a message that "Christianity is primarily concerned with this world, and it is the mission of Christianity to bring to pass here a kingdom of righteousness." For this purpose, technical knowledge of the workings of the American economy would be required, and thus the heart of religion "in its elaboration, becomes social science." Ely recommended that economics departments be located in schools of theology, declaring that "it is as truly a religious work to pass good laws, as it is to preach sermons; as holy a work to lead a crusade against filth, vice and disease in slums of cities, . . . as it is to send missionaries to the heathen."[33]

Economic progress was the key, not just the economic benefits themselves. With more and more material production, wide redistribution of the benefits of an expanding economy equally among all Americans would become politically feasible. Relieved of the severe stresses of material deprivation, American democracy would work better and better. No longer subject to the intense historical pressures of economic scarcity of the past, individuals would truly come to behave according to the Ten Commandments. As American historian Samuel Haber wrote, the Progressive Era early in the 20th century was characterized by an "efficiency craze" that represented "a secular Great Awakening."[34] A leading political scientist, Dwight Waldo, commented that "it is yet amazing what a position of dominance 'efficiency' assumed, how it waxed until it had assimilated or over-shadowed other values, how men and events came to be degraded or exalted according to what was assumed to be its dictate."[35] In the American Progressive Era, "efficient" and "inefficient" came to replace for many modern men and women the older Christian categories of "good" and "evil." Efficiency was so important because it was the operative measure of economic progress and, as J. B. Bury wrote in 1932, the idea of progress "belongs to the same order of ideas as Providence or personal immortality," the route to a new heaven on earth.[36]

The Progressive Heresy

For Rachel Carson, such forms of modern worship of progress were a grave heresy.[37] Human beings were overstepping their bounds. While the social gospel may have been a product of American Protestantism, it actually had no real need for any Christian God. Indeed, as time passed American progressivism more and more rejected the overtly Christian elements, becoming instead a secular religion. If human beings could save themselves by their own economic actions, they had no need for a distant God in the hereafter whose existence in any case could never be proven by valid scientific methods.

For Carson, however, the corruption of human nature in the "garden" was much more fundamental than the progressives understood. Material explanations were superficial; human behavior had deeper sources than the influence of the surrounding economic environment. Thus, while economic progress had greatly expanded human powers to alter the world, it had done little to change the basic sinfulness of the human condition. Indeed, the Holocaust had shown with great clarity how terrible outcomes could still be reached in an economically advanced nation in "economically efficient" ways; the evils of old-fashioned anti-Semitism had been married to modern economic efficiency to far worse effect. Modern physics had created nuclear energy, giving human beings a vast new power to alter the natural world, but one that also contained the terrifying possibility of destroying most life on earth. *Silent Spring* opens with a dedication to Albert Schweitzer, quoting him: "man has lost the capacity to foresee and forestall. He will end by destroying the earth."

Silent Spring is not, of course, explicitly a work of theology or philosophy. Carson does offer brief strong warnings about the false worship of progress. But her primary argument was to show in one specific area—the spraying of pesticides to control mosquitoes and other insect populations—how the government application of progressive principles of "scientific management" had gone wrong. When Carson was writing, belief in economic progress was still the reigning national religion of America. Thus, for large numbers of Americans, she was a dangerous heretic. Since *Silent Spring* was published, however, her views have become much more common. Not only those in the environmental movement question the basic tenets of progressive religion; Evangelical and Pentecostal Protestants, the most rapidly rising groups among institutional Christianity in American life, share a skepticism that economic progress is the true path to salvation. Indeed, the libertarian movement offers a related critique: economic progress has created vast new powers, but in the hands of frail political leaders and institutions this poses an even greater threat to personal liberties (as events in Germany in the 1930s and 1940s had so dramatically demonstrated).[38]

In 1998, James Scott in *Seeing Like a State* presented what had by then become almost a mainstream viewpoint, a negative verdict based on solid empirical grounds: the failed history in the 20th century of "high modernism."[39] Communism was seemingly not the only economic "god that failed":

> Much of the great state-sponsored calamities of the twentieth century have been the work of rulers with grandiose and utopian plans for their societies. . . . There is no denying that much of the massive, state enforced engineering of the twentieth century has been the work of progressive, often revolutionary elites. Why?

> The answer, I believe, lies in the fact that it is typically progressives who have come to power with a comprehensive critique of existing society and a popular mandate (at least initially) to transform it.

> What is high modernism, then? It is best conceived as a strong (one might even say muscle-bound) version of the beliefs in scientific and technical progress that were associated with industrialization in Western Europe and in North America from roughly 1830 until World War I. At its center was a supreme self-confidence about continued linear progress, the development of scientific and technical knowledge, the

> expansion of production, the rational design of social order, the growing satisfaction of human needs, and, not least, an increasing control over nature (including human nature) commensurate with scientific understanding of natural laws. *High* modernism is thus a particularly sweeping vision of how the benefits of technical and scientific progress might be applied—usually through the state—in every field of human activity.[40]

Progressive modernism may have achieved its widest acceptance in the years prior to the severely disillusioning events of World War I. But it continued to exert a great influence on the political and economic history of the 20th century. Indeed, while there were growing doubts, there were few clear alternatives until the latest "great awakening" of the 1960s onwards. Economist Robert Fogel (winner of the Nobel prize in economics in 1993) wrote in his 2000 book *The Fourth Great Awakening and the Future of Egalitarianism* that "the theory projected by the Social Gospel, and embraced by modernism generally, held that cultural crises could be resolved by rising incomes. That theory has been given a long trial [in the 20th century] and has turned out to be incorrect."[41]

The Pesticide Wars

DDT was originally seen as a "miracle" chemical, yet another marvelous product of modern science that was capable of relieving human beings from the scourge of malaria—as well as the annoying if less dangerous presence of nonmalarial mosquitoes over other wide areas. Until *Silent Spring*, DDT was generally seen as another symbol of progressive religion, one more example of the application of modern science to achieve wonderful results for human beings. Hence, for the advocates of greatly expanded DDT spraying, *Silent Spring* was not just a practical critique of the effectiveness of DDT for controlling mosquitoes and other insects; Carson's book and other criticisms were also a religious challenge.

Indeed, in practice, the progressive religious enthusiasm of DDT advocates often surpassed their actual understanding of the biology of insects in nature. Along with agency interests in winning larger budgets, more employees, and more bureaucratic power, DDT spraying all too often became an end in itself. In the 1940s and 1950s, while spraying did offer significant benefits in some places, DDT also failed in many others. Carson and other skeptics of the religion of progress could easily point to specific instances of DDT failures as testimony to the falsity of the modernist utopian dream.

As Carson wrote in *Silent Spring*, after DDT use began in the 1940s, insects often developed resistance in a matter of just a few years. DDT advocates had failed to consider adequately how rapidly insects could breed and evolve. In Italy, for example, DDT was intensively applied in the mid-1940s to control flies and mosquitoes. But after a heavy application in 1945, Carson reported, "only a year later the first signs of trouble appeared. Both houseflies and mosquitoes of the genus *Culex* began to show resistance to the sprays." In 1948, another strong pesticide, chlordane, was used to supplement the DDT, but it worked for only two more years before strong resistance again developed. Carson reported that, "as rapidly as new chemicals were brought into use, resistance developed. By the end of 1951, DDT, methoxychlor, chlordane, heptachlor, and benzene hexachloride had joined the list of chemicals no longer effective. The flies, meanwhile, had become 'fantastically abundant,'" the result of DDT overwhelming of the balance of nature.[42]

Besides the many cases where resistance soon developed, DDT and other pesticides often had further unanticipated consequences. Intensive spraying of DDT killed not only target insect species, such as mosquitoes, but also other species. Some of those other insect species, however, might themselves be useful in controlling the target species—one insect often preys on or competes with another. Matters could become even worse if resistance developed first in the target species. In that case, DDT would no longer work on the target population, but its natural enemies would be suppressed by DDT. Mosquitoes or other target populations might proliferate well beyond even the levels found prior to the commencement of DDT spraying. As Carson wrote, "In America, farmers have repeatedly traded one insect enemy for a worse one as spraying upsets the population dynamic of the insect world."[43]

In *Silent Spring*, Carson offered a number of such examples. She described how "the spider mite . . . has become practically a worldwide pest as DDT and other insecticides have killed off its enemies." In 1956, for example, the U.S. Forest Service had sprayed 885,000 acres of national forest with DDT as a means of controlling the spruce budworm. But the next year it was discovered that "vast blighted areas could be seen where the magnificent Douglas firs were turning brown and dropping their needles," precisely in those areas where the spraying had occurred. The trees were dying because the intensive DDT spraying had killed off the natural enemies of spider mites, thus altering the dynamics of the insect world to yield "the most extensive and spectacular infestation of spider mites in [the] history" of the area.[44]

Carson's greatest concern, to be sure, was not the failure of the insect control programs as such. Rather, she was horrified by the widespread collateral damage to birds and other kinds of wildlife. Again, she offered a host of compelling examples of government spraying with tragic results for many of the wildlife in the target areas. Carson wrote that "in 1954 the United States Department of Agriculture and the Illinois Department of Agriculture began a program to eradicate the [invasive] Japanese beetle," supported by large public "funds for chemical control [that] came in never-ending streams." Government officials used scare tactics (rather like the Department of Homeland Security today in justifying its own "war" against terrorism) in seeking to communicate "a spirit of crisis, as though the advance of the beetle presented an extreme peril justifying any means to combat it."[45] With memories of World War II still fresh, perhaps the "Japanese" origin of this particular beetle made its "invasion" of the United States all the more frightening to many Americans.

Like the disastrous results of many other grandiose modernist projects, the taxpayer-financed spraying failed to achieve its objectives but did have many counterproductive consequences. Indeed, it decimated many local bird populations in Illinois. As Carson described the scene, "as the chemical [pesticide] penetrated the soil the poisoned beetle grubs crawled out on the surface of the ground, where they remained for some time before they died, attractive to insect-eating birds." Local bird populations of "brown thrashers, starlings, meadowlarks, grackles, and pheasants were virtually wiped out" in the sprayed areas. Pesticide-filled worms were also a threat. "Robins were almost annihilated, according to the biologists' report. Dead earthworms had been seen in numbers after a gentle rain," tempting the robins to a near certain death. For other types of birds as well, the presence of the pesticides represented an "evil power of . . . poison introduced into the world," converting the previously gentle rain "into an agent of destruction" for large parts of the natural world.[46]

With the exceptions of eagles and falcons, government spraying admittedly did not affect large enough areas or enough birds in total to have any real impact on the overall survival prospects of bird species (many, in fact, increased nationwide over the period of most intensive pesticide spraying).[47] But this was little consolation for homeowners and other local people who saw the bird populations decimated in the immediate areas where they lived and worked. The bird watchers and others who loved the presence of birds in their daily lives were in a sense victims, too. The government pesticide wars thus produced widespread collateral damage for many thousands of people who had never been asked to give their consent to the massive spraying programs in their localities. The government had simply "drafted" them involuntarily into the insect-control war it was waging. Where people's property was directly sprayed against their wishes, the government provided no compensation for the losses that occurred.

In the end, after all the devastating local consequences for wildlife, and for the many people who enjoyed being surrounded by birds and animals, as Carson reported, the government's efforts "resulted in only temporary suppression of the insect, which continues its westward movement." To be sure, the Japanese beetle damages turned out to be much smaller than the government had originally warned. This was also less of a surprise than might have been suspected from the dire government predictions. Further east in states such as New York—where the influx of Japanese beetles had occurred considerably earlier—the problem had been effectively contained, partly by using biological control methods. In Illinois, however, that success was ignored by officials of government agricultural agencies who were determined to wage a full-scale frontal attack on the Japanese beetle.

In another dramatic example of a government out of control, Carson related the story of the government campaign to rid the South of the fire ant, an invasive species that originally arrived from South America in the 1920s. As Carson explained,

> In 1957 the United States Department of Agriculture launched one of the most remarkable publicity campaigns in its history. The fire ant suddenly became the target of a barrage of government releases, motion pictures, and government inspired stories portraying it as a despoiler of

> southern agriculture and a killer of birds, livestock and man. A mighty campaign was announced, in which the federal government in cooperation with the afflicted states would ultimately treat some 20,000,000 acres in nine southern states.

> Never has any pesticide program been so thoroughly and deservedly damned by practically everyone except the beneficiaries of this "sales bonanza." It is an outstanding example of an ill-conceived, badly executed, and thoroughly detrimental experiment in the mass control of insects, an experiment so expensive in dollars, in destruction of animal life, and in loss of public confidence in the Agriculture Department that it is incomprehensible that any funds should still be devoted to it.

> Congressional support of the project was initially won by representations that were later discredited.[48]

Carson could be compared with Jane Jacobs, a kindred spirit of the time whose classic study, *The Death and Life of Great American Cities*, came out the year before *Silent Spring*.[49] Both were attacks on modernist follies as they had spurred large and ambitious U.S. government programs of the 1950s. In her book, Jacobs revealed how government urban renewal and other urban improvement campaigns had resulted in the wholesale destruction of many vital urban neighborhoods. The architects of all this urban mayhem were the professional experts who preached their own urban planning version of the progressive gospel. Carson's stories were about rural America, but the bottom line was much the same: great damage was done by government programs designed and implemented by planners and other professional experts, all in the name of "progress."

As Jacobs explained, once they were in place, government urban renewal programs acquired a momentum that made them very difficult to halt. Carson similarly reported on the government campaign against the fire ant: "As the program continued, facts began to accumulate from studies made by biologists of state and federal wildlife agencies and several universities. The studies revealed losses running all the way up to complete eradication of wildlife on some of the treated areas. Poultry, livestock, and pets were also killed." Hunters also suffered major losses: "Some of the most upsetting news for southern sportsmen concerned the bobwhite quail.

The bird, a ground nester, was all but eliminated on treated areas."[50] Again, the government never asked the hunters for their permission or compensated them for the losses imposed. It simply declared a pesticide war and in effect invoked emergency powers, ignoring any curtailments of individual freedoms resulting from the often arbitrary government exercises of power.

Soon, "urgent protests were made by most of the state conservation departments, by national conservation agencies, and by ecologists and even by some entomologists." Ignoring the protests, the U.S. Department of Agriculture willfully plunged ahead. This was all the more bizarre given how little evidence of any major threats the fire ants posed. One Alabama scientist who had closely studied fire ants reported that "damage to plants in general is rare." Remarkably enough, the overall influence of fire ants might even have been positive. As Carson reported, those who had "actually observed the ants in the field and in the laboratory, say that the fire ants feed chiefly on a variety of other insects, many of them considered harmful to man's interests. Fire ants have been observed picking larvae of the boll weevil off cotton. Their mound building activities serve a useful purpose in aerating and draining the soil."[51] But it took years to stop blanket rural pesticide spraying directed at the ants. The government and other advocates of spraying were all too often possessed by a progressive religious zeal that transcended any practical consequences on the ground.

The Dam and the Wilderness

The wonders of modern pesticides such as DDT were only one among many prominent progressive symbols. Progressive religion had its own artwork and cathedrals that served to provide religious inspiration. Many Americans made pilgrimages to places such as Hoover Dam on the Colorado River or Grand Coulee Dam on the Columbia River. Such modern pilgrims experienced a sense of awe and reverence in seeing the dramatic evidence before them of the newfound power of human beings to bring wild nature under control for human benefit. With this power, it appeared, humanity was no longer dependent on God to save the world but could achieve this wondrous result through its own scientific and economic efforts.

It is easy to forget that the current era of human control over nature commenced not much more than 150 years ago with the rise of organized technological advance based on the systematic development and application of physics, chemistry, and other theoretical sciences. Electricity and its wide uses seemed to many people a wondrous miracle. It was in the Progressive Era (1890–1920) that American intellectuals first sought to come to terms with the implications. If the initial response was a burst of optimism, today the reaction is often more pessimistic.

The former executive director of the Sierra Club, David Brower, was another contemporary of Carson who played a leading role in the rise of the environmental movement.[52] In the early 1960s, he led a successful fight to block a Colorado River dam that would have backed water into Grand Canyon National Park—an epic moment in the rise of American environmentalism. Brower declared, "I hate all dams, large and small."[53] He was not concerned that many dams were pork barrel projects that served narrow interest groups and could not pass a simple economic benefit-cost test. (He once published a full-page ad in the *New York Times* headlined "Economics is a form of brain damage.")[54] Rather, he hated dams for the very fact that they powerfully symbolized the new human power to control nature—the very opposite of the old progressive feeling of reverence in the presence of a dam. Brower's widely publicized attacks in the early 1960s on the "evils" of dams were the equivalent in the field of water policy of Carson's message in *Silent Spring* about the evils of pesticides.

Although their language is less certain and less righteous, economists today are by and large still true believers in progressive religion. This goes far to explain the tensions often seen when economists and environmentalists come together. They are waging a secular version—fortunately without bloodshed—of religious warfare. The Roman Catholic theologian Robert Royal writes that "in the modern environmental debate, those who would permit use and those who advocate wilderness preservation have become virtual warring denominations."[55] For many environmentalists such as Brower, a symbol of human control over nature filled them with disgust and regret. In recent years, moreover, the environmental antagonism toward dams has been winning. Congress has remained fully addicted to pork barrel in other areas of government spending, but it largely stopped funding new dams in the 1970s. Indeed, a recent trend is to tear some of them down—the planned removal (as I write) of the Elwha Dam in Olympic National Park in Washington State is one example.

Reflecting the influence of Carson, Brower, and other 1960s environmental leaders, "anti-progressive" symbols have become the leading religious objects in American life. For environmental religion, wilderness areas are the new "cathedrals."[56] Like a dam, a wilderness area makes a symbolic statement about the desirable form of human interaction with nature. In this case, however, rather than showing an aspiration to greater mastery of nature, the creation of a wilderness area renounces such human powers. As defined by Congress in the Wilderness Act of 1964 (another key 1960s event in the rise of environmentalism), a wilderness area is a place "untrammeled by man" where any signs of a past human presence should be at a minimum. The protection of the Arctic National Wildlife Refuge in Alaska has been so symbolically important to the environmental movement (despite the presence of many hundreds of billions of dollars' worth of oil) because it is said to be one of the last remaining places on earth still "untouched by man."[57] *Silent Spring* also seeks to protect nature from unnatural human impacts; in its case, the protection is against the impacts of artificial chemicals such as DDT and other pesticides.

Cancer Looming Everywhere

If Rachel Carson had limited herself to detailing the common 1950s failures and abuses of government pesticide spraying for insect control, there would be much less to criticize in *Silent Spring*. Perhaps she exaggerated the negative side of pesticides somewhat. Perhaps she ignored or minimized other important instances where DDT did have positive results. But her critique would have been within the bounds of permissible public rhetoric in making a strong argument. On the whole, moreover, she was correct; indiscriminate intensive pesticide spraying as practiced in the 1950s by government agencies over wide areas of the United States was a good example of the failures of modernism and its religious aspirations for the scientific management of society and the natural world.

Much of *Silent Spring*, however, went well beyond the damaging impacts of past episodes of ill-conceived pesticide spraying. Carson did not limit herself to the failings of progressive economic religion in this one area of government action. Rather, she ventured into much broader realms of dire prediction and alarmism about the future. She devoted large parts of *Silent Spring* to making the case that the widespread use of chemicals of all kinds was about to precipitate a plague of cancer in American society (as will be discussed in detail in Chapter 6 in this volume). This was even more devastating evidence of the heretical if not altogether diabolical character of American progressive religion.

But Carson's claims in this area had much less basis in science. In this case, she committed the same error as her modernist foes, using weakly biased scientific assertions as a means of communicating what was in reality a form of religious zeal. The problem was compounded because some of her central scientific speculations about modern chemicals and cancer, while appearing plausible enough at the time she made them, simply turned out to be in error. In making a religious argument in the implicit form of popular science, Carson left her environmental theology exposed to the risk of scientific refutation. It was a bet that she lost.[58]

In *Silent Spring*, Carson wrote that "the contamination of our world is not alone a matter of mass spraying" of pesticides and herbicides. Rather, we are increasingly faced in our daily lives with a "birth-to-death contact with dangerous chemicals" of all kinds, resulting in a "progressive buildup of chemicals in our bodies and so to [the] cumulative poisoning" of ourselves. Because it occurs so slowly and in such small increments, "the average citizen is seldom aware of the deadly materials" being introduced into his or her body. The foods routinely sold in supermarkets contain small residues of many chemicals that will have a cumulative, "death-dealing power."[59] If supermarkets were required to be honest with their customers, they would have to display a "huge skull and cross-bones" above many of the seemingly ordinary products for sale that, in fact, include in their contents "death-dealing chemicals."[60]

In *Silent Spring*, Carson was especially concerned that many of the deaths that would result from our ever-growing exposure to chemicals would be from cancer. She explained that "the chemical agents of cancer have become entrenched in our world." We are constantly exposed to "carcinogens that now contaminate our food, our water supplies, and our atmosphere . . . minute exposures, repeated over and over throughout the years." Given the levels of exposure to carcinogenic chemicals, she guessed that about 25 percent of Americans would develop cancer—even as the epidemic of cancer could be "greatly mitigated" by reducing those exposures.

This would be practicably feasible—indeed, the cost would not be great—because "a very large proportion" of the carcinogenic chemicals to which humans are being exposed "are by no means necessities of life."[61]

Carson never seriously attempted to demonstrate that her assertions had a well-developed scientific basis in the literature. She presented a number of specific examples where exposures to radiation or to chemicals had a severe human health impact. But these were generally of limited scope and at higher levels of exposure than most people would ever experience. Rather, her speculations about the looming cancer epidemic in American life were based on ad hoc theories of her own that belong more to environmental religion than to environmental science. (Carson was suffering from breast cancer as she wrote *Silent Spring* and died of the disease two years after its publication, a possible further influence on her thinking.)

Carson's environmental theology as developed in her popular science parable of chemicals and cancer goes as follows. Human beings lived for many thousands of years in "a natural environment" that, given the very limited tools available at the time, could not be altered in any essential way by human actions.[62] Although there were cancer causing elements in this environment such as the radiation of the sun, "over the eons of unhurried time that is nature's, life reached an adjustment with destructive forces" through the workings of biological evolution. While some cancers were caused by exposure to natural forces, they were "few in number and they belong to that ancient array of forces to which life has been accustomed from the beginning."[63] Left to the happy workings of nature, cancer was therefore a minor factor in human existence. (This may well have been true since, until recently, few people lived to the advanced ages where cancer becomes widespread.)

In Carson's parable, however, the moment of the fall came with the spread of economic progress over the world. As she explained, "with the dawn of the industrial era the world became a place of continuous, ever-accelerating change. Instead of the natural environment there was rapidly substituted an artificial one composed of new chemical and physical agents, many of them possessing powerful capacities for inducing biologic change." Having turned away from the possibility of living in a natural and thus ecologically balanced world, modern human beings now received large exposures to "carcinogens which his own activities had created" and against which "man had no protection."[64] In an older version, Adam and Eve had rebelled against God, lost their natural innocence, and had been thrown out of the Garden to live out their lives in a newly hostile environment of widespread pain and suffering.

The very gene structure of human beings, for example, had been "shaped through long eons of evolution." Our natural "genetic heritage" is "infinitely more valuable than individual life." Here again, however, through their misplaced human pride and greed, ending up in the pervasive unnatural assaults on nature of modern industrialization, human beings faced a bleak future. The terrible impacts of nuclear radiation on human beings had been seen at Hiroshima and Nagasaki; nuclear power was perhaps the ultimate act of human beings playing God with the world. Moreover, in their capacity to produce genetic damage, "the parallel between chemicals and radiation is exact and inescapable," Carson declared. Indeed, *Silent Spring* warns that "genetic deterioration through manmade [chemical] agents is the menace of our time, 'the last and greatest danger to our civilization.'"[65]

Those who challenge God's authority, seeking to remake His world for their own purposes, must know that His punishments will be severe. In both the Bible and the environmental writings of today, God's wrath is often seen as taking the form of an environmental calamity. In *Silent Spring*'s contribution to this message, chemicals spread through the environment would be a terrible instrument of human pain and suffering.

Large parts of *Silent Spring* are thus devoted to telling this story of human beings creating their own unnatural world in place of the previously healthy and sustainable environment of original nature. If present trends continued, the only places where true nature might still be found would be the wilderness areas officially protected by government agencies. Carson did not create this message of human sinfulness as manifested in the drive for ever more rapid growth and development (in its secular versions it is at least as old as Jean Jacques Rousseau), perhaps eventually encompassing the entire earth, altogether destroying "the creation" originally put there by God. But the popularity of *Silent Spring* and the large readership it achieved in the 1960s first introduced such ways of thinking to many Americans, people who had previously been more accustomed to thinking of modern economic progress as the salvation of the world.

Cancer Science versus *Silent Spring*

Carson's great fear that the spread of chemicals would soon yield a new cancer epidemic became a staple of environmental writings through the end of the 1970s. The Environmental Protection Agency, like other government agencies hoping to increase budgets, personnel, and authority, and also possessed of a sense of religious mission, actively spread the cancer scare story in the late 1970s. But that was the high point. A particularly influential skeptical note was the 1981 publication in the *Journal of the National Cancer Institute* of a study by Richard Doll and Richard Peto, both epidemiologists of unimpeachable international reputation.[66] It concluded that overall chemicals in the environment played a small role in causing cancer. Among cancers that could be attributable to some form of direct outside exposure, Doll and Peto estimated that environmental pollution was responsible for only 2 percent of those cancers and occupational exposures for another 4 percent. Food additives and industrial products were responsible for less than 1 percent each. By far the overwhelming cancer threats—among those factors which human beings could directly influence through their actions—were tobacco smoking and dietary choices, responsible in combination for 65 percent of potentially avoidable cancers.

A few years later, another large blow to the popular science of *Silent Spring* came from Bruce Ames, another leading scientist of international reputation. Ames struck directly at Carson's portrayal of a sharp dichotomy between the "natural" and the "unnatural," the former a source of good in the world, the latter a source of evil, including the attribution of a looming cancer epidemic. As Ames wrote (with Lois Gold) in 1993, "the public has many misconceptions about the relationship between environmental pollution and human cancer" (spread with perhaps the widest impact by *Silent Spring*, although Ames did not mention Carson by name). "Underlying these misconceptions is an erroneous belief that nature is benign." Ames and Gold observed that, despite the increasingly common exposures of Americans to at least small doses of a large number of chemicals, "cancer death rates in the United States (after adjusting for age and smoking) are steady or decreasing." Indeed, "there is no persuasive evidence that life in the modern industrial world has in general contributed to cancer deaths."[67] Remarkably, and altogether contrary to Carson's supposed dichotomy between benign natural and life threatening unnatural chemicals in *Silent Spring*,

> About 99.99 percent of all pesticides in the human diet are natural pesticides from plants. All plants produce toxins to protect themselves against fungi, insects, and animal predators such as humans. Tens of thousands of these natural pesticides have been discovered, and every species of plant contains its own set of different toxins, usually a few dozen. When plants are stressed or damaged (when attacked by pests), they greatly increase their output of natural pesticides, occasionally to levels that are acutely toxic to humans.[68]

Carson had speculated that biological evolution would have meant that humans and other animals would have evolved natural defenses against natural toxins in the environment. But Ames and Gold found that, using the very same methods of testing that were being used to attribute carcinogenic properties to artificial chemical substances, testing of natural toxins found essentially the same carcinogenic properties. It made no difference: exposures to high doses of the toxins found in common foods such as apples, lettuce, plums, celery, and mushrooms produced equally cancerous results in experimental populations of mice, rats, and other test animals. Ames and Gold wrote of one of their studies that "of the 77 natural chemicals tested, about half (37/77) are carcinogenic to rodents; a similar fraction is observed for synthetic chemicals (212/350)."[69] Contrary to the message of *Silent Spring*, the workings of natural evolution over the ages had not meant that the animals being used for test purposes were any less susceptible to natural toxins in their tendency to develop cancerous growths.

Of course, those findings did not answer the question of whether natural toxins actually produce cancer. The problem might be in the manner of testing for carcinogenic properties. Whether a natural or unnatural substance, the very high doses to which animals were exposed might in and of themselves have produced the cancerous results. At the much lower doses likely to occur in real-world exposures, neither natural nor artificial toxins might actually cause significant amounts of cancer. That is one interpretation. Alternatively, many current cancers might, in fact, be attributable to the large human exposures to natural toxins.

Either way, these new studies undermined Carson's popular science of cancer as especially attributable to unnatural chemicals. Carson, in short, had it wrong scientifically, and since her science was the vehicle for an implicit theology, her theological arguments were undermined as well. Despite Carson's intent, *Silent Spring* provided little support for the 1960s substitution of "natural" and "unnatural" as synonyms for "good" and "evil" in environmental religion.

Humans versus Nature

To be sure, the failure of Carson's popular science of chemicals and cancer did not prove the opposite, that the modern claims for economic progress were sustained. Progressive economic religion would have to stand or fall on much larger considerations than Carson ever addressed in *Silent Spring*. Indeed, as explored above, there was much to be said for Carson's specific criticisms of DDT and other pesticide use in the 1950s. In those parts of *Silent Spring*, Carson provided some useful case evidence in the wider clash between economic religion and environmental religion—the "new holy wars," as I have described it.[70]

But Carson sought to go much further. *Silent Spring* offers not only an indictment of progressive scientific management but also presents a strong affirmative case for a rising new faith in American life, environmental religion. She was not the first person to do so. Aldo Leopold in 1949 in *Sand County Almanac* laid out perhaps the most poetic statement of the theology of 20th-century environmentalism. Still earlier, John Muir, the founder of the Sierra Club in 1892, had helped to set the stage. Muir himself was a self-avowed disciple of New England transcendentalists such as Ralph Waldo Emerson and Henry David Thoreau.

The tenets of environmental religion are found throughout *Silent Spring*. In some cases, they appear as explicit comments. More often, they are seen in the overarching implicit framework of assumptions relating to humans and nature that underlies the whole book.[71] The first chapter, only a few pages long and titled "A Fable for Tomorrow," could be regarded as the Genesis story of *Silent Spring*, portraying an original nature that is then corrupted by the fall.

Paradise is lost, humans have been condemned to live in sin and suffering, but salvation is still possible.

The very first sentence of *Silent Spring* reads as follows: "There was once a town in the heart of America where all life seemed to live in harmony with its surroundings"—Carson's version of Eden. Carson described a happy world where "the town lay in the midst of a checkerboard of prosperous farms. . . . In autumn, oak and maple and birch set up a blaze of color that flamed and flickered across a backdrop of pines." For a traveler along these roads, "laurel, viburnum and alder, great ferns and wildflowers delighted the traveler's eye through much of the year."[72]

But an "evil spell had settled on the community," destroying the original natural paradise. A "shadow of death" had fallen on the people and their land. Children "would be stricken suddenly while at play and die within a few hours." The roadsides "were now lined with browned and withered vegetation. . . . Even the streams were now lifeless." How had this fall from paradise occurred? As Carson related, "no witchcraft [of the devil], no enemy action had silenced the rebirth of new life in this stricken world. The people had done it [to] themselves." Like Adam and Eve, they had rebelled against God, worshiping a false god of economic progress; and, once again, they were punished for their disobedience. Carson acknowledged that she was not reporting on an actual historical town, but nevertheless "it might easily have a thousand [real] counterparts in America or elsewhere in the world." Fallen human beings all over the earth must confront "a grim specter [that] has crept upon us almost unnoticed" and might become "a stark reality we all shall know."[73]

She lamented how "the voices of spring" have already been "silenced . . . in countless [real] towns in America." How did this happen? Carson declared that she knew; she could lead us to the Promised Land: "This book is an attempt to explain," reads the closing sentence of Chapter 1. *Silent Spring* is thus presented as our new environmental Bible. It will tell us how we fell so far, and if we humbly accept our past sinfulness and corruption, how we can hope to rise again.

The Corruption of Original Nature

Chapter 2, another short chapter, is the only other direct statement of environmental religion in *Silent Spring*. Over hundreds of millions of years, as Carson related it, natural evolution slowly produced "the life that now inhabits the earth—eons of time in which that developing and diversifying life reached a state of adjustment and balance with its surroundings." This was a popularization of ideas once widely held in the professional field of ecology, that trends in evolutionary systems move toward a single natural "climax state." Disturbances do occur from time to time, but then equilibrating forces reassert themselves and bring ecological systems back to their long-run natural condition. Or, as Carson put it, "given time—time not in years but in millennia—life adjusts, and a balance has been reached."[74] This sustainable balance of nature is not only a scientific reality but was for Carson, and for environmental religion, an ethical norm. In their interactions with the natural world, the guiding moral rule for modern human beings is that they must avoid, or at least minimize so far as humanly possible, any actions that would alter (or, even worse, irreversibly destroy) the natural happy equilibrium of the nonhuman world.[75]

Until the past few hundred years, this commandment was not difficult to obey. The whole circumstance, however, has been radically changed by the rise of modern science and industry. As Carson related, "only within the moment of time represented by the present century has one species—man—acquired significant power to alter the nature of his world." Given humans' fallen natures, and given the very flawed character of the political systems by which collective human decisions are made around the world, the results have been disastrous. *Silent Spring* tells us that there has been a pervasive "contamination of air, earth, rivers, and sea with dangerous and even lethal materials." This contamination has produced a "chain of evil" afflicting the natural world that is "for the most part irreversible." Human beings in their greed and indifference have declared and have been aggressively waging a "war against nature."[76] In their blinded condition, many of them have even sought to justify these evils in the highest terms of religion, as the advancement of economic progress that will bring heaven on earth.

Hence, rather than the natural workings of the earth as they had occurred for hundreds of millions of years, the new human powers over the earth have meant that "the rapidity of change and the speed with which new situations are created follow the impetuous and heedless pace of man rather than the deliberate pace of nature." Natural radiation from the sun has always been present, but now modern nuclear physics has led to "the unnatural creation[s] of man's tampering with the atom." There are also "synthetic creations of man's inventive mind, brewed in his laboratories, and having no counterparts in nature." There are, Carson estimated, around "500 new chemicals to which the bodies of men and animals are required somehow to adapt each year, chemicals totally outside the limits of biologic experience." All these changes and creations are not only a grave offense against nature but also contain an "incredible potential for harm" to human beings themselves. As Carson warned, "future generations," assuming we even survive that long, "are unlikely to condone our lack of prudent concern for the integrity of the natural world that supports all life."[77]

How have modern men and women failed to recognize and to act against such a terrible threat to their very existence? It is partly a matter of simple greed; we live "in an era dominated by industry, in which the right to make a dollar at whatever cost is seldom challenged." But there are other leading causes. The "so-called control agencies" in the government all too often demonstrate a "fanatic zeal on the part of the many specialists" who run them to assert a human mastery over nature. Modern university education is also partly to blame. It fails to teach the future leaders of America how to think broadly and ethically. Instead, it produces the technocratic manpower to staff "an era of specialists, each of whom sees his own problem and is unaware of or intolerant of the larger frame into which it fits."[78] All told, between private greed, excesses of government zeal, and the blindness of the experts, the result has been that "there is still a very limited awareness of the nature of the threat" posed to the earth by modern science and economics and to the human beings who depend on its natural systems.

In short, we have committed many evils, we have worshipped false idols, we have shown an excess of human pride, and God is angry. If we do not reform our ways, he will impose many severe punishments. Environmental calamities, much like those foreseen in the Old Testament when God expressed his wrath, will surround us. But Rachel Carson was a new prophet who had come to show us a better way.

Religion in the Guise of Science

Silent Spring was part of a wider religious phenomenon of the time. Cultural historian David Williams writes in *Searching for*

God in the Sixties that the baby boomers then reaching adulthood believed that there is "some basic, knowable truth" and that it "exists in what we call nature, and that nature is both, as the Beatles sang, 'within us and without us'" to be discovered there. The 1960s harked back to events in American history preceding the progressive era: "The Sixties . . . became the latest instance of the American cycle of the sojourn from Egypt into the wilderness in search of the Promised Land. It followed the same pattern of the awakenings of the Transcendentalists of the 1840s and the Great Awakening of the 1740s."[79] Once again during the 1960s, an era of religious ferment produced upheavals in many areas of American life, including marriage and divorce, the role of women in society, music, drug use, personal dress, civil rights, university education, and many more. It was the beginning of decline for mainstream Protestantism, which had made too many large compromises with progressivism modernism. There was a return to older forms of Protestantism that were, in fact, much closer to the original Protestantism of Martin Luther and John Calvin.

Environmentalism was itself a kind of fundamentalism that represented a turn away from economic religion and other progressive modernist ways of thinking. In this setting, *Silent Spring* was intended for a particular audience, a mostly secular elite in American society that would have rejected any explicit religious proselytizing in the language of old-fashioned Calvinism. *Silent Spring* thus had to employ a rhetorical trick. In its essence, it presented a classically Protestant message of doom and gloom, of fallen humans living in a state of moral corruption, of a world facing God's wrath. But all this had to be done largely—allowing for occasional invocations of the language of old-fashioned Protestantism—with a modern veneer.

In *Silent Spring*, this new environmental fundamentalism was communicated in the language of popular science. Therein lies a problem for Rachel Carson's legacy. Her underlying theology may have held some important elements of truth. Undeniably, the Protestant Reformation changed the world. Calvinism and Puritanism have exerted a great influence on American history. Progressive optimism challenged that influence, but the worship of economic progress did not hold up well given the wide death and destruction seen so often in the 20th century. And despite what many economists profess, although economic forces are important, ultimately, they do not shape the world. The implicit messages of old-fashioned Protestant religion expressed in *Silent Spring* put Rachel Carson in some very good company.

The problem was therefore not so much the religious message itself. Rather, it was the popular science disguise that Carson used to try to convert her largely secular readership. Just 50 years later, most of the popular science of *Silent Spring* has turned out to be wrong as a matter of scientific truth. As examined above, her dire warnings of a looming cancer epidemic created by the unnatural spread of modern chemicals in American society turned out to be grossly overstated if not altogether false. In the developing world, the limitations on DDT inspired by Carson's greatly exaggerated fears have often had tragic consequences.[80] The science of ecology offered up in *Silent Spring* has also been largely invalidated, in this case by ecological scientists themselves.

Discordant Harmonies

Mirroring much of the mainstream thinking of environmental religion from the 1960s to today, Carson presented a picture of the natural world as one of natural harmony and balance—a constant flow of movement to sustain the healthy equilibrium of a true natural state (if often varying greatly from place to place according to the natural conditions of each location). But the dominant paradigm of ecology has shifted dramatically since Carson's time. The natural world is now seen as typically in constant flux, a succession of disturbances showing no natural tendency to return to some happy equilibrium of forces in nature. Rather than the clear and simple idea of an original natural order envisioned by Carson and environmental religion, the actual natural order, as discovered by the field of ecology, more closely resembles a world of chaos.

Daniel Botkin explored this idea in his influential 1990 book, *Discordant Harmonies: A New Ecology for the Twenty-First Century.*[81] An ecologist himself, Botkin wrote about the old way of environmental thinking—the message of *Silent Spring*—which envisioned a "highly structured, ordered, and regulated steady-state system." That view was part of the "1960s and 1970s mythology about conservation, environment, and nature"—a central set of faith assumptions for environmental religion. It was not only a scientific understanding but an ethical precept, that "what is natural is constant and what is constant is good." Environmental policy for too long, Botkin observed, was based on the "belief that everything natural (i.e., nonhuman) is desirable and good." That provided a mooring of the faith to which most environmentalists still clung, despite the accumulating scientific evidence to the contrary. Indeed, Botkin wrote, "to abandon a belief in the constancy of undisturbed nature is psychologically uncomfortable" or, even worse, might leave some environmentalists in a position of "extreme existential" anxiety.[82] Botkin did not put it precisely this way, but he was describing the situation of a religious true believer who finds that events in the real world are contradicting some core elements of faith.

Botkin argued that, however distressing it might personally be, it will be necessary—at least for those who are to be intellectually honest with themselves—to make a basic paradigm shift.[83] The fact is that "change appears intrinsic and natural at many scales of time and space in the biosphere, and that nature changes during all time scales." In the past, ecology had offered a view of "nature as a Kodachrome still-life" picture; but in the future, we would have to see the processes of nature as a "moving picture show," where one frame rapidly succeeds another. Once they have made this leap and no longer have a one-natural-state to pursue as a goal, human beings will also have to accept a new human responsibility to shape and manage nature themselves. An objectively desirable state defined as nature untouched by human hand is simply a myth. Hence, as Botkin wrote, "nature in the twenty-first century will be a nature that we make."[84] The only question is "the degree to which this molding" of the future of the natural world by human beings "will be intentional or unintentional, desirable or undesirable." The hope of *Silent Spring* that humans can retreat from managing and controlling nature can now be seen as a practical impossibility.

Donald Worster is a distinguished American environmental historian who has also written widely on developments in the field of ecology.[85] As he observed, ecology (like economics) is much more than a science: "its ideas . . . have been reflections of ourselves as much as objective apprehensions of nature." The old idea, the one that shaped Carson's thinking in *Silent Spring*, Worster wrote, was that "ecology was basically a study of equilibrium, harmony and order," all this the natural order of things in the absence of human actions to alter it. The new and radically different idea, however, is that ecology is "a study of disturbance, disharmony, and chaos." Indeed, this recognition became the consensus among ecologists in the 1990s, that "nature . . . is *fundamentally* erratic, discontinuous, and unpredictable." Worster noted that for John Muir "the clear lesson of cosmic complexity was that humans ought to love and preserve nature just as it is"—and ought to work to restore it when human actions may have unfortunately altered its basic character in the past.[86]

Worster doubted, however, whether any such environmental outlook can be maintained given the understanding of ecological science that disorder is the natural state of the world. He asked, "does the tradition of environmentalism to which Muir belonged, along with so many other nature writers and ecologists of the past, people like Paul Sears, Eugene Odum, Aldo Leopold, and Rachel Carson, make sense any longer?"[87] Given the virtually existential implications, Worster may have been reluctant to cast aside the old environmentalism (one suspects that Worster would be forced to rethink some of his own convictions), but in the interests of intellectual honesty, he clearly acknowledged a fundamental challenge to a core tenet of the faith.

In 1907, Harvard University acquired nearly 3,000 acres of forestland in central Massachusetts for research purposes, resulting in perhaps the longest and most intensive study of forest in the United States. About 5,000 years ago, as Harvard researchers discovered, an insect pest virtually wiped out the hemlock trees, leaving a new forest condition that lasted for about 1,000 years. Even when hemlocks recovered, it was "with considerable geographic variation in the rate and extent of recovery." Then another drastic change occurred: "the arrival of chestnut [trees] around 1,500 to 2,000 years ago" significantly altered the successional patterns that followed. Furthermore, evidence showed that "powerful hurricanes" and other tropical storms "episodically disrupt and shape New England forests," along with "less intense disturbance resulting from northeasterlies, downbursts, ice storms, and late-season snowstorms."[88] Impacts of American Indians were also substantial and changed considerably over time, owing to such developments as the widespread "adoption of corn, or maize, a Central American plant" by the Indians of New England, beginning 1,000 years go.[89] Indians also made common use of fire as "the major mechanism through which they could affect forests on a broad scale."[90] The Harvard forest researchers summarized the overall results of their research as follows:

> Interpretations based primarily on records of pollen and other fossils preserved in the sediments of lakes and wetlands confirm that the environment and vegetation of New England have changed continually through time. Although the rate and extent of change have varied since the last Ice Age, precipitation, temperature, storminess, and growing season length have all been dynamic as a consequence of long-term changes in solar, orbital, global, and atmospheric processes. The changing environment has initiated shifts, some subtle and others quite substantial, in the range and relative abundance of plant and animal species and in the composition, structure, and function of forest ecosystems.

> We now recognize that environmental changes are multifaceted and complex and often lack any modern equivalents. Not only the amount but also the seasonal and daily distributions of rainfall or temperature change through time, and these may vary as factors, such as storminess, atmospheric CO_2 concentrations, or animal and human populations, also change. As a consequence, the environmental conditions that have occurred in the past, and will develop in the future, may have no close parallels in any current landscape. In fact, the continual development of novel environmental settings through time is a major reason that fossils and other historical records attest to a long and changing sequence of unique and "nonanalog" plant and animal assemblages and ecosystem dynamics.[91]

In order words, the idea of "restoring" a single uniquely "natural" environment of the past—typically defined operationally in environmental religion as a "pre-European" natural order—is based on a large fiction, however central it has been to the theology of environmental religion as developed in writings such as *Silent Spring*.[92] This fiction survives, however, and despite frequent scientific refutations such as the Harvard research, because it has such great appeal. It offers an implicit Christian message of "the Creation," and then the fall, in the supposedly more sophisticated and scientific language of ecology. Michael Crichton once wrote that environmentalism is "the religion of urban atheists." In a secular age, even "non-believers" apparently require a source of meaning to their lives and, if forced, will choose a purposeful scientific myth over a purposeless ecological nihilism. Perhaps more excusably because she was writing in 1962, when much less was known, Rachel Carson has been a leading source of the environmental myths of our time.

The Trouble with Wilderness

The environmental religion of *Silent Spring* was undermined from yet another direction. This was not a problem of its scientific validity but of something outside science, its basic theological (and philosophical) logic.[93] The leading critic is this case was one of America's leading environmental historians, William Cronon, author of *Changes in the Land* and other well-regarded writings (and president of the American Historical Association).[94] Cronon believes that the idea of the separation of human beings and nature, found throughout environmental writings, exposes the environmental movement to the damaging charge of being misanthropic in some of its core beliefs.

If environmental good and evil are defined according to a criterion of natural and unnatural, combined with a view of human actions as outside nature, that would seem to put the presence of human beings in the world in the evil category. Then, Cronon noted, if the underlying assumptions of environmental religion are carried to their fullest extent, "it is hard not to reach the conclusion that the only way human beings can hope to live naturally on the earth is to follow the hunter-gatherers back into a wilderness Eden and abandon virtually everything that civilization has given us." Indeed, it might be even most logical to conclude that, "if nature dies because we enter it, then the only way to save nature is to kill ourselves." The vast majority of environmentalists, including Rachel Carson, would surely reject this conclusion, if presented so baldly. But Cronon finds the line of thinking of "radical environmentalists and deep ecologists all too frequently come[s] close to accepting" an ending of the human presence on earth "as a first principle," the best outcome imaginable.[95] Perhaps, if human beings ever accepted their highest ethical obligations, in the newest version of utopia, they would agree among themselves to cease reproducing altogether, and eventually disappear.[96]

Illustrating Cronon's point, as mainstream an environmental writer as Bill McKibben can declare that "it is not utter silliness to talk about ending—or, at least, transforming—industrial civilization." McKibben is prepared at least to hope for "a different world, where roads are torn out to create vast new wildernesses, where most development ceases, and where much of man's imprint on the earth is slowly erased" (and ultimate perfection, at least in concept, would mean erasing all of it).[97] Another prominent figure in mainstream environmental thought, the historian of the American wilderness movement, Roderick Nash, declared in 1991, "I'm sorry people are starving but I'm much more concerned with members of the species smaller than Homo sapiens."[98] In the 20th century, the numbers of human beings on earth expanded exponentially, while the presence of many other living creatures—the wildest ones especially—decreased correspondingly. Environmental religion tells us this must now be reversed.

Silent Spring was one of the earliest and strongest statements of the natural-unnatural dichotomy in environmental religion. Indeed, *Silent Spring* suffers from the basic philosophical/theological problems that Cronon identifies. In the original Calvinism, human beings are depraved but God will eventually save them (or many of them) in the hereafter. In a modern "Calvinism without God," human beings are simply depraved with no hope of a divine rescue—a good reason to get rid of them altogether.[99]

Conclusion

Silent Spring is outwardly a work of popular science. More fundamentally, it is a message of environmental religion in disguise. That has been the standard pattern for secular religion in the modern age. Remarkably enough, Karl Marx even claimed a strict scientific status for his apocalyptic vision of history. It seems that many people have found it difficult to accept Jewish or Christian religion in their traditional forms. Yet, they also seem to have an undiminished desire for a strong sense of meaning in their life. Furthermore, many of them have retained more of the Jewish and Christian worldviews than they themselves realize.

The compromise solution has been secular religion, which has shaped the lives, thoughts, and feelings of its followers no less than traditional Christianity. But it is a form of religion without the presence, at least explicitly, of a God in the hereafter. Instead, it seeks to ground its authority in science. It is this combination of religion in the name of science that explains the great popular appeal of *Silent Spring* and its large influence on the future development of the environmental movement. In this sense, it was an immense success.

Judged by more rigorous and exacting standards of science, however, even as *Silent Spring* made some valid criticisms of the damaging consequences of many specific applications of DDT, it was otherwise gravely flawed. Judged by the standards of theology, it may fare better. Its negative verdict on the progressive gospel of efficiency, and on economic religion in general, is today widely shared, even by people who are not followers of the environmental gospel (libertarians, for example). In seeking to elevate "natural" and "unnatural" to the environmental moral equivalent of good and evil, however, it has fallen short theologically. The distinction is not well grounded in either scientific analysis or theological coherence.

Thus, in the final analysis, *Silent Spring* was a great accomplishment as a popular religious performance of sorts. As a work of serious science or theology, the verdict must be considerably less favorable.

5. The Selective Silence of *Silent Spring*: Birds, Pesticides, and Alternatives to Pesticides

Pierre Desrochers and Hiroko Shimizu

Shortly before Thanksgiving 1959, the secretary of the U.S. Department of Health, Education and Welfare, Dr. Arthur Flemming, announced that aminotriazole, a pesticide that could cause thyroid cancer in rats if they were fed excessively large doses (equivalent to a human eating 15,000 pounds of cranberries every day for several years), had been detected in Oregon cranberries.[1] Asked what advice he would give a hypothetical housewife, he stated that to be on the "safe side," she should eschew cranberries. For authority, he cited the Delaney clause, which had been passed the previous year as an amendment to the Food and Drug Act[2] and banned any chemical food additive that had been "found to induce cancer in man, or, after tests, found to induce cancer in animals." Mothers stopped buying cranberries, supermarkets and restaurants suspended sales, and some state officials went so far as to ban the product, notwithstanding exhortations from the president and the secretary of agriculture. Even presidential candidates John F. Kennedy and Richard M. Nixon distanced themselves from Flemming's diagnosis by publicly ingesting portions of the maligned fruit.[3]

Far from occurring in a political vacuum, the Delaney clause and the "Great Cranberry Scare of 1959" were responses to growing concerns about the "chemical peril," "persistent pesticides" and "carcinogens," that had been raised for years by proponents of organic farming, environmentalists working for organizations such as the Audubon Society and the Conservation Foundation, and influential individuals within government agencies such as the Food and Drug Administration and the Fish and Wildlife Service.[4] Growing distrust of men in white lab coats and industrialization had also been fed by the powerful atomic

97

imagery of Hiroshima and Nagasaki, periodic warnings of nuclear fallout and Strontium-90 in milk from nuclear weapons tests,[5] and the "killer smog" episodes of Donora (Pennsylvania) in 1948; London in 1952; New York in 1953; and Los Angeles in 1954,[6] among others. "Mouse-as-little-man" stories (i.e., the premise that "any substance that causes cancer in rodents at extraordinarily high doses will also cause cancer in humans at more moderate doses") were also becoming regular features in newspapers and broadcast news.[7] Despite unprecedented advances in human health and standards of living in previous decades, the most affluent and healthiest populace in human history was beginning to question the miracles of science and the promise of a better life through chemistry.

It was against this backdrop that the *New Yorker* published its three-part serialization of Rachel Carson's *Silent Spring*, starting with its June 16, 1962, issue. The forthcoming book garnered additional attention when the author(s) of a sympathetic July 2 *New York Times* editorial noted:

> "Miss Carson will be accused of alarmism, or lack of objectivity, of showing only the bad side of pesticides while ignoring their benefits. But this, we suspect is her purpose as well as her method. We do not . . . find a cure for disease by boasting of the reduction in mortality rates. Miss Carson does not argue that chemical insecticides must never be used, but she warns of the dangers of misuse and overuse by a public that has become mesmerized by the notion that chemists are the possessors of divine wisdom and that nothing but benefit can emerge from their test tubes. If her series helps arouse public concern and [mobilize Government agencies to enforce] adequate controls, the author will be as deserving of the Nobel Prize as was the inventor of DDT."[8]

Then the thalidomide tragedy landed with full force on the nation's front pages, accelerating an already smoldering fire. Thalidomide had been touted as a Wonder Drug for a variety of ailments such as insomnia, pains, cough, and cold,[9] and had also been prescribed for, among other things, morning sickness during pregnancy in Europe, Australia, and Canada.[10] Prior to July 1962, the *Washington Post* and the *New York Times* had each carried a couple of stories linking the drug to the birth of thousands of deformed babies in Germany and the United Kingdom. On July 15, the *Washington Post* and the *Times Herald* broke the story that, but for a vigilant physician employee of the FDA, Dr. Frances Oldham Kelsey, the United States may also have approved the drug, and that her prescience may have saved thousands from similar tragedies in the United States. The frenzy over thalidomide was phenomenal.

The descriptions and images of the infant victims accompanying reports on thalidomide propelled swift action on the part of the government. Within weeks, on August 7, 1962, Dr. Kelsey, hailed as a heroine, had received the Distinguished Federal Civilian Service Award from President John F. Kennedy, and hearings were held in Congress.[11] By the time *Silent Spring* was released as a book 73 days later, there were over 90 additional articles on thalidomide in the *Post* and 132 pieces in the *New York Times*. In August alone, the *New York Times* carried an average of over three pieces per day. In early October, Congress unanimously modified FDA's drug approval procedures.[12] According to Wallace Janssen, an FDA historian, "[I]t was recognized that no drug is truly safe unless it is also effective, and effectiveness was required to be established prior to marketing—a milestone advance in medical history."[13]

Meanwhile, perhaps aided by these tragic events, *Silent Spring* was also garnishing attention. In response to a question at a news conference on August 29, both the book and author were mentioned by President John F. Kennedy.[14] The following day—still weeks before *Silent Spring* was due to hit the bookshelves—it was announced that the Federal Council on Science and Technology Committee was looking into the use and control of pesticides.[15]

Rachel Carson recognized that her book's popularity owed not a little to the furor over thalidomide. Writing in the *New York Times* Christmas edition of its Book Review, she observed that "[f]or many reasons the climate of 1962 seems to have been far more favorable for its reception than that of . . . any earlier year. . . . Almost simultaneously, with the publication of *Silent Spring*, the problem of drug safety and drug control, which had been simmering many months, reached its shocking culmination in the thalidomide tragedy."[16]

However, timing wasn't the only reason for her tremendous success. While her major claim that we should, in the words of the *New York Times*, be wary of "misuse and overuse" of pesticides was beyond reproach, her shocking title and lyrical presentation of worrying anecdotes left little doubt in most minds that synthetic chemists' hubris and corporate greed had triggered an ecological catastrophe of epochal proportion. But while the general public can be expected to panic over complex issues, a science-trained writer such as Rachel Carson should be held to higher standards. Our goal in this chapter is to assess whether or not, based on the data available at the time she was researching and writing *Silent Spring*, some of her implications and generalizations seemed warranted. In particular, we will look at Carson's take on bird populations, various omissions and internal inconsistencies on the role and benefits of pesticides (especially in terms of habitat loss and hunger), and suggested alternatives to synthetic pesticides. Along the way, we will also point out some logical inconsistencies in the book and its author's broader worldview. Our conclusion is that many of Carson's explicit and implicit claims were (and remain) shaky.

Bird Populations and Synthetic Pesticides[17]

It is at the end of her frightening "Fable for Tomorrow" that opens her book that Rachel Carson finally confesses to her reader that the town she described

> does not actually exist, but it might easily have a thousand counterparts in America or elsewhere in the world. I know of no community that has experienced all the misfortunes I describe. Yet every one of these disasters has actually happened somewhere, and many real communities have already suffered a substantial number of them. A grim specter has crept upon us almost unnoticed, and this imagined tragedy may easily become a stark reality we all shall know.
>
> What has already silenced the voices of spring in countless towns in America? This book is an attempt to explain.[18]

This passage and other anecdotes elsewhere in the book leave the reader with the definite impression that various American bird populations—if not all bird populations—were crashing at the time and that synthetic pesticides were the perpetrators of the coming silent spring.

As was observed by some of Carson's early critics even before *Silent Spring* was available in book form, however, trend data on avian population suggested to the contrary that many bird populations were *not* decreasing but rather increasing or rebounding. One of Carson's earliest and most persistent critics was the University of California biochemist (although frequently identified as a former employee of American Cyanamid by his critics) Thomas J. Jukes who, in the September 1963 issue of *The American Scientist*, addressed head on the rhetoric of the "many conservationists [who] have expressed deep concern" over the "image of a fragile and exquisite songbird dying in paralytic convulsions from the callous and unjustified application of a repulsive and deadly chemical sprayed broadcast over a defenseless landscape." Jukes observed that not only were counts up for several bird species, he also marshaled other supporting evidence, such as quoting a Pennsylvania Department of Agriculture bulletin whose author had observed that in the gypsy moth eradication project in this state "not a single case of poisoning attributable to the DDT treatment at one pound per acre was reported. Officials of the National Audubon Society were satisfied that no damage was done to bird life, including nestling birds."[19] As he would later specify, the "National Audubon Society in 1961 had declared DDT harmless to birds when used at 1 pound per acre for control of the gypsy moth in Pennsylvania."[20] In a paper titled "Bird Populations Are Increasing" published the following year in the *Bulletin of the Entomological Society of America*, the entomologist Philip H. Marvin noted that "[f]ar from declining during the past 15 years of expanded insecticide use, bird numbers have multiplied several fold."[21]

Both Jukes and Marvin based their observation on the Audubon Society's Christmas Bird Census (CBC), which had been conducted every year around Christmas time since 1900 and was cosponsored by Carson's employer, the U.S. Fish and Wildlife Service, during Carson's employment there and in the years preceding the publication of *Silent Spring*. As they and other critics observed in the years that followed the publication of *Silent Spring*, the available data suggested that between 1941 (pre-DDT) and 1960 (after DDT use had waned), at least 26 different kinds of birds had become more numerous.[22] This source was not ideal and was rapidly dismissed by Carson's supporters on the grounds that, among other things, it did not cover insect-eating migratory birds that spent winters outside the continental United States, that the omnivorous feeders that remained often changed behavior (by aggregating in large flocks), that the number of amateur bird watchers might have increased, watchers might have devoted more time to their hobby, and better observations sites might have been found.[23] It was nevertheless the only database available to gain a notion of bird population trends at the time and should not have been ignored. Notably, Rachel Carson was not only an active member of the organization, she also held an appointment on her local Audubon society's board of directors and participated in the bird census herself.[24] Yet she did not even allude to the existence of the Audubon Bird Census. We will now revisit some of the numbers raised by some of Carson's detractors in the 1960s.

Among the species featured in various bleak anecdotes in her book with the implication that their loss was a harbinger of things to come but whose numbers, according to Jukes and Marvin, had increased from the 1940s to 1961–1962 were robins,[25] starlings,[26] meadowlarks,[27] and cardinals.[28] This is approximately the period over which "[t]he production of synthetic pesticides in the United States soared from 124,259,000 pounds in 1947 to 637,666,000 pounds in 1960—more than a fivefold increase."[29]

The Marvin study showed that bird counts per observer in 1961–1962 were 2.7 times their 1949–1952 levels. While bird numbers could be assessed per number of Audubon census volunteers, it did not adjust for the average number of hours spent by observers during each census. It is, however, unlikely that the average number of hours per observer increased equally dramatically between these periods. Thus, the upward trend reported by Marvin casts doubt on the notion of a general decline in bird populations.

Another species that figures in *Silent Spring* is the "national symbol, the eagle."[30] It states that "reports by the Florida Audubon Society, as well as from New Jersey and Pennsylvania, confirm the trend that may well make it necessary for us to find a new national emblem."[31] Figure 5.1, based on data from the Audubon Society's website, which makes data from the CBC available,[32] shows trends in bald eagle populations from Christmas 1939 through Christmas 1961. The figure accounts for the number of observers and the length of time over which observations were taken. Despite the spike for the bird count from Christmas 1949 (which, in any case, was during the organochlorine pesticide era), it does not indicate a declining national trend in bald eagle counts. If anything, the

Figure 5.1
BALD EAGLE TRENDS IN NUMBERS COUNTED PER
PERSON-HOURS, CHRISTMAS 1939–CHRISTMAS 1961,
UNITED STATES EXCLUDING ALASKA

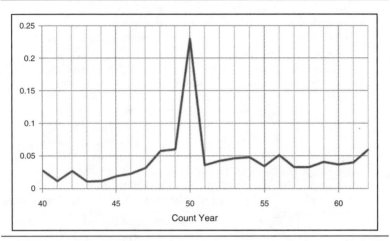

NOTES: point 40 on the graph corresponds to Christmas 1939, and point 62 corresponds to Christmas 1961. We start at 40 in order to get an idea of trends prior to the advent of organochlorine pesticides, and stop at 62 because that would be the latest data possibly available for inclusion in *Silent Spring*, although 60 or even 59 would have been more likely.

SOURCE: Christmas Bird Count, *Historical Results*, available at http://birds.audubon.org/historical-results, visited March 2012.

national count was somewhat higher in the late-1950s and early-1960s than in the early-1940s.

Rachel Carson discussed a study by a retired banker, Charles Broley, of bald eagle nests in a stretch of Florida's west coast from Tampa to Fort Myers that showed a decline in reproductive success.[33] However, she failed to note that the decline commenced prior to the mid-1940s,[34] perhaps due to habitat destruction and increased disturbance and contact with humans.[35] Observations by Howell,[36] who had also been studying bald eagle nest sites in east-central Florida since 1935, showed that nest occupancy had been declining since his first set of data in 1935.[37] Synthetic pesticides could have exacerbated an already deteriorating situation in Florida, but that does not explain the lack of a declining national trend during the 1945 through 1962 period shown in Figure 5.1.

Yet another bird that gets considerable play in the book is the brown thrasher:

> Perhaps no community has suffered more for the sake of a beetleless world than Sheldon, in eastern Illinois, and adjacent areas in Iroquois County. In 1954 the United States Department of Agriculture and the Illinois Agriculture Department began a program to eradicate the Japanese beetle along the line of its advance into Illinois, holding out the hope, and indeed the assurance, that intensive spraying would destroy the populations of the invading insect. The first "eradication" took place that year, when dieldrin was applied to 1400 acres by air. Another 2600 acres were treated similarly in 1955, and the task was presumably considered complete. But more and more chemical treatments were called for, and by the end of 1961 some 131,000 acres had been covered. . .[38]

> [By 1955] the chemical had been changed to the even more toxic aldrin, 100 to 300 times as toxic as DDT in tests on quail. By 1960, every species of wild mammal known to inhabit the area had suffered losses. It was even worse with the birds. In the small town of Donovan the robins had been wiped out, as had the grackles, starlings, and brown thrashers. These and many other birds were sharply reduced elsewhere.[39]

Data from the Christmas Bird Count (CBC) for the brown thrasher in Illinois does not indicate a population decline consistent with the *Silent Spring* narrative (see Figure 5.2). However, Sheldon, Illinois, is on the Illinois-Indiana border, and Indiana is generally downwind of Illinois. So it is possible that brown thrasher populations may have been declining in Indiana. But the CBC data do not show any consistent trends for this species in Indiana (see Figure 5.3). In any case, Figure 5.4 indicates that brown thrasher population generally increased nationwide during the period in which organochlorines came on the scene.

Thus, while one does not dispute that the eradication campaign might have overused pesticides in many areas which needlessly poisoned many non-target birds and animals, in the broader context,

104

Figure 5.2
BROWN THRASHER TRENDS FOR ILLINOIS
CHRISTMAS 1939–CHRISTMAS 1961

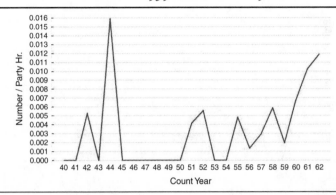

NOTE: point 40 on the graph corresponds to Christmas 1939, and point 62 corresponds to Christmas 1961. Japanese beetle eradication program was commenced between points 54 and 55 and continued at least through point 61 (*Silent Spring*, pp. 91–93).

SOURCE: Christmas Bird Count, *Historical Results*, available at http://birds. audubon.org/historical-results, visited March 2012.

Figure 5.3
BROWN THRASHER TRENDS FOR INDIANA
CHRISTMAS 1939–CHRISTMAS 1961

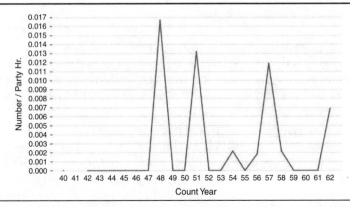

SOURCE: Christmas Bird Count, *Historical Results*, available at http://birds. audubon.org/historical-results, visited March 2012.

105

Figure 5.4
Brown Thrasher Trends for the United States
Christmas 1939–Christmas 1961

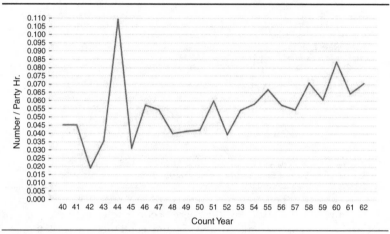

Source: Christmas Bird Count, *Historical Results*, available at http://birds. audubon.org/historical-results, visited March 2012.

the CBC seems to contradict the impression of a spring in which brown thrashers were being silenced throughout the United States. More importantly, they confirm that while anecdotes are compelling, they can seriously mislead if they are used to generalize.

To summarize, the best (albeit imperfect) information available at the time on bird population trends did not support the "Silent Spring" thesis but often pointed instead in the opposite direction. An open-minded science writer could thus have legitimately suggested that DDT was actually beneficial to many birds by protecting them from a wide range of diseases (avian malaria, Newcastle disease, encephalitis, rickettsialpox, and bronchitis), that it might have played a useful role in controlling carcinogens such as aflatoxins, and that DDT and the broader synthetic insecticidal package of the time not only made more seeds and fruits available to humans but also to birds.

The Audubon data were readily available to Carson, and her lack of discussion of it is especially puzzling in light of her long-time association with the organization, including as a volunteer in their bird count census. Furthermore, she must have known that the

Audubon Society had been created in the late 19th century out of a similar concern about the disappearance of American birds. Of course, the problem at that time had nothing to do with synthetic chemicals but rather everything to do with women's fashion (the aim of the society ladies who gathered over tea to create—or rather re-launch—Audubon was "to save birds from being slaughtered for the hat trade"[40]), over-hunting (sometimes done deliberately, e.g., legal or illegal shooting by fishermen bent on eliminating competition for their catches or by hunters trying to protect ducks from birds of prey), trapping (e.g., for controlling birds of prey populations around fish hatcheries), egg collection, and habitat destruction.

These other considerations had long been known to those with an interest in bird population trends, such as the founders of the American Ornithologists' Union (1883) and several turn-of-the-century nature writers. To give one illustration of warnings of impending avian doom at that the time, in his 1913 classic *Vanishing Wildlife*, William Hornaday denounced the disastrous culture of immigrants whose origins could be traced back to "the lower classes of southern Europe." The worst among these were the Italians, who were not only "then root[ing] out the native American and [taking] his place and his income" wherever they settled but were also "human mongoose[s]" towards wildlife. Give the Italian laborer power to act, Hornaday wrote, "and he will quickly exterminate every wild thing that wears feathers or hair. To our songbirds, he is literally a 'pestilence that walketh at noonday.'" Of course, "the great increase in the slaughter of song birds for food, by the negroes and poor whites of the South" had also become "an unbearable scourge to our migratory birds."[41]

Even if there had actually been declining bird populations at the time Rachel Carson wrote *Silent Spring*, a fair-minded and scientifically trained writer should have given more weight to long-standing and more recent alternative hypothesis (which, apart from those that existed in the late 19th century, would later include powerline electrocution and climate change in the 1960s[42]) along with other potentially harmful substances (such as polychlorinated biphenyls (PCBs), mercury, oil, and lead), if only to dismiss them.

Allegedly vanishing birds might have given *Silent Spring* its title, but its real target were the synthetic "biocides" that Carson contrasted to the allegedly "simpler"—because produced by nature rather than man—pesticides of earlier times. Because her treatment of the latter category is rather casual, we first discuss briefly a few facts that any fair-minded and reasonably informed commentator of the time should have known on the subject.[43]

Pesticide Use in Historical Perspective[44]

Afflictions of all kinds have always been able to, and can still, significantly reduce the quality and value of agricultural production and stored food. The problems include animals (birds, rodents, insects, mollusks, mites, nematodes, slugs, and snails), fungi (blights, mildews, molds, and rusts), microorganisms (bacteria and viruses), algae, or weeds. For instance, Egyptian farmers in Pharaonic times wrestled with swarms of locusts while their 19th-century counterparts in the United States found themselves besieged by chinch bugs, currant worms, cotton army worms, codling moths, plum curculios, Colorado potato beetles, and Rocky Mountain locusts.

The impact of these pests obviously always varied depending on several factors, from local climate and agricultural practices (for instance, wet tropical zones producing more than one crop a year without crop rotations—or "break crops" that "break" pest cycles—were always more susceptible to pests than temperate regions where one crop a year was produced and crops rotated from time to time) to availability and know-how in handling pesticides. To get a sense of what life was like before the development and widespread availability of modern pesticides, consider that perhaps as much as one third of the potential global agricultural production (food, feed, and fiber) in less advanced economies is thought to be destroyed annually by over 20,000 pest species, a loss of approximately $300 billion.

To give more specific illustrations, the maize of African farmers is nowadays subjected to the massive predation of army worms, ear borers, grain moths, cutworms, beetles, weevils, grain borers, rootworms, and white grubs. By far the most devastating are various species of stem borers that can cause losses ranging between 20 and 40 percent during cultivation and 30 and 90 percent during storage. Another problem for corn growers (and other crop plants such as sorghum, sugarcane, rice, and millet) is various parasitic weeds that can occasion major yield losses, even sometimes wiping out an entire crop.[45] (A small consolation is that maize is more resistant to bird depredation than sorghum.)

The potato blight not only caused the Irish potato famine but is also responsible for total yield losses of approximately $10 billion worldwide every year, in large part because, despite its name, it also affect tomatoes and other solanaceous crops.[46] Overall, mold spoils approximately 10 percent of the world's annual harvests, and without crop protection, almost 75 percent of the attainable potato crop worldwide would be lost to pests.[47] In Asia, rodents eat approximately 6 percent of the annual rice harvest (from munching on seedlings to eating stored grain), a volume roughly equivalent to what is needed to feed all of Indonesia (approximately 240 million people) for a whole year.[48]

Historically, agriculturalists achieved some success in reducing the impact of pests through a variety of ways such as encouraging pests' natural enemies, rotating crops, using crop diversity patterns, natural forage and trees when possible and appropriate, and, in the specific case of weeds, through repeatedly plowing fallow land and the use of herbicides. To illustrate how old Rachel Carson's alternative path to pest control truly was, consider that as far back as 324 BC, China ants were released on orchard trees to control caterpillars and boring beetles.

Because such "biocontrols" never proved completely adequate and exhibited other problems of their own,[49] agriculturalists have also long relied on pesticides, which are, technically speaking, any substance or mixture of substances that kill, repel, control, or mitigate the actions of any pest harmful to humans and crops. (Fungicides, insecticides, rodenticides, germicides, herbicides, acaricides (or miticides), nematicides, molluscicides, and virucides are thus all pesticides; some classifications also include avicides (bird poisons) in this category.) Suffice it to say that pesticides could typically control a much broader array of problems than a target agent (e.g., a pathogenic fungus might be an effective control for a single weed species, whereas some herbicides can control hundreds of different kinds) and considerably reduce the demand for labor to control insects another old-fashioned way— which was crushing them by hand.[50]

Among older discussions of the subjects, readers of the *Odysseus* are given a description of how the main protagonist, after having slain several suitors and slave-maids, asked for "sulfur, which cleanses all pollution," and fire in order "to burn it" and fumigate the "cloisters and both the inner and outer courts."[51] At about the same time, the Chinese were preparing solutions of arsenic and water to protect crops. Much later on, lead and mercury salts were used as agricultural pesticides from at least the early-15th century. Nicotine (from tobacco and related plants) was used on pears to protect them from insects in the late-17th century. The substance was used more widely afterwards, especially in the early-20th century, when it was discovered that its lethality to insects could be significantly increased by chemically sulfating it into nicotine sulfate, approximately five million pounds of which were used each year by American farmers in the 1940s and 1950s.

Pyrethrum (from the pyrethrum flower, a member of the chrysanthemum family) was first used to kill body lice on people in the early-19th century and then household pests. By the second half of the 19th century, large scale production in areas such as Japan and Kenya made the insecticide affordable enough to be used in agriculture. In 1886, over 600,000 pounds of the substance were imported into the United States for farm use.

The late-19th century, however, was mostly the era of inorganic poisons, or "chemical pesticides" as they were then labeled. They included lead arsenate (used especially by apple growers) and hydrogen cyanide (orange growers) and specific products such as Bordeaux mixture[52] (copper sulfate, lime, and water), London purple (mostly calcium arsenite, a former waste of the synthetic dye industry previously dumped at sea), and Paris Green (copper aceto-arsenite, a combination of copper acetate and arsenic trioxide), which were all used by a wide range of horticultural producers. Among other practices that might worry modern readers, in 1918 a home garden pest control handbook recommended the use of broadly and highly toxic lead arsenate, Bordeaux mixture, nicotine sulfate, mercury bichloride, and formaldehyde.[53]

Contrary to Carson's contention, these old-fashioned pesticides—now rechristened "biological extracts" and "rockdusts" by today's organic farmers who use them because they are "manufactured by nature" even though they are more expensive, more likely to promote insect resistance than synthetic alternatives because they are less effective, have higher toxicity for mammals, persist longer in the environment, and do more collateral damage to non-pests—were typically more problematic than many synthetic alternatives. For instance, pyrethrum has a chemical composition very similar to military nerve weapons, while DDT was actually 40 times less toxic to humans than nicotine sulfate.[54] Whether or not this information was available to Carson, she had no scientific grounds to argue that some pesticides were inherently less problematic than others because they had been manufactured in a flower or through geological processes rather than in a chemical plant.

Overlooked Benefits of Pesticides

In our view—and that of many of her contemporary critics—the major flaw of *Silent Spring* is that it overlooked the benefits of pesticides for not only human well-being but also for the environment. These include (a) reductions in habitat loss, which impoverishes biodiversity; (b) reductions in hunger, which is the first step toward ensuring a healthy population and an environmental consciousness that is not limited to elites; and (c) an increase in no-till farming, which reduces erosion and agricultural run-off into water bodies and limits the loss of agricultural productivity.

Habitat Loss

One of Rachel Carson's reasons for writing *Silent Spring* was to shine a spotlight on "permanent destruction of wildlife habitat" through the poisoning of the land and water that various organisms relied upon.[55] Paradoxically, by increasing agricultural yields, pesticide use also reduces the amount of land that would be converted to cropland. By releasing land to be "rewilded" or preventing the conversion of forestland or grassland, pesticides contribute to habitat conservation,[56] especially in light of the fact that such habitat conversion is deemed to be the single largest threat to terrestrial biodiversity worldwide.[57]

U.S. yields for cotton, wheat, and corn grew very slowly, if at all, from the 1860s to until just before 1940, after which they increased very rapidly with a vigorous burst from the late 1940s through the early- to mid-1960s.[58] In the 15-year span from 1945–1947 to 1960–1962, yields for wheat, corn, and cotton grew at an annual rate of 2.6 percent, 2.0 percent, and 4.7 percent, respectively.[59] By contrast, in the 76-year span from 1866–1868 to 1942–1944, these yields increased by 0.5 percent, 0.4 percent, and 0.9 percent annually. See Figure 5.6.

These increases in yields helped reduce land planted in crops (which excludes fallowed land) over the same period from 353 million acres to 309 million acres, that is, a decline of 12 percent

Figure 5.6
COTTON, CORN, AND WHEAT YIELDS, UNITED STATES, 1866–2010

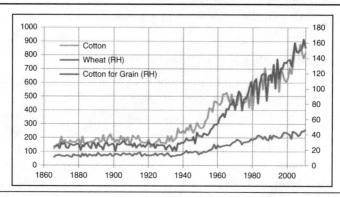

SOURCE: National Agricultural Statistics Service, *QuickStats 1.0 (2010)*, available at http://www.nass.usda.gov/Statistics_by_Subject/index.php?sector=CROPS, downloaded December 28, 2011.

Figure 5.7
LAND PLANTED IN CROPS (MILLIONS OF ACRES), POPULATION (MILLIONS), AND GDP PER CAPITA (IN $100S), UNITED STATES, 1910–2006

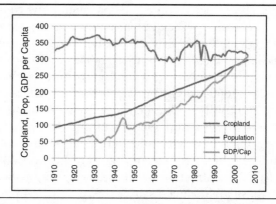

SOURCES: Economic Research Service, Major Land Uses 1910–2006, downloaded from http://www.ers.usda.gov/Data/MajorLandUses/spreadsheets/croplandusedforcrops.xls on 11 July 2008; Indur M. Goklany, "Have Increases in Population, Affluence and Technology Worsened Human and Environmental Well-being?" *Electronic Journal of Sustainable Development*, 1(3) (2009).

even as population and GDP per capita, both determinants of food demand, increased 29 percent and 16 percent, respectively (see Figure 5.7).

Of course, pesticide use was not the only factor contributing to these reductions in habitat conversion.[60] Greater fertilizer use, increased irrigation, greater mechanization (e.g., horses and mules consumed about a fifth of American crops before they were replaced by tractors[61]), and improved seeds and agronomic practices also contributed. So too did the development of a wide range of synthetic products, from textile fibers to dyes, that eliminated the need for many non-edible agricultural crops and commodities (from wool and silk to natural dyes and flax). And it should be noted that the mix of pesticides employed by farmers is continually evolving based on changes in, among other things, conditions on the farm and feedback based on performance of various practices, technology, supply and demand domestically and worldwide, and regulations. That is, because of farmers' ability to adapt, Carson's suggestions—that yields might decline[62]—have failed to materialize.

Pimentel et al. estimated that crop losses to all pests (including insects, diseases, and weeds) varied from 31.4% in 1942–1951 to 33.6 percent in 1974.[63] However, these estimates do not provide an indication as to how much more would have been lost absent pesticide usage. While more recent estimates are available,[64] Zilberman et al. provide estimates of the reductions in yield if a pesticide ban were to be applied to various major crops that are closer in time to the publication of *Silent Spring*.[65] They indicate that yield reductions would vary from 20 percent for sorghum to 70 percent for rice (see Table 5.1). If one assumes that these estimates hold for the period from 1945–1947 to 1960–1962, but for pesticides, as much as 30 percent

Table 5.1
PERCENT DECLINE IN YIELD DUE TO A PESTICIDE BAN ON MAJOR COMMODITIES

Wheat	Barley	Rice	Corn	Cotton	Soybean	Sorghum	Peanut
25%	29%	57%	32%	39%	37%	20%	70%

SOURCE: David Zilberman, Andrew Schmitz, Gary Casterline, Erik Lichtenberg, and Jerome B. Siebert, "The Economics of Pesticide Use and Regulation," *Science* 253 (1991): 518–522, table 3.

or more cropland would have been needed to maintain U.S. crop production. This, in addition to increasing the cost of food generally (see below), would have been quite detrimental for U.S. biodiversity.

Hunger around the World

It may be argued that the extra production enabled by pesticides was unnecessary since all it did was contribute to the United States' overproduction of food. As noted in *Silent Spring*, "We are told that the enormous and expanding use of pesticides is necessary to maintain farm production. Yet is our real problem not one of over-production? Our farms, despite measures to remove acreages from production and to pay farmers not to produce, have yielded such a staggering excess of crops that the American taxpayer in 1962 is pay-ing out more than one billion dollars a year as the total carrying cost of the surplus-food storage program."[66]

Carson's stance on this issue strikes us as very parochial. While the United States may have had surplus production in the early 1960s, the rest of the world was struggling to meet its food needs. As with all of human history up to that point in time, the 1940s and 1950s were times of hunger—and occasionally starvation—for less developed economies. From 1955–1961, there were famines in Somalia, China, Tunisia, Indonesia, East Pakistan (now Bangladesh), Algeria, Ceylon (Sri Lanka), Haiti, India, Laos, Nepal, Peru, the Congo, Crete, and Kenya.[67] Such episodes, plus the need to put its food surpluses to use, propelled U.S. efforts to establish a World Food Bank to relieve hunger and famine worldwide.[68] Notably, despite the overall drop in cropland, the acreage of cropland estimated to be used for exports increased from 42 million acres in 1945 to 66 million acres in 1962.[69] So while the United States may have been able to forego its food surpluses, the rest of the world depended on them.

No-Till Farming

Yet another overlooked benefit of pesticides (more specifically in this case, herbicides) is that it enabled no-till farming. For millennia, farmers had prepared their land for sowing and planting by tilling the earth. This loosens the soil, aerates it, kills weeds, and mixes nutrients, crop residue and other organic matter evenly in the soil. However, it also makes the soil susceptible to erosion and loss of nutrients from wind and water action, problems that were exacerbated by the use of tractors and other heavy machinery. These problems, highlighted among others by Edward Faulkner in his 1945 book, *Ploughman's Folly,* led to the development of no-till farming.[70] However, its use was limited until the advent of relatively cheap synthetic herbicides that enabled efficient removal of weeds without resorting to more expensive human labor or its mechanical substitutes.

While *Silent Spring* decries the use of "chemical weed killers" for "chemical plowing,"[71] it does not mention its potential for reducing erosion, which not only leads to loss of agricultural productivity but can also foul the air and water.

The "Other Road"

The last chapter of *Silent Spring,* "The Other Road," lays out alternatives to chemical pesticides that are, for the most part, throwbacks to practices that existed before the development of agricultural chemicals. These include use of other living organisms (including other insects, small mammals, birds, and carriers of insect disease, such as bacteria, viruses, and fungi), mass introduction of sterile insects, pheromones, and sound. While all of these should be part of a comprehensive agricultural production package, they were obviously insufficient by themselves—indeed, had this not been the case, there would have been no need to develop modern pesticides in the first place. Besides, despite the banning of specific products and widespread fears about their uses, the absence of effective alternatives to synthetic pesticides means that approximately 3 billion kilograms of several hundred different kinds of such substances are still applied each year.[72]

Carson, however, glossed over some rather obvious potholes in her discussion, most notably that these anti-pest organisms could themselves turn out to be invasive pests, do much damage on non-target insects, and might prove impossible to eradicate once established. As she notes, "Nearly half of the 180 or so major insect enemies of plants in the United States are accidental imports from abroad . . . it is no accident that our most troublesome insects are introduced species. . . . These invasions, both the naturally occurring and those dependent on human assistance, are likely to continue indefinitely. Quarantine and massive chemical campaigns are only extremely expensive ways of buying time."[73] Notably, "invasive-introduced species" are generally ranked second to habitat "destruction" in terms of their threat to biodiversity.[74] Yet, in her last chapter, Carson throws these considerations out of the window and makes no attempt to reconcile her recommendation to use biotic agents (including insects) instead of pesticides with the unintended consequences the former might bring in their wake.

Bacillus Thuringiensis

In a stroke of inspiration, Rachel Carson suggested, as one of the biological control alternatives to chemical pesticides, the use of *Bacillus thuringiensis* (Bt), a soil bacterium which can kill various insects.[75] It had been discovered in the early-20th century in Japan and Germany,[76] and at the time *Silent Spring* was being written, Bt was just beginning to be used in the United States. It has the advantage that, for practical purposes, it has no effect on human beings and wildlife. Today, genes from Bt have been incorporated into some of the more popular genetically modified crops (e.g., Bt corn and Bt cotton) to combat various insects. These genes produce proteins that immobilize the gut of the target pest, with different proteins being effective against different pests. Humans and wildlife lack the receptors that the proteins can bind to, hence their immunity to that bacterium. In the United States, in 2010, 63 percent of corn and 73 percent of cotton were planted with genetically modified Bt varieties.[77]

One wonders whether Rachel Carson would have been as adamant against the use of genetically modified Bt crops as many environmentalists have been in more recent times. Moreover, given the book's ambivalence over the use of chemical pesticides, it raises the question of how far she would have traveled on this branch of the Other Road that she herself pointed out.

Are Chemical Pesticides a Necessary Evil?

On the one hand, Rachel Carson averred that she was not opposed to chemical pesticides on principle, only to their overzealous application that had "potentials for harm."[78] On the other hand, she argued that, "to establish tolerances is to authorize contamination of public food supplies with poisonous chemicals . . . But if . . . it is possible to use chemicals in such a way that they leave a residue of only seven parts per million (the tolerance for DDT), or of one part per million (the tolerance for parathion), or even of only 0.1 part per million as is required for dieldrin on a great variety of fruits and vegetables, then why is it not possible, with only a little more care, to prevent the occurrence of any residues at all? This, in fact, is what is required for some chemicals such as heptachlor, endrin, and dieldrin on certain crops. If it is considered practical in these instances, why not for all?"[79] This sentiment was shared by many environmentalists who argued for a global ban on all uses of DDT in the run up to the Stockholm Convention's ban on persistent organic pesticides.[80]

In Chapter 6, Meiners suggest that the above contradiction could be reconciled by striving to balance the risks of not using pesticides against those of using them by employing a risk-risk framework of the precautionary principle. Using such a framework, the human health costs of a global ban on DDT would exceed the reduction in environmental and human health costs of such a ban. Many of Rachel Carson's disciples, however, do not favor such balancing of the risks of using DDT versus the risk of eschewing its use. This is evident from their support of a global ban on all DDT uses prior to the signing of the Stockholm Convention's ban on persistent organic pesticides) and their continuing efforts to phase out DDT despite its potential public health benefits.[81] But it does not follow that she herself would be averse to such a balancing.

Conclusion

Although a trained scientist, if not a practicing one, Rachel Carson had become an advocate by the time she wrote *Silent Spring*. This, at any rate, seems to be an inescapable conclusion in light of her blatant disregard for data she must have known disproved her main thesis (most notably the Audubon Christmas Bird Count) and her virtual silence on the real past, present, and future benefits of synthetic pesticides for humanity (by making food more abundant and affordable) and the environment (by increasing yields and sparing wilderness in the process). Perhaps, as suggested by the *New York Times*, this had become part of "her method."[82] Her apparent lack of consideration for what were then well-publicized famines in other parts of the world is also unsettling. After having made its case against synthetic pesticides, the book offers another road that is in the end a one-way lane to past practices whose deficiencies motivated the development of synthetic pesticides as people struggled to feed themselves.

6. Rachel Carson's Health Scare

Roger E. Meiners

Rachel Carson begins *Silent Spring* by reminding her readers of a simpler, happier time: "There was once a town in the heart of America where all life seemed to live in harmony with its surroundings."[1] But as "A Fable for Tomorrow" continues, she forecasts a grim future: children stricken while playing and dying within a few hours, no fish living in the stream, chicks not hatching, few birds heard, no bees pollinating, and vegetation turning brown and withered. Although she explains that the story is just a fable and no town had suffered such a fate, she cautions, "Yet every one of these disasters has actually happened somewhere, and many real communities have already suffered a substantial number of them."[2] This "grim specter has crept upon us almost unnoticed" and "may easily become a stark reality we all shall know."[3] To catch a reader's imagination and attention, it is hard to imagine a more effective opening.

The view of a formerly healthy and happy America expressed at the opening of *Silent Spring* was not new, as Desrochers and Shimizu discuss in Chapter 3. And as Nelson discusses in Chapter 4, some people today take as an article of faith that heaven on earth has been despoiled by modern technology. Nostalgia is a powerful theme— nostalgia for a time when families gathered to read in the evening by candlelight and everyone communed with nature, suggesting we have been fools to think we could improve upon the natural state of affairs enjoyed by our ancestors. But nostalgia ignores the improvements to living standards that accompany the disruptions of change.

When Rachel Carson was born in 1907, life expectancy was about 49 in the United States, the same as enjoyed in Guinea-Bissau and Chad today.[4] When Carson was writing *Silent Spring*, life expectancy in the United States had risen by more than 20 years.[5] Americans were healthier and wealthier than ever. She knew that. But her world view was a glass half empty and going dry. Exactly why were we headed for the environmental cliff? Carson writes, "This book is an attempt to explain."[6] This chapter considers the major human health issue she raised.

Better Living through Chemistry

Chapter 3, titled "Elixirs of Death," opens with the following ominous statement:

> For the first time in the history of the world, every human being is now subjected to contact with dangerous chemicals, from the moment of conception until death. In the less than two decades of their use, the synthetic pesticides have been so thoroughly distributed throughout the animate and inanimate world that they occur virtually everywhere.[7]

Subsequent chapters elaborate on this theme with respect to the impact of pesticides on birds and other creatures. Carson believed that "natural cancer-causing agents are still a factor in producing malignancy; however, they are few in number."[8] What explained the increase in cancer she observed in her lifetime? She believed it was the effect of pesticides and other man-made (synthetic) chemicals:

> No longer are exposures to dangerous chemicals occupational alone; they have entered the environment of everyone—even of children as yet unborn. It is hardly surprising, therefore, that we are now aware of an alarming increase in malignant disease.
>
> The increase itself is no mere matter of subjective impressions. The monthly report of the Office of Vital Statistics for July 1959 states that malignant growths, including those of the lymphatic and blood-forming tissues, accounted for 15 per cent of the deaths in 1958 compared with only 4 per cent in 1900. Judging by the present incidence of the disease, the American Cancer Society estimates that 45,000,000 Americans now living will eventually develop cancer.[9]

The U.S. population in 1960 was 180 million, hence the title of Chapter 14, "One in Every Four."

The 20th century saw an increase in cancer deaths and death rates in the United States as in other developed countries. However, Carson ignored major factors in evaluating the matter. First, the population by 1958 was 175 million, compared to 75 million in 1900. Thus, all else being equal, the number of deaths (but not death rates) would have increased. Second, the 20th century saw a continual decline in all-cause death rates (see Figure 6.1). Consequently, life expectancy had increased from 47.3 years in 1900 to 69.6 years in 1958.

Relatively few young people die from cancer. The risk of death from cancer increases sharply with age.[10] Because people were living longer, cancer was becoming a more common cause of death until near the end of the 20th century, when improved diagnosis and treatment stemmed the tide, along with the gradual decline in smoking.

Figure 6.1
U.S. CRUDE DEATH RATES FOR ALL CAUSES AND CRUDE DEATH RATES FOR CANCER (PER 100,000 POPULATION)

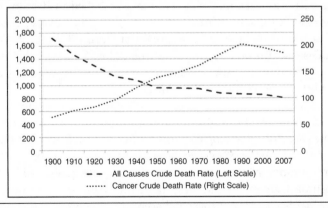

SOURCES: Jiaquan Xu et al., "Deaths: Final Data for 2007," *National Vital Statistics Reports* 58, no. 19 (2010), www.cdc.gov/nchs/data/nvsr/nvsr58/nvsr58_19.pdf; "Leading Causes of Death, 1900–1998," www.cdc.gov/nchs/data/dvs/lead1900_98.pdf; and *Health, United States*, 2010, (Hyattsville, MD: National Center for Health Statistics, 2011), www.cdc.gov/nchs/data/hus/hus10.pdf#032.

Because of its increasing prevalence, cancer was high on the public health agenda in the 1950s.[11] There was substantial debate at that time over the cause of the increase in cancer death rates—was it smoking or some other substance?

Silence on Tobacco Smoking

Silent Spring entirely ignores the debate. Carson indicts man-made "new chemical and physical agents" against which man has "no protection" as these "powerful substances . . . easily penetrate the inadequate defenses of the body."[12] Not once does she mention that smoking tobacco might be a carcinogen. The closest Carson comes to suggesting a connection to smoking and cancer is when she mentions that arsenic compounds are known to cause cancer. She suggests that use of arsenic-based pesticides (which was common in the pre-DDT era) in tobacco farming could lead to increased cancer, not because of smoking but because of exposure to arsenic.[13]

The relationship between smoking and cancer was under active debate when Carson was writing *Silent Spring*. For example, between January 1, 1959, and March 31, 1962, the *New York Times* carried 133 articles dealing with "smoking" and "cancer." These pieces carried headlines ranging from, "War on Smoking Asked in Britain; Royal College of Physicians Links Cancer of Lung to Heavy Cigarette Use; Curb on Ads Is Sought; Report Also Terms Tobacco Factor in Heart Disease, Bronchitis and TB"[14] and "New Study Adds Data on Smoking, Confirms Cancer-Tobacco Link,"[15] to "Experts on Cancer Voice Differences on Heavy Smoking."[16]

Perhaps Carson overlooked this controversy because she adopted as her cancer guru Dr. Wilhelm Hueper, a protagonist in the debate over the cause of increasing cancer. Originally from Germany, Hueper was a distinguished pathologist who did major work on occupational and environmental cancer that is heralded for its quality.[17] However, at the time Carson was writing, he firmly believed environmental contaminants were the culprits; tobacco smoking was not a concern.[18]

From today's vantage point, most people would scoff at Hueper's ideas. However, an Internet search of his name yields evidence of adherents who still preach that doctrine: chemicals cause cancer. There is a conspiracy between the government, chemical makers, and research scientists who are on their payrolls. Books, such as *The Secret History of the War on Cancer*,[19] tell all about the corporate profiteers and their toadies in government who suppress the truth about cancer. Science makes little difference for those who hold such ideas as a matter of faith (see Chapter 4).

Given the state of knowledge at that time, Hueper had reasons for his skepticism of the tobacco hypothesis.[20] Talley et al. suggest that the controversy over the role of tobacco in cancer was not considered settled until publication of the Surgeon General's report, *Smoking and Health*, in 1964.[21] Other observers claim that the controversy in the scientific community over smoking as a major cause of cancer was settled well before official government recognition was pronounced.[22]

Carson, ignoring tobacco, clearly implies that many entomologists supported the use of chemical pesticides for pecuniary reasons:

> The major chemical companies are pouring money into the universities to support research on insecticides. . . . Inquiry into the background of some of these men reveals that their entire research program is supported by the chemical industry. Their professional prestige, sometimes their very jobs depend on the perpetuation of chemical methods. Can we then expect them to bite the hand that literally feeds them? But knowing their bias, how much credence can we give to their protests that insecticides are harmless?[23]

It seems to have escaped her that her cancer guru, Hueper, as a professional researcher at a university that received grants, could have been susceptible to the same failing. In any case, her statement about the researchers constitutes an ad hominem attack on people with opposing viewpoints rather than an argument based on the science and the facts. It is difficult to believe she was unaware that the majority of the relevant cancer researchers were sure tobacco was a major culprit among the causes of cancer, despite tobacco company funding of some research.

The Contribution of Environmental Contaminants to Cancer

Various quotations from *Silent Spring* indicate that Carson believed that man-made carcinogens in the environment were responsible for the bulk of the increase in cancer during the 20th century and that, in the future, cancer could strike "one in every four" Americans. However, once cancer death rates are adjusted for the aging of the population, and confounding factors such as smoking and diet are considered, cancer death rates did not show upward trends.[24] Cancer death rates for nonsmokers aged 35–69 declined at least from the 1950s onward, at just about the time they should have been increasing if synthetic pesticides (such as DDT) were the major cause of cancer.[25]

Similarly, age-adjusted cancer death rates for all cancers, excluding lung and bronchus, declined from 1950 to 1990 for all age groups except those above 85.[26] The decline ranged from 71 percent for the 0–4 year age group and 8 percent for the 74–85 year age group.[27] The declines would have been greater if only nonsmoking-related cancers were considered, since smoking is also implicated in cancer of the mouth, esophagus, pancreas, bladder, leukemia, and possibly colon,[28] as suggested by Figures 6.2 and 6.3.

Figure 6.2
AGE-ADJUSTED CANCER DEATH RATES (MALES, BY SITE, 1930–2006)

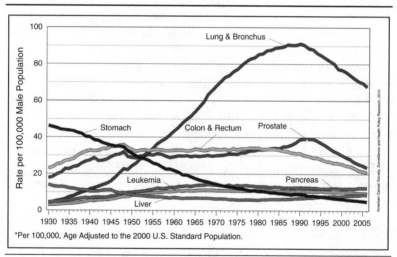

*Per 100,000, Age Adjusted to the 2000 U.S. Standard Population.

NOTES: Due to changes in ICD coding, numerator information has changed over time. Rates for cancer of the liver, lung and bronchus, and colon and rectum are affected by these coding changes.

SOURCE: American Cancer Society, *Cancer Facts & Figures* (2010), http://www. cancer.org/acs/groups/content/@epidemiologysurveilance/documents/ document/acspc-026208.pdf.

Figure 6.3

AGE-ADJUSTED CANCER DEATH RATES (FEMALES, BY SITE, 1930–2006)

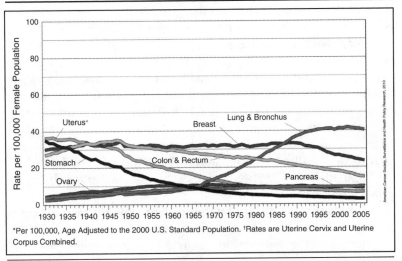

*Per 100,000, Age Adjusted to the 2000 U.S. Standard Population. †Rates are Uterine Cervix and Uterine Corpus Combined.

NOTE: Due to changes in ICD coding, numerator information has changed over time. Rates for cancer of the lung and bronchus, colon and rectum, and ovary are affected by these coding changes.

SOURCE: American Cancer Society, *Cancer Facts & Figures*, (2010), http://www.cancer.org/acs/groups/content/@epidemiologysurveilance/documents/document/acspc-026209.pdf.

Carson did not have the benefit of the Internet to look up the graphs here, which were compiled by the American Cancer Society, but she did have available the annual mortality data cited by the Cancer Society for 1930 and forward. A leading killer of women was cancer of the uterus. Carson could have eyeballed the data to see the trends. For example, the data for 1936 lists 16,280 deaths from malignant uterine cancer.[29] By 1956, the raw (not age-adjusted) number was 9,690.[30] Could Hueper and Carson have been blind to the fact that lung cancer among men was the only form of cancer rising rapidly among men in the 1950s, while among women it barely moved? They breathed the same air. We now know, as did most researchers by 1960, that lung cancer jumped because the percentage of men who smoked increased significantly during World War II. The share of women addicted to tobacco did not

125

rise as rapidly until the liberating 1960s, so lung cancer shows up later among women.

In their authoritative paper on the causes of cancer in the United States, published 19 years after *Silent Spring*, Richard Doll and Richard Peto[31] estimate that less than 1 percent to as much as 5 percent of cancer deaths were due to pollution (with a best estimate of 2 percent). For occupational exposures, they estimate a range of 2 to 8 percent (best estimate of 4 percent). They also calculate that the share of cancer deaths due to tobacco was 30 percent and to diet, 35 percent.

Although the Doll and Peto estimates are generally accepted, not all researchers agree with them. Clapp et al. note that other scholars estimate that occupational hazards could contribute as much as 10 percent of cancer incidents.[32] In a later survey article in *Nature* in 2001, Peto provides fresh estimates of the share of cancer deaths that could be attributed to specific causes and avoided through appropriate interventions (see Table 6.1).[33]

Peto's estimates show that more than half of cancer deaths among nonsmokers are unavoidable (based on current knowledge). For smokers, the corresponding figure is 25 percent. Smoking

---

Table 6.1
U.S. CANCER DEATHS AVOIDED BY ELIMINATING KNOWN RISKS

Cause	Deaths (percent avoided after removing each cause)	
	Current Smokers	Nonsmokers
Smoking	60	—
Known infections	2	5
Alcohol	0.4	1
Sunlight	0.4	1
Air pollution	0.4	1
Occupation	0.4	1
Lack of exercise	0.4	1
Diet (overweight)	4	10
Other dietary factors	4–12?	10–30?
Presently unavoidable	≈25	>50

SOURCE: Julian Peto, "Cancer Epidemiology in the Last Century and the Next Decade," *Nature* 411 (2001): 390–95.

accounts for 60 percent of cancer deaths among smokers. Reduced air pollution, better occupational controls, and sunlight avoidance could lower cancer deaths by 1 percent among smokers and 3 percent among nonsmokers.

More recently, in a survey of cancer trends in France, Boffetta et al. come to qualitatively similar conclusions.[34] They attribute 2.4 percent of cancer deaths in France to occupation, 0.7 percent to ultraviolet light, and 0.2 percent to pollution. By contrast, they attribute 23.9 percent to smoking, 6.9 percent to alcohol, and 3.6 percent to infectious agents.

In sum, the scientific evidence of a half-century has not borne out Carson's notion that man-made environmental carcinogens would cause an explosion of cancer. Why did she think this was happening? She believed it was because of "man's search for a better and easier way of life" and "because the manufacture and sale of such chemicals has become an accepted part of our economy."[35] That is, unless we returned to the days of (alleged) harmony with nature, we would pay the price.

What accounts for the disparities between Carson's prognostications about cancer and the current understanding of the causes of cancer? Perhaps she was misled by a misconception combined with a hypothesis. The misconception was that natural carcinogens "are few in number and they belong to that ancient array of forces to which life has been accustomed from the beginning."[36] The hypothesis may have been that since these new synthetic pesticides were designed to kill various organisms, they could cause biological changes in humans, and humans had not yet developed defense mechanisms against their toxic effects.[37]

Since publication of *Silent Spring*, however, research has shown that 99.99 percent of the carcinogens we ingest are natural in origin.[38] Plants manufacture them to defend against pests that would otherwise injure or kill the plant. That is, they are the products of plants' self-defense mechanisms. That does not mean that natural carcinogens do not harm humans. Belladonna and many other plants are toxic. Just as natural species produce chemicals to defend themselves from harm, human beings often rely on synthetic pesticides to help protect them from harm. This harm includes death and disease from vector-borne diseases, such as malaria, and loss of food supply (which is the first line of defense in ensuring and maintaining public health).

127

At the high doses at which chemicals are tested for carcinogenicity in rats, about half of natural chemicals are carcinogens—the same percentage as for synthetic chemicals.[39] The high doses in these animal studies cannot, without heroic assumptions, be extrapolated downward to the much smaller doses received by the general public. Similarly, much of the data on acute and chronic doses that Carson relied on came from studies in occupational settings where, typically, much higher doses than the general population is exposed to are found.[40] Even if rats are a good model for human beings when it comes to cancer—which is debatable—the contribution of synthetic chemicals to cancer among the general population is slight, and certainly nothing approaching "one in every four." As Boffetta et al. note:

> Many chemicals have been postulated as human carcinogens (pesticides, dioxin, endocrine disruptors, etc.). The clinical and experimental data are, however, not consistent with a substantial role of pollution in human cancer. Moreover, the concentrations to which the public is exposed are very low and biological data show that great caution is required before extrapolating from high to low exposure. . . . Even if the action of air pollution [including fine particles] is taken into account, the total proportion of cancers attributable to pollution would not exceed 1%, a figure consistent with that reported in Nordic countries and the UK.[41]

Leukemia

Silent Spring singled out leukemia for special attention:

> There is, however, one presently known exception to the fact that a long period of latency is common to most malignancies. This exception is leukemia. Survivors of Hiroshima began to develop leukemia only three years after the atomic bombing, and there is now reason to believe the latent period may be considerably shorter. . . .
>
> Within the period covered by the rise of modern pesticides, the incidence of leukemia has been steadily rising. . . . In the year 1960, leukemia alone claimed 12,290 victims. Deaths from all types of malignancies of blood and lymph totaled 25,400, increasing sharply from the 16,690 figure of 1950. In terms of deaths per 100,000 of population, the increase is

from 11.1 in 1950 to 14.1 in 1960. The increase is by no means confined to the United States; in all countries the recorded deaths from leukemia at all ages are rising at a rate of 4 to 5 per cent a year. What does it mean? To what lethal agent or agents, new to our environment, are people now exposed with increasing frequency?[42]

However, an analysis by Gilliam and Walter (published several years before *Silent Spring*) of trends in age-specific leukemia death rates suggests that the increase commenced in the 1920s (or earlier), before organochlorines such as DDT came on the scene.[43] These death rates moderated after about 1940, with the greatest reduction in the younger age groups.[44] Gilliam and Walter's take-away message is that the "trends . . . provide no support whatsoever for a theory which postulates a sharp increase within the last 15 years in leukemogenic factors affecting the environment of Americans in general. On the contrary, the data suggest that such exposure has either become stabilized or has actually decreased during this period, if exposure to environmental factors is in fact responsible for the disease."[45]

Consistent with the Gilliam and Walter study, Milham and Ossiander later showed (in a study responding to the assertion that another factor of modernity—electricity—caused leukemia) that the increases in age-specific death rates for childhood leukemia (in males) slowed down in the 1940s and peaked in the 1960s.[46] Although this paper was published long after the appearance of *Silent Spring*, the data through the 1950s were available in public health reports at the time Carson was writing.

The Ultimate Fear: Cancer in Children

Carson raised the specter of an increasing toll of cancer among children: "A quarter century ago, cancer in children was considered a medical rarity. *Today, more American school children die of cancer than from any other disease.*"[47] (Emphasis in original.) It is hard to imagine anything more disturbing to parents than this claim.

There are several problems with this assertion. Table 6.2 shows mortality rates from all-causes and cancer among children less than 1 year old, ages 1–4 years, and ages 5–14 years for 1900, 1935, and 1960. The major reason cancer deaths in these age groups loomed larger in 1960 than in 1935 or 1900 was less the increase in cancer death rates than the dramatic decline in all-cause death rates. Common

129

Table 6.2
ALL-CAUSE AND CANCER MORTALITY RATES AMONG CHILDREN (PER 100,000 POPULATION, AGES 0–14 YEARS, 1900–1960)

Age Group	Year	< 1yr	1–4 yrs	5–14 yrs
All-cause	1900	16,240	1,980	390
	1935	5,740	370	150
	1960	2,880	110	50
Cancer	1900	3.2	2.9	1.8
	1935	3.1	4.1	2.0
	1960	7.2	10.9	6.8

NOTE: Rates are based on population in each age group.

SOURCES: Public Health Service, *Vital Statistics Rates in the United States, 1900–1940* (Washington, D.C.: Government Printing Office, 1947), pp. 181, 250; Public Health Service, *Vital Statistics of the United States, 1960* (Washington, D.C.: Government Printing Office, 1963), pp. 5–182, 5–192; and U.S. Bureau of Commerce, *Statistical Abstracts of the United States 1961* (Washington, D.C.: Government Printing Office, 1961), pp. 29, 58.

"childhood diseases" which had killed many children were being brought under control. For instance, for the 5–14 year age group, deaths dropped from 150 per 100,000 in 1935 to 50 per 100,000 in 1960. Over the same period and for the same age group, cancer death rates increased from 2.0 to 6.8 per 100,000, a big increase in percentage terms from a relatively low base but one that is dwarfed by the large reduction in the broader context of all-cause death rates.

Another problem with Carson's argument in *Silent Spring* is that cancer is not one disease but a class of diseases. Thus, to compare all-cancer death rates with the death rate for other diseases is somewhat misleading. There is also no way of knowing if some children who died of cancer in 1960, when diagnoses were better than in earlier years, might have been classified differently in the past. That is, an individual death may involve multiple causes, but only one cause is entered in the record for statistical purposes. In earlier times, a child with cancer might well have succumbed to pneumonia or some other disease, so cancer rates may actually have been higher than reported—and not as readily recognized as in later years. Although death statistics are quite accurate, the cause-of-death statistics are a bit less accurate, and likely less so the further back in time one goes.

Even if the cancer numbers are accepted as accurate, the timing of increases in cancer death rates is inconsistent with the narrative in *Silent Spring* regarding DDT:

> [T]he first exposures to DDT date from about 1942 for military personnel and from about 1945 for civilians, and it was not until the early fifties that a wide variety of pesticidal chemicals came into use. The full maturing of whatever seeds of malignancy have been sown by these chemicals is yet to come.[48]

As seen in Figure 6.1, overall cancer death rates had been increasing at least since 1900, long before DDT and other synthetic organic pesticides came on the scene. In fact, the increase in the crude cancer death rate started to moderate in the early 1950s, just after DDT and organochlorines came into widespread use.

Evolving Pesticides

The use of arsenic-based pesticides waned as the new organochlorines (later largely replaced by organophosphates) came on the market. As shown in Figure 6.4, DDT and other organochlorines were rapidly displacing pesticides containing arsenic (as well as lead and other metals) by the 1950s.[49] Carson did not care for any of the new products. "Can anyone believe it is possible to lay down such a barrage of poisons on the surface of the earth without making it unfit for all life? They should not be called 'insecticides,' but 'biocides.'"[50] She did not expressly advocate banning the products, but the implication was clear; and, as Desrochers and Shimizu discuss in Chapter 5, she was sure there were natural alternatives.

As Carson notes in *Silent Spring*, "One of the earliest pesticides associated with cancer is arsenic, occurring in sodium arsenite as a weed killer, and in calcium arsenate and various other compounds as insecticides. The association between arsenic and cancer in man and animals is historic."[51] Moreover, arsenic compounds were implicated in more than cancer—they were associated with conditions of the liver, skin, and gastrointestinal and nervous systems.[52] One of the major arsenical pesticides was lead arsenate.[53] Because arsenic compounds had long been in use, Carson portrayed the

Figure 6.4
Volume of Conventional Insecticide/Miticide Active Ingredient Usage in the United States (Millions of Pounds, 1935–1960)

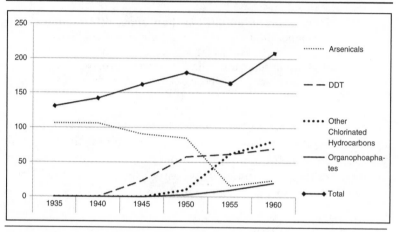

Notes: The major categories shown do not create the total; other minor categories are not included. Data are once every five years.

Source: Adapted from Arnold S. Aspelin, *Trends in Pesticide Usage in the United States*, Part 4 (Raleigh, NC: Center for Integrated Pest Management, North Carolina State University, 2003), p. 19.

human health-related problems associated with them as being known with relative certainty.[54] The consequences of organochlorines such as DDT were still speculative.[55] The displacement of pesticides containing arsenic (and other heavy metal) compounds by organochlorines may have provided a public health benefit. But Carson did not explore whether the change, which she knew was occurring, might provide a silver lining to what she saw as a dark cloud.[56] The failure to consider this possibility is a lapse in scientific logic.

One of Carson's criticisms of pesticides in general, and DDT in particular, is that they are temporary fixes: sooner or later target pests will develop resistance, and the pesticide will become ineffective.[57] Pesticide users know that, so most use the products judiciously. Overusing a pesticide would not only be more costly but also reduce its long-term effectiveness. Similarly, the likelihood of resistance provides an incentive for pesticide manufacturers to advocate prudent use to stretch the period over which they can sell their product and develop substitutes. If pests indeed became resistant, the pesticide's use would be curtailed, which would allow the environment to cleanse itself.

Domestic DDT use had begun to decline in the late 1950s, prior to publication of *Silent Spring*, partly because of its decreasing cost-effectiveness relative to other options, partly because of regulations in a few states. Proof that discontinuing the use of a pesticide will indeed cleanse the environment of its pollutant load is seen in trend data for various organochlorines—DDT and its residues, aldrin and dieldrin—indicating that their concentrations have declined in the environment, in human adipose tissue, and in human breast milk by as much as an order of magnitude or more since their use was phased out (for whatever reason).[58]

Weak Analysis

The reader of *Silent Spring* would be led astray on the significance and contribution of pesticides to cancer in the United States. Carson's lopsided view stems, in part, from her reliance on Wilhelm Hueper as her cancer guru. His views reinforced her prejudice against pesticides (confirmation bias). Her reliance on Hueper, however, is less of a problem than her silence regarding the possible role of smoking. That constitutes a sin of omission.

Other problems with the book's cancer narrative are twofold: it failed to explore more fully the consequences of (a) replacing arsenic-based pesticides, (e.g., lead arsenate, a known carcinogen) with pesticides whose carcinogenicity was uncertain, and (b) the development of resistance to specific pesticides on the future pollution burden in the environment and in organisms. Carson compounded these failings by ignoring the effects of a longer life expectancy on cancer rates, the spatial distribution of cancer rates between rural and urban populations, and the backdrop of rapid elimination of many of the biggest causes of deaths, which automatically magnified the relative importance of cancer. Had she considered these elements, her perception of the urgency of the pesticide problem perhaps might have diminished. Contrary to the suggestion in a July 1962 *New York Times* editorial—that Carson might have good reasons for ignoring the benefits of pesticides[59]—there was little scientific basis for these oversights.

Since Carson's condemnation of DDT, numerous studies have been done to establish the relationship, if any, between DDT (and its metabolites, DDD and DDE) and cancer. As the Agency for Toxic Substances and Disease Registry reports, "Issues inherent to epidemiological studies, such as the role of cofounders [sic[60]] for example, make it difficult to draw definite conclusions about exposure to DDT/DDE/DDD and cancer. However, taking all factors into consideration, the existing information does not support the hypothesis that exposure to DDT/DDE/DDD increases the risk of cancer in humans."[61] Notably, the Environmental Protection Agency classifies DDT, DDE, and DDD as *probable* human carcinogens; the International Agency for Research on Cancer classifies them as *possible* human carcinogens; and the Department of Health and Human Services has determined that they *may be anticipated* to be human carcinogens.

Thus, even after more than a half century of work, the status of DDT as a carcinogen remains shrouded in uncertainty, suggesting that public policy might better focus on substances where the evidence of a marked negative effect is clearer. As Roberts and Tren explain in this volume, DDT continues to be an effective weapon in many locales and situations against malaria and other vector-borne diseases. Efforts to discontinue its use for public health purposes are misguided and clearly not based on the evidence of DDT's benefits when it is properly applied.[62]

Ambivalence about the Use of Chemical Pesticides

In *Silent Spring*, Carson explains that she is not against the use of chemical pesticides, only their overzealous application by users unaware of their "potentials for harm"[63]—and who could disagree with that? But she attributes only horrors to pesticides and notes that even exposure to "one molecule" might be problematic.[64] Carrying this thought to its logical conclusion, she argues that

> to establish tolerances is to authorize contamination of public food supplies with poisonous chemicals. . . .
>
> But if . . . it is possible to use chemicals in such a way that they leave a residue of only 7 parts per million (the

tolerance for DDT), or of 1 part per million (the tolerance for parathion), or even of only 0.1 part per million as is required for dieldrin on a great variety of fruits and vegetables, then why is it not possible, with only a little more care, to prevent the occurrence of any residues at all? This, in fact, is what is required for some chemicals such as heptachlor, endrin, and dieldrin on certain crops. If it is considered practical in these instances, why not for all?[65]

For practical purposes, a "no-residue" policy is tantamount to a no-use policy. Essentially, *Silent Spring*'s rhetorical question was an articulation of the Delaney Clause (a zero-risk standard imposed on the Food and Drug Administration that was so impractical Congress had to repeal it). It lives on in present day environmentalists' version of the precautionary principle, as Katzenstein and Marchant discuss in their respective chapters.

Can this apparent contradiction within *Silent Spring*—between acknowledging a role for pesticides while arguing for a no-residue policy—be reconciled? Perhaps, if "no residue" meant no measurable residue based on the detection technology available in the early-1960s (and no one could have anticipated that subsequent advances in technology would lower detection levels by orders of magnitude). But even that rationale runs counter to the "one molecule" narrative.

From a practical perspective, the contradiction could be reconciled by attempting to balance the risks of *not using* pesticides against those of *using* them. Many of Carson's disciples are reluctant to do such balancing, as is evident from the events preceding the decision to allow a public health exemption for DDT in the Stockholm Convention's ban on persistent organic pesticides and continuing efforts since then to eliminate DDT completely. This campaign continues despite the broad range of public health benefits that DDT can provide.[66] Given Carson's contradictory statements, it is unclear whether she would oppose an attempt at balancing.

Endless Threats

During Carson's life, the use of chemicals and metals in the United States rose from the modest levels that would be expected of a country with a low standard of living in 1900 to the higher levels needed for ordinary people to enjoy a better life by 1960. Figure 6.5 shows that between 1900 and 1960, despite the five-fold increase in the use

Figure 6.5

U.S. TRENDS IN USE OF SYNTHETIC ORGANIC CHEMICALS AND
PRIMARY METALS COMPARED TO LIFE EXPECTANCY (1900–1960)

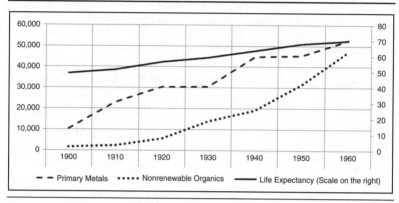

SOURCES: Grecia R. Matos, "Use of Minerals and Materials in the United States from 1900 through 2006," U.S. Geological Survey Fact Sheet 2009–2008, http://pubs.usgs.gov/fs/2009/3008/; and National Center for Health Statistics, *U.S. Decennial Life Tables for 1989–1991*, vol. 1, no. 3 (Hyattsville, MD: CDC, 1999), http://www.cdc.gov/nchs/data/lifetables/life89_1_3.pdf.

of primary metals (ranging from aluminum to beryllium to cadmium to indium to mercury to selenium to tin to zinc) and a 30-fold increase in the use of nonrenewable organic compounds (ranging from asphalt to lubricants to petroleum coke to benzene to ethylene to xylene), U.S. life expectancy increased steadily (from 49.2 years in 1900 to 69.9 years in 1960). Cancer increased over those decades as well, but little evidence attributes that rise to the substances tagged by Carson. Whatever public health problems may have been created or exacerbated by the mass production and use of metals and nonrenewable organics, technological developments and economic progress reduced public health problems overall.

These data cast doubt on the premise inherent in the question in *Silent Spring:* "The question is whether any civilization can wage relentless war on life without destroying itself, and without losing the right to be called civilized."[67] This rhetorical question suggests another: whether any civilization that hobbles new technology that could reduce hunger and disease, on the chance that the new technology might have negative consequences—essentially giving up a real bird in hand for a hypothetical bird in the bush—should lose the right to be called civilized.

Conclusion

Desrochers and Shimizu (Chapter 5) identify several shortcomings in Carson's *Silent Spring* that stem from major omissions. These include her silence on the benefits of chemical pesticides, such as higher agricultural production—which reduced hunger in a world of chronic starvation and limited the loss of wildlife habitat. Another flaw is her reliance on anecdotes rather than systematic analysis of available information. But perhaps the book's biggest failing is its discussion of cancer.

Carson attempted to create in the reader's mind the impression that pesticides (and other man-made chemicals) were the drivers of the increase in cancer deaths in 20th-century America. At the time she was writing *Silent Spring*, the causes of cancer and the relative role of various potential causes were widely debated. Yet Carson was silent on that debate. She focused on the views of a researcher whose ideas matched her own. She omitted any discussion of the role of smoking and compounded that sin by engaging in unbalanced speculation on how pesticides and other pollutants might lead to an increase in cancer (accompanied by a few well-told anecdotes).

She overlooked relevant factors affecting the overall impact of organochlorine pesticides on cancer rates. For example, she should have considered the net result of replacing arsenic-based pesticides—known carcinogens—with organochlorine pesticides of uncertain carcinogenicity. Besides ignoring risk tradeoffs, Carson also overlooked key factors that magnified the 20th-century increases in cancer death rates relative to all-cause death rates. The spectacular reduction of many causes of death meant that cancer death rates automatically accounted for a larger share of deaths. That increase in share was further exaggerated because people were living longer and because cancer deaths are compounded with increasing age. An increasing cancer death rate can be a sign of society's success in reducing deaths from diseases that are more prone to strike younger people. This is one reason why, despite increases in cancer deaths, life expectancy has continued to improve in the half century since the publication of *Silent Spring*.

Today we know that—contrary to Carson's speculation—while man-made pollutants (in general) and chemical pesticides (in particular) can increase cancer deaths, they contribute only a small fraction of total cancer deaths and an even smaller fraction of all-cause deaths. As life expectancies continue to increase and medical science advances, the share of deaths attributable to cancers will also likely increase—we must all die of something eventually.

Finally, although Carson claimed that she was opposed not to chemical pesticides but only to their misuse, her book suggests that exposure to even "one molecule" might be problematic, and her rhetoric is consistent with a zero-residue policy. This apparent inconsistency might be resolved by balancing the risks of *not using* pesticides against the risks of *using* them. Many environmentalists today oppose such balancing and indulge in one-sided application of the precautionary principle to justify a ban on life-saving chemicals. It is unknown whether Carson would be among them.

The National Academy of Engineering, a part of the National Academies, uses *Silent Spring* in its online ethics training for engineering and research: "Undaunted by the chemical companies' hostility and by the public's high enthusiasm for pesticides, she wrote a book called *Silent Spring*, which caused a major shift in public consciousness about the environment."[68] If the scholarship evidenced in *Silent Spring* is a paragon of judicious research then we have fallen victim to what Robert Nelson in his chapter calls a "secular religion" in the guise of science.

7. The Balance of Nature and "The Other Road": Ecological Paradigms and the Management Legacy of *Silent Spring*

Nathan Gregory

"The 'control of nature' is a phrase conceived in arrogance, born of the Neanderthal age of biology and philosophy, when it was supposed that nature exists for the convenience of man."[1] So begins the final paragraph of Rachel Carson's *Silent Spring*, a statement that has been characterized as a rejection of what were then the conventional views on science and the widely held belief in a dichotomy of man versus nature.[2] It is also a deeply personal comment and may express one of the main reasons why Carson wrote her book. As Kaufman notes in Chapter 1, Carson learned about the potential environmental risks of DDT at least as early as 1945. She was repeatedly exposed to reports about the ecological effects of chemical pesticides while serving as an editor at the U.S. Fish and Wildlife Service, and she witnessed a trend of "hubris and intoxication" with technological advancement that deeply disturbed her[3] and compelled her writing about the dangers of pesticides.

In addition to the impact the book had on the research and regulation of chemical pesticides,[4] *Silent Spring* has been credited with introducing the public to ecological principles and popularizing the science of ecology. At the time, few people knew the meaning of ecology; the discipline of conservation biology did not yet exist, although its roots had been established at the end of the 19th century. However, the application of ecological principles to environmental problems did not suddenly occur with the book's publication; ecology and its uses have much older origins.[5]

Maril Hazlett has credited Carson with confronting a cultural ideology that held humans as separate from nature.[6] Throughout *Silent Spring*, Carson presents everyday examples and images of

139

nature that resonated with her audience: flocks of robins, idyllic waterfalls, and pastoral landscapes. Additionally, she challenged this "dominant scientific paradigm" through her portrayal of the human body as the link that joins humans with nature[7] and thus adopted an anti-mechanical view of the environment. Such assertions exaggerate Carson's role as an iconoclast. Carson was a part of the scientific community, as were many of her critics, and she was an ecologist. Therefore, she was part of a tradition of thinkers who study the relationships among living things and sometimes apply their findings to practical problems. Even before the publication of *Silent Spring*, the contributions of ecologists to agriculture were overshadowed by the advancements of the industrial age and postwar technological developments.[8] Breakthroughs in chemistry found applications in agriculture, including the Haber-Bosch process, which brought the first large-scale manufacture of ammonia for synthetic fertilizer in 1913 and then for the development of explosives during World War I. Similarly, the advent of World War II spurred advances which led to the availability of cheap organic pesticides.

To claim that Carson repudiated science is not strictly accurate, but it is fair to say that the discipline of ecology was misunderstood at the time. It operated under its own organizing assumptions, just as other sciences, such as applied entomology, were guided by a paradigm that held humans as separate (and in constant conflict) with the forces of nature.

Silent Spring's central metaphor of a "balance of nature" has been credited with being an essential factor in the book's success. It presents a vision of the world that resonated well with readers.[9] In a particularly dramatic example, Carson describes a woman's reaction to a destructive pesticide application:

> "I'm dreading the days to come soon now when many beautiful birds will be dying in our back yard," wrote a Milwaukee woman. "This is a pitiful, heartbreaking experience . . . It is, moreover, frustrating and exasperating, for it evidently does not serve the purpose this slaughter was intended to serve . . . Taking a long look, can you save trees without also saving birds? Do they not, in the economy of nature, save each other? Isn't it possible to help the balance of nature without destroying it?"[10]

140

Carson avoids most discussions of the political or economic factors that brought about the use of and reliance on pesticides. Instead, she employs an argument that invokes nature as a complex web of interrelationships of which humankind is part.[11] While it has been argued that Carson reworked conventional perceptions about the balance of nature,[12] the metaphor is ancient and ubiquitous.

The balance, or economy, of nature dates back to Herodotus and holds at its core the belief that nature is continuously directed toward a relatively stable, balanced state. Whenever humans intervene in natural processes, this delicate balance is upset, but the system can recover if left alone. Numerous authors[13] have effectively critiqued and explored the history of this idea. However, since this metaphor is central to *Silent Spring* as well as to the science of ecology at the time, it is worth discussing in some detail.

Linnaeus is credited with using the term "economy of nature" as far back as 1751 to both describe a balanced state, or equilibrium, and to convey the idea of a divine plan providing direction and purpose to the natural world. This idea has been associated with ecology since Ernst Haeckel named the discipline in 1869 and wrote, "By ecology we mean the body of knowledge concerning the economy of nature—the investigation of the total relations of the animals both to its inorganic and its organic environment."[14]

In ecology, the balance of nature metaphor is enshrined in the assumption of equilibrium that underlies many theoretical models. Examples include the model of plant succession in a community as conceived by Frederic Clement in 1916. In this model, termed *dynamic equilibrium*, nature will progress in an orderly fashion to a climax community that will persist unless a disturbance knocks it back to an earlier stage, and the process begins again. Clement approached ecology as the "study of harmony, continuity, gradation, and equilibrium" where nature had a definite and perfectly predictable direction.[15] In a similar vein, Eugene Odum and Arthur Tansley drew a link between biological communities and their associated abiotic or nonliving environmental factors and developed the concept of the ecosystem. As with the model of the climax community, ecosystems have a strategy and develop toward a stable, self-regulating state. At the heart of the balance of nature paradigm is the complex web of relationships that link all plant and animal populations. The key assumptions are that natural systems are closed and self-regulating and develop to an equilibrium point. Succession is fixed, disturbances to natural systems are rare, and humans are generally considered outside of these natural processes.

Through her invocation of the balance of nature, Carson fairly represents the dominant views in ecology at the time—generally grounded in the equilibrium assumption.[16] Much of the focus of the discipline centered on understanding the mechanisms that regulate biological populations. Consistent with the balance of nature paradigm, abiotic factors were the disruptors of balance and considered relatively unimportant to the regulation of populations. "Populations are kept in check by something the ecologists call the resistance of the environment, and this has been so since the first life was created," Carson writes in "Nature Fights Back,"[17] referring to the forces of competition and predation that were assumed to keep populations at their carrying capacity, a natural limit on population size. Throughout the book, many examples are explained within the framework of either equilibrium competition or, more often, predator/prey models. "Sometimes the problem is one of upsetting that delicate balance of populations by which nature accomplishes far-reaching aims. Explosive increases in some kinds of soil organisms have occurred when others have been reduced by insecticides, disturbing the relation of predator and prey."[18]

This passage neatly ties the human-caused disturbance of insecticide application to the disruption of a predator-prey dynamic, which interferes with nature's greater purpose. Furthermore, Carson quotes the influential ecologist Charles Elton who, in *The Ecology of Invasions by Plants and Animals*, writes that the rise in the use of chemical pesticides threatens "the very delicately organized interlocking system of populations."[19] This notion of interdependence among populations was a central assumption of the balance of nature. As Carson writes:

> In some quarters nowadays it is fashionable to dismiss the balance of nature as a state of affairs that prevailed in an earlier, simpler world—a state that has now been so thoroughly upset that we might as well forget it. Some find this a convenient assumption, but as a chart for a course of action it is highly dangerous. The balance of nature is not the same today as in Pleistocene times, but it is still there: a complex, precise, and highly integrated system of relationships

between living things which cannot safely be ignored any more than the law of gravity can be defied with impunity by a man perched on the edge of a cliff. The balance of nature is not a *status quo*; it is fluid, ever shifting, in a constant state of adjustment. Man, too, is part of this balance. Sometimes the balance is in his favor; sometimes—and all too often through his own activities—it is shifted to his disadvantage.[20]

This most likely was written in anticipation of critics who accused Carson of arguing for a rejection of technology and progress. Despite the anti-pesticide message of the book, Carson insisted that she was not advocating a wholesale ban on pesticides but was arguing for more careful and targeted use and greater research on their effects.

A Delicate Balance?

While Carson's idea of the balance of nature was not out of the mainstream, we see an interesting set of exchanges involving the language itself. In Carson's view, the world was a delicate, stable organic system prone to destruction by humans.[21] For her critics, the balance of nature meant something else, a perpetual war of humans against nature, particularly agricultural pests. A classic attack was the parody of *Silent Spring* published by Monsanto in 1962, which depicted a world overrun by insects after an imagined ban on pesticides.[22] Carson's more substantive critic, biologist I. L. Baldwin, had a similar reaction and wrote, "It is certain that modern agriculture and modern public health, indeed, modern civilization, could not exist without an unrelenting war against the return of a true balance of nature."[23] Similar language permeates literature promoting DDT before *Silent Spring* was published. R. M. McPherson characterized the human species as engaged in a never-ending battle against hordes of insects and rodents, although he does concede that nature has seen fit to aid humans in this struggle through the production of natural enemies that have perhaps saved us from destruction.[24] Whether Carson should be characterized as confronting the dominant scientific paradigm of the day depends on context.

Despite Carson's understanding of a dynamic equilibrium, thought at the time to be at the heart of all natural systems, other elements of Carson's representation of ecology are problematic. The balance of nature was historically tied to theology,[25] and aspects of Carson's writing come across as teleological and even mystical.[26] One particular example is surprising in its portrayal of evolution. In contrast to the fluid balance of nature outlined in "Nature Fights Back," Carson's portrayal of the sagebrush ecosystem in Chapter 6, "Earth's Green Mantle," is wholly static and disconnected from theory. Describing the formation of the community over evolutionary time, she writes:

> As the landscape evolved, there must have been a long period of trial and error in which plants attempted the colonization of this high and windswept land. One after another must have failed. At last one group of plants evolved which combined all the qualities needed to survive. . . . It was no accident, but rather the result of long ages of experimentation by nature that the great plains of the West became the land of the sage.

> Along with the plants, animal life, too, was evolving in harmony with the searching requirements of the land. In time there were two as perfectly adjusted to their habitat as the sage. One was a mammal, the fleet and graceful pronghorn antelope. The other was a bird, the sage grouse—the "cock of the plains" of Lewis and Clark . . . The sage and the grouse seem made for each other. The original range of the bird coincided with the range of the sage. . . .[27]

These passages create a mental picture of a suite of candidate colonizers eagerly waiting at the edges of the fully formed ecosystem, testing it and their ability to thrive until an ecological soul mate steps forward and triumphantly takes up residence. The process of adaptation seems rigid, as if the environment and the occupying organisms are predetermined as opposed to being part of a dynamic adaptive landscape[28] where species constantly evolve in response to changing environmental conditions. This narrative seems surprising given Carson's frequent description of pesticides as selective agents for insects and the co-evolutionary arms race between pests and their natural enemies.

Despite the popularity of the deterministic and equilibrium notions of ecology depicted in *Silent Spring*, some ecologists were skeptical of the balance of nature and embraced a more chaotic view.

For example, in contrast to Clement's orderly model of succession, Henry Gleason[29] proposed an individualistic model of plant succession where community organization arose due to chance. Elton himself declared, "'The balance of nature' does not exist, and perhaps never has existed. The numbers of wild animals are constantly varying to a greater or lesser extent, and the variations are usually irregular in period and always irregular in amplitude. Each variation in the numbers of one species causes direct and indirect repercussions on the numbers of the others, and since many of the latter are themselves independently varying in numbers, the resultant confusion is remarkable."[30] These were rumblings in what was soon to become a major paradigm shift in ecology from the balance of nature to the flux of nature.

Another alternative viewpoint to the balance of nature paradigm during Carson's time came from Herbert Andrewartha and Charles Birch, who observed that resources are seldom fully exploited by species in natural environments, implying that density-independent factors may be important to the regulation of populations.[31] Increasingly, it was recognized that even if populations do reach equilibrium, they are constantly challenged by abiotic processes which are often localized.[32] As abiotic disturbances affect the landscape stochastically, they can create a mosaic of changing habitat patches across space and time. Indeed, consideration of scale is essential[33] to the flux of nature paradigm as it provides a framework for integrating equilibrium, multiple equilibrium, and non-equilibrium perspectives.[34] The flux of nature paradigm does not preclude equilibrium dynamics, but they may be limited in time and space.[35] For instance, over small areas and short time periods and, conversely, over very large areas and broad temporal scales, otherwise stochastic ecological processes may exhibit some regularity. This model is inherently dynamic and emphasizes the importance of ecological processes and chance events over species interactions. The paradigm helps account for environmental heterogeneity and is more effective at predicting ecological properties such as community assembly, patterns of species diversity, and population dynamics.

The science of ecology has flourished in recent history, perhaps in part due to increased public interest traceable to the ideas expressed in *Silent Spring*. Carson popularized the dominant ideas of ecology at the time and effectively used the balance of nature metaphor to alter the public's perception of their relationship with their environment. However, despite the balance of nature paradigm's appeal to the general public, it lacked useful applications. The fundamental assumption of equilibrium and the implied exclusion of human influence allowed for the creation of elegant, deterministic population models that ultimately misrepresented the foundations of resource management, nature conservation, and environmental protection.[36] In management, ignorance of both natural and anthropogenic disturbances can lead to destructive, unintended ecological consequences. The balance of nature paradigm has been largely rejected in the field of ecology, but it persists in the popular perception of ecological principles and its legacy can be seen in management, including practices promoted by Carson in "The Other Road."[37]

"The Other Road": Biological Control

In *Silent Spring*, Rachel Carson argues that human actions, particularly the use of chemical pesticides for the control of native and invasive agricultural pests, harm ecological systems, which in turn lead to serious public health consequences since humans are inextricably linked to the environment. According to the balance of nature paradigm, systems will recover and return to equilibrium if the disturbance, such as chemicals, is removed. Carson argues that the problem of agricultural pests is, at its core, one of upsetting the balance of nature because large farmlands and their vast monocultures are unnatural. "Nature has introduced great variety into the landscape, but man has displayed a passion for simplifying it. Thus he undoes the built-in checks and balances by which nature holds the species within bounds. One important natural check is a limit on the amount of suitable habitat for each species."[38] Large-scale land conversion for farming creates a situation favorable for insect pests, and their natural enemies are suppressed through the use of pesticides.

In "The Other Road," Carson strongly argues for the use of biological approaches to pest control as an alternative to chemical pesticides. Echoing the prevailing opinion of the time, Carson writes that "in contrast to chemicals, insect pathogens are harmless to all but their intended targets." *Silent Spring* generated renewed interest in the practice of biological control,[39] which had largely fallen out of favor after World War II when the rise in pesticide use helped generate rapid increases in agricultural output.[40] However, biological control has a long history and has been the subject of considerable controversy in more recent years. Here, I briefly consider the history of biological control, how its implementation has been influenced by developments in ecological thinking, and to what degree "The Other Road" has lived up to its promise.

Biological control can include the release or the manipulation of natural enemies for the suppression of host population densities. Four strategies are generally recognized: classical biological control, inoculative control, inundative control, and conservation biological control.[41] The distinctions are important, as the method by which biological control is conducted has implications for both the duration of the treatment and the persistence of the control organism in the environment.

Perhaps the most familiar technique, classical biological control, is the intentional introduction of an exotic, usually co-evolved, control agent with the goal of providing a long-term, self-perpetuating solution. Inoculation biological control is the intentional release of an organism as a control agent with the expectation that it will multiply and control the pest for an extended period but not permanently. Inundative control is the mass release of living organisms, and control is achieved exclusively by the released individuals. In contrast to inoculation, the successful reproduction of the control agent is unnecessary for inundative control, such as the use of *Bacillus thuringiensis* spores as a biopesticide.[42] Finally, conservation biological control involves the modification of the environment or existing management practices to enhance specific natural enemies or organisms to control pests, such as through habitat manipulation. The effects of inoculation and inundation are typically meant to be temporary, while classical and conservation biological controls are intended to be long-term solutions. Classical biological control is the strategy described in the greatest detail in *Silent Spring* and will be explored in the greatest detail here.

On the surface, biological control appears consistent with the equilibrium view of ecology; insect populations are assumed to grow and become a threat because they are not being properly regulated by predators. Since agro-ecosystems are human-altered ecosystems, the solution is to either enhance existing predator populations in the case of native pests or import a predator from the native range of an exotic pest. However, Carson's promotion of a biological solution for pest control has potentially complicated and wide-reaching consequences. First of all, returning to the paragraph at the end of *Silent Spring* that opens this chapter, manipulating a biological community in such a fundamental way is as rife with hubris as the technological solutions that Carson condemns. It also raises the need for an examination of Carson's distinction between natural or biological and technological or chemical approaches to the problem. Along with her promotion of the balance of nature metaphor, this demonstrates that Carson struggled with and propagated the false dichotomy of nature versus culture in spite of her success at illustrating the link between human actions and environmental degradation. For example, the original title of *Silent Spring* was *Man against the Earth*. Garb also seized upon this problem.

> Terms like the "natural" or the "balance of nature" can obscure the social relations and priorities that go into evaluating environmental practices. Take, for example, Carson's preference for biological rather than chemical methods of pest control as less disturbing of "nature's balance." This term reifies judgments about the respective benefits and costs—to humans—of these methods, creating internal contradictions in Carson's account. Why, for instance, is the importation of an exotic pathogen (a bacteria) to kill the Japanese beetle a "natural" means of control? Is this intervention—which Carson notes in passing kills not only the target species but at least forty other species in the scarabaeid family—more respectful of the balance of nature than certain pesticides? [43]

It is stunning to think that Carson or the practitioners of biological control did not see a problem or contradiction in the classical approach of sending one exotic species to control another. As a one-time invasive species manager and student of biological control, I find one of the most shocking passages in *Silent Spring* to be Carson's lauding of Newfoundland's efforts to import masked shrews to the islands to control sawflies. Generalist predators, particularly vertebrates, are typically disastrous biocontrol agents. A short time in Hawaii, for example, will reveal the presence of mongooses that were imported for the control of exotic rats but instead spend their days consuming native birds. In the case of the Newfoundland shrews, their introduction has been linked to

148

increased prevalence of a parasite that causes skull lesions in native short-tailed weasels.[44] However, Carson was once again communicating the conventional wisdom of her time, and it was not until nearly two decades after her death that the wisdom of biological control was seriously challenged. Why did it take so long for a serious debate over the merits of biological control to develop? Perhaps biological control enjoyed its initial uncritical acceptance due to a rush to find alternative means of pest control amid the backlash against chemical pesticides.[45] Perhaps the delay reflected a general bias and lack of understanding about the ecology of insects. Part of the answer may be found through an examination of the history of biological control and the eventual paradigmatic shift away from the balance of nature in ecology.

The term biological control was first coined in 1914 but did not gain popularity until after DDT was recognized as environmentally problematic. The use of natural enemies to control agricultural pests goes back at least to 324 BC in China when ants were released on orchard trees to control caterpillars and boring beetles.[46] Most historical examples of biological control involved the recognition and augmentation of native natural enemies (inoculative or inundative biological control).

No discussion of biological control can be complete without describing the vedalia beetle and its successful suppression of the cottony cushion scale insect in the 1850s. Carson used this example to highlight the effectiveness of biological control in contrast to the negative consequences of spraying for Japanese beetles. In honor of the so-called centennial of biocontrol, L. E. Caltagirone and R. L. Doutt write, "In retrospect, one could not have purposely designed a more dramatic, effective, public demonstration of biological control."[47] The California citrus industry was being threatened by the scale, and the control agent—the vedalia beetle—was a highly visible and brightly colored *Coccinellid* (ladybug) that could be easily observed feeding in the trees. The vedalia beetle happened to be an especially effective colonizer and was thus able to become established and control the scale insect. This successful case marked the beginning of classical biological control as the ladybug was a natural enemy of the pest insect in its native Australia. As a result of this success, which is credited with saving the citrus industry, California farmers became very supportive of biological control.

In the aftermath, an infatuation with biological control led to mass importations of different species with little knowledge or consideration of their life history. Subsequent successes were few. However, the success of the vedalia was repeated outside of California and had an important influence in the acceptance of biological control, and the number of biocontrol programs increased worldwide.[48] Unfortunately, early importations were undertaken with little guidance.

Consistent with the example described in *Silent Spring*, Caltagirone and Doutt confirm that scale insect resurgences are common after application of pesticides toxic to vedalia, presumably due to the slower reproductive rates of the beetles relative to the scales.[49] While this phenomenon ties in directly to what would be expected from equilibrium population ecology, the authors also point out that the beetles can be impacted by extreme weather events as well. Thus the flux of nature model promotes the persistence of the scale insect and changing numbers of vedalia. The range of the vedalia does not have the same environmental tolerances as the scale insect, which allows populations of the scale to escape predation in space and time.

The vedalia beetle was not only the first modern attempt at classical biological control but the first biological control program with scientific and institutional backing.[50] Following the success of the beetle, a huge effort went into exploration for and collection of potential biocontrol agents. In fact, many orchard farmers stopped spraying altogether, which actually set back the California pest control effort overall.[51] These early importation efforts focused largely on ladybugs, but no other *Coccinellid* emerged as such an effective control agent.

Nevertheless, the vedalia beetle remains a flagship example of what effective biological control could be. "In the long pursuit of these goals, no single achievement has more thoroughly, soundly, and significantly established a major pest control tactic than the vedalia project. All subsequent projects, programs, advances, and refinements in the theory and practice of biological control have sprung from this single event."[52] Carson points out that much of the success of this project was ultimately forgotten with the advent and availability of chemicals after World War II.

From 1900 to 1930, significant biocontrol programs for gypsy moths began in New England. Carson holds up the gypsy moth as an example of a pest being adequately managed by a biological control program that was later disrupted by pesticide spraying. During this time, separate biological control programs were also initiated in Hawaii. Both cases resulted in significant nontarget effects that contributed to the debate over the costs and benefits of biological control.

Biological control activity in the United States reached its peak in 1930–1940 but soon collapsed with the onset of World War II. The war put an end to global exploration for natural enemies and spurred the production of inexpensive organic pesticides. As pesticide research became the focus of applied entomology, funding for biological control became scarce. However, this period did see the founding of two international institutions that promote research and provide guidance for biocontrol programs. This was an important step because, as Carson admits, "Perhaps for want of support biological control through insect enemies has not always been carried out with the scientific thoroughness it requires—exacting studies of its impact on the populations of insect prey have seldom been made, and releases have not always been made with the precision that might spell the difference between success and failure."[53] It is important to note that her criticism focused on procedural shortcomings rather than anticipating any of the ecological concerns, such as nontarget effects, that now dominate the debate over the merits of biological control.

After the publication of *Silent Spring*, the increased public interest in ecology and the environment also led to a resurgent interest in biocontrol.[54] During this time, integrated pest management also developed as, essentially, a decision support system for the selection and use of pest control tactics either singly or in concert. Biological control forms the centerpiece of this system, but judicious pesticide use is often part of the strategy, along with cultural and mechanical controls. Finally, the 1970s brought about the development of plant pathogens for use as mass applied bioherbicides.

The original theoretical underpinnings of biological control were firmly grounded in the balance of nature paradigm; pest species were first depressed by the control agent followed by stabilization of both populations at low, equilibrium levels. Biological control does not aim to eradicate the pest but to reduce its numbers and maintain smaller, less harmful population sizes over the long term. Originally, it was believed that the hosts were able to avoid extinction because of refuges generated in space and time. The control agents were thought to respond to spatial density-dependence and maximize their efficiency by searching for prey nonrandomly in accordance with the predictions of optimal foraging theory; nonrandom searches allowed some pests, particularly those in low-density populations, to escape. Now it is understood that pest populations survive as a result of stochastic processes that create habitat patches in space and time and allow subpopulations of the pest species to persist.[55] In fact, an understanding of the flux of nature paradigm as well as the natural history characteristics of control agents and their targets help explain the successes and failures of biological control programs over the years.

Until the early 1980s, biocontrol proponents, such as Paul DeBach, whom Carson quotes in *Silent Spring*, maintained that classical biological control was completely safe, with the potential for substantial economic benefits and no adverse effects.[56] That widespread opinion of the practice as environmentally benign received its first serious challenge in 1983 with the publication of Francis Howarth's "Panacea or Pandora's Box."[57] In this paper and subsequent work,[58] Howarth, an expert on Hawaiian insects and ecosystems, targeted classical biological control of insect pests as opposed to cultural practices aimed at invasive species control or the mass rearing of native natural enemies. He pointed out that the euphoria over the promise of biocontrol mirrored that surrounding chemical pesticides in the 1940s and 1950s. In both cases, widespread adoption of the techniques came without an understanding of the potential environmental consequences.

Howarth's argument paralleled *Silent Spring*'s critique of chemical control. He expressed concern over the phenomenon of biological pollution in which communities become increasingly populated by nonnative species. And like Carson, Howarth expressed grave concern over the reversibility, specificity, and area covered by classical biological control. Unlike chemical pesticides, which presumably do not persist in an ecosystem once application has ceased, the goal of biocontrol is the establishment of a self-sustaining population of exotic insects. Admittedly, establishing such populations is difficult, but when successful, eradication becomes nearly impossible. One of the main thrusts of Carson's argument was that chemical pesticides affected living organisms indiscriminately, and this was especially problematic when they were applied over vast areas. However, contrary to what biocontrol proponents, including Carson, espoused at the time, the degree of host specificity exhibited by a biocontrol agent is the product of its natural history, and introduced animals are known to switch hosts. Furthermore, the application of introduced agents cannot be limited to a specific area, whereas pesticides can be. Introduced insects will expand to occupy the entirety of a suitable range—which may not encompass the entire range of the target pest. More important, the host may not be restricted to agricultural landscapes and may expand into native habitats. More species extinctions have been blamed on invasive species than on pesticides.[59] In the end, chemicals, for all of their negative impacts, are more tractable because they do not mutate or reproduce, meaning that their impacts may be much different than those of biocontrols over the long term. A large part of the problem lies in the fact that most biocontrol agents have been poorly studied, while the effects of chemicals are better understood (almost certainly due to the influence of *Silent Spring*).

Finally, and in step with Carson, Howarth invoked the precautionary principle,[60] citing suspected extinctions of nontarget species. Specifically, he described the devastating effects of introduced vertebrates to island ecosystems and the possible contribution of parasitoid biocontrols to the extinction of native Hawaiian butterflies. Since species are often linked through complicated webs of direct and indirect connections, Howarth questioned whether an appropriate level of understanding could be achieved to allow for the safe use of biocontrol. Howarth's papers called for legislation to better regulate the importation of exotic insects. As a result of his work, classical biocontrol programs in Hawaii were sharply curtailed. The controversy over biocontrol, the importance of its nontarget effects, and outcomes for biodiversity gained international prominence following the Rio Convention on Biodiversity in 1992.

The debate has progressed and become more polarized, but the main arguments have remained fundamentally unchanged. Critics of biocontrol programs argue that predicting outcomes is an extraordinarily complicated undertaking, made more so by indirect interactions within and between species and nonequilibrium ecological dynamics.[61] Proponents of biocontrol argue that there is, in fact, little evidence of nontarget effects. Skeptics of Howarth's conclusions point out that islands, which inspired Howarth's criticism, are special cases, and few examples of nontarget effects exist in mainland ecosystems.[62] They repeat Carson's endorsement of the practice as promoting long-term reductions in pest numbers, the elimination of chemicals, and the associated low cost-benefit ratio.[63] One author, in an appeal for continued use of exotic bio-control agents, even invoked outdated notions of equilibrium by titling his paper, "Restoring Balance: Using Exotic Species to Control Invasive Exotic Species."[64]

One of the legacies of *Silent Spring* has been an increase in the use of biocontrol agents: numerous but poorly monitored releases of potential exotic biocontrol agents have resulted in an unknown number of establishments. Most authors writing on the subject agree that significant research gaps continue to obscure the issue, particularly a lack of monitoring following release.[65] Nontarget effects from vertebrate introductions are much better understood than those resulting from exotic plants and arthropods.[66] However, current research efforts have documented some of the natural history characteristics that influence the success and likelihood of nontarget effects. The most important is the host-specificity of the control agent,[67] but this is no guarantee of success, as native relatives of target organisms may still be vulnerable.[68]

The debate over the relative benefits and harms of exotic biocontrol agents has become part of a larger discussion about the threat that invasive species pose to biodiversity. Many authors maintain that alien invasive species present one of the gravest threats to biodiversity today. Alien species cause more than $120 billion in losses each year from agriculture or altered ecosystem function and productivity. They have also been implicated in the decline of about 42 percent of listed threatened and endangered species.[69] In recognition of the threat, President Clinton created an Interagency Invasive Species Council in 1999.

As with the debate over biocontrol, skeptics maintain that there is little evidence introduced species actually cause extinctions, and that instead they may actually increase local biodiversity.[70] Furthermore, they maintain this is beneficial since species richness correlates with desirable ecosystem properties such as productivity and stability in the face of changing conditions.[71] These arguments are somewhat bogged down by semantics. Richness, or the number of species, is not the same as diversity, which takes into account the relative abundances of species. And while it may be true that introduced species are seldom directly responsible for extinction, they can lead to significant reductions in local populations, leaving those populations vulnerable to stochastic effects.[72] An introduced species is not necessarily the same as an invasive species, which can dominate communities and significantly affect ecosystem function. For example, cheat grass has invaded vast expanses and significantly altered the hydrology of the water-starved grasslands and deserts of the American West. Such species may ultimately fulfill the predictions of Carson and Elton and lead to the simplification of the natural world.[73] Finally, growing evidence indicates that native ecosystems and species provide significant ecosystem services. Cropland located near fragments of native habitat may benefit from enhanced pollination and crop yields.[74]

A great irony of Carson's promotion of biocontrol is that there have been so many unintended consequences. The debate over classical biological control is far from resolved, yet despite significant concerns over nontarget effects from exotic species and the risk of aggressive invasions, there is still a surprising lack of a clear regulatory framework for biocontrol.[75] Before biological control agents for invasive plants can be imported, they are required by federal law to undergo host-specificity testing. That is not the case for arthropod biocontrol agents whose importations are only guided by nonlegally binding agreements. The justification has been that there is little need for regulation of parasitoids due to their coevolution and specificity with their hosts.[76] However, parasitoids have indeed been implicated in nontarget extinctions in the United States. Given the widespread use of arthropod biocontrol agents, including in widely utilized integrated pest management strategies, greater regulatory oversight is clearly necessary.[77]

Given *Silent Spring*'s role in the resurgence of biocontrol as a management technique, it is instructive to briefly review the history of some of the case studies that Carson held up as justification for alternative approaches to pest control. The sterile insect technique, developed by Edward Knipling, is the least problematic of the nonchemical alternatives. The practice involves releasing large numbers of sterile male insects into a target pest population with the hope that they will outcompete fertile males and cause reproductive failure in the population. It is an inoculative form of biocontrol and thus the least disruptive method in terms of nontarget impacts since it involves using members of a pest species against each other. No exotic agents or new genetic material enter the environment. It is, however, an inefficient endeavor, and was particularly so in the early days of the technique when sex separation was more difficult and the radiation used to sterilize the males also left them weak and less competitive.[78] Advances in genetics have greatly simplified the process by making it possible to raise only males and to sterilize them without the loss in competitive ability.

The sterile insect technique is firmly grounded in equilibrium ecology and is thus very scale-dependent. It is only effective when the entire population of the pest can be targeted, and application must be sustained to prevent recolonization of the pest.[79] The technique is particularly effective on islands, as demonstrated by its successful use in the eradication of tsetse fly from Zanzibar[80] and the limited control of malaria vectors in Africa.[81] However, one success of the sterile insect technique cited by Carson is the successful eradication of screw-worm from the southeastern United States. In her narrative, Carson describes how freezing temperatures had reduced screw-worm populations and confined them to a small area, providing the ideal conditions for the release of the sterilized flies.[82] It is noteworthy that she ignores this clear example of the importance of abiotic conditions for the control of pests.

Another example involves the fire ant. According to Carson, fire ant populations did not constitute a significant problem before the disastrous pesticide campaign she describes. She portrays them as being of little notice and valuable biocontrol agents "picking larvae of the boll weevil off cotton."[83] Contrary to Carson's portrayal, the fire ant problem has developed considerably since *Silent Spring*. In an age of increased globalization, the southern United States has been a source for fire ant invasions in California, Asia, and Australia.[84] Fire ant densities in the southern United States are 5 to 10 times higher than in their native South America and are blamed for causing hundreds of millions of dollars of damage every year, in addition to being a public health nuisance.[85] A satisfactory solution has yet to be found. Since the 1970s, fire ants have been the targets of biocontrol agents, including imported pathogens. A decapitating fly has been employed as a biocontrol, although nontarget effects on native fire ants have limited use on both the fly and pathogens.[86]

Fire ants are typically among the most abundant predators in agro-ecosystems and do, in fact, feed on plant pests as Carson describes. However, they also attack beneficial insects and arthropods such as native natural enemies of pests and can compromise biocontrol efforts.[87] This fact illustrates a tension that arises between introduced species and ecosystem services. For instance, Mark Sagoff has argued that invasive species provided essential ecosystem services such as the water filtration provided by invasive zebra mussels in the Great Lakes.[88] In this case, while the fire ant may contribute to the control of crop pests, it has also been shown to invade nonagricultural habitats and exert major impacts on community composition at multiple scales.[89] Where nontarget effects are involved, invasive species management often involves complex cost-benefit analyses and valuations of function versus native biodiversity.

Finally, Carson uses the example of the gypsy moth to illustrate how a mass spraying program led to the proliferation of a pest that had been effectively controlled by imported parasites and predators. Unfortunately, and consistent with the flux of nature paradigm, the history and dynamics of the gypsy moth are much more complicated. The gypsy moth was the target of both classical and inundative biocontrol as the parasitoid *Compsilura concinnata* was first introduced as a control agent beginning in 1906. The moth was also targeted with *Bacillus thuringiensis* (Bt) beginning in the 1920s. Introductions of the parasitoid continued until 1986 despite the fact that the parasitoid is, in fact, a generalist. The agent produces multiple generations per year and must overwinter in its larval stage, meaning it needs a winter caterpillar host. Because the gypsy moth overwinters as an egg, the parasitoid spread to other hosts and attacked both other crop pests and native nontarget species. The parasitoid, along with habitat destruction and Bt spraying, has been implicated as one of multiple reasons for the decline and even extirpation of lepidopteran species in the northeastern United States, particularly native silk moths.[90]

Finally, and consistent with nonequilibrium dynamics, gypsy moths are also regulated indirectly by acorn production in the oak forest. In years of high acorn production, termed *masting*, populations of white-footed mice become more abundant and exert significant predation pressure on gypsy moth caterpillars, but their numbers and influence decline during nonmast years.[91] This example illustrates the hidden complexity in population regulation and the interactions with density-independent factors and argues for caution in the further implementation of biocontrol.

The Balance of Nature Paradigm and the Consequences for Management

Although ecologists have largely acknowledged the rarity of equilibrium conditions and the relative frequency of disturbance events in most ecological systems, the idea of a balance of nature continues to pervade the public's perception of ecological principles.[92] This persistence is due, in part, to the long history of the concept but also because the notion of a self-regulating ecosystem with a fixed equilibrium endpoint is comforting.[93]

The flux of nature paradigm is a more disturbing view of the world than the deterministic balance of nature. If stochastic abiotic processes exert a major role over everything from population regulation and community assembly to disease spread and climate fluctuations, the world is much less predictable and considerably more difficult to understand. Uncertainty in ecology and evolution challenges conventional views of human purpose. There is no orderly march toward some evolutionary endpoint. In addition to being less comforting than the view espoused by Carson and others, the nonequilibrium assumption in ecology is difficult to communicate because understanding requires consideration of ecological dynamics over multiple spatial and temporal scales.

In one sense, the paradigm of the flux of nature may appear to undermine our perceptions of the value of species and ecosystems. As discussed above, if all systems are chaotic and the composition of natural communities is the product of chance events, then what is the value of biodiversity? Beyond practical ecosystem services valuations, arguments for the intrinsic worth of species might be boosted by the acknowledgment that chance events may add to the fragility of earth's ecosystems.

A more practical concern relates to how effective our conservation and management practices can be in light of so much uncertainty. The incorporation of chance events may seem to undermine ecology's role as a predictive science and limit its application to conservation.

Rather than being crippling, the understanding of stochastic processes requires an understanding of ecological dynamics at multiple scales—the equilibrium assumption may still hold for certain times and places or over very narrow or very broad temporal and spatial scales. Today, the best population models for the conservation of species must take into account not only the probability of chance fluctuations in environmental conditions but similar changes in a population's demography or genetics. Such stochasticity, depending on its severity, impacts the statistical likelihood that a population will persist over time. Theoreticians create models incorporating a variety of initial conditions and probabilities of chance events and generate a range of predictions. When these models are applied in conservation, management actions can be adjusted to respond to a greater range of possible outcomes and thereby improve their effectiveness. Typically, results show that target population sizes or conservation areas must be larger to account for unforeseen circumstances, or the landscapes must be intensively managed to maintain environmental processes. Ultimately, the practice forces us to take a larger, more comprehensive view that mandates both greater management flexibility and greater human intervention.

In their landmark paper, S. T. A. Pickett and J. N. Thompson[94] applied the Theory of Island Biogeography to the planning of nature reserves. The theory holds that species richness on an island is the product of a dynamic between species colonization and species extinction. Pickett and Thompson recognized that national parks and other protected areas exist in a larger land-use mosaic; as development and habitat destruction proceeded, reserves would become increasingly isolated, and extinction would become the dominant population process. They argued that it is essential to maintain internal disturbance dynamics in such cases and that a variety of habitats in the reserve would ultimately maintain a higher degree of diversity. This incorporation of nonequilibrium landscape processes into management has been a defining characteristic of modern stewardship.

Nature in Flux: A Story from Kenya

Applying equilibrium assumptions to the management of dynamic systems has had devastating consequences. The suppression of forest fires in the American West has resulted in catastrophic fires such as those in Yellowstone National Park in 1988. In the

159

oceans, ignorance of stochastic fluctuations in abiotic conditions and fish populations coupled with a stubborn adherence to unchanging, theoretically sustainable harvest limits—termed *maximum sustainable yields*—led to the collapse of numerous fisheries. Much of my own research has been conducted in the savannas of central Kenya, which exemplify how the interaction of density-independent factors such as rainfall and fire can change the structure of communities and how ignorance of these processes can result in negative outcomes for wildlife and human health.

In much of East Africa, rainfall fluctuates unpredictably over multiple scales,[95] which creates temporary hotspots of productivity that drive both local and landscape-scale movements of grazing ungulates. When they think of savannas, most people don't realize that their modern character is the product of a long history of frequent human-generated disturbances. Indeed, our ancestors may have converted the landscape from tropical forest to grassland through intentional burning beginning as early as 2.5 million years ago.[96] Off the coast of East Africa, marine sediments from the present interglacial period show a distinct increase in elemental carbon, which indicates that humans have dominated fire regimes in East African savannas for at least the last 10,000 years.[97] Natural fires are uncommon in East Africa due to infrequency of lightning strikes[98] during rainy seasons when levels of fuel moisture are high.

Cattle herding began in East Africa around 2000 BC,[99] and pastoralists have occupied the region for much of the last 2,000 years.[100] Pastoralism coupled grazing with managed fire, which helped remove rank vegetation and promote fresh growth as well as control shrubs and livestock parasites.[101] In many areas, pastoralists further altered the landscape by clearing trees and building *bomas*, temporary thorn-scrub corrals that afforded increased mobility and allowed the herders to follow the rains and sustain large cattle herds.

Historically, this was the case on the Laikipia Plateau of central Kenya, where my research is based. What is today a landscape mosaic of mixed land use ranging from large-scale cattle ranches to smallholder agriculture was once open savanna dominated by the Masai and other pastoral peoples. Since rainfall varied dramatically in space and time, herders would roam far from their home settlements in search of good forage. Joseph Thomson, the first European to explore the area, remarks in his memoirs in 1895, "The greater part of Lykipia—and that the richer portion—is quite uninhabited, owing in large degree, to the decimation of the Masai of that part, through their wars. . ."[102] While it is true that what are now known as the Laikipia Masai had essentially disappeared as the result of fighting, the area was far from uninhabited. On the previous page of his book, Thomson explains that "great herds of cattle, or flocks of sheep and goats are seen wandering knee-deep in splendid pasture." Thomson made a mistake common in the history of colonialism and assumed that the land was being underutilized. This belief was the primary justification for what was to come.

In the early 20th century, a desire for prime grazing land and a belief that the traditional system was inherently destructive[103] led European colonists to undertake a large-scale resettlement of pastoralists. In Kenya, Masai were moved from the central part of the country to reserves in the south.[104] Large ranches were created and left in the hands of European colonists while the remaining herders were eventually relegated to communal ranches. The perception that the traditional system was unsustainable derived from the equilibrium paradigm that predicted that the number of livestock on the range was limited by a carrying capacity and that the high livestock densities of the traditional pastoralists were negatively impacting the condition of the savanna.[105]

The belief that grasslands are equilibrium systems persists in much of the world, and there is an ongoing controversy about whether pastoralism can coexist with wildlife.[106] Most contemporary ranchers practice a form of range management that maximizes livestock production by equally distributing grazing pressure in space and time and by promoting the growth of a few key forage species at the expense of plant species diversity and structural heterogeneity.[107]

As a result, historically mobile pastoralists in East Africa have become increasingly sedentary while population growth and agricultural conversion are pushing many people away from livestock herding[108] with potentially severe consequences for the ecosystem. The large mobile herds of the Masai and other East African pastoralists were part of a strategy aimed at coping with patchy rainfall and frequent drought.[109] Now when the rains fail, pastoralists have no recourse apart from allowing their livestock to graze in the water-stressed landscape, and this has brought about a conversion from grassland to shrubland or resulted in desertification. Additionally, fires in the area have been actively suppressed since at least the 1950s. Bomas are still used throughout the region for cattle management and are one of the only sources of regular disturbance and habitat heterogeneity. The breakdown of traditionalist pastoral practices has negatively impacted biodiversity.

My research has examined the influence of prescribed fire and bomas on bird biodiversity across several large cattle ranches. These properties actively manage for wildlife and have much lower densities of livestock then the communal areas. My collaborators and I set a series of controlled, replicated fires, and I compared changes in the bird community on the burned plots and recently abandoned bomas to unburned control plots. The results were dramatic. The disturbed patches—the burned areas and bomas—attracted greater numbers of both individual birds and species, and the community assemblages were significantly different than those in the unburned areas. Some species, particularly migrants, specialized in the burned plots. The most illuminating finding was observed in the aftermath of a drought during the second year of the study. While the newly burned plots seemed to provide the highest quality habitat under circumstances of normal rainfall, both abundance and species richness declined during the drought year. However, bird communities remained relatively stable on the abandoned bomas in spite of the drought. The thick layer of dung that builds up during a boma's occupancy fuels the productivity of the patch for years, so these abandoned settlements may offer refuges for wildlife during harsh times.[110] Traditional pastoralist practices developed in response to an uncertain environment and promoted landscape heterogeneity and, by extension, biodiversity.

I wanted to better understand the environmental history of the Laikipia Plateau, and I had the good fortune to develop relationships with pastoralists on the communal properties. Many of the elders have been herding cattle since before colonial policies aimed at restricting mobility and suppressing fire were actively enforced. It is difficult to overstate the changes to the land witnessed by these people. The boundary between a private ranch and a communal property is stark. In contrast to the large private operations, communal ranches have little in the way of grass cover, are more heavily dominated by shrubs, and are home to almost no large species of wildlife. Instead of the large herds of cattle so intrinsically tied to the cultural identity of the Masai, livestock holdings are now dominated by small stock such as sheep and goats, animals better able to exploit the lower quality forage.

This overgrazed and degraded habitat is also favorable to the establishment of invasive species. Friends told me stories of goats becoming sick or dying from ingesting the spine-covered fruit of the invasive prickly pear cactus. The fine hairs that cover the leaves can fill the air, and I met a toddler during one of my visits whose stomach and sides were covered in a painful rash. Landscapes are the products of the environment but also of history. In this case, the prickly pear is exploiting an environment created by a suite of environmental and socio-political factors. If the land were being managed in a way suited to the flux of nature, the cactus would be unable to proliferate to the point where it threatens human health. The plant is almost entirely absent from the large, foreign-owned ranches. The prickly pear is only one symptom of a larger development issue. For instance, the lack of vegetation cover and the high density of people and livestock on communal properties has affected the hydrology and likely increased the frequency of local droughts.

In Laikipia, both the large, wildlife-friendly ranches and the communal properties suffer from the legacy of the balance of nature, and the lessons learned on the savanna are relevant to management in the United States as well. The Great Plains have been shaped by the same biotic and abiotic factors as the African savannas. Traditional pastoralism in East Africa parallels Native American land use in New England when the first European colonists arrived. In fact, the historic New England landscape was a patchwork generated by anthropogenic fire, and the native inhabitants stayed mobile to better exploit seasonal resources.[111] To sound a hopeful note, studies elsewhere in Africa and North America have demonstrated that an opportunistic management strategy including managed fire and livestock grazing can increase habitat heterogeneity, benefit wildlife communities, and still meet management and livestock production goals in these unpredictable systems.[112]

Managing Uncertainty

While Rachel Carson may have helped popularize the science of ecology through her persuasive book, part of her legacy may be the continued belief by most people in the balance of nature. The idea is an old one, and other authors since Carson have promoted the same vision,[113] but the continued influence of *Silent Spring* has important implications for education and conservation.

The persistence of the balance of nature metaphor in culture and science creates misconceptions about ecological concepts among students, educators, environmental activists,[114] and skeptics. In a survey of a large, unnamed midwestern university, Corinne Zimmerman and Kim Cuddington found that both the majority of science majors enrolled in an introductory ecology course and the general student population believe that balance of nature describes the dynamics of real ecological systems.[115] Additionally, most students believe protected areas will regain balance and recover from environmental damage.[116] This is frustrating at a time when the fortress conservation model of protected areas and parks has been shown to fail.

As discussed earlier in this chapter, unless development around them is managed, protected areas will become increasingly isolated, and without active management, extinction will become the dominant process.[117] However, the more basic problem is that the majority of national parks and protected areas in the United States were established to protect areas of scenic beauty or geological value as opposed to biodiversity. In much of Africa, protected areas are the legacies of colonialism, places first established as hunting preserves for the elite after the eviction of the native inhabitants from the land.[118] Human access to these areas is thus a matter of social justice, and anthropogenic disturbances can be critical to the maintenance of these systems. Furthermore, few protected areas anywhere in the world are large enough to fully encompass the ranges of the largest animals. Nor will the established boundaries shift to match the changing distributions of species in response to climate change. National parks and other refuges should continue to function as sanctuaries of natural beauty, but greater attention and planning must be devoted to the landscapes surrounding these areas. Future conservation solutions require partnerships with private landowners and the creation of integrated and actively managed multi-use landscapes if we hope to protect not only species but environmental and evolutionary processes.

Finally, the traditional balance of nature metaphor continues to create roadblocks for environmental decisionmaking, particularly for global issues such as climate change. Policymakers and the public often seem to expect conclusive results from scientists and have a low tolerance for uncertainty even where the uncertainty is inherent in the science. For example, predictions of environmental consequences from climate change are the product of theoretical models that must be based on numerous assumptions or starting conditions ("contingencies" in the language of the flux of nature). The complexity and high degree of uncertainty are often causes for these predictions to be ignored or at least misunderstood, especially if the uncertainty is compounded across multiple temporal and spatial scales. Convincing some members of the public and policymakers that climate change is at least, in part, anthropogenic in origin and therefore requires management-based solutions has been complicated by the recognition of historical fluctuations in temperature and climate. Identifying and addressing environmental challenges under the flux of nature paradigm always requires the identification and justification of a baseline or target, which can seem arbitrary and be difficult to communicate. Additionally, an anthropogenic cause for climate change seems implausible under the balance of nature metaphor—how could humans as one cog in the machine affect a fully-integrated and self-regulating system at that scale?

In contrast, the flux of nature paradigm embraces complexity and unpredictability. The example from Kenya illustrates how altered disturbance regimes can alternately lead to bush encroachment or desertification depending on the circumstances. Contrary to the idea of a balance of nature, these systems will not return to an earlier equilibrium state if left alone. Instead, disturbance-prone ecosystems may transition to alternative stable states if ecological processes are disrupted,[119] with irreversible consequences for biodiversity and ecosystem function.

Our species has the ability to alter ecosystem function at speeds and scales never before seen. Increases in global temperature and extinction rates are orders of magnitude higher than the historical background, and the loss of agricultural productivity and other ecosystem services will have consequences for human welfare. Much of the global change we are experiencing may not be reversible, but it may be managed and mitigated only if we reject the outdated concept of the balance of nature.

8. Did Rachel Carson Understand the Importance of DDT in Global Public Health Programs?

Donald R. Roberts and Richard Tren

Introduction

Memories of DDT and its controversies have faded. Many who do remember may be tempted to think any talk of need for DDT is an anachronism of a bygone era. Some may remember Joni Mitchell's classic and catchy song "Big Yellow Taxi," where she implores farmers to "put away the DDT now, give me spots on my apples, but leave me the birds and bees, please."

It may be unreasonable to expect Joni Mitchell to sing about the benefits of DDT and the astonishing way in which it saved countless millions of lives from insect-borne diseases. Mitchell was a folk singer and artist, and few people would expect from her a balanced, nuanced, science-based treatment of insecticides. Rachel Carson, however, promoted herself as a scientist; and at its time of publication, *Silent Spring* was—and even now is still—considered by many as a scientific treatise.

Silent Spring achieved its iconic status largely through its long and involved critique of DDT and other man-made chemicals. However, as we explain in this chapter, Rachel Carson's poetic vilification of DDT reveals a serious ignorance about the chemical and the way it works. Carson's interpretation of the development of insecticide resistance is fundamentally flawed, and the book is littered with statements about insect biology and evolution that are false and misleading. She hardly recognizes the great benefits, most dramatically in public health, that DDT provided for mankind—even though those benefits were widely known at the time. Still, a generous and sympathetic historian might excuse this important omission, concluding that Carson genuinely believed that the benefits were overstated and that DDT made the fight against diseases and crop pests more difficult. But excusing Carson on the basis of beliefs reveals a fundamental flaw of *Silent Spring*. The scientific record shows DDT's benefits were not overstated, and the fact that it is still needed and remains a superlative disease-control chemical even today attests to its extraordinary benefit to humanity. Any fair examination of *Silent Spring* will reveal that Carson's arguments against DDT were scarcely more serious than those of Joni Mitchell, while the lasting legacy of her book for countries and communities reliant on DDT has been devastating.

We have collaborated on this chapter, and on other publications that have strongly defended the use of DDT for malaria control, and have been critical of groups and individuals that seek to prevent or halt the use of this chemical and others in malaria control programs. We each arrived at this common point from divergent paths. Roberts's interest in DDT evolved slowly in the 1960s and 1970s. He studied malaria and malaria control programs in Brazil during the 1970s. His collaboration with Brazilian researchers on how DDT protected people inside sprayed houses led to a startling finding that DDT functioned mostly as a powerful repellent, stopping mosquitoes from entering houses and transmitting disease while people slept. The research eventually culminated in a major paper detailing a model on how DDT actually functioned to control malaria.[1] That research experience changed his professional life because DDT's spatial repellent action made it unique among all man-made insecticides. Today, the modern arsenal of public health insecticides includes no chemical equivalent to DDT as a spatial repellent or as a chemical that will continue to protect people in houses for months after it is sprayed on inside walls.

Roberts's search of literature showed DDT's repellent actions were repeatedly discovered and quantified by field and laboratory researchers, even as early as 1943. Yet those findings were systematically ignored. Environmental activists forced most malaria endemic countries to abandon DDT during the 1980s and 1990s. Disease rates increased as a result. Roberts monitored those changes as they occurred and, in response, became increasingly involved in insecticide advocacy, and DDT advocacy in particular—eventually combining his efforts with those of Richard Tren and others to restore countries' freedom to use DDT and other public health insecticides in disease control programs.

Tren is an economist. While writing about development and environmental issues, he became engaged and interested in the way in which international treaties and agreements, spearheaded by the rich developed world, affect the poor developing world. In the late 1990s, the Stockholm Convention on Persistent Organic Pollutants was being negotiated, and it seemed certain that DDT would be banned completely. The issue of DDT and the fight against malaria provided an excellent example of the way in which first world sensibilities affect third world lives. In researching the issue for a policy paper, in 1999 Tren travelled to northern KwaZulu Natal, South Africa, which was in the grip of a severe malaria epidemic. The epidemic's primary cause was traced to changes in insecticide use: DDT had been removed from the malaria control program and replaced with insecticides to which mosquitoes rapidly developed resistance. The beds in all the clinics and hospitals in the region were full to overflowing, with many people, including children and pregnant women, forced to sleep on the floor or outside on verandahs. The sight of children dying needlessly made a lasting impression and kept Tren motivated to ensure that malaria programs around the world would be free to use the best and most appropriate tools for their circumstances. Then, as now, this has meant defending the right to use DDT. More than a decade later, the issue of DDT for malaria control remains controversial, and anti-insecticide activist groups along with the U.N. Environment Program are working to shut down all DDT production and use even though there is no true replacement chemical available.

The Advent of DDT

DDT was first created in 1874, 33 years before Rachel Carson was born. It was synthesized by a German graduate student, Othmar Zeidler, as part of a research project and then essentially forgotten until the 1930s, when Dr. Paul Müller re-discovered DDT and its insecticidal properties.

Müller was an employee of J. R. Geigy, a Swiss chemical company that, among other things, was searching for a commercially viable chemical to control clothes moths. In his work on this project, Müller found that flies died when exposed to DDT.[2]

169

Shortly after Müller's discovery, World War II broke out. While most of Europe was struggling under and fighting against Nazi tyranny, the Swiss were using DDT to fight beetles. As early as 1941, Geigy scientists and other Swiss researchers had discovered that DDT was effective against a great many important insects, including body lice. The importance of this discovery should never be underestimated, as one enduring lesson of history is that insect-borne diseases flourish during times of war. Typhus, which is spread by body lice, is a leading example. Under the squalid conditions of war, the disease struck with spectacular ferocity. Typhus killed more soldiers and civilians in World War I than all the shell-fire combined.[3]

By 1942, the Swiss were reporting remarkable results with DDT, and reported that it killed fleas, mites, lice, and mosquitoes as well as flies.[4] In verification of Swiss studies, the Allies found that DDT was toxic to lice at doses that were safe for humans. Furthermore, it remained active against lice for many days after application, depending on personal hygiene. The Americans and the British soon conducted their own toxicity tests, which confirmed the Swiss reports.[5]

With DDT, the Allies had a powerful tool for preventing deadly outbreaks of typhus,[6] and by early 1943, the United States and British governments were working to ramp up DDT production. The U.S. military was projecting even larger DDT requirements for 1944.[7] By early 1944, Geigy's U.S. subsidiary, the Cincinnati Chemical Works, was producing DDT, along with 14 other American chemical companies and several British corporations.[8]

The advent of DDT in 1943 forever changed the role of typhus in warfare. Later on it would have dramatic impacts on other diseases. In a reflection of the life-saving properties of DDT as an insecticide, Müller won the Nobel Prize in Physiology or Medicine in 1948 for his discovery.[9]

DDT: A Wartime Necessity

One might assume the discovery of a chemical that changed the face and outcome of warfare and revolutionized man's ability to combat significant diseases like malaria involved extraordinary chemical wizardry. Actually, it didn't. DDT is a remarkably simple compound, in both structure and production. Here is a technical description of its chemical production:

> It was first synthesized by Zeidler on the following lines: 225 parts of chlorobenzene are mixed with 147 parts of chloral or the corresponding amount of chloral hydrate and then 1,000 parts sulphuric acid mono-hydrate are added. Whilst stirring well, the temperature rises to 60° C., and then sinks slowly to room temperature, the mass then containing solid portions. It is poured into a large excess of water whereupon the product separates in solid form. It is well washed and can be crystallized from ethyl alcohol forming fine white crystals having a weak fruity odour.[10]

And there it is, the most cost-effective insecticide known to man—produced in a simple two-step chemical process. This simple process produces the white crystals that, when sprayed on house walls, can stand guard and protect residents from mosquitoes and malaria for months on end.

DDT gained fame with the beginning of a typhus epidemic in Naples, Italy, in December 1943. The Allies set up DDT delousing stations in January 1944. During that month, 1,300,000 civilians were dusted at two delousing stations (72,000 on the peak day), and within three weeks the outbreak in the city of Naples was completely under control.[11]

Success against the typhus epidemic in Naples was an unprecedented achievement[12] and particularly remarkable because the Swiss had only released the formula for DDT in 1942. From WW II onward, DDT was in common use as a powder for spraying or sprinkling into the clothing of soldiers and refugees for typhus prevention. Almost overnight, DDT went from being unknown to being a critical military necessity.

DDT played an important role in the liberation of concentration camps as well. One example was the delousing of liberated populations from the Belsen concentration camp in 1945. At the time of liberation, typhus had been rampant for four months in the camp, with an estimated 20,000 cases. Those liberated from the camp doubted that British efforts to control typhus would work.[13] One former prisoner stated:

> After two-three days at the hospital, we have our first encounter with the pesticide DDT. When the English soldiers enter the hospital room with sprayers filled with this product, we all look at them with contemptuous

171

> superiority. They're planning on using this puny white powder to destroy all these millions of lice! But hundreds of the most radically conducted Entlausungs [delousing chambers that ineffectively used heat to kill body lice in clothing] hadn't helped. Yet, right in front of our eyes, something close to a miracle starts to happen! Slowly, the incessant itching, so painful on our pus-infected, ulcerated skin, starts to vanish, and this great relief finally convinces us that we have really been liberated. O Great, Powerful Benefactor, Inventor of the White Powder![14]

For many years after WW II, travelers were commonly provided a small container of DDT powder for sprinkling into underclothes to control body lice, other arthropods, and disease transmission. It became a standard issue for State Department officials.[15] In spite of extensive use over many years, with untold millions of individuals directly treated or otherwise exposed, there are no documented cases of harm among WW II soldiers or war refugees who were doused with DDT to prevent typhus, or among U.S. State Department officials who, in later years, also used DDT in their underclothes to prevent typhus when they visited typhus endemic areas.

Critical uses of DDT during and immediately after the war set the stage for DDT to become a peacetime commodity and a game changer for many life style issues of the mid-20th century. We have described DDT's impact on body lice and typhus, but another ancient burden on humanity was the ever present and vexing problem of bedbugs. Mankind had achieved little progress against bedbugs, as revealed in the following authoritative text from a public health paper published in 1945. Given the importance of the ongoing global re-emergence of bedbug infestations and modern society's apparent inability to effectively combat the problem, the full description of DDT efficacy in control of bedbugs during that era is presented here:

> Bedbugs—The superiority of DDT over all other treatments for bedbugs has now been amply demonstrated. The use of a 5 per cent DDT solution in deodorized kerosene will largely replace the expensive and dangerous hydro-cyanic acid gas fumigation and the less effective insecticide sprays.
>
> The main advantage of DDT over pyrethrum and other sprays is its persistence. DDT sprayed thoroughly on

mattresses and bedsteads will continue to kill all bugs coming in contact with it for many months. In tests at the Orlando laboratory of the Bureau of Entomology and Plant Quarantine, infested sleeping quarters were sprayed with a 5 per cent DDT oil solution. The bugs present were exterminated and 25 vigorous bugs were put on the mattress each week for 16 weeks. Not a single living bug was recovered on subsequent examinations, but a large percentage of them were found dead on the floor under the bed.

DDT sprays have been used extensively to combat bedbugs in military barracks. The results have been uniformly and remarkably successful. Tests carried out in cooperation with the National Pest Control Association in about 20 cities have shown 10 per cent DDT dust and 5 per cent kerosene solutions when applied to infested beds and adjacent walls to eliminate the pest.

The spraying of bug-infested theater seats, railway coaches, and Pullman cars has given striking and lasting results."[16]

Revealed in this text is a vivid picture of how the bedbug held forth in the everyday lives of people in the mid-1940s, even in the United States. Against that recalcitrant problem, DDT changed completely the balance of power between the "bug" and man's desire to be rid of it. The key to DDT effectiveness was its persistence, not its toxicity. Other compounds were far more toxic, but far less effective.

DDT and Public Health in the United States

In addition to being an essential tool for protecting deployed soldiers and travelers abroad, DDT also became an indispensable commodity for protecting the lives and health of people in the United States. At the turn of the 20th century, the continental United States was intensely malarious. The disease was an immense cause of human death, human illness, and economic loss. In 1916, malaria was estimated to reduce economic productivity in the United States by $100 million (in 1916).[17] The economic loss from malaria in the state of California alone was estimated to be $3 million, and California was not even considered a highly malarious state.[18] A conservative estimate of malaria cases for the country as a whole was one million or more cases per year.[19]

Malaria rates declined gradually in the United States through the first half of the 20th century, with occasional increases as a result of war and other events. The overall decline was in large part due to improvements in housing, better standards of living, and improved control of mosquito-breeding sites, which together reduced contact between man and mosquito. Notwithstanding this trend, during the 1940s, infectious diseases still caused major public health problems throughout the country. In the southeastern states, malaria control was possible only in urban settings where draining and eliminating aquatic habitats for mosquitoes and using larvicides to kill mosquito larvae was cost-effective. In contrast, the only real progress made in poor rural areas was screening houses to prevent mosquitoes from entering and transmitting disease.[20]

The office of Malaria Control in War Areas was created in 1942 right after the bombing of Pearl Harbor "to prevent or reduce malaria transmission around Army, Navy, and essential war industry areas [in the United States] by extending the control operations carried on by military authorities within these reservations."[21] Spraying houses with DDT quickly became established within the program as the most effective method of stopping malaria transmission in and around military installations in the United States.

Then, beginning in 1945, the MCWA launched its Extended Program of Malaria Control. This program was not limited to military posts, camps, and stations, but instead was extended to more malarious civilian areas.[22] It consisted of spraying DDT on interior walls of homes and privies. The spraying program covered large areas of the southern United States. From January 1945 to September 1947, 3.2 million houses were sprayed.[23] This number apparently did not include houses sprayed through use of local funds. As described in a 1946 report, "a number of larger cities have contributed sufficient funds to spray the cities in the 2,500–10,000 population group. The entire cost of this type of residual house spraying is paid from local funds."[24] After 1945, investigators discovered they could increase performance and get longer protection by spraying a greater concentration of DDT on house walls. Thus, as a result of the change in formulation, the number of sprayings per house varied from nearly 2.0 in 1945 to 1.5 in 1947.[25]

The MCWA was a wartime organization. With demobilization of military forces in 1945 and 1946, the MCWA went into a phase of rapid liquidation.[26] That led to the creation of the Communicable

Disease Center (now the Centers for Disease Control and Prevention) of the U.S. Public Health Service on July 1, 1946.[27] The CDC was created to capture the unique resources and expertise of the MCWA and was tasked with continuing and expanding MCWA programs in all areas of public health in the United States.[28]

The MCWA's Extended Program of Malaria Control had already been successful in reducing numbers of malaria cases in areas where houses were sprayed (see Figure 8.1).

To build on that success, the CDC started a National Malaria Eradication Program, commencing operations on July 1, 1947. It was referred to as the Residual Spray Program, and spraying DDT on inner walls of rural homes in malaria-endemic counties was the key component. From July 1947 to the end of 1949, the program sprayed over 4,650,000 houses. On the basis of surveys conducted in 13 southeastern states, the CDC concluded that "over-all control (reduction in houses infested) was approximately 90 percent for the 5-year period [1945–1949]."[29]

Overall, beginning in 1945,[30] millions of houses were sprayed for malaria control throughout the southern United States. DDT spraying broke the cycle of malaria transmission and, in 1949, the United States was declared free of malaria as a significant public health problem.[32] Despite this background of accomplishments from the use of DDT, arguments still abound that DDT was not a factor in malaria elimination from the United States.

Figure 8.1

MAP OF U.S. COUNTIES WHERE HOUSES WERE SPRAYED WITH
DDT FOR CONTROL OF MALARIA (1946–1947)[31]

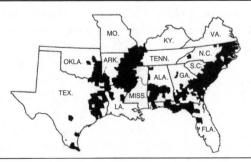

SOURCE: U.S. Public Health Service, Atlanta, Georgia, 1948.

One such argument is presented in *The Fever*, in which author Sonia Shah states, "By the time . . . the United States created the Malaria Control in War Areas program in 1942 (which would later become the Centers for Disease Control), the weaknesses of their antimalarial methods didn't matter anymore. Malaria had already nearly vanished."[33] The author is not alone in this assessment and like her colleagues is seriously wrong in her conclusion. As described above, malaria control was only possible in urban settings; in poor rural areas, the only option was to screen houses to prevent mosquitoes from entering and transmitting disease. Unfortunately, screening required rural people to spend money they didn't have.

In fact, malaria was still an entrenched problem at the time broad spraying began. As late as 1945, for example, Arkansas reported 1,182 malaria cases. With spraying of houses in 1945, malaria cases dropped to 849 in 1946. Those statistics are for just one of several states with deeply entrenched rural malaria. Broad spray coverage provided other health benefits, too. In 1945, Missouri sprayed 85,000 homes, and from 1945 to 1946, numbers of cases of fly-borne diseases dropped by 66 percent in sprayed areas.

The author of *The Fever* should have perused some original sources of historical data. As we explain below, Rachel Carson wrote *Silent Spring* when the memory of these successes was much more fresh, and although she gives a restrained nod to DDT's role in malaria control, she is dismissive of the whole idea of using chemicals in disease control.

The remarkable successes against malaria by 1949 did not mean that house spraying ended. DDT was used in many other public health endeavors.

Typhus

Control of murine typhus, which was an important public health problem in southern states, was one such endeavor. Unlike epidemic typhus, which is spread by lice, murine typhus is transmitted by fleas that infest rats. The control of murine typhus was achieved by dusting rat burrows and runways with DDT to kill fleas (oriental rat fleas) (see Figures 8.2 and 8.3).[34] Over time, hundreds of thousands of premises were dusted with DDT for control of this disease.

A total of 448,297 residences were dusted with DDT for typhus control in calendar year 1946.[37] Dusting of premises continued for

176

Figure 8.2
MAP OF COUNTIES WITH RESIDUAL DUSTING PROJECTS USING DDT FOR CONTROL OF MURINE TYPHUS (1946 AND 1947)[35]

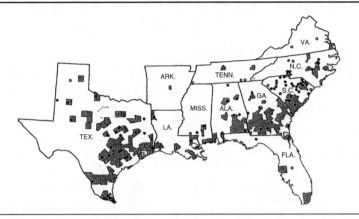

SOURCE: U.S. Public Health Service, Atlanta, Georgia, 1948.

Figure 8.3
COMPARISON OF NUMBERS OF TYPHUS CASES IN U.S. COUNTIES WITH AND WITHOUT DDT DUSTING (1945–1946)

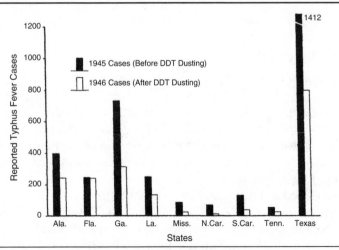

NOTE: The comparison data for not dusting were drawn from 1945 case data.[36]

SOURCE: U.S. Public Health Service, Atlanta, Georgia, 1948.

several more years and declined only when risk of murine typhus had been greatly reduced or eliminated. Examples of extensive DDT use are 1) from September 1 to November 22, 1947, when 91,083 premises were dusted,[38] and 2) from March 20 to July 2, 1949, when 150,705 premises were treated.[39]

Housefly and Dysentery Control

Although houseflies eventually became resistant to DDT, it was used for a time to control them successfully. Control of houseflies also helped reduce problems of dysentery. Some housefly control was a byproduct of the residual spray program for eradicating malaria. As stated in a Missouri State Health Department publication (cited in a CDC report) in 1946:

> [L]ast year the U.S. Public Health Service sprayed 85,000 homes with DDT in the delta country of Mississippi. It was chiefly a malaria control project to kill mosquitoes. But so many flies died as a result of the spraying project that the infant death rate from fly-borne diseases such as dysentery, typhoid fever, diarrhea, and enteritis, was cut to less than one-third that of the year before.
>
> This means that approximately 50 children in Mississippi who otherwise would have died as a result of these diseases are alive today.[40]

Aedes Aegypti *Control*

For many years, DDT was sprayed in towns and cities for control of the mosquito that transmits dengue fever and urban yellow fever, *Aedes aegypti*. Sporadic efforts to control this important vector were converted into a national eradication program in the 1960s.

The United States, along with other countries of North, Central, and South America, first signed a resolution of the Pan American Health Organization to eradicate *Aedes aegypti* in 1947. The United States signed a similar resolution in 1961. Funds were appropriated to initiate a U.S. eradication program in 1963.[41] The CDC coordinated the program, and with rare exception, it was based on spraying DDT as a matter of official public health policy in urban residential areas. The program continued until 1969.[42]

Plague Control

Like murine typhus, plague is transmitted by fleas, which were controlled effectively with DDT. The insecticide was used even in areas of western Texas and in a broad swath of the western United States for dusting prairie dog colonies and ground squirrel burrows as a means of plague control.[43]

Scope and Intensity of Public Health Use of DDT in Texas

Most Americans living in the 21st century are likely unaware of the historic extent and severity of malaria, murine typhus, dengue, and yellow fever in the United States. Media reports of West Nile virus outbreaks or of Lyme disease may give some pause to consider the threats posed by disease-spreading insects. Public health agencies respond to these outbreaks, usually with a targeted, local intervention. Given the contemporary response to insect-borne disease outbreaks, few will appreciate the scale of the response in the 1940s and 1950s. But then for most Americans, diseases like malaria, to say little of plague and typhus, are probably viewed like sepia photographs, as curiosities of the past.

The scale and urgency of the responses to malaria and other public health threats by U.S. agencies was enormous, and none of the programs described above that used DDT were trivial in scope. Texans, not known for their timidity or modesty, were residents of just one state that used DDT on a grand scale and to great effect. We review here the sequence of public health endeavors for Texas as an example of what occurred in many disease endemic states in the mid-1940s.

Malaria in San Antonio, Texas, from 1904 to 1908 caused a death rate of 17.5 per 100,000 population. In the interval from 1909 to 1913, the rate was 13.9 per 100,000 population.[44] To put these death rates into a modern framework, the rates for malaria infections alone were two- to fourfold higher than the modern death rate for all cancers combined in the 0- to 19-year age group in the United States.[45] A comparison of these age groups is justified because, in 1922, the deaths of children under age 5 from malaria were several-fold more than any other 10-year age group except the elderly.[46] However, malaria and other infectious diseases did more than just kill people, they also reduced their economic wherewithal.

Even in the 1940s, malaria remained a large public health problem in the United States. As stated in a 1941 update on status of malaria in the United States:

> Conservative evidence indicates that malaria is today indig-enous in 36 of the United States. These include all of the southeastern states (i.e., Virginia, North Carolina, South Carolina, Georgia, Florida, Kentucky, Tennessee, Alabama, Mississippi, Arkansas and Louisiana); a large portion of Oklahoma and Texas; Missouri (especially the southeastern section; . . ."[46]

For Texas in particular, malaria remained a formidable public health problem, even in the 1940s. In 1941, the most malarious areas in Texas were "situated chiefly around the Rio Grande, Red and Sabine Rivers."[47] Public health officials believed in 1941 that malaria was "more widespread and probably more prevalent [in 1941] than in 1930."[48]

Spraying houses with DDT to control malaria started at least by 1945. Between the latter half of 1945 and mid-1947, more than 200,000 houses in Texas were sprayed with DDT.[49] The CDC malaria eradication program, based on DDT spraying, continued beyond 1947, but in 1948 the program was altered. As with the national program described above, spray cycles were reduced from two per year to just one per year. The amount of DDT applied to house walls was 200 mg/ft^2, which is about two grams per square meter of wall surface,[50] which to this day is the international standard for malaria control treatments.

The numbers of houses sprayed in Texas were 89,600 in 1947; 94,905 in 1948; and 71,870 in 1949.[51] For part of 1948 and after, house spraying became less costly and better tolerated by residents because spraying was limited to one time per year opposed to the earlier strategy of spraying at six-month intervals. In 1950, a total of 85,355 houses in Texas were sprayed with DDT.[52] As stated in a CDC report for July, August, and September 1952, "a total of 145,138 spray appli-cations have been made this season."[53] Texas was one of the states that continued spraying houses in the 1950s. For example, 23,885 and 41,273 premises were sprayed in 1952 and 1953, respectively.[54]

Spraying continued in Texas during 1950–1953, in part because malaria was still endemic in South Korea during the Korean War, and several U.S. bases were located in Texas. With the military returning from the Korean War, the United States had to maintain vigilance to prevent large re-introductions of malaria.[55]

DDT also was used in many other public health endeavors in Texas, including the dusting of premises to control murine typhus. In the 1951 review of murine typhus control, public health officials concluded that "semiannual DDT dusting of rat runs and harborages in rat-infested business buildings and annual DDT dusting in the residential areas" contributed to reduction of rats and prevalence of murine typhus. All told, through those and other preventive measures, Texas reduced the incidence of murine typhus "from 1,844 cases in 1945 to 222 [cases] in 1950."[56] This was an 88 percent reduction in disease.

Aedes aegypti control was essential to halt the spread of dengue and yellow fever, and Texas and CDC initiated DDT spraying to control this mosquito in 1946.[57] Spraying DDT in and around the mosquito breeding sites in backyards and next to houses continued throughout the 1940s and 1950s.[58] Spraying was intended not only to control mosquito breeding but to eradicate the mosquito.

Funds were appropriated for a national *Aedes aegypti* eradication program in the fall of 1963.[59] The CDC-coordinated program got underway in 1964. As described in a 1964 annual report, the program had two objectives:

> It will protect this country against outbreaks of yellow fever and dengue, and it will eliminate this reservoir of *Ae. aegypti* as a possible source of reinfestation of countries that have rid themselves of the species.[60]

When the U.S. program was initiated in 1964, a total of 16 countries within the hemisphere had already used DDT to successfully eradicate *Aedes aegypti*.[61] Thus, the second of the two objectives had great significance for many countries in the Americas. Simply stated, eradicating *Aedes aegypti* from the United States would have ended the export of the mosquito back into *Aedes aegypti*-free countries.

The U.S. *Aedes aegypti* eradication program was based on the use of DDT, and southern Texas was one of several pilot test sites. Pressure from environmental activists and resultant government actions were the proximate cause of ending the *Aedes aegypti* eradication program in 1969; in turn, that action was the proximate cause for the collapse of successful eradication efforts in the rest of the hemisphere. A measure of the devastating, but perhaps indirect, consequences of the 1969 decision to end the eradication effort in the United States is the nearly one million cases of dengue that occurred in Brazil in 2010.[62] Furthermore, the tragedy is ongoing, with the reoccurrence of millions of cases each year in countries that were once—through use of DDT—free of dengue and the risk of urban yellow fever.

In summation, the historical record shows how DDT was heavily relied upon in public health programs in the United States. It was indubitably a key element in the successful elimination of malaria, and it was an important contributor to the control of murine typhus, dysentery, and other diseases.

DDT was saving lives in the United States when Rachel Carson was in her early 30s and was editor-in-chief of all publications for the U.S. Fish and Wildlife Service. While her focus was not public health, the facts presented above could not have escaped her attention. This makes the dismissive attitude Carson exhibited toward the public health use of DDT, as we describe below, inexcusable.

Public Health Use of DDT Overseas

The United States was not the only country to gravitate to DDT for use in public health. Many other countries quickly put the magical white powder to work in national public health programs, especially for malaria and, in the Americas, for eradicating *Aedes aegypti* mosquitoes. DDT's ability to prevent disease transmission and, in some cases, eradicate the disease vectors led a National Academy of Sciences committee in 1970 to conclude: "To only a few chemicals does man owe as great a debt as to DDT. . . . In little more than two decades, DDT has prevented 500 million human deaths, due to malaria, that otherwise would have been inevitable."[63]

The effectiveness of DDT for disease control convinced various countries throughout the world to create national malaria control programs. Their successes eventually stimulated the World Health Organization to coordinate a global eradication program.

DDT and Malaria Control in the Americas

Almost all countries in the Americas started using DDT in their malaria control programs. The experiences of countries like

Venezuela and Guyana demonstrate the powerful benefit of spraying house walls with small amounts of DDT. In the mid-1940s and before, malaria rates in countries in the Americas were dangerously high. Venezuela had a national malaria program but was still reporting more than 800,000 cases per year.[64] Venezuela started spraying DDT in houses in 1946. The protection was immediate, and malaria rates dropped precipitously in all sprayed areas. From the period 1941–1945 (pre-spray period) to 1948, DDT spraying reduced the number of malaria positive slides per 100,000 people from an average of 1,083 to just 82 for 1948, a 91.25 percent drop in malaria.[65]

In the neighboring country of Guyana, during 1943–1945, more than 37 percent of the rural population and 27 percent of the urban population were stricken with malaria. Accompanying these high infection rates was a death rate among newborns of 126 per 1,000 live births. Guyana started experimental spraying of DDT inside houses in 1945, expanded the program in 1946, and initiated countrywide spraying in 1947.[66] By the 1948–1949 time period, as a result of house spraying alone, infant mortality declined by 39 percent.[67] In urban areas, malaria declined by 99 percent. Even in the highly endemic rural areas, malaria infections declined by a stunning 96 percent.[68]

By the early 1950s, both Venezuela and Guyana had used DDT to eliminate malaria from large areas.[69] Soon malaria infections could be found only in sparsely populated forested areas of both countries. Malaria completely disappeared from heavily populated coastal regions and from much of the interior savannas.

Health workers in other countries also recognized the particular value of DDT. The head of malaria control in Brazil characterized the changes that DDT offered in the following statement:

> Until 1945–1946 [when DDT became available for malaria control], preventive methods employed against malaria in Brazil, as in the rest of the world, were generally directed against the aquatic phases of the vectors (draining, larvicides, destruction of bromeliads, etc. . .). These methods, however, were only applied in the principal cities of each state, and the only measure available for rural populations exposed to malaria was free distribution of specific drugs.[70]

In the late-1950s, under guidance from the World Health Organization and the Pan American Health Organization, most national malaria programs were converted into malaria eradication programs.

DDT in National Malaria Control Programs in Africa and Asia

Historical data from many countries outside the Americas also show the huge beneficial impact of spraying houses with DDT. As documented here, many countries started their own malaria control programs. These countries, like those in the Americas, pioneered house spray methods, and laid the groundwork for what would become a WHO-coordinated global malaria eradication program.

Africa

The vector control programs in southern Africa adopted DDT shortly after the end of WW II. Residual spraying with DDT brought rapid reductions in the number of malaria cases. In the Transvaal province of South Africa, hospital admissions "fell from 1,177 cases during the 1945–1946 transmission season to 601 in 1946–1947 coinciding with the availability of DDT in 1946, and falling to 454 in 1948 and to a low of 61 cases in 1951."[71] Similar successes were echoed in other southern African countries where DDT was used. While DDT resulted in plummeting malaria rates in many parts of southern Africa, the spraying programs were not scaled up in most of the highly endemic areas of central Africa where health infrastructure was poor and levels of development remained low. However, it is safe to assume that had donor countries, and the governments of malarial countries, invested in such projects, the impacts would have been dramatic. According to World Health Organization data, pilot projects of DDT spraying combined with distribution of chloroquine in the Kigezi district of Uganda reduced malaria parasite prevalence from 22.7 percent to 0.5 percent between 1959 and 1960. In southern Cameroon, parasite prevalence among children was reduced from 28.5 percent to just over 5 percent in one year using DDT alone.[72] WHO reports that equally impressive results were achieved in other countries of the region.

Sri Lanka

After DDT was introduced for control of malaria in Sri Lanka (then Ceylon) in 1946 and over a three-year period, the spleen rate (malaria infections cause enlarged spleens) dropped from 77 percent to 2.7 percent, and general infant mortality dropped by 62 percent.[73] By 1954, infections had declined from 413 per 1,000 to 0.85 per 1,000 people.[74] These statistics reveal reductions in millions of malaria cases per year.

Taiwan

The newly-formed Republic of China (Taiwan) adopted DDT use in malaria control shortly after World War II. In 1945, there were more than one million cases of malaria on the island; by 1969, there were only nine cases.[75] Shortly thereafter, the disease was eradicated from the island (and remains eradicated today).[76]

In summary, extensive use of DDT for malaria control preceded the global eradication program. As shown by the statistics presented above, countries used DDT to combat malaria and greatly improved the health of their residents. Over a third of a billion people were freed of endemic malaria even before the WHO-led eradication effort began.[77]

DDT and WHO's Global Malaria Eradication Program

The 8th World Health Assembly in 1955 directed WHO to coordinate a global program to eradicate malaria. As revealed in statistical reports of malaria eradication in the Americas, the program was fully underway in 1959.

Nepal was just one of several countries that benefited from malaria eradication. One report noted that "dramatic, nationwide reduction of malaria [in Nepal] was perhaps the greatest technical and logistic triumph of the 1960s."[78] That triumph over malaria was based largely on use of DDT as the exclusive preventive measure of the eradication program.

Each year in the early 1950s, there were more than two million cases of malaria in Nepal, with a mortality rate of 10 percent. The burden of deaths fell most heavily on children. At that time, malaria was Nepal's most serious public health problem, and it contributed to increased deaths from other diseases as well. The U.S. Agency for International Assistance started the malaria program in Nepal in 1959. Spraying of houses in the central zone began in 1960. Spraying in the eastern zone was underway in 1964 and in the western zone in 1965.[79]

Whereas previously more than two million cases of malaria a year had been the norm, only 2,468 cases were found in 1968. Before the malaria control program, life expectancy in Nepal was 28 years. By 1962, life expectancy was 33 years, and by 1970 it was 42.3 years.[80] Malaria in Nepal had been an enormous problem in many areas—so bad that it had prevented people from occupying land and producing crops. Once malaria was brought under control, previously unoccupied areas became available for agricultural productivity. As land became available, large numbers of people moved into new areas. The total cost of the multiyear program in Nepal was a mere $13 million, which brought vast improvements in health, dramatically reduced death rates and increased population longevity, and ultimately, vastly increased agricultural productivity and wealth.[81]

All told, from the mid-1940s to 1969, almost one billion people worldwide were freed from endemic malaria by DDT-sprayed house walls.[82] This achievement is unequaled in the history of arthropod-borne disease control. DDT was used to change the global distribution of endemic malaria. In those countries that coupled malaria eradication with economic growth and development, the disease remained banished after spraying stopped.

Today this eradication program is often referred to, disparagingly, as a public health failure. One cannot, of course, deny that the program failed to eradicate the disease from the entire planet and thus did not achieve its ultimate goal. But characterizing the program as a failure ignores the fact that well over a billion lives were spared the burden of endemic malaria, an extraordinary success by any measure. However, DDT did more than just save lives. Life expectancy for people in Nepal grew from 28 years before DDT to 42.3 years by 1970. The house spray program produced, on average, an extension of 14.3 years of human life. The population of Nepal in 1970 was 11.232 million.[83] That value times 14.3 years of improved longevity equates to 160,617,600 additional years of human life. And these statistics describe how DDT improved health and life for people of just one country. These simple statistics reveal how the offhand and cheap dismissal of the global malaria eradication program does a grave disservice to the thousands of hard working professionals who were involved in the program. They should instead be lauded; millions of people are alive today thanks to their efforts.

Rachel Carson and DDT for Public Health

Carson would have known of the great public health achievements of DDT and that it was saving lives; indeed she describes some of the programs in *Silent Spring*. But the bulk of the book is a singular attack on DDT and other insecticides with scarcely any recognition of their actual and potential benefits. Although Carson didn't actually call for a ban on DDT, it happened nonetheless, thanks to a ruling by the U.S. Environmental Protection Agency. The EPA ban on most uses of DDT allowed its use only in emergencies in the United States—and of course EPA has no jurisdiction in other countries. Nevertheless, disease control programs in developing countries that relied on DDT were shut down. If unintended consequences are defined as outcomes that are unexpected, then we must emphasize that the devastating harm to malaria programs cannot be accurately described as an unexpected consequence of EPA's action. Historical records show EPA was firmly and repeatedly warned by top public health officials of the United States, the WHO, and the Pan American Health Organization of disastrous consequences of a DDT ban.[84] The EPA administrator ignored those warnings and banned DDT anyway. The movement against the public health use of DDT was, in most ways, a direct result of environmental activist pressure against insecticides. In the wake of this activism, lives have been lost, and the struggle to improve human health and well-being has suffered setbacks.

Given her iconic status within the environmentalist movement and the importance of *Silent Spring* in the fight to ban the use of DDT, it is tempting to blame Carson for the problems that befell malaria control programs as a result of anti-DDT activism. That would be too easy, however. Carson died eight years before the U.S. Environmental Protection Agency issued its ruling—seen as laudable by some, notorious by others—banning most uses of DDT. Carson states in *Silent Spring* that it is not her contention "that chemical insecticides must never be used."[85] Toward the end of *Silent Spring*, in Chapter 16, Carson explains that mosquitoes transmit diseases like malaria and yellow fever and states:

> The list of diseases and their insect carriers, or vectors, includes typhus and body lice, plague and rat fleas, African sleeping sickness and tsetse flies, various fevers and ticks, and innumerable others. These are important problems that must be met. No responsible person contends that insect-borne diseases should be ignored.[86]

These statements, while accurate and important, stand almost alone in over 250 pages vilifying insecticides and generating great fear about modern chemicals, and DDT in particular. The problem we have in excusing Carson's role in the banning of DDT is that she dismisses the great achievements that resulted from using DDT, and she also gets some basic facts and theories wrong. For these, she can and must be blamed.

Understandably, *Silent Spring* deals mostly with the agricultural use of insecticides such as DDT. The control of crop pests consumed vastly greater amounts of insecticide than the targeted use of insecticides in public health. Carson was also primarily concerned with the effects of insecticides on wildlife, and as spraying insecticides inside houses results in almost no biologically significant environmental contamination, this use would interest her less. However, as most of the book discusses DDT, it is curious that she ignores the most important use of DDT, from a humanitarian perspective, until one of the final chapters.

Readers of *Silent Spring* will go through many pages of Carson's lyrical prose describing one horrifying consequence of using DDT after another. Her words are well chosen to strike fear into any reader's heart as she describes her speculations about insidious harm to both man and wildlife from the use of modern pesticides. Not until Chapter 15, "Nature Fights Back," does Carson explain that DDT was used in the South Pacific during World War II to control malaria. Unlike the concentration camp survivor quoted earlier, however, she does not dwell on the life-saving properties of DDT; the reason she brings up this example is to claim that the mosquitoes soon developed resistance to the insecticide.

Her treatment of disease control programs in Chapter 16, "The Rumblings of an Avalanche," is equally designed to claim that using insecticides like DDT will actually make disease control harder. Carson continues the quotation from above, with this:

> The question that has now urgently presented itself is whether it is either wise or responsible to attack the problem by methods that are rapidly making it worse. The world has heard much of the vectors of infection, but has heard little of the other side of the story—the defeats, the short-lived triumphs that now strongly support the alarming view that the insect enemy has been made actually stronger by our efforts. Even worse, we may have destroyed our very means of fighting.[87]

Later (on page 233), Carson describes the famous use of DDT in Naples, Italy, to control typhus during World War II. Again her reason for describing the usefulness of DDT against body lice is merely to claim that eventually lice developed resistance.

Throughout the book, Carson dismisses the beneficial uses of DDT. In the final paragraphs of Chapter 13, "Through a Narrow Window," she describes the potential for chemicals to lead to genetic mutations and "strike directly at the chromosomes. . . ."[88] Carson concludes this paragraph with, "Is this not too high a price to pay for a sproutless potato or a mosquitoless [sic] patio?"[89] Though Carson doesn't finger DDT as one of the chemicals in this passage, she refers to it elsewhere in the chapter and throughout the book, and it can be taken that DDT was one of the chemicals to which she was referring. The problem with her statements is that at the time she was writing *Silent Spring*, as now, there is no evidence that DDT acts in this way and "strikes directly at the chromosomes." While Carson was writing this passage, millions of people were being saved from diseases and were enjoying a longer lifespan, better nutrition, and as a result, a brighter future, thanks to the chemicals she attacks. Yet Carson trivializes these benefits and stokes up fears for which she had little or no evidence.

Unfortunately, *Silent Spring* is littered with inaccuracies about the way in which DDT works and the biology of insecticide resistance. In her defense, Carson was not alone in misunderstanding the way that DDT functions. However, given that so much of the book is devoted to DDT, this is hardly an excuse.

From the very early uses of DDT in disease control in the 1940s and ever since, scientists and field workers have reported in the peer-reviewed literature and elsewhere that DDT functions as a powerful spatial repellent.[90] In other words, DDT stops mosquitoes from entering sprayed houses. In addition to these spatial repellent properties, DDT also acts as a contact irritant so that if a mosquito lands on a surface sprayed with DDT, it will quickly move away. Lastly, DDT also acts as a toxicant, and if exposed to the chemical long enough, the mosquito will die.

These three powerful modes of action are unique among public health insecticides; no other chemical used in malaria control functions in these ways. For these reasons and others, public health professionals value DDT and its remarkable ability to keep disease spreading insects away from people, thereby interrupting transmission of parasites and other disease agents, and saving lives.

Carson, like others, eagerly noted the spatial repellent properties of DDT, explaining, "Some malaria mosquitoes have a habit that so reduces their exposure to DDT as to make them virtually immune. Irritated by the spray, they leave huts and survive outside."[91] Carson was not a medical entomologist and perhaps could be forgiven for misinterpreting the results of DDT spraying; indeed some entomologists and public health professionals fell into the same trap.

The major species of malarial mosquitoes have evolved their patterns over the millennia to feed on humans inside their houses, normally late at night. The fact that disease-spreading mosquitoes exit houses and are kept away from people means that they are no longer transmitting the malaria parasite; this breaks the disease transmission cycle. The evidence from countless malaria programs around the world, over many years, shows that as a result of the spraying, malaria rates plummet. Carson thought that she found some Achilles' heel of the DDT malaria programs, when in fact she described one of its strongest attributes.

Carson focused on insecticide resistance because she seemed to view it as a cunning way to turn public health triumphs into potential disasters. Insecticide resistance is a problem for vector control programs. In a similar way, resistance to antibiotics is also a serious and ongoing medical problem. In the face of resistance to medicines, however, few people argue that we should eschew them altogether. Rather, well-publicized, well-funded, and popular campaigns seek to invest both public and private funds in the search for new drugs. Although insecticides, when used in public health, save lives just as medicines do, they do not benefit from the same kind of popular support and funding. This has much to do with the negative view that most people have of modern chemicals, thanks in large part to *Silent Spring* and fear mongering of anti-insecticide advocacy.

Notably, Carson fails to explain that in almost all cases, mosquito resistance to DDT did not result from its use in public health, but from chemical use in agriculture. Resistance in a population is driven by mortality. As the susceptible insects die, those with the resistant genes survive and gradually dominate in the population. Because DDT is, in fact, a weak toxicant and mainly functions as a spatial repellent when used for malaria control, the mosquitoes often do not die from their exposure to DDT. Therefore, the resistant gene is not driven through the population via the force of selective mortality. This is important because then, as now, insecticide resistance is used as an argument against DDT and indeed against other insecticides.

In several instances, Carson writes that as mosquitoes develop resistance to DDT, they become "tough" and that "a process of escalation has been going on in which ever more toxic materials must be found."[92] Carson relies on Darwinian evolution to explain that the use of insecticides results in the survival of the fittest. Yet her understanding of this topic was weak. The mosquitoes are not more "tough," they are more resistant to a given chemical, and in the absence of that chemical, they are no more fit to survive than nonresistant mosquitoes. In fact, in the absence of the chemical, the mosquitoes may even be less fit than others.

Carson is also wrong in her assessment that resistance requires "ever more toxic materials." This statement can only be designed to frighten readers, who would rightly be worried about more and more dangerous chemicals in the environment. In reality, the presence of resistance does not call for ever more toxic chemicals; it calls for chemicals that have different modes of action and act differently on the insect. Malaria control professionals now largely agree that combining different insecticides in spraying programs and/or rotating spraying with different classes of chemicals, is a useful means of stopping the spread of resistance through a population. This same principle holds true for management of drug resistance. The modern protocols for the treatment of malaria and other diseases, like tuberculosis and HIV/AIDS, call for combinations of different drugs with different active ingredients.

Silent Spring may have gotten these basic fundamentals wrong, but such was the power of the book that it started a renewed push for the use of biological, supposedly environment-friendly methods of disease control. The final chapter, "The Other Road," lays out Carson's vision for a world free of man-made chemicals. Since her death, public health policies have been greatly influenced by her agenda and the idea of insecticide-free malaria control. Despite a dearth of evidence to support this idea, it remains alive and well and continues to undermine malaria control and thereby cost lives. Also, emphasis on biological control has diverted precious resources from the development of new and improved public health insecticides and from research to improve the methodology of chemical use. Instead, those resources have gone to a single-minded program of research aimed at demonstrating efficacy of nonchemical methods of disease control. We cannot blame Carson for changes in public health policy enacted by the global health bureaucracies after she died. However, as countless environmental groups celebrate and almost sanctify Carson's legacy, it is useful to examine her anti-insecticides legacy with respect to global public health.

Changing Public Health Policies

In May 1970, two years before EPA banned DDT and six years after Carson's untimely death, the World Health Assembly, the governing body of the World Health Organization, met in Geneva and debated malaria. The WHA sets the agenda for WHO and represents the interests of ministers of health from around the globe. The 1970 WHA adopted a resolution on malaria, which includes a statement recognizing the importance of insecticides for effective control of malaria.[93] Furthermore, the WHA urged "the countries manufacturing insecticides to continue to make available to the developing countries insecticides for malaria control."[94] These basic statements were presumably encouraging to malaria control program managers in developing countries who were already seeing growing opposition to the use of DDT and were no doubt deeply concerned about the increasing pressure not to use insecticides—and DDT in particular.

These issues had played out several months prior to the WHA at the WHO executive board meeting in January 1970. During this meeting, a report was presented from WHO's Regional Committee for South-East Asia. The regional committee had adopted a resolution "which encouraged countries producing DDT to continue to do so until a less toxic and equally effective insecticide became available."[95]

The minutes of the executive board include the following:

> Dr. Layton [Canada's representative] said he had been struck by a series of statements made on the question of DDT all within a brief space of time. In the first place, the Director-General [of WHO], in his introduction to Official Records No. 179 (page XVII), had stressed the desirability of

> continuing to use DDT for malaria eradication. Almost simultaneously, the Canadian Prime Minister [Pierre Trudeau], in a formal statement on the matter, had said that research showed the environment to be widely contaminated by DDT residues; while there was no evidence that the present levels of DDT in the diet had caused injury to humans, it was only prudent, in view of the persistent use of DDT and the lack of clear-cut evidence, to limit contamination of the environment.[96]

Thus, despite the clear and unambiguous need for DDT voiced by public health experts—including WHO's director general—Canada's representative invoked the "precautionary principle" and advocated against the use of DDT. This would not be the last time that developed countries and anti-insecticides groups would use official meetings of WHO to push their agenda, even if it went against the views of disease control experts and undermined malaria control.

The malaria control specialists pushed back against this anti-insecticide activism. One year later, WHO's Expert Committee on malaria issued its 15th report, which included a resolution stating that the committee recommended . . . "that every effort be made to ensure the continued availability of residual insecticides, particularly DDT, for malaria eradication, which is an essential health activity."[97]

However, in a reflection of the growing popular opposition to DDT, by 1972 WHO was subjected to growing criticism in the media for its support of DDT use. The 1972 report, *The Work of WHO*, reflects the ideological importance of insecticide use. WHO states:

> Press cuttings received in 1972 amounted to roughly twice the volume received in 1971. A considerable increase in press coverage of WHO activities was achieved, especially in the African Region. Comment on WHO continued to be largely favourable. Such criticism as was noted related to the Health Assembly's action regarding the German Democratic Republic [East Germany] and WHO's position on DDT.[98]

The report goes on to explain that WHO was counteracting the criticism on DDT and had held a televised debate in the United States, which concluded favorably for the use of DDT in developing countries until a suitable substitute could be found. Notably, the

193

debate about the use of DDT appears to have been as important and controversial for the media as the great ideological battles of the Cold War.

WHO's technical health specialists continued their defense of DDT, but in many respects, this defense became quixotic. DDT production dwindled, and prices rose after EPA's 1972 ban (an outcome EPA had been judiciously warned would occur). DDT became increasingly difficult to acquire for use in malaria programs. At the same time, the cost of developing new insecticides kept rising, and the prospect of a new public health insecticide dimmed. By the mid-1970s, WHO understood this well, stating:

> The number of new pesticides received in 1975 for evaluation by WHO for use in vector control was considerably lower than in previous years. The great increase in the cost of developing and testing new chemical pesticides has caused industry to limit the number of compounds being developed to those which can be shown to have wide potential use in agriculture as well as in public health.[99]

The report goes on to explain that "much attention is now being paid to the ecology of vectors and animal reservoirs, the fate of pesticides in the environment and their effects on nontarget species, and the feasibility of using biological or other nonchemical means of control."[100]

In his report to the WHO executive board in May 1976, Dr. Jacques Hamon, director at the time of WHO's Division of Vector Biology and Control, noted that "regrettably, costs of research and development of new products had increased to such an extent that the chemical industry had reduced its research efforts on pesticides because the prospects of recovering the investment by marketing new insecticides were also decreasing."[101]

By the late 1970s, WHO began to include biological and environmental controls as more mainstream strategies for malaria control. The 1976–1977 report, *The Work of WHO*, states:

> In recent years vector control has been achieved mainly through the use of chemicals. This approach has given rise to problems such as pesticide resistance, hazards to non-target organisms including man, and environmental contamination. A program of research is now underway to develop better chemical and non-chemical methods of control.

> The Organization carried out a review of the situation and
> prepared a statement on pest/vector management systems
> in collaboration with [the U.N. Environment Programme]
> and WHO.[102]

Insecticide resistance was and is a real and pressing problem.
However, the impact of resistance to DDT was no doubt
overstated because of DDT's spatial repellent properties. Regardless, the solution to resistance is not to stop the use of pesticides, but
to find new pesticides and ensure that resistance is managed and
contained. Unfortunately, although development of new public health
insecticides is the proper solution, that avenue was blocked by
anti-insecticide activism. Instead, efforts were directed at avenues
of research that were destined to fail, namely methods of environmental management and biological control. Throughout this period,
malaria control based on the sound and effective use of public health
insecticides gradually unraveled. In the meantime, layer upon layer
of new costs were piled onto research and development of new
insecticides, making discovery of a new public health insecticide
more and more unlikely. All of this occurred as a direct consequence
of the ever-growing influence over disease control by environmental
agencies and environmental activists.

During the 1985 75th WHO executive board meeting, Dr. Norman
Gratz, WHO's then-director of the Division of Vector Biology and
Control, recognized that chemicals would remain "the mainstay of
vector control in the developing and developed world for the fore-
seeable future. Nevertheless, substantial resources had been transferred to biological control; in addition the program had received
additional funding through its collaboration with the Special
Program for Research and Training in Tropical Diseases, which
would be used for the development of biological control methods
and materials."[103] These methods were to include fish in the control
of mosquito larvae.

Regrettably, WHO bowed to the increasing public pressure and
pressure from the developed nations that pay WHO's bills. WHO
began withdrawing support for DDT and other insecticides in
public health. As an organization reliant on donations, WHO also
began chasing the money, which by then was flowing towards environmental control and away from insecticides. No one can blame

Carson for WHO's failings, but based on content of *Silent Spring*, it is fair to say that she would have been pleased with this outcome.

As described in the preceding paragraphs, since the 1970s, numerous WHO reports[104] have emphasized the use of biological and other environmental controls. Yet, despite decades of research and funding, the evidence that these methods are able to contribute meaningfully to disease control is largely absent. The 1980 review of malaria control for WHO's executive board includes a statement that unequivocally points to the growing power of the anti-insecticides movement: ". . . in some countries where coordinated insecticidal spraying could be important in the control of malaria there has been political pressure to restrain its use, although malaria could be seen as an environmental polluter."[105]

In 1997, the anti-insecticides movement achieved a significant victory, lobbying strongly for a WHA resolution that called on countries to reduce their reliance on insecticides for public health. Consumers International, a leftist group opposed to insecticides, made presentations during the WHO executive board meeting prior to the WHA. We can find no record of any presentation by disease control specialists at this meeting. The UNEP, which began collaborating with WHO in the 1970s, had apparently succeeded in keeping out anyone with actual experience in controlling disease-spreading insects while allowing in activists with an ideological opposition to insecticides.

Roll Back Malaria, a partnership among various UN agencies, including WHO, as well as donor agencies and the World Bank, developed its Global Malaria Action Plan in 2008. After decades of research on and funding for environmental and biological controls to prevent malaria, the undeniable truth remains that public health insecticides are needed and form the foundation of malaria control. The main methods of delivering these insecticides are either to spray them inside houses or to provide insecticide treated bed nets, under which people sleep. GMAP includes environmental management and biological controls but notes that "their sustainability relies on the ability to conduct continuously reliable surveillance and mapping activities to identify areas where these interventions are most appropriate."[106]

Investment, both public and private, in the search for new public health insecticides has been totally inadequate, largely as a result of Carson's agenda and the growing expense of insecticide development. By comparison, the much-needed funding for new malaria treatments and even for a malaria vaccine has been substantial. In 2004 alone, malaria vaccine development received almost $80 million in funding, and in that same year the search for new malaria drugs received $120 million.[107] A recent report published by the Program for Appropriate Technologies in Health reveals that the annual investment in research and development (R&D) for new tools to fight malaria quadrupled between 1993 and 2009 to a level of $612 million. Even though malaria is a vector-borne disease that requires vector control measures, between 2004 and 2009, only 4 percent of total R&D expenditures was devoted to vector control; most funds went toward the search for vaccines and new medicines.[108] Included in that 4 percent was funding from the Bill & Melinda Gates Foundation for the Innovative Vector Control Consortium. That is the only partnership to discover new public health insecticides, and in 2005 it was granted $50 million over a five-year period. While this is a valuable initiative, regrettably the consortium is not investigating or developing any chemicals with the spatial repellant action exhibited by DDT. The prospects of finding a true replacement for DDT, therefore, are slim.

Regulatory barriers and the costs of developing medicines and vaccines have risen, just as they have with insecticides. However, unlike insecticides, WHO, other health agencies, charities, foundations, advocacy groups, and the private sector have successfully lobbied for funding. And unlike insecticides, there is no organized, effective, and richly funded opposition to medicines and vaccines.

Environmental and biological controls—the preferred path sketched out by Rachel Carson in *Silent Spring*—have failed to provide any credible method of controlling malaria and thereby saving lives. Naturally, the modern day individuals and groups that have taken up Carson's anti-insecticide crusade claim great successes in insecticide-free malaria control. But these groups, including Pesticide Action Network and the UNEP, hide behind a thin veil of misinformation and are particularly damaging to serious disease control efforts—which require new and effective public health insecticides.

An excellent example of the way in which the success of environmental control of malaria is not only exaggerated, but fabricated, is found in a malaria project in Mexico and seven Central American countries funded and managed by UNEP and the environmental health unit of the Pan American Health Organization (PAHO). With funding from the Global Environment Facility, UNEP and PAHO set out to show that malaria could be controlled without DDT and indeed without any insecticides. After the completion of the project, in 2008, UNEP, GEF, and the environmental sector of PAHO claimed that their environmentally sound approaches reduced malaria by more than 60 percent. Malaria had declined in these countries, but as we explained in a peer-reviewed paper,[109] the decline was due to the widespread distribution of malaria treatments and totally unrelated to UNEP's efforts. In fact, an epidemiologic review of the UNEP project showed that its environmentally sound methods made absolutely no difference to the transmission of malaria.

Almost 70 years after it started saving lives in war-torn Europe, DDT is still being used in malaria control, mostly in southern Africa and India. The great irony of the anti-DDT and anti-insecticides campaign started by Carson and carried forth by so many others, is that while dampening research into new public health insecticides and diverting resources into a fruitless quest for biological controls, WHO continues to recommend DDT as one of the few effective vector control insecticides. And several malaria programs have few options other than to use it.

Conclusion

Unlike some environmental writers and doomsayers of the time, such as William Vogt or Paul Ehrlich, Carson never advocated against disease control and never specifically suggested that people in poor countries should die to arrest population growth. But Carson did get her facts wrong. And though she may not have intended to harm people suffering from insect-borne diseases, her ideas, as mistaken as they were, have inflicted great and lasting harm. As we have explained in this chapter, the evidence of the great and unprecedented way in which DDT helped save lives and lift people out of the misery of poverty and disease was overwhelming. Carson should have known better than to disparage the disease control successes and use false arguments against insecticides.

Today, we still rely on DDT, and in spite of the political risks to governments involved, it is still being produced and used in malaria control programs. Carson's scare tactics produced great fears about insecticides, which led to a dearth of investment in new public health insecticides to replace DDT. The ultimate irony is that DDT remains a valuable and necessary tool in our malaria control arsenal precisely because no legitimate DDT replacement has been found. And this, in turn, is a consequence of Carson's anti-insecticide advocacy.

9. Agricultural Revolutions and Agency Wars: How the 1950s Laid the Groundwork for *Silent Spring*

Roger E. Meiners and Andrew P. Morriss

Silent Spring has acquired iconic status in the history of the environmental movement. Rather than just a popular science writer, Rachel Carson is virtually a secular saint, having been martyred by her death from cancer shortly after completing her *magnum opus*.[1] A half-century after publication of the book, most people agree that Carson and *Silent Spring* appear to have changed public opinion about pesticides in general and DDT in particular.

But, as Desrochers and Shimizu discuss in Chapter 3, debates about pesticides began long before Carson's book. In this chapter, we will show that *Silent Spring* is a populist expression of a struggle over the regulatory authority governing American food production between two federal agencies with dramatically different visions: the Food and Drug Administration (FDA) and the federal Department of Agriculture (USDA). This struggle took place at the same time as important technological changes in food production and delivery were remaking rural America. Just as agriculture underwent a dramatic productivity revolution that changed the face of American farming, marketing, new home appliances, and increased participation in the labor force by women radically changed the kinds of food Americans ate. The consumption of processed foods increased significantly, and, concomitantly, concern about the purity of those foods increased as well. (Food purity was central to the "guinea pig muckraking" discussed in Chapter 3.)

The combination of these trends with the agencies' turf conflicts created the conditions in which powerful parties with conflicting interests in pesticide policy would have clashed regardless of whether Carson had written *Silent Spring*. Institutional entrepreneurs at the FDA used public concern over food safety, and the processing industry's desire for protection from public perception of food safety threats, to gain advantages in its struggle for power with USDA. This conflict aided in the organization of environmental pressure groups already coalescing over opposition to publicly funded pesticide spraying. *Silent Spring* was one more expression of conflicts unleashed by larger changes in agriculture.

DDT provided a particularly convenient target for both the FDA and the nascent environmental pressure groups because it was in widespread use. Its ubiquity and cheapness meant there were few organized interests to defend it. As a commodity in the 1950s, DDT was a low-margin product that competed successfully with higher margin, less effective, and more dangerous products.[2] As a result, agricultural chemical producers had little interest in spending resources to protect DDT. The primary costs of restrictions on DDT were ultimately borne not by American agricultural interests but by residents of developing countries where malaria and other diseases are persistent problems. Being poor, nonwhite, and far away, those people had little influence in the debate over DDT. Indeed, some environmentalists ultimately argued against DDT's use even for malaria control precisely because it lowered death rates in developing countries.[3]

In this chapter, we first sketch out the larger changes in agriculture and federal regulation of agriculture that set the stage for the debate over DDT in the late 1940s and 1950s. We then use the record of hearings held in 1950 and 1951 to explore how the competing interests at FDA and USDA used the issue in their larger struggle for control over the growing processed food market. Finally, we use these materials to put *Silent Spring* into a broader context, showing how conflicts over pesticides in the 1950s helped position *Silent Spring* to create a movement. Carson was not a voice in the wilderness; she had powerful allies in government and industry. We conclude by fitting this explanation into economist Bruce Yandle's "Bootleggers and Baptists" theory of regulation.

The Second Agricultural Revolution

Farms in 1930 were not much different from farms 50 years earlier.[4] Productivity had slowly improved through better tools and better crops, but tractors would not outnumber horses and mules until 1950.[5] Most farms were diverse operations. Many farmers produced much of their own food and sold the surplus eggs, butter, milk, chickens, vegetables, and other products to local customers and retailers, as well as raising a primary cash crop.[6] This changed rapidly after the war, as increases in "the efficiency of production in almost every specialized area of agriculture and marketing of foods made it cheaper to buy almost any type of food than to grow one's own."[7] Even for farm families, commercial food processing replaced much of the home processing previously used to store food for the winter, partly as a result of increased labor force participation by women during the war.[8] An even faster transformation occurred in urban areas. Sixty-five percent of food sold at retail was partly or fully processed by 1940, rising to more than 80 percent by 1960, making food processing one of the nation's largest industries.[9] One measure of the expansion was the spread of frozen foods. Frozen foods were limited in the 1930s, in part because of a lack of freezers in stores and homes. By 1944, over 70 percent of households had refrigerators and freezers, and "frozen foods were widely accepted."[10]

Just as the market for farm products was shifting as food processors became the primary buyers of farm output, the labor shortages resulting from the war led to "a virtual explosion in production per acre and per worker."[11] Labor productivity in agriculture grew almost three times as fast as labor productivity in manufacturing from 1950 to 1970;[12] total factor productivity growth after 1935 rose at six times the rate from 1900 to 1930.[13] This growth resulted in part from the post-war recovery's luring of labor out of agriculture, which spurred further efforts to substitute capital for labor.[14] In the 30 years after World War II, only communications, electrical machinery, and chemicals surpassed agriculture's productivity growth.[15]

The revolution in agricultural productivity was driven by the spread of mechanical equipment, vastly increased fertilizer use, improved crops, and the new insecticides, herbicides, and fungicides widely available after World War II.[16] These were not accidental innovations. Beginning in World War I, a "formidable dual system" promoted innovation in agriculture, with public institutions funding research[17] and training agricultural engineers and private manufacturers turning these inputs into improved technology.[18] Major companies such as Hercules invested heavily in developing synthetic pesticides in the 1930s.[19] Mechanization freed the 72 million acres used for work animal feed crops in 1910 for other crops.[20] Increases in fertilizer production during and after the war meant that, "for the first time in human history, the average farmer could grow crops on the same fields year after year."[21] By the end of World War II, there had been a widespread "chemical revolution" in agriculture.[22] This revolution helped agriculture expand on the intensive production demanded by war needs.[23]

The chemical revolution was a critical part of broader changes in agriculture. In the 1920s, both public research institutions and private manufacturers "assumed greater authority in determining biological and chemical resources (seed, chemical fertilizers, pesticides) and for new machinery (tractors, combines, and mechanical corn pickers). In part, this was spurred by discoveries during World War I of the pest-killing properties of substances manufactured as explosives and for gas warfare."[24] As a result, from 1920 to 1940, farmers began to shift their focus: "they dwelled less on questions of innovation and more on problems of adoption."[25] Thus, just as farmers' markets were changing to meet the rising demand from food processors, the source of agricultural productivity increases was shifting from farm to laboratory.

The new technologies from the labs transformed how crops were produced. For example, post–World War II herbicides allowed dramatic reductions in labor by eliminating the need to cultivate row crops for weed control. "For corn, herbicides raised production more than had hybridization. Farmers could now reduce the width of corn rows from three feet or more to as little as twenty inches, in some cases almost doubling production."[26] Aerial crop dusting—a technology pioneered about 1921—made widespread use of pesticides possible in many more crops than hand sprayers had allowed.[27] By 1926, aerial spraying of several thousand acres of potatoes threatened by pests accomplished with just two pilots, a mechanic, and a single plane what would have taken 2,000 ground workers.[28] By the early 1950s, more than 5,000 airplanes were involved in aerial spraying.[29]

This revolution in agricultural technology meant that the 1950s were a time of significant change in American agriculture. Farms grew larger, used less labor, and sold to large commercial buyers rather than consumers or local stores. Growing a crop involved new seeds, new fertilizers, new herbicides, and new insecticides. Not only was agriculture more mechanized than before the war, production was becoming a sequence of complex, interrelated decisions about appropriate application rates of fertilizers and pesticides. Livestock operations were undergoing similar changes, as large commercial feedlots displaced smaller farm-based operations.[30] Similarly, farmers' relationships with the market and the government were also changing. Such shifts create uncertainties, in which policy entrepreneurs have openings.

Regulating Agriculture

Prior to the New Deal, the federal role in agriculture was largely limited to support for research intended to boost productivity.[31] But farmers were unhappy with this limited role and had been lobbying to change that focus for more than a decade. While *farms* in 1930 were not much different from farms 50 years earlier, *farmers* in 1930 were better organized politically than farmers had been in 1880. In particular, falling agricultural prices after World War I prompted agricultural interests to organize politically in search of "parity" in prices, that is, a price level for their crops relative to other goods (especially those they bought) that was the same as during the "golden era" of 1910–1914.[32] The formation of a powerful, bi-partisan "Farm Bloc" in Congress after World War I was one of the more visible results of increased focus on politics by agricultural interests.[33] In a short period, the Farm Bloc passed "the Packers and Stockyards Act, the Futures Trading Act, the Agricultural Credits Act of 1921, amendments to the Federal Farm Loan Act, the Capper-Volstead Cooperative Marketing Act of 1922, and the Agricultural Credits Act of 1923," before splitting during bitter battles over the McNary-Haugen bill[34] that sought to bring prices back to pre–World War I "parity."[35]

While the split temporarily reduced farm interests' clout in Congress, the Farm Bloc's successes gave powerful evidence of farmers' political clout when they did agree. Further, many of the new agricultural programs themselves prompted additional organizing efforts. For example, the Farm Board created by President Herbert Hoover in 1930 had a director representing each major crop and a staff distributed around the country whose job was to organize farmers into cooperatives and cartels to boost farm income.[36] Government efforts at promoting political organization by farmers predated even the Farm Bloc. USDA had begun efforts to organize farmers in 1914, attempting to create an analogue to a chamber of commerce for agriculture. In 1917, it called a meeting of all farm organizations that led to the creation of the National Board of Farm Organizations and an early attempt to create a "national rural policy."[37] Such efforts further encouraged political organization by helping farm interests coalesce into organized groups.

By the time Franklin Roosevelt was preparing to take office, agricultural interests were powerful enough that he directed that whatever program his underlings designed for agriculture, it be one that was acceptable to farm interests.[38] One measure of agriculture's clout was that the task of writing production codes for agriculture was given to USDA rather than the National Recovery Administration.[39] The regulatory program that emerged still shapes agricultural policy today in two important ways.[40]

First, New Deal agricultural policy furthered organization among farm interests, requiring farmers to join local groups to participate in programs under the Agricultural Adjustment Act of 1933 and putting AAA offices in "every farming county in America."[41] Moreover, because the "confusing array" of agricultural programs adopted during the New Deal had no guiding principle,[42] interest group politics could be given free rein. There were thus good reasons for farmers to pay close attention to politics: "by the 1930s, the USDA was one of the largest governmental agencies in the world and was the most powerful one for a single occupational interest. In 1931, it had 25,000 employees . . ."[43] As historian Paul Conkin summarized,

> In no period of American history has the federal government undertaken so many initiatives or inaugurated so many programs to aid one economic sector. Farmers received payments for cutting production and subsidies to carry out necessary conservation practices; they received price supports for five basic commodities and crop insurance as a form of disaster relief. In fact, the sheer number of new programs still confuses most historians, just as they confused the legislators who approved them and the farmers who benefited from them.[44]

Second, the New Deal married farm incomes to government policy. By giving the federal government a major role in determining commodity prices, it created a powerful alliance between USDA and farm constituencies. This alliance's efforts at promoting higher prices through programs that gave farmers incentives to produce more intensively expanded the use of pesticides dramatically. The one constant in the farm policies inaugurated by the New Deal was the tying of participation to production levels. As a result,

> [p]roduction controls made it more difficult for small farmers to compete with larger ones, and larger and more efficient farmers gained the greatest benefits from farm policies. In the long run, the most enduring benefits of price-raising subsidies were an increase in the value of farmland and an even greater importance for base acres. One long-term effect of this product-based system was a tendency for small, less competitive farmers to leave agriculture, often selling their land to more commercially successful neighbors. At the same time, the large and expanding Department of Agriculture, despite internal battles, continued to cater to its prime constituency—the most affluent and capable farmers.[45]

The labor shortages produced by World War II furthered this movement and reduced federal investment in efforts to keep people on the land[46] as well as generating ever more opportunities for lobbying.[47] As farms got larger, technology improved the ability to increase yields. This was reinforced by the many farm policies that encouraged intensive production such as the 1950s Soil Bank, which limited the land farmers could use, encouraging more intensive cultivation of their remaining acreage.[48]

As a result, by the 1950s the federal government's relationship to agriculture was different than it had been in 1930. The USDA now played a major role in determining farm income through its many programs, federal agencies were significant sources of farm credit, and federal policies reinforced trends toward larger farms focused on commodity production.[49] Further, both public- and private-sector research provided agriculture with a steady stream of technological improvements that continued to raise productivity. Finally, consumers' preferences for high standards of appearance in produce also pushed farmers toward greater chemical use.[50] In response to these changes (and partially a cause of them), agricultural interests were well organized politically and paid close attention to the federal policies that played such an important role in determining their income. The early 1950s were marked by constant struggles over the level of price support the federal government would provide.[51] Moreover, constant increases in production as a result of subsidies during the fifties drove farmers toward more intensive techniques in efforts to maximize yield.[52] This kept farmers in a "cost-price squeeze" and heightened the importance of federal assistance, focused on those USDA thought most likely to succeed.[53]

The creation of a powerful federal agency dealing with agriculture and the transformation of agriculture into an area of the economy dependent on federal policy did more than create incentives to speed the transformation of a nation of small farms using animal power to produce a broad range of products into a nation of large farms relying on mechanical power, fertilizers, and pesticides to produce single crops. It transformed many agricultural decisions into political questions, to be settled (at least in part) through bureaucracies and legislatures rather than in the marketplace. As USDA's size and budget grew, and rural populations continued to shrink, farm interests developed a growing interest in making alliances with nonfarm interests to protect the farm programs that had become a key source of farm income.[54] Pesticide issues became a part of this politicized and rapidly changing landscape.

The Growth of Pesticide Use

DDT played its first major role in World War II, sparing servicemen and civilians from scourges of pests, such as mosquitoes and lice, and the diseases they carry, such as malaria and typhus. As Donald Roberts and Richard Tren explain in this volume, immediately after the war, DDT was used for mosquito control both at home and abroad. Its use quickly expanded into agricultural pest control, where its combination of safety for humans, toxicity for insects, and low cost made it popular.[55]

DDT was not the first agricultural pesticide, of course. Insect pests had been problematic during the last half of the 19th century; many of these pests were non-native species that had been brought to North America by cargo and immigrants.[56] The most common solutions to pest problems were inorganic poisons, substances such as "Paris Green" (copper acetoarsenite) and lead arsenate.[57] By the 20th century, problems included the peddling of ineffective products by scam artists to unsuspecting farmers[58] and free-riding by some farmers, whose failure to spray their crops with effective insecticides allowed insects to harm their neighbors' crops.[59] To address effectiveness issues, federal and state governments imposed consumer protection regulations, most often requiring labels to disclose the active ingredients.[60] Free riding was addressed by mandatory spray laws in the Pacific Northwest.[61]

Those commercial insecticides developed in the 19th century and used before World War II required high enough doses that they could cause acute medical problems for people who ate food with pesticide residues still on them.[62] Because the effective ones were based on highly toxic chemical substances such as arsenic, farmers, consumers, regulators, and food processors worried about residues. This was a particular problem in the apple market, where high loss rates were common, especially for apples shipped from the Northwest to eastern and foreign markets. People wanted fruits free of worms, but worries about residues caused some governments to restrict the sale of sprayed crops not fully washed. For example, in 1925 two shipments of apples from the United States to London were rejected because of spray residue.[63]

Hence, farmers and food processors were aware of the potential problems posed by agricultural chemicals well before DDT appeared on the scene. James Whorton quotes an 1891 contributor to *Garden and Forest* who worried about the long-term impact of the use of "a most virulent mineral poison,"[64] a concern similar to Carson's worries over the aggregate impact of DDT. During the 1920s and 1930s, the medical profession took increasing notice of the dangers of the arsenical pesticides.[65] And in *100,000,000 Guinea Pigs*—discussed by Desrochers and Shimizu in Chapter 3—Arthur Kallet and Frederick Schlink devoted a chapter to the dangers of arsenic and lead residues and blamed the FDA for failing to be more aggressive. Similarly, *The American Chamber of Horrors*, authored by the FDA's information officer, included a chapter on "How Much Poison Is Poisonous?" which cast the FDA as heroically attempting to save children from foods with pesticide residues.[66]

Indeed, the new pesticides coming into use during World War II represented a step toward solving these problems, since they were not acutely toxic to humans and were applied at lower doses than earlier pesticides. DDT and other organochlorines[67] rapidly grew in use, as they appeared to be safe for both farmers and consumers as well as effective.[68] By the end of the war, DDT and the other

209

members of its chemical family had almost completely replaced most other insecticides in agricultural use.[69] Moreover, tax incentives for DDT production and federal money to build plants created a ready infrastructure for DDT when peace came.[70]

Not surprising, farmers loved the new generation of pesticides. As the USDA was fond of noting in its congressional testimony in the postwar years, damage to agricultural output from pests cost $4 billion a year, almost 1 percent of GDP at the time.[71] The new pesticides offered significant savings. For example, using DDT to control the horn fly increased milk and beef output by $45 million in the states that kept statistics on the matter.[72] Where DDT was used, the USDA estimated that cattle gained an average of 50 pounds more.[73]

While agricultural interests and the USDA focused on the benefits of increased productivity from the new pesticides, other agencies were less enthusiastic. Beginning in the late 1940s, both the Fish and Wildlife Service and the FDA began to raise questions about DDT and other new pesticides. Early FWS involvement is important to the *Silent Spring* story because Carson worked at FWS for many years, where she headed publications and developed a reputation as a science writer for the public. As Desrochers and Shimizu note, Carson edited some FWS publications that were critical of DDT. Although her own work about DDT appeared many years later, she was aware of negative views about DDT at a time when most people were still celebrating its benefits in agricultural use and the relief it provided to millions of people suffering from many diseases.

What Carson Saw

DDT received good publicity during the war. For example, *The Saturday Evening Post* titled one article "How Magic Is DDT?"[74] Prof. Edmund Russell of the University of Virginia concludes that hundreds of such articles "cemented DDT's reputation as a miracle worker."[75] But not everyone shared the popular press's enthusiasm. The day after Nagasaki was bombed, the FWS warned that "DDT is toxic to both human beings and animals."[76] The degree of the problem was not well understood, and tests were begun. A week after the surrender of Japan, Secretary of the Interior Harold Ickes and FWS Director of Wildlife Research Clarence Cottam both warned of damage to wildlife, beneficial insects, and crops from DDT use.[77] They asserted that even a single application could do significant harm to nature. While its benefits during the war may have warranted ignoring the side effects, that was no longer the case in peacetime. Cottam unsuccessfully sought to prevent DDT's release for civilian use until the FWS could assess its impact.[78]

In 1945, Carson wrote to *Reader's Digest*, proposing an article on FWS research about what DDT "will do to insects that are beneficial or even essential; how it may affect waterfowl, or birds that depend on insect food; whether it may upset the whole delicate balance of nature if unwisely used."[79] That same year, the Audubon Society (of which Carson was an active member) held a conference on DDT at which C. H. Curran of the American Museum of Natural History warned that the pesticide could "kill almost [all], if not all, cold-blooded animals."[80] In 1946, the FWS issued a "warning" that "care must be taken in applying DDT to field and forest areas if wildlife is not to be endangered."[81] Marine life—an area of particular concern to Carson, as Kaufman describes in this volume—was thought to be most at risk as high kill rates were observed among fish in ponds sprayed with DDT at multiple test sites. Carson wrote a series of articles for the *Baltimore Sun* "whose theme was often the same—marine ecologies in some state of crisis" while she worked at FWS.[82]

The agency's annual report for 1948 noted that its studies of DDT began in 1945 and that "it is unsafe to apply by airplane more than two pounds of DDT per acre if harm to birds, mammals, and amphibians is to be avoided."[83] For many years to come, the agency continued tests and lobbied for increased funding for tests of DDT and other pesticides.[84] By 1965, the agency was reporting that "amazingly small amounts of pesticides can kill shrimps, crabs, and other aquatic life," such as "one part of DDT in one billion parts of water."[85]

Meanwhile, the Public Health Service was singing in praise of the glories of DDT. The experience in World War II at controlling malaria, yellow fever, dengue, and other diseases was a wonder.[86] While not advocating willy-nilly use of DDT, the PHS saw huge potential benefits in extending its use. The PHS and U.S. Army issued a "Joint Statement of Policy" for the "Use of DDT for Mosquito Control in the United States," advocating spraying DDT on houses to kill adult mosquitoes, using it as a larvicide where it would not harm fish and wildlife, and applying it by aircraft in large areas when needed.[87]

A test spraying of 513 rural houses in the South noted the cost was only 74 cents per house, and the mosquito population remained reduced for months.[88] The PHS soon reported that "the highly effective insecticide, DDT powder, obtained through the Public Health Service, is being used to spray the workers [seasonal migrant workers who were often infected with lice] before they board the train in Mexico City [to come work in the United States]."[89] A year later, in 1946, a report from the new Communicable Disease Center (which replaced the Office of Malaria Control) noted that "the advent of DDT wrote a new chapter in the history of insect control, yet the surface of this important subject is barely scratched."[90] The next year the British reported success in ridding a prison of bed bugs by application of DDT: "It is . . . no mean achievement to obliterate bugs from an infested prison. . . ."[91]

Not unmindful of the criticism of injury to wildlife, the PHS did its own investigation of the impact on wildlife from spraying a swamp with DDT. The mosquitoes died but, presaging Rachel Carson, it reported in 1947 that bird "singing continued into July and August" after months of spraying.[92] In 1948, the PHS was reporting on the beneficial effects of aerial spraying with DDT in urban areas to reduce the population of flies.[93] In the 1950s, the PHS was still reporting health benefits from DDT spraying, such as in outhouses and in areas subject to flooding,[94] but more impressive in those years were many reports from around the world of the huge impact on disease control, especially malaria, from the spraying of DDT.[95] The effects were a near miracle from the viewpoint of public health experts.

Scrap among Agencies

FWS was casting doubt on DDT because of its impact on wildlife. Soon, and more important to the long-run debate, it gained a potent ally. The FDA claimed that the new pesticides had serious human health consequences, as described below. The FDA had begun as the Bureau of Chemistry within USDA, then changed its name to the Food and Drug Administration in 1930, and finally separated from USDA in 1940.[96] Solving a botulism outbreak in 1919–1920 (ultimately traced to a California packing plant) and ending sales of a new antibiotic that turned out to be fatal for some users in 1937 were high-profile successes for the agency.[97]

Even before DDT appeared on the scene, the FDA was heavily involved in pesticide residues, spending over a third of its budget on residue enforcement in 1933.[98] Food regulators generally had focused on residue issues—which became their "single most serious concern"—at least since a 1919 conference on the topic.[99] The 1925–1926 publicity in Britain over arsenic residue on American apples also prompted concern among exporters, who saw the potential for disaster.[100] That incident prompted the bureau to consider establishing a publicly acknowledged tolerance for residues; previously, the agency's tolerance levels had not been released to the public.[101] In 1927, the bureau convened a conference in Salt Lake City to discuss tolerances, which it hoped would settle the issue.[102] It did not.[103]

The residue issue gained additional traction when Assistant Agriculture Secretary Rexford Tugwell, a key member of Franklin Roosevelt's "brain trust," pushed the issue to the forefront after receiving a citizen complaint about the use of lead arsenate on food crops.[104] Moreover, there were other constituencies outside the shrinking population that earned its living in agriculture worried about chemicals in food. Organic farming entrepreneur J. I. Rodale launched the magazine *Organic Gardening and Farming* in 1942,[105] and his 1948 book *Pay Dirt* attacked DDT.[106] Indeed, Russell argues that investigations into charges of war profiteering during World War I transformed chemical companies generally into "iconographic 'merchants of death'" for much of the public by the 1930s.[107] Consumers might not have wanted to grow their own organic tomatoes, and welcomed the convenience offered by the new processed foods, but the postwar years were also the time when protoenvironmentalist books such as Fairfield Osborn's *Our Plundered Planet* (1948) and William Vogt's *Road to Survival* (1948) were best sellers (whose impact is discussed by Desrochers and Shimuzi in this volume), evidencing some broader disquiet among the general population.[108]

These concerns prompted the federal government to revisit its pesticide regulatory strategy after the war. One of the first battles was over the proper approach to investigating the scientific issues, and the National Academy of Sciences prevailed over USDA in the organization of the academy's Insect Control Committee. Particularly irksome to USDA was that the committee "was dominated by medical doctors and chemists who had specialized in chemical weapons" while entomologists were deliberately excluded as committee members.[109] USDA did not lose every battle, as it succeeded in shaping the 1947 Federal Insecticide, Fungicide, and Rodenticide Act (FIFRA) to its liking. The 1947 Act gave USDA primary control of pesticide regulation and focused on notification and informational labeling.[110] Crucially, the new statute did not mandate testing of substances before marketing, as the FDA had urged. Most importantly, Congress rejected the FDA's bid for control of the entire pesticide regulatory process. But FIFRA's passage did not end the struggle for regulatory turf. USDA had regulatory authority that the FDA wanted. DDT and other chemicals would serve as a vehicle in that fight. And from the start of that struggle, while the FDA assailed many pesticides as dubious, it gave DDT special attention, as we discuss below.

The 1947 version of FIFRA required that product labels include the product name, name of maker or distributor, list of ingredients, net contents, warning about use, and directions for use.[111] USDA was given, but rarely exercised, authority to require testing to demonstrate safety when used as directed. In a minor victory for the FDA, the statute required USDA to consult with the FDA to determine if residuals on food were acceptable, as the presence of residuals could put a chemical, or at least certain uses of it, under the authority of the Federal Food, Drug and Cosmetic Act of 1938 (FFDCA). In practice, however, USDA rarely interacted with the FDA on pesticide issues.

The FDA did not abandon its quest for regulatory authority after its defeat by USDA in 1947. As early as 1949, FDA Commissioner Paul Dunbar argued that DDT's war use had been a "reasonably calculated military risk" but that the civilian calculus would be different.[112] The agency began a campaign to discredit USDA's administration of FIFRA. Bit by bit, FDA was successful, as the 1958 amendments to the Food, Drug and Cosmetics Act gave the FDA power to establish residual clearances for pesticides [113] so that, from that point forward, USDA had to coordinate registrations with the tolerances set by the FDA for food and animal feed crops.[114] The key with respect to DDT was not the final outcome but the dynamics of the struggle for regulatory authority, to which we now turn. Moreover, the FDA needed an issue on which it could win public support, because it had made powerful enemies in Rep. Clarence Cannon, a Mississippi Democrat, and Rep. John Taber, a New York Republican, both of whom sat on the House Appropriations Committee. In the mid-1930s,

Cannon—who raised apples—barred the FDA from spending money on investigating harmful effects of pesticide residues on humans.[115] In the 1950s, annoyed at the FDA's unwillingness to compromise on a label for canned beets to allow a company from his district to sell cut-up regular beets as "baby beets," Taber cut the agency's budget by 15 percent from 1951 to 1954.[116]

The House Select Committee Hearings

The House of Representatives passed a resolution in 1950 calling for an investigation into chemicals in food products and named Rep. James J. Delaney of New York as chair of the House Select Committee to Investigate the Use of Chemicals in Food Products.[117] Delaney chose Vincent A. Kleinfeld, the FDA's general counsel, to be the committee's chief counsel. Kleinfeld played an important role in pesticide law from this point forward. Not only did he co-found a law firm in 1953 that specialized in FDA-related law, he served as plaintiffs' counsel in the landmark (and unsuccessful) suit against DDT spraying on Long Island to control gypsy moths in 1957.[118] (Carson relied on materials collected by the plaintiffs in that suit in her research for *Silent Spring*.[119]) Kleinfeld's firm notes in its history that Kleinfeld served as counsel to the "Delaney Committee" and helped craft concepts incorporated into the FFDCA relating to pesticides, chemicals, and food additives.[120]

Kleinfeld masterfully ran hearings for the select committee, which received major coverage in the media as hearings moved around the country.[121] Agricultural interests were represented on the committee and, as we noted, powerful in Congress, and those members were fearful of costly regulatory controls that could limit farmers' access to useful chemicals or raise their costs, or could reduce USDA's authority. Kleinfeld was therefore constrained in his ability to directly challenge those interests. A frontal assault on USDA's authority would have been futile. Instead, Kleinfeld used USDA and agricultural witnesses' testimony to paint USDA as a biased agency beholden to agricultural interests and ignorant of the harms that were being inflicted on, or might be inflicted on, the public by the use of toxic chemicals that tainted food. The hearings effectively built a case that the FDA needed greater authority to protect the public from toxic risks by enhanced testing of chemicals present in the food production process.[122]

At the hearings, the assistant secretary of agriculture discussed the importance of chemicals in agriculture but noted USDA's concern that sprays should be safe.[123] The director of USDA's Plant, Soil, and Nutrition Laboratory discussed soil conditions around the country and agreed with Kleinfeld that organic farming could be productive and healthy.[124] Physicians from CDC and NIH discussed their concerns about DDT, attacking the USDA standard of five parts per million in foodstuffs as too generous given the lack of knowledge of safety for human consumption.[125] Witnesses noted that the *Journal of the American Medical Association* had discussed whether "Virus X," a health scare sparked by a New York physician's articles, could be caused by DDT poisoning.[126] A professor of medicine from the University of Cincinnati who focused on environmental health hazards testified that not enough was known about DDT, but that "it is probably responsible for such conditions as suicidal tendencies, aplastic anemia, pneumonia, leukemia, "Virus X", arteriosclerosis, and even cancer."[127]

Kleinfeld carefully built a case that agricultural chemicals should not be sold until proven safe and that DDT was the tip of the chemical iceberg.[128] His proposed remedy was for an "impartial board" of scientists to determine what should be allowed on the market[129] and to subject products to extensive premarketing testing, beginning with animal tests and then, for products that passed the first hurdle, human testing to search for safe exposure levels.[130] In short, Kleinfeld sought an FDA standard for agricultural chemicals that mimicked the FDA standards for drug approval. Without such standards, he argued, public health was threatened and, thereby, agriculture was threatened because of the possible backlash against chemically tainted foods.[131]

Agricultural representatives fought back. Dr. George Decker, the head of economic entomology at the Agriculture Experiment Station, University of Illinois (a major land grant university), testified that while about 200 farmers were killed every year, and 300 debilitated, by farm machinery in Illinois alone, none had ever died from chemicals used on farms and FIFRA regulations were adequate safeguards.[132] He noted that most food shipment seizures ordered by the FDA were due to insect infestations, not excessive levels of spray residue.[133] Kleinfeld responded that just because there was no evidence of current deaths from DDT and other pesticides, that did not mean pesticides did not cause "chronic illnesses" that had not yet been discovered.[134] Foreshadowing one of Rachel Carson's main themes (see Meiners, in Chapter 6, reviewing cancer evidence), a committee member noted that the incidence of cancer was rising in the United States over time and speculated that there "might be a connection between some of these insecticides and chemicals being used."[135] Kleinfeld cited a British scientist who stated that DDT and other insecticides upset the balance of nature (another key theme in *Silent Spring*; as discussed by Gregory in Chapter 7),[136] and asked the witness if there should not be extensive testing of all chemicals before use.

Dr. Decker addressed several key issues. Americans had come to expect quality produce. Not only did that expectation dominate the market, it was part of the law. The public "will no longer accept the old scabby apple or the wormy apple. When you and I were young the worm had to look out for himself when we ate an apple. Today, the Department of Agriculture would not let that apple move in interstate commerce. As a matter of fact . . . the Food and Drug Administration could take action on an apple moving in interstate commerce because it had a worm in it."[137] As to Kleinfeld's assertion that new chemicals should be tested for perhaps 15 years before being certified for use, Decker replied that the notion was good in theory but not in practice. "Such would be desirable, but such is utterly prohibitive and impossible. If every new and potential chemical that may be valuable as a pesticide . . . had to have fifteen years of study we would never have a new chemical introduced."[138] In fact, chemicals were field tested by scientists, just not under such prohibitive conditions. As to the claim that insecticides upset the balance of nature, Decker stated that the result, even if a chemical was worse than anticipated, was not catastrophic. There was no evidence that such a problem had happened. "But if I wiped out every insect in an entire county in my state this year, every insect beneficial and bad . . . next year or the year after, the population would be approaching normal, and within five years the balance would be right back where it started."[139] Nature is tougher than city folks might think.

Arguments at the hearings went back and forth. Agriculture experts from various colleges generally defended the then-current practices and cited evidence that DDT and other sprays were not harmful to humans as currently used. A Utah State professor testified that evidence from rat studies showed that DDT at high levels is harmless. A member of the committee blasted the notion, saying that rat studies did not mean that DDT was not harmful to humans.[140]

The attack on DDT was weakened by evidence from agriculture researchers which showed that DDT was not present in food products consumed by humans. Kleinfeld countered this point with testimony from a junior researcher from a new organization, the Texas Research Foundation (TRF). Although numerous senior researchers from universities and USDA had testified that DDT residue in plant and animal foods was consistently within the 5 ppm level believed to be safe, a TRF representative with a recent master's degree from Oklahoma A&M University (now Oklahoma State) reported DDT levels up to 14 ppm in milk and up to 69 ppm in beef.[141] Furthermore, he testified that DDT was absorbed into cereal crops such as corn, making its way into many other foodstuffs. This testimony reframed the issue as how to resolve contradictory scientific evidence. Crucially, this testimony—cited for years to come—was buttressed by testimony from food processors, who expressed concern about toxins making their way into the products they sold. Beech-Nut worried that baby food could be tainted.[142] A lawyer representing numerous food processors noted a lack of effective regulation.[143] Not only was more publicly funded research needed, but standards like those employed by the FDA for drugs before approval should be employed.

A final theme in the testimony came from a representative of the organic farming community. An organic farmer testified that organic agriculture was an alternative that avoided the problem of toxic residues in food: "The use of poisons in the growing and processing of our foods has steadily increased until today millions of pounds of these poisons are used, of which a considerable amount is consumed by our people."[144] Tying organic agriculture to the commercial food processing industry, he reported that some food processors demanded organically grown crops so they would know there would not be chemical residue. Furthermore, he asserted that organic farming was better for the environment and sprays were unnecessary because nature was "in balance" on organic farms. Such techniques were viable, based on the example of French farmers, who he claimed had never used sprays.[145] Finally, the organic farmer repeated the concern that DDT caused "Virus X"[146] and accused agriculture colleges of pushing chemical use.[147]

The testimony cast the credibility of agricultural experts in doubt. For example, when a USDA poultry expert explained that chemicals used in and around egg-laying facilities did not get inside the shells and any residues were generally washed away in cleaning, the committee expressed skepticism about his certainty.[148] The next witness, a doctor from the American Cancer Society, testified that while rising U.S. levels of cancer were due partly to longer life spans, the increase might also have been caused by the millions of pounds of chemicals being used on crops.[149] Indeed, he even suggested that the chemicals used in growing tobacco might result in it causing cancer.[150] He concluded that, given the myriad risks, more research and regulation, especially by the FDA, was needed. This conclusion was echoed by a researcher from the National Cancer Institute.[151]

As the 19 days of hearings moved around the country, similarly conflicting testimony was presented. Agriculture representatives, while never opposed to more research, pointed to the lack of evidence of harm from current spray levels and the great increase in output allowed by the use of sprays—not only increasing agricultural productivity but saving forests as well. They also noted that the new generation of sprays was clearly less harmful than the lead arsenates and other sprays used in previous years.[152]

Critics of agriculture widened the assault, raising the issue of hormone use in animal production. A scientist from Swarthmore called for a complete ban.[153] UCLA dermatologists agreed, saying that hormones were unsafe and extensive testing was needed because latency issues might exist that could not be known for years.[154] A medical professor from the University of Southern California testified that estrogen in animals could cause a sex change in people consuming such food products.[155] A California doctor reported that while he did not think estrogen caused cancer, it caused cancer to spread.[156] A scientist from the drug industry, testifying about the hormone issue, recommended expanded FDA powers to ensure public safety.[157] Other testimony on the issue was in conflict; there seemed to be no scientific consensus about the matter, but if the critics were right, the risks were substantial.

Witnesses raised multiple food safety issues. People were reminded of a mass poisoning at an Oregon state hospital in 1942 that killed 47 people.[158] Regular themes included the dangers of mislabeled products,[159] the need for the burden of proof of safety to be on manufacturers, the inadequacies of FIFRA, and the need for stronger FDA oversight.[160] Kleinfeld found an instance of a commercial chemical in use in agriculture that was not registered under FIFRA; this was evidence of sloppy USDA practice and, he noted, people die from improper use of chemicals.[161] Kleinfeld was not the only one concerned. Industry representatives from the National Canners Association and the Grocery Manufacturers Association testified about their concerns over chemical toxicity.[162] As the director of the National Canners Association Research Laboratories noted, "Industries are concerned primarily with the unavoidable presence of pesticide residues on certain crops."[163]

As the hearings drew to a conclusion in California, conflicts persisted. A University of California professor of agriculture testified that existing controls were sufficient; the FDA process would be too long and costly and, besides, FDA proceedings had all the fairness of a kangaroo court.[164] Kleinfeld attacked him, and others, who questioned the wisdom of expanded FDA control. He used witnesses from the cosmetics industry, who, his questioning implied, knew little about the scientific testing of the chemicals they were selling. The chemicals could be toxic, Kleinfeld regularly implied, citing, for example, the case of a woman who died during a hair permanent procedure in Georgia in 1941.[165] The hearings ended with a California allergist testifying that DDT and other sprays made people sick. He claimed people suffered from a strange lethargy after exposure and that DDT was particularly bad, present in the milk supply, and steps were needed to "protect our infants."[166] Committee chair Delaney went so far as to publish an article in *American Magazine* entitled "Peril on Your Food Shelf."[167] Ultimately, the hearings helped the FDA secure passage of a 1954 amendment to the Food, Drug, and Cosmetic Act, requiring inclusion of toxicity and residue studies in petitions to the secretary of Health Education and Welfare for permission to market a new pesticide.[168]

This review of the 1951 hearings illustrates three important parts of the saga of the regulation of DDT. First, it illustrates how prominent the criticisms of modern pesticides generally, and DDT in particular, had become soon after widespread use of these products began and long before *Silent Spring* crystallized these concerns.

The themes voiced in these criticisms continued into the 1960s and 1970s: the need for caution in adopting new technologies that affected the food supply, the promotion of organic farming as an alternative, and a reliance on scientific uncertainty created by an unwillingness to make judgments between any points of view that could marshal someone in a lab coat to defend it. Stories about "Virus X" or a strange lethargy, put forward by witnesses with weak credentials seemingly counted equally with the views of the agricultural establishment and thereby served as a basis for caution. The testimony suggested science was in conflict. At a minimum, there should be more money for research, and extensive federal oversight might be warranted.[169] The committee gave a junior researcher at an unknown Texas foundation the same credibility it gave many experienced scientists with more impressive credentials. The committee treated impracticable ideas, such as reliance on lower-productivity organic farming techniques, as worthy of consideration. *Silent Spring* was the most noteworthy attack on DDT and pesticides through 1962, but virtually all of the criticisms it made were well developed and being articulated more than a decade earlier.

Second, powerful interests within the government saw pesticides as an important issue long before *Silent Spring*. Considerable attention has been paid to USDA's promotion of pesticide use in the 1950s, including its subsidizing of public spraying programs aimed at eradicating pests like the fire ant and gypsy moth,[170] while FDA's role has not received as much. As the records of the 1950 and 1951 hearings demonstrate, Delaney and Kleinfeld were masters of congressional and regulatory techniques. They made a case for expanded FDA authority, which enhanced Delaney's power in Congress and Kleinfeld's authority as general counsel of FDA, which he would soon leverage in private practice. Indeed, Kleinfeld's questioning of the witnesses at the hearings foreshadowed his questioning of government witnesses in the 1957 Long Island case involving the spraying of gypsy moths.[171] This does not require imputing bad motives to them; we have no reason to doubt they believed in what they were doing. Rather, the point is that their beliefs were aligned with their career interests. The result was that Delaney and Kleinfeld laid important groundwork for *Silent Spring* by stoking the public's fears of the new technologies.

221

Third, food processing companies were crucial players in the debates over pesticides. Organic farmers, a few researchers, and individuals who feared "Virus X" would not be a sufficient constituency to attract much congressional attention, and the millions who had bought *Our Plundered Planet* or *Road to Survival* were not yet organized into an effective political constituency, as they would be by the end of the 1960s. Beech-Nut and other food processors were rightly concerned about the issue. If, in fact, toxins were present in foodstuffs, food processors would be the main defendants as easily identifiable parties with deep pockets. Not only was food processors' liability for contaminated products well-established in American tort law,[172] but the issue was receiving attention in the legal press.[173] Moreover, getting chemicals out of the food supply was costly. At the hearings, Beech-Nut reported that it spent $668,000 over six years (more than $5.5 million in today's dollars) removing pesticide residue from baby foods and peanut butter.[174] The director of toxicology for Swift & Co., a major brand name meat packer, supported more controls: "It is my opinion that any food processor proposing to incorporate a new nonfood material into a food product that is to be made for commercial use should be required to pretest such a material to assure adequate evidence of innocuousness in the human dietary."[175] And the new FDA commissioner appointed in 1954 focused on cultivating the industries regulated by the agency, in an effort to build support for the agency. As his deputy put it, "in order to administer a regulatory law, the regulator has to have a constituency; he has to have someone who will back him before Congress."[176] The 1959 controversy over cranberries contaminated with aminotriazole—a controversy that Carson biographer Mark Lytle says Carson followed "[d]ay by day . . . especially the fortitude shown by HEW Secretary Arthur S. Flemming in the face of hostile industry reaction to the ban"[177]—drove the issue home to the food processors.

Although tighter controls on pesticides could mean higher agricultural prices paid by food processors, they appeared to prefer to reduce the likelihood of tort litigation and the possible damage to their brands that litigation could cause. For example, Beech-Nut was a major food processor. Even one story that babies were poisoned by pesticide residues in their baby food, let alone a successful suit, could cause sales to collapse.[178] All industry, and consumers, would pay higher prices if input costs rose, but as long as everyone in the industry shared the cost, the impact on profits would be minimal. Moreover, the larger firms were the ones with the most at stake, and they were the firms that testified at the hearings.[179] Regulations can be costly, but in almost all regulatory experiences, large firms have an easier time bearing the costs than smaller competitors.

Why Was DDT the Primary Target?

DDT was the first, and most widely used, of the new class of insecticides discovered around the time of World War II. That alone made it a logical target. Moreover, unlike many other chemicals used only in agriculture, DDT's nontoxicity for humans meant that it was widely used in insect control programs outside rural areas— as Carson highlighted in *Silent Spring*—making it highly visible to those not directly involved in agriculture and so lacking a direct economic benefit from its use. Farmers, on the other hand, who were profiting from the new pesticides, and whose regular contact with them provided personal experience that contradicted claims like those about "Virus X" and other ills would prove to be a much more difficult audience for pesticide critics throughout the battles over pesticides.

While DDT use was extensive, its use in the United States peaked in 1959, well before *Silent Spring*;[180] DDT production peaked in 1962, the year the book appeared. Production dropped 40 percent by 1966, and domestic use fell by half between 1958 and 1966.[181] By 1966, DDT, toxaphene, and aldrin, members of the same chemical family, constituted just half of the pesticide market. One reason was that pesticide producers preferred alternatives because newer products had intellectual property protection that increased profits. In contrast, the World War II bargain between the military and pesticide producers to secure sufficient production of DDT to meet military needs included grants to multiple companies of the right to produce it,[182] reducing those companies' incentive to invest heavily in DDT's defense. The five major DDT producers[183] would suffer lost sales of DDT from restrictions on DDT, but as makers of substitutes, they would gain sales of their more profitable proprietary products. The substitutes were more costly than DDT, which was one reason farmers had not previously switched to such alternatives.

These tradeoffs were recognized during the later fight over banning DDT. For example, USDA reported in 1970 that the ban meant winners and losers in the industry.[184] A few years later, reviewing the ban on DDT, the Environmental Protection Agency concluded that the largest impact was on cotton.[185] The 1975 EPA review concluded that DDT was still in use on 17 percent of cotton farms in 1971 and that those farmers doubled their pesticide cost by 1973 as a result of the ban.[186] So certain farmers suffered greater economic injury than others, but the impact was not draconian, as pesticide cost was estimated to be just 5 percent of the production cost of cotton.[187]

There are costs and benefits to any change. The new generation of more costly pesticides that replaced DDT and its chemical siblings were short lasting, so the problem of residual effect was lessened, but were more potent at the time of application. USDA reported that the new pesticides were more dangerous to the users and would cause increased injury to wildlife and to beneficial insects at the time of application.[188] The new insecticides were more costly, in part because of the more stringent permission process. As early as 1970, only 1 in 1,800 new compounds tested made it to market after years of research.[189] "The requirements for registering new pesticides are likely to increase. This would tend to reduce the competition in the pesticide industry. On the other hand, the markets for new products created by banning organocholorines would be attractive to manufacturers."[190]

DDT's most important use was in mosquito control in anti-malaria programs, as described in detail by Roberts and Tren in Chapter 8. Carson barely mentioned its public health use in *Silent Spring*. This may have been partly because the primary public health uses by that time were in Africa, Asia, and Latin America, out of sight of Carson and her readers. Indeed, by the time of the ban, most of the DDT produced in the United States was exported. At no point in the debate over DDT begun by *Silent Spring* was there more than passing discussion of DDT's huge impact in reducing malaria and other scourges. One reason was that foreigners suffering from malaria do not vote in U.S. elections. Even taking this into account, there was less sympathy for the foreign ill and dying than might be expected, given the commitments the United States made during the same period to development aid, the Marshall Plan, Food for Peace, the Peace Corps, and other programs that were at least nominally aimed at improving the lives of nonvoters. The ugly truth is that the writers who were articulating nascent environmentalism in the late 1940s and early 1950s saw overpopulation as an overriding threat and so were harshly critical of the use of DDT precisely *because* it would save lives.[191]

Finally, again and again, while organochlorides were condemned as a group, DDT was held up for special attention by Kleinfeld and others. While other sprays of the same chemical group, such as aldrin, were used in agriculture as much as DDT and seemed to have the same environmental characteristics, there may have been an element of marketing involved in singling out DDT. "DDT" is simple. "Organochlorides" does not have much of a ring to it. And while "chlorides" may sound suspicious, "organo" sounds, at least to ears today, like "organic," which is "good," like organic farming.

Putting the Battle over DDT in Context

Silent Spring may have been the spark that ignited the modern environmental movement, but it was one of many sparks thrown off by the post–New Deal realignment of American agriculture. The industry had moved from multicrop, relatively small, non-capital-intensive operations using traditional agricultural methods and selling in local markets into monocrop, relatively large, capital-intensive operations using modern techniques, selling to commercial food processors, and dependent on federal programs for portions of farm income. The combination of this transformation and the parallel transformation of the American diet created conditions under which interest groups both inside and outside the federal government sought advantages.

Inside the government, USDA and its farm-state allies engaged in high stakes battles for resources and control over agricultural policy. As part of that conflict, they had to contend with the FDA and its allies' efforts to expand their authority. DDT, in particular, and pesticides, in general, provided the FDA coalition with a useful tool with which to assert a claim to authority, playing off popular concerns over chemicals and the uncertainties created by the transformation of agriculture. Those battles—illustrated by the hearings we described—both reacted to and expanded public concern

225

about food safety and the role of pesticides in agriculture, laying important groundwork for *Silent Spring* as well as likely introducing Carson to the topic through her work at FWS. Outside the government, the food processing industry sought a safe harbor against the impact of possible contamination both on sales and in tort actions.

The economist Bruce Yandle coined the term "Baptists and Bootleggers"[192] to explain how interest alignments among otherwise opposing or nonaligned groups could facilitate regulation. Traditional models of regulation posited that regulations emerged because they were in the "public interest" or, in the alternative, they evolved because politicians had been "captured" by economic interests. Yandle posited that some voters support regulatory controls that have no particular economic benefit to them but do provide economic benefits to others. He developed a model of unwitting political cooperation among divergent groups in support of particular regulatory measures. The name he gave the phenomenon, for purposes of alliteration, not disparagement, came from Baptists who support restrictions on the sale of alcoholic beverages on Sunday. They support such regulation for the good of society. But such legislation has hidden supporters, the bootleggers, who earn their living by skirting the regulations that make their livelihood possible. The two groups have nothing in common and do not explicitly cooperate, but their different interests combine to strengthen the incentives for politicians to regulate. One group has a publicly acceptable interest but insufficient clout to achieve its aims; the other group has an economic interest but lacks a publicly acceptable justification for action. Both provide political support for regulations that limit certain economic activity that would otherwise occur.

The creation of a coalition that ultimately would succeed in obtaining a federal ban on DDT in 1972 had aspects of a bootleggers and Baptists coalition. Environmentalists were the "Baptists." Pesticide manufacturers, looking to move beyond generic products such as DDT, played the role of the bootleggers, accepting enhanced regulatory authority by the new EPA as the price of creating significant barriers to entry in order to protect their markets. USDA ceded environmental authority to EPA but preserved its larger agricultural policies. That is not to suggest that the battles over DDT in the late 1960s and early 1970s were not heated and intense, for they were. But the ultimate resolution—by Richard M. Nixon, the politician to whom environmentalists ought to award the title "greatest environmental president" for his role in creating EPA, the Clean Air Act of 1970, the Clean Water Act of 1973, and the Endangered Species Act of 1973—largely disadvantaged poor malaria victims in Africa and had relatively little impact on American farmers.

At the risk of mixing metaphors, the future "Baptists" were still wandering in the wilderness in the 1950s. As we have shown here, it was the FDA and its congressional allies' efforts to expand their authority that helped bring the dispersed interests opposed to pesticide use together around DDT as an issue. There is no doubt that policy entrepreneurs in Washington saw *Silent Spring*'s publication as an opportunity. For example, Interior Secretary Stewart Udall, soon to author his own environmental classic, *The Quiet Crisis*,[193] "assigned a member of his staff to track the book's reception and report ideas for future policy initiatives."[194] Continuing Yandle's metaphor, Rep. Delaney and his general counsel played the roles of Roger Williams and John Clarke, the originators of the Baptist denomination in America.[195] Their work prepared the way for Carson and *Silent Spring*, whose impact on environmentalism can be analogized to the religious Great Awakenings of the 18th and 19th centuries. And no doubt policy entrepreneurs in Washington saw *Silent Spring*'s publication as an opportunity. We thus offer an addition to Yandle's theory, illustrating how regulatory "Baptists" can come into being as a result of policy entrepreneurs' efforts.

Silent Spring is properly credited with a major role in changing Americans' attitudes toward the environment. But the context of the changing nature of American agriculture and the conflict for regulatory authority between USDA and the FDA also suggests that *Silent Spring* was as much an expression of those changes and struggles as it was an innovation.

10. The False Promise of Federalization

Jonathan H. Adler[1]

Coupled with other seminal environmental events of the 1960s, *Silent Spring* fueled the push for federal environmental regulation. Many hoped the federal government would be a more vigilant guardian of environmental concerns than the states had been. Shifting regulatory authority to the nation's capital was not an unmitigated environmental advance, however. State and local environmental efforts preceded federalization and were often based on localized knowledge and ecological insight. Uncle Sam did not always have the greenest thumb, particularly when compared to alternative policies based on the concerns of those most affected by environmental problems.

Pesticide regulation began long before publication of *Silent Spring*. The first generation of laws governing "economic poisons," as pesticides were called, focused on protecting producers from "unfair" competition and consumers (i.e., farmers) from mislabeled or ineffective products. There was little concern about health, beyond general concern for excessive residues or "impure" foods. Later efforts put increased attention on residues and potential threats to farm workers, but policymakers largely ignored environmental effects. Carson's exposé helped change that, encouraging regulators, legislators, and citizen-activists to call for greater controls on agricultural chemicals in order to protect wildlife, ecosystems, and even human health. DDT, in particular, went from "miracle" to "menace" and began to symbolize the potential costs of uncontrolled pesticide use.[2]

Even before publication of *Silent Spring*, some state and local governments were attuned to the environmental effects of excessive pesticide use. Though far from perfect, state and local policymakers were often more environmentally protective than federal officials— and the federal government was not particularly protective until prodded by federal courts. Congress and much of the administrative bureaucracy were responsive, if not beholden, to agricultural interests, and the pesticide industry was more than happy to centralize greater regulatory authority in Washington, D.C. Increased federal regulation did not automatically translate into increased environmental protection. As Carson herself recognized, state officials could be more attuned than were federal regulators to the ecological consequences of unrestrained chemical use on local environments.

Origins

Federal regulation of agricultural chemicals began at the dawn of the 20th century. Early federal regulations did not target environmental concerns. If anything, they sought to encourage pesticide use.[3] Early pesticides consisted of inorganic materials, such as copper sulfate or arsenic, which were relatively easy to produce.[4] Larger manufacturers feared that fraud would discourage farmers from purchasing and using pesticides, and some farm groups wanted greater assurances the "economic poisons" purchased by their members were as advertised.[5] As political scientist Christopher Bosso noted, "Farmers feared increasingly that their purchases might be ineffectual or outright dangerous, while chemical makers worried about 'unbridled competition' and less scrupulous competitors."[6] Federal regulation was a way to reduce the chaos of unbridled market competition to the benefit of incumbent firms.

In 1910, Congress passed the Federal Insecticide Act.[7] The law prohibited the sale of any misbranded or adulterated insecticide or fungicide in interstate commerce. The act was neither a public health nor an environmental statute.[8] It "made no specific reference to the possibility of injury to humans or domestic animals, nor did it require directions for use or caution statements."[9] In a similar vein, Congress had passed the 1906 Pure Food and Drug Act to protect the public from "impure" food and to protect food producers from "less scrupulous operators."[10] The Insecticide Act was not particularly controversial and prompted minimal debate, as it was directly responsive to the concerns of pesticide users and producers.[11]

For the next 30 years, federal regulatory efforts focused on protecting industry and agricultural interests more than the public; the environment was not even a concern. The Department of Agriculture had been formed in 1862 for the express purpose of promoting agricultural development, and as Meiners and Morriss discuss in the previous chapter, it continued to operate in this vein with the support of its congressional patrons. It sought to protect farmers and so did not make public its enforcement actions or safety concerns. For example, the agency warned apple growers in 1925 about the threat of "British sanctions against excessive arsenic residues on American fruit" but did not inform the press, let alone the public, lest public concern have a "chilling effect" on sales. And a 1937 USDA appropriations bill barred the use of funds for "laboratory investigations to determine the possibly harmful effects on human beings of spray residues on fruit and vegetables."[12]

Early State Action

The first state and local laws governing "economic poisons" predated federal efforts. In the late 19th century, some local health agencies policed food products and occasionally took action to remove adulterated or potentially harmful foodstuffs from the marketplace. In what may have been the first such action, the New York City Board of Health condemned 258 crates of grapes in 1891 after the discovery of pesticide residues sparked public concern.[13] Other local health boards began inspecting grapes from New York to make sure they were pesticide-free, and the grape market suffered until USDA officials declared that the residues, a combination of lime and copper sulfate, posed no risk to the grape-consuming public.[14]

Early state laws required manufacturers to register and label their products. A few states had laws regulating the sale of particular poisons prior to 1910.[15] California, for instance, adopted regulations governing Paris Green in 1901.[16] While states took the lead in adopting measures to protect consumers, few focused on environmental protection any more than the federal government did. In some cases, state or local governments actually required pesticide spraying to ensure effective regional pest control.[17] A few, however, adopted measures to control local spillovers from pesticide application.[18] States also did relatively little to address emerging concerns about the risks posed by pesticide residues on foods.[19]

As has often been the case in environmental policy, California was a far more aggressive environmental regulator than the federal government. California began requiring pesticide registrations in 1911[20] and revised the law in 1921 to incorporate early environmental concerns.[21] California's law required manufacturers to register all pesticides sold within the state with the director of agriculture. Among other things, the law also authorized the director of agriculture to revoke a pesticide's registration if the pesticide was found to be dangerous to public health or animals, even if used properly.[22]

In 1927, California began regulating pesticide residues,[23] and in 1949, California adopted legislation requiring pest control specialists and pesticide applicators to obtain state licenses.[24] This licensing role had previously been filled by local governments. Imperial County, for instance, imposed a pesticide permitting system in 1938 to protect other farmers and beekeepers from those using pesticides.[25] Even before World War II, amid growing concern about localized effects of agricultural chemical use, some local governments enacted measures in response.

FIFRA and Federalization

The federal government made little effort to regulate pesticides between passage of the Insecticide Act (1910) and the Federal Insecticide, Fungicide, and Rodenticide Act (1947). Congress held only two hearings on pesticides between 1910 and 1945.[26] However, both the use and production of "economic poisons" exploded after World War II. An estimated 22,000 pesticides were registered with USDA between the end of hostilities and 1950, and pesticide production increased approximately three-fold between 1945 and 1950.[27] With the increase in pesticide use and production came increased demand for government regulation—particularly from pesticide manufacturers.

Manufacturers opposed comprehensive regulation but "had long supported the modest regulatory system enacted in 1910, which allowed the sale of any product, no matter how dangerous, as long as it was honestly labeled." This regulatory system worked to the advantage of larger, more established producers and helped build confidence in the reliability of pesticide products. In the 1940s, the industry "had even lobbied Congress for increased appropriations so that the division could enforce the rules more effectively."[28]

One reason manufacturers sought greater federal regulation was to blunt state regulatory efforts. States were beginning to regulate "economic poisons" but not always in the same way. Industry found state regulations increasingly burdensome, particularly because the specific requirements or common law liability rules could vary from one state to the next.[29] By 1946, manufacturers claimed, pesticides were subject to 270 state laws across more than 30 states.[30] New federal legislation had the potential to relieve manufacturers of those burdens without imposing too many new requirements. Federal regulation could also further "screen out those fly-by-night operators who might sully the industry's reputation" and could help convince farmers that agricultural chemicals were a good investment.[31]

Thus, in 1947, Congress enacted the Federal Insecticide, Fungicide, and Rodenticide Act. Like the Insecticide Act it replaced, FIFRA was largely the product of negotiations among farm and chemical interests and the U.S. Department of Agriculture.[32] More than any other agency, USDA was concerned with promoting a single sector of the economy. USDA was "the farm community's earth mother and government nanny" and worked aggressively to safeguard agricultural interests.[33] The relevant congressional committees and subcommittees were also fully aligned with the interests of agriculture. Environmental concerns, as such, were not a major issue. The environmental movement of the time, still largely a conservation movement, was focused on other concerns such as wildlife, wilderness protection, and sustainable resource use.[34] As noted in earlier chapters, there were always organic farmers who opposed the use of chemicals, but they were swamped by the dominant agricultural interests that favored increased yields in a market increasingly dominated by large-scale operations.

Given the alignment of interests, it was no surprise the federal emphasis "remained almost entirely on providing economic protection for the commercial farmer, and reputable manufacturers."[35] FIFRA's express goals were to protect pesticide consumers by requiring useful and accurate labels, and "to protect the reputable manufacturer or distributor from those few opportunists who would discredit the industry by attempting to capitalize on situations by false claims for useless or dangerous products."[36] It was also intended to "serve as a model for future state laws."[37]

The 1947 law was, in many respects, "self-regulatory."[38] Pesticide manufacturers were required to label their products with the contents and use instructions, and those pesticides sold in interstate commerce had to be registered with USDA. Yet USDA lacked the resources or authority to investigate and analyze industry claims. Although registration was supposed to benefit consumers, pesticide manufacturers were not allowed to reference pesticide registration on product labels.[39] FIFRA authorized the federal government to deny pesticide registrations, but placed the burden of demonstrating the need for a rejection or cancellation on the federal government. Moreover, FIFRA specifically provided for "protest" registrations, under which manufacturers could continue to market pesticides the federal government had rejected unless the USDA sought criminal prosecution. Though rarely invoked, this provision almost certainly would have undermined USDA's regulatory authority—had it sought to exercise any.[40]

If the goal had been to protect public health or the environment, registration would not have been a particularly effective tool. As it was, the requirement's primary purpose was to further standardize the national pesticide market. In 1980, the National Research Council described the act as follows:

> The crucial assumption underlying FIFRA was that the major problem associated with the use of pesticides was their efficacy. The major basis for denying registration was that the label contained claims that differed from those made to the USDA. The only protection against undesirable effects of the pesticide to nontarget species and plants was afforded by the requirement that the label identify the pesticide as a poison. The USDA administered FIFRA on the assumption that efficacy was the major problem and, as a consequence, the bulk of the USDA's regulatory activity was concerned with ensuring that pesticides were labeled accurately. Few chemicals were barred from the market.[41]

FIFRA was not much more controversial than the law it replaced, and its passage escaped widespread notice. The New York Times ran a short, "innocuous" Associated Press item on page 26, noting that pesticide powders would be colored to prevent accidental confusion with benign products, such as baking powder.[42] The law was enacted by voice vote "without 'significant comment or debate,' reflecting the widely shared political perception that pesticide policy was mostly a matter of accommodating the interests of growers and the emerging chemical industry."[43] The public was simply not much concerned with pesticide policy at the time. Industry, however, was concerned. Pesticide producers were encouraged by the law, and invested heavily to expand pesticide production—nearly $4 billion between 1947 and 1949.[44]

Silent Spring

Awareness of the potential health and environmental costs of pesticide use was growing even before publication of *Silent Spring*. Yet Rachel Carson's book served to concentrate and focus that awareness, seizing on the public's sense of unease about emerging environmental concerns. *Silent Spring* challenged the prevailing, albeit waning, notions that pesticides were an unmitigated blessing and that the federal government invariably promoted the public good. Her writing prompted the creation of "a series of presidential commissions" and legislative hearings addressing concerns about the long-term health and environmental consequences of pesticide use.[45] Whereas public concern about pesticides had historically been confined to concerns about poisoned or "impure" foods, Carson's work broadened that focus to include potential effects on ecosystems and other species.

The book provoked substantial public debate and prompted some local protests against federal spraying campaigns, but it had relatively little immediate impact on law or policy. According to historian Thomas Dunlap, "Neither *Silent Spring* nor the subsequent public controversy over Carson's charges changed pesticide use and regulation in any significant way."[46] USDA scaled back some of its aerial spraying campaigns, but farmers and government agencies continued to use DDT and other suspect chemicals. Some members of Congress were spurred into action by Carson's call, but others—most notably those in charge of the relevant congressional committees, and the Agriculture Committees in particular—had little interest in revising federal pesticide law.

The controversy over DDT, to which *Silent Spring* contributed, may have helped build support for revising FIFRA in 1964, but the changes were exceedingly modest. The most meaningful change was the elimination of protest registrations. Pesticide manufacturers agreed to this reform in return for greater federal preemption of state regulation.[47] This was not much of a sacrifice on their part, as the protest provision was almost never invoked—in no small part because pesticide registrations were rarely suspended. It was a "symbolic change."[48] Further, the 1964 revisions granted pesticide manufacturers an alternative means of challenging adverse regulatory decisions.

Perhaps more significantly, Congress revised the definition of what constituted a "misbranded" pesticide to include substances that could injure nontarget species "when used as directed or in accordance with commonly recognized practice." This was a dramatic, if unintended, expansion. As one commentator noted, the new definition, if applied literally, "would have precluded the use of most pesticides," as virtually all such substances could have negative effects on nontarget species, even when used as intended. "Congress had never anticipated such a strict translation."[49]

The elimination of protest registrations did not sate the demand for increased environmental action. Newly formed environmentalist groups juxtaposed Carson's warnings with those made by other environmental authors and pointed to apparent environmental disasters to encourage greater legislative action, particularly at the federal level. Although Congress would not enact greater federal pesticide regulation, it could mandate other changes. For example, Congress authorized federal controls on air emissions from new motor vehicles (also supported by industry) and enacted the National Environmental Policy Act in 1969.

Relatively early in his presidency, Richard Nixon decided to burnish his environmental credentials. So, in 1970, he created the federal Environmental Protection Agency by Executive Order, relocating various environment-related responsibilities from other parts of the federal government. Among other things, responsibility for enforcing FIFRA was transferred from USDA to the newly formed EPA. This was potentially significant, as USDA had developed a reputation for being quite the lax regulator and for failing to review industry registration submissions with any diligence.[50] Nixon also proposed new federal pesticide legislation in 1971.

The debate prompted by *Silent Spring* largely ignored the state role in pesticide regulation, even if Carson herself did not. The book detailed numerous instances in which state and local officials or experts were more attuned to ecological concerns and the consequences of excess pesticide use than was the federal government. State conservation officials protested USDA's aggressive campaign to eradicate fire ants, while local forestry officials questioned federal encouragement of pesticide spraying to control Dutch elm disease.[51] "Effective and inexpensive methods of local control have been known for years," wrote Carson of the fire ant campaigns. USDA's "mass control program" was "the most expensive, the most damaging, and the least effective program of all."[52]

Testifying before Congress, Carson encouraged greater consultation with state officials and concurred with Senator Ribicoff that "local people" were often more knowledgeable about local needs and ecological conditions than federal authorities were.[53] Even before publication of *Silent Spring*, some local communities opposed the widespread spraying of DDT.[54] Some were even able to stop it. Nonetheless, most federal policymakers assumed solutions had to be found in Washington, D.C. The Mrak Commission, ignoring the fact that state environmental regulation often preceded federal action, simply asserted that "in all probability most State regulation will follow Federal guidelines and will likely be less demanding."[55] In fact, many states had enacted more stringent pesticide regulations than those in place at the federal level, and states were substantially ahead of federal efforts to account for the potential environmental effects of pesticide use.

Back in the States

As concern about the broader environmental impacts of pesticide use increased in the wake of *Silent Spring*, California again acted ahead of the federal government. The Golden State's pesticide registration law specifically imposed restrictions on the use of pesticides that had uncontrollable adverse environmental effects.[56] At the local level, officials in Imperial County imposed severe limitations on DDT use in 1961, and state-wide limitations were imposed in 1970.[57] California was hardly alone, however. By 1968, 47 states had registration laws, many of which were modeled on the Council of State Governments' "Uniform State Pesticide Act."[58] Even after the adoption of federal registration requirements, state regulators continued to argue that state registration was necessary "to permit consideration of local conditions and to impose more stringent requirements for the protection of public health and the environment."[59] California, for instance, barred the registration of any pesticide determined to endanger the environment.[60] Thirty-six states also had statutes governing pesticide use or application.[61]

States also began to act on DDT while the federal government pondered the problem. Many local communities objected to excessive and indiscriminate pesticide spraying, often conducted with federal encouragement. "Bans on DDT began to dot the national landscape," worrying industry.[62] Local activists in Wisconsin convinced officials in some towns to stop using DDT.[63] Eventually, attorneys from the newly formed Environmental Defense Fund joined them in seeking an end to DDT spraying. In 1969, the Wisconsin Department of Agriculture announced it would no longer recommend DDT use for control of Dutch elm disease.[64] Shortly thereafter, the Wisconsin Natural Resources Board decided it would no longer issue permits for DDT use during growing season.[65] That year the Michigan Department of Agriculture also cancelled most DDT registrations, largely in response to fears about high concentrations of DDT residues in fish.[66] Arizona also imposed a one-year ban on the agricultural use of DDT.[67]

New state efforts to control pesticide use were not limited to DDT. In the late 1960s and early 1970s, states continued to tighten regulation of pesticide sale and use. In 1971 alone, more than a dozen states enacted pesticide laws of varying scope and strength, including several statutes that included controls on pesticide application and otherwise sought to control the environmental effects of pesticides. New Hampshire, for instance, authorized its Pesticide Control Board to regulate or ban the use of pesticides that could harm nontargeted species, and Georgia imposed detailed reporting requirements to enable local officials to monitor environmental effects.[68]

While both the federal and state governments enacted registration laws, in the 1960s, laws governing the use and application of agricultural pesticides were still "peculiar to the states."[69] The precise requirements of these laws varied greatly from state to state. Some commentators found this "lack of uniformity" to be "disturbing," echoing the concerns of industry, even though some of the variation could explained "by the varying needs and desires of the people in different areas."[70]

One reason to be suspicious of early state regulation was that regulatory authority was typically bestowed upon state agricultural departments—as was true at the federal level. No federal environmental agency regulated the potential environmental effects of pesticides until President Nixon created the EPA in 1970. And while federal courts pushed EPA to take a more aggressive stance toward those pesticides with potentially harmful environmental effects, Congress did not mandate such measures until it amended FIFRA with the 1972 Federal Environmental Pest Control Act. Yet that act further limited state regulatory authority and, by some accounts, called for less stringent regulation than had been demanded by the courts. State regulators, some of whom had been working to control the harmful effects of pesticide use for decades, were not happy.[71]

State common law also provided remedies for improper or negligent use of pesticides, particularly by aerial spraying.[72] As a general rule, farm owners were liable for damage to others and others' property caused by negligent aerial spraying of their land.[73] Tort suits were successfully filed in various states for damage to crops, and even for harm to animals or wildlife.[74] Tort suits were not a perfect source of protection and did relatively little to sanction broader environmental damage, but liability seemed to "do a reasonably adequate job of protecting persons and property from injury" resulting from pesticide use.[75] State-level litigation was sometimes successful at stopping the use of DDT. Lawsuits filed by EDF halted the spraying of DDT in several Michigan municipalities.[76] Lawsuits in Long Island, on the other hand, failed, as Rachel Carson chronicled in *Silent Spring*.[77]

Taking DDT to Court

Litigation was a relatively new weapon in the environmentalists' arsenal. The Sierra Club had filed the occasional lawsuit in the 1950s and 1960s, but few yet saw the courts as a partner in programmatic policy change. That changed in the 1970s as new environmentalist groups emerged to bring legal actions against polluting industries and recalcitrant government agencies. Among these new groups was the Environmental Defense Fund, mentioned above, which grew out of failed local anti-DDT-spraying efforts on Long Island. EDF began a legal and publicity campaign against DDT and other agricultural chemicals shortly after it was formed.

EDF's actions began in the states, where it challenged local pest eradication programs and administrative support for DDT use. Most significantly, EDF arranged for an administrative proceeding in Wisconsin to consider whether DDT was a water pollutant. In effect, EDF put DDT on trials and was able to make its case in public.

Ultimately, however, unsatisfied with state-level actions—which were unpredictable and could only help one region at a time—EDF turned to the federal government.

In October 1969, EDF petitioned USDA to cancel all pesticide registrations for DDT, notice of which would trigger a series of administrative proceedings, and to immediately suspend all authorized DDT use pending the outcome of such proceedings. The Secretary of Agriculture initially refused to rule on the petition and instead issued a notice of cancellation for nonessential DDT uses. EDF sued and won, forcing the secretary to rule on the petition. He then denied the request for suspension, and EDF sued to overturn that decision in 1970.

By the time the U.S. Court of Appeals for the D.C. Circuit issued its opinion in *EDF v. Ruckleshaus*,[78] authority over pesticide registrations had shifted to EPA. This placed regulatory authority in the hands of a bureaucracy more willing to challenge agricultural interests. More important, the lawsuit had landed in a court willing to reinterpret FIFRA "to impose a major reassessment of pesticide policy."[79] For the first time, FIFRA was interpreted as a public health statute. Judge David Bazelon interpreted the 1964 FIFRA revisions to require EPA to initiate cancelation proceedings "whenever there is a substantial question about the safety of a registered pesticide."[80] In effect, Judge Bazelon's decision shifted the burden of proof to a pesticide's manufacturer to demonstrate that a pesticide was safe and effective once a question about a pesticide's safety had been raised.[81] As such questions had been raised about DDT, the court held, EPA was required to initiate cancellation proceedings for all remaining uses of DDT.

After the court's decision, EPA held several months of hearings, reviewing the relevant scientific evidence on DDT. The hearing examiner, Edmund Sweeney, initially concluded that the threat to humans or wildlife from DDT had not been demonstrated and that ample reasons remained to continue DDT use. EPA Administrator William Ruckleshuas disagreed with this conclusion, however, and cancelled DDT registrations for all agricultural and other non-health-related uses. Industry groups appealed, but to no avail.

From FIFRA to FEPCA

The decision in *EDF v. Ruckleshaus* increased the pressure for further legislative revisions to FIFRA. Agricultural interests and their congressional sponsors recognized that FIFRA reform was "inevitable."[82]

Industry was unhappy with the way federal regulatory requirements under FIFRA had been tightened by the courts and found judicial mandates too unpredictable.[83] A federal court had given environmental advocates a set of legislative controls that would not have passed Congress—at least not yet. The court had, in effect, given EPA authority to ban pesticides on the basis of unproven environmental risks; Congress intervened to ensure that such risks were balanced against the potential benefits of pesticide use.[84]

Congress enacted the Federal Environmental Pesticides Control Act to amend FIFRA in October 1972. The revisions extended federal authority to cover pesticides sold in intrastate commerce and explicitly instructed EPA not to register pesticides that posed unreasonable adverse environmental effects, though framing this standard in a way that ensured EPA would also consider a pesticide's benefits. Specifically, FEPCA defined "unreasonable adverse effects on the environment" as "any unreasonable risk to man or the environment, taking into account the economic, social, and environmental costs and benefits of the use of any pesticide." It further authorized EPA to impose additional restrictions on the use of some pesticides, mandated additional recordkeeping requirements, and called for EPA review of existing registrations. At the same time, FEPCA provided indemnification for pesticide manufacturers and applicators should they be stuck with unusable supplies after a decision to cancel or suspend a previously registered pesticide.

Although FEPCA was more explicitly directed at environmental effects than FIFRA had been, at least as written by Congress, it was not clearly more regulatory or precautionary than the D.C. Circuit's interpretation in *EDF v. Ruckleshaus*. Though often characterized as the result of a "republican moment" in Congress, motivated by *Silent Spring* and broader environmental concerns, FEPCA also represented a compromise and retrenchment, as it did not meaningfully enhance the federal government's regulatory authority at the expense of pesticide producers. FEPCA included language authorizing broader environmental regulation, but EPA was not given the funding necessary to implement such requirements.[85] As William Reukauf, a senior attorney who dealt with pesticides at the EPA explained, the General Accounting Office concluded in the 1976 that EPA lacked the data to fulfill its statutory mandates to regulate agricultural chemicals.[86]

FEPCA was not the last revision to FIFRA. In 1975, Congress amended FEPCA to address state and agribusiness dissatisfaction with EPA's attempts to take effective, forceful action to protect public health and the environment."[87] The legislative revisions of 1975 and 1978 were intended to force EPA to give more attention to the economic consequences of limitations on pesticide use and to restore some state flexibility.

Federalism Lessons

The rash of federal regulations adopted between 1969 and 1976 is often seen as an overdue federal response to the failure of state and local governments to provide adequate environmental safeguards. This is the standard fable of federal environmental regulation.[88] The historical record tells a different story. State and local regulations addressing environmental concerns ranging from urban air pollution to wetland development predated federal efforts—and were sometimes superior. Fear of stringent and potentially variable state standards often led national industry groups to support the centralization of environmental policymaking in Washington, D.C., particularly where federal action could preempt state legislative initiatives or common law tort liability.

The standard fable miscomprehends the history of pesticide regulation as well. State and local efforts were variable and inconsistent, but they largely preceded federal efforts to confront the potential environmental consequences of agricultural chemical use. Federal regulation was initially driven by industry concerns, not the protection of public health or the environment, and that history was hard to shake. Congress showed little inclination to adopt broad environmental controls on chemicals until well after state governments and the courts had taken substantial steps—and even then the legislative efforts were inconsistent.

That states were often ahead of federal regulators—and even more often ahead of federal legislators—at addressing the environmental consequences of pesticide use is not surprising. Local officials have greater access to local knowledge about ecological conditions and may be more attuned to emerging evidence of environmental harm. Particularly before policymakers became aware of the potential latent effects of pesticide spraying and the bioaccumulation of chemicals within humans and other organisms, state and local officials were likely to be more attuned to the practical effects of different approaches to pesticide use. As Carson herself noted, state and local officials often resisted federal spraying initiatives. Further, the potential consequences of pesticide use vary from place to place based upon a wide range of factors, including local geographic and environmental conditions, land-use patterns, and types of crops or produce grown in a given area.

The rationale for federal regulation of pesticide residues is strong and long-acknowledged, as even a half-century ago food products were distributed and marketed nationally.[89] A national regulatory framework for residues is particularly good for larger, national companies. Historian Thomas Dunlap notes, "Some of the most serious complaints about the contamination of food by insecticide residues came from officials of the Beech-Nut Packing Company."[90] Yet the FDA was not particularly proficient at setting pesticide residue tolerances, and it is possible Congress wanted it that way.[91]

The environmental justification for federal pesticide regulation was relatively weak so long as the environmental effects at issue were localized. Once scientists and environmentalists began to express concern about the accumulation of residues and the potential for pesticide use in one area to impact ecosystems elsewhere, a clear rationale for federal involvement to control such interstate spillovers became evident. Yet when Congress enacted legislation authorizing the environmental regulation of pesticide use, it did not focus on addressing such spillovers and complementing preexisting state and local efforts. Instead, Congress created a broad, untargeted regulatory structure and then failed to appropriate the resources necessary to enforce the newly created scheme. The result was by no means ideal. Though subsequent reforms sought to expand state-level flexibility, it is difficult to provide a sound institutional rationalization of the current regulatory structure.

While current federal regulation adopts a cooperative federalism model that offers states some flexibility to adopt more stringent regulations or policies tailored to local conditions, the federal regulatory structure imposes "significant constraints" on states' abilities to "develop new, potentially more effective forms of handling the environmental problems pesticide use creates."[92] States retain the ability to obtain special local needs registration, but this has not led to significant state-level policy innovation.

The federalization of pesticide regulation may have itself discouraged greater state and local efforts and crowded out more finely tuned approaches to environmental protection. As Carson observed, federal officials do not often consider local conditions or effects. At the same time, federal intervention may discourage greater policy investments by state and local policymakers. Why should they devote time to an issue once the federal government has entered the field, enacted the easiest policies, and taken credit for solving the problem? Even non-preemptive federal regulation may discourage the adoption or maintenance of more stringent state-level regulation and reduce the benefits of attempting policy experimentation.[93] Insofar as the environmental regulation of pesticide use is best when it accounts for local effects and ecosystem properties, premature federalization can produce less optimal environmental regulation.

Conclusion

Intentionally or not, *Silent Spring* contributed to a broader political push for the federalization of environmental regulation in the 1970s. It initially spurred state and local efforts, then it reinforced growing concerns about the environmental consequences of agricultural chemicals and a latent demand for greater federal regulation. Even though Carson herself was somewhat skeptical that much environmental wisdom would be found in Washington, D.C., her book contributed to the federalization of pesticide regulation and the tightening of federal rules—first by the courts and then by Congress. "The first casualty of the battle over DDT was the old system of federal regulation of pesticides and the interest-group control over that policy."[94] Yet the new system still had some things in common with the old. If the old system was too dominated by agricultural interests, the new was too inflexible and overly centralized—in part because of the continuing legacy of agricultural interests used to plowing ground in Washington, D.C. Ecological harms may have been an unintended consequence of uncontrolled pesticide use. Overly centralized and inflexible pesticide regulation may have been an unintended consequence of *Silent Spring*.

11. The Precautionary Principle: *Silent Spring*'s Toxic Legacy

Larry Katzenstein

The publication of Rachel Carson's *Silent Spring* in 1962 triggered repercussions that resonate to this day—from creating the modern environmental movement to spawning federal laws governing air and water quality, protection of endangered species, worker safety, and much more. But a crucially important "contribution" of *Silent Spring* has gone largely unrecognized: it gave birth to the "precautionary principle," a philosophy for regulating chemicals and technologies and arguably one of the late-20th century's more pernicious doctrines.

The Extended Shadow

By general consensus, *Silent Spring* led President Richard Nixon in 1970 to establish the Environmental Protection Agency, charged with regulating the pesticides and herbicides that Rachel Carson criticized for endangering the environment and human health. On its website, EPA had this to say about the book that led to its creation:

> *Silent Spring* played in the history of environmentalism roughly the same role that *Uncle Tom's Cabin* played in the abolitionist movement. In fact, EPA today may be said without exaggeration to be the extended shadow of Rachel Carson.[1]

The precautionary principle in many ways can be considered the "extended shadow" of *Silent Spring*. In this chapter, I'll make the case that *Silent Spring*—thanks to the precautionary principle it created—continues to bias public policy and attitudes against new products and technologies because of the dangers they allegedly pose to the environment and public health. I'll offer evidence that the spirit of this 50-year-old book continues to animate calls for "precautionary" measures.

Defining the Precautionary Principle

The precautionary principle is a strategy for coping with scientific uncertainty. Its proponents contend that governments should prohibit or restrict technologies or activities "when they are suspected of posing some harm to human health or the environment, even if the probability and magnitude of such harm has not been demonstrated scientifically."[2] And it requires that "the main burden of providing evidence for safety" rests on "the proposers of a new technology or activity"[3] rather than on government regulators or society.

The precautionary principle embodies familiar and commonsensical ideas such as "better safe than sorry" and "look before you leap." At first blush, the societal response that is called for—plan ahead to avoid threats that damage the environment or human health— seems reasonable. But as this chapter will show, the precautionary principle on closer scrutiny is far from benign. Jonathan Adler has nicely summarized the dangers of this doctrine:

> More and more, environmental policy incorporates the "precautionary principle," which calls upon governments to impose regulatory measures based upon the barest potential of environmental harm. If a chemical substance *might* be causing harm, it should be controlled or eliminated. If a new technological innovation *could* have unknown environmental effects, it should not be permitted. The precautionary principle may appeal to common-sense notions of safety, but its application will not produce a safer, cleaner world. Quite the opposite. The incorporation of the precautionary principle in environmental, health, and safety regulation is itself a threat to environmental protection and optimal safeguards for public health.[4]

As Adler suggests, the precautionary principle is not just an abstract concept floating in the intellectual ether. Indeed, the principle is written into international environmental declarations and agreements such as the Rio Declaration on Environment and Development, the United Nations Framework Convention on Climate Change, and the Convention on Biological Diversity. In Europe, where it holds particular sway, "the precautionary principle is now written into law,"[5] and "has emerged as a critical component of the new European approach to risk regulation."[6] The European Union's resistance to genetically modified foods and hormone-treated beef and its activist role in opposing global warming are clear expressions of the principle.

Coming up with a definitive definition of the precautionary principle is difficult: A 1999 study found 19 formulations of the precautionary principle expressed in international treaties, laws, and academic writings.[7] In choosing the iteration of the principle that best exemplifies its precautionary spirit, I defer to Indur Goklany, author of the acclaimed book *The Precautionary Principle: A Critical Appraisal of Environmental Risk Assessment.* He has written that "a popular and reasonably good definition" of the precautionary principle appears in the so-called Wingspread Declaration,[8] which emerged from the Wingspread Conference on the Precautionary Principle—a three-day meeting held in January 1998 in Racine, Wisconsin.[9]

The statement announcing the conference called its 31 participants "treaty negotiators, activists, scholars and scientists from the United States, Canada and Europe."[10] But the attendees have also been described as "a panel of activists with an agenda."[11]

Following are key sections from the Wingspread Consensus Statement on the Precautionary Principle. I have italicized the sentence expressing the principle itself.

> The release and use of toxic substances, the exploitation of resources, and physical alterations of the environment have had substantial unintended consequences affecting human health and the environment. . . . We believe there is compelling evidence that damage to humans and the worldwide environment is of such magnitude and seriousness that new principles for conducting human activities are necessary. . . . Corporations, government entities, organizations, communities, scientists, and other individuals must adopt a precautionary approach to all human endeavors. Therefore, it is necessary to implement the Precautionary Principle:
>
> *When an activity raises threats of harm to human health or the environment, precautionary measures should be taken even if some cause and effect relationships are not fully established scientifically.*

In this context the proponent of an activity, rather than the public, should bear the burden of proof.

Theoretically, the precautionary principle protects the public health and the environment by curbing the threats posed by newer technologies such as genetically modified foods or nuclear energy. But applications of the precautionary principle can actually cause more harm to health and the environment rather than less.

A Brief Digression: My Personal Brush with Precaution

Before describing *Silent Spring's* role in creating the precautionary principle, it may be instructive to describe my own evolution—from a disciple of the precautionary principle to a dissenter—during my career at *Consumer Reports*, where I worked as a health and environment writer from 1978 to 1990.

My first major article for the magazine was the cover story for the August 1979 issue, entitled "Are Hair Dyes Safe?" After a six-month investigation, I concluded that the answer was a resounding no. Hyping hypothetical risks in the best tradition of the precautionary principle, I wrote that "the problem consumers face is that the NCI [National Cancer Institute] has tested only a minority of the coal-tar dyes now used in hair dyes. Many of those not yet tested could prove just as hazardous as some of those already tested."[12]

In December 1986, I learned that the National Association of Science Writers' holiday party in New York City would be preceded by a talk on food irradiation. I had never heard of the technology, but judging from its name, I was sure I could turn it into another fear-inducing cover story for *Consumer Reports*. Instead, the talk turned around my career and my life.

The speaker, food irradiation consultant George Giddings, discussed irradiation's proven ability to rid food of pathogenic bacteria and—if widely used on raw meat and poultry—to prevent thousands of deaths and hundreds of thousands of cases of foodborne illness due to *E. coli*, salmonella, listeria, and other microbes each year.

Giddings also reviewed the risks raised by irradiation's opponents—from their prediction that thousands of dangerous irradiators would spring up around the country to their claims that irradiating food produces toxic residues that could cause serious health effects, including cancer—and explained why those risks were vanishingly small or nonexistent.

After the talk, I knew that I had a good story, but not the one I'd expected. This story would inform readers about the life-saving benefits of food irradiation and debunk the irresponsible allegations of its opponents. Such an article, I was sure, could help win national acceptance for food irradiation and would further *Consumer Reports'* goal of protecting the public's health. I lobbied my editors for a year and a half and finally got the go-ahead. But soon the food irradiation article I'd fought so hard for hit a roadblock in the form of the precautionary principle.

Rhoda Karpatkin, executive director of Consumers Union of the United States (the publisher of *Consumer Reports*) at the time, was also serving then as president of the International Organization of Consumers Unions. IOCU (now known as Consumers International) is a federation based in The Hague, Netherlands, consisting of Consumers Union and 164 other consumer organizations from 63 countries.

Europe in the 1980s was already under the sway of the precautionary principle, and European-based organizations such as IOCU were by no means immune. IOCU had issued two resolutions calling for a worldwide moratorium on food irradiation. In the best tradition of the precautionary principle, IOCU's major objection to food irradiation was that it "has not yet been proved sufficiently safe."[13] Ms. Karpatkin was clearly not pleased at the prospect of a pro–food irradiation article appearing in *Consumer Reports* during her stint as IOCU president. Before I could even start on the article, she walked into the editor's office and—as I was later informed—told him, "I don't want Katzenstein writing that article on food irradiation."

Disappointed and disgusted, I immediately began looking for another job. I left *Consumer Reports* and became medical editor at *American Health* magazine, where I finally did get to write "my" article. "Food Irradiation: The Story behind the Scare" appeared in the December 1992 issue of *American Health*[14] and was later condensed in *Reader's Digest*.[15] *Consumer Reports* got around to writing about food irradiation in 2003.[16] Not surprisingly, the article was decidedly negative, calling for "further tests of chemical byproducts created by meat irradiation." Another victory for precaution, another defeat for public health.

Tracing the Precautionary Principle's Origin

The premise of this chapter—that *Silent Spring* gave birth to the precautionary principle—first of all requires that the book preceded the principle, and here there is good consensus. Articles dealing with the history of the precautionary principle trace its creation to the late 1960s, several years after *Silent Spring*'s publication in 1962. There is also agreement that the earliest versions of the precautionary principle were formulated in Germany and Sweden in response to local environmental concerns.

The first legal use of the term is said to be the 1969 Swedish Environmental Protection Act, which required Swedish industries to demonstrate the safety of their products to regulators instead of regulators having to prove harm.[17] At around the same time, the German government was developing its environmental policy on the basis of Vorsorgeprinzip, a concept that has been translated as "foresight planning."[18] The Vorsorgeprinzip concept influenced legislation approved in the 1970s to prevent acid rain from damaging German forests.

One reason that Europe is credited with the precautionary principle is that the principle arguably is better entrenched there than elsewhere in the world. Versions of the precautionary principle have been written into important European laws, including the 1992 Fifth Environmental Action Program and the 1992 Maastricht Treaty.[19]

Despite these codifications in European law and the roles of Germany and Sweden in articulating the principle around 1969, I contend that "credit" for the precautionary principle's conception rightfully belongs to an event that occurred several years earlier: the publication of *Silent Spring*. Those who claim the precautionary principle as a European creation, promulgated in response to European concerns, fail to appreciate the tremendous impact that resulted from *Silent Spring*'s publication, not only in the United States but internationally.

In his introduction to the 1994 edition of *Silent Spring*, then Vice President Al Gore noted that the book "achieved enormous popularity and broad public support" and "planted the seeds of a new activism that has grown into one of the great popular forces of all time"—the environmental movement. "Without this book," Gore wrote, "the environmental movement might have been long delayed or never have developed at all."[20]

The following passage, from *Rachel Carson: The Environmental Movement*, by John Henricksson, powerfully describes *Silent Spring's* success in planting those "seeds of a new activism" among interest groups that would eventually "blossom" into the modern environmental movement:

> Ad hoc groups—groups organized for one specific purpose—have opposed the building of nuclear power plants, the dumping of toxic wastes into rivers, and the systematic poisoning of coyotes in the West or wolves in Alaska.
>
> All of these groups profoundly mistrust the idea of progress through new technology. They take *Silent Spring* as their bible. Rachel Carson had described one environmental issue with such clarity and precision that they could use it as a model for other issues. . . . Their own battles were extensions of the one that she had fought. . . .[21]

Among the battles listed as being inspired by *Silent Spring* is "the battle against acid rain"—the concern that led Germany (as noted above) to pass one of the earliest instances of legislation incorporating the precautionary principle.[22]

Other supporting evidence for the book's impact and influence include the following:

- After its publication, *Silent Spring* not only spent weeks atop the U.S. best seller list but also became an international best seller that has been described as "one of the most influential books in the modern world."[23]

- The *New York Times* included *Silent Spring* on its list of the 20th century's 100 most important books;[24] and in 1992, a panel of distinguished Americans selected *Silent Spring* as the most influential book of the previous 50 years.[25]

- *Silent Spring* was translated into 22 languages.[26]

- In the United States *Silent Spring's* popularity spurred enactment of key federal laws that embody aspects of precautionary regulation: the National Environmental Policy Act; the Clean Air Act; the Clean Water Act; the Federal Insecticide, Fungicide and Rodenticide Act; the Safe Drinking Water Act; the Environmental Pesticides Control Act; the Toxic Substances Control Act;[27] and the Endangered Species Act.[28]

Thus, it is not difficult to imagine that *Silent Spring*—one of the most notable books of the 20th century—inspired the Europeans who articulated the earliest iterations of the precautionary principle as well as the authors of the many versions that followed.

Silent Spring's Long Reach

Somewhat more direct evidence that *Silent Spring* reached across the Atlantic Ocean to create the precautionary principle comes from a book on risk assessment of chemicals, published in the Netherlands in 2007. Chapter 12, "The Management of Industrial Chemicals in the EU,"[29] recounts the history of Europe's long-awaited chemical policy: a law known as REACH (Registration, Evaluation, Authorization, and restriction of Chemicals). Enacted in 2005, REACH created a single system for evaluating all EU industrial chemicals and was designed to "ensure a high level of protection of human health and the environment."

In laying out the key developments culminating in REACH, Chapter 12 cites both *Silent Spring* and the precautionary principle. The introductory section contains the following passage:

> The use and releases of chemicals increased enormously in the 20th century. It has become apparent that this increase was not without "cost" to health and the environment, particularly in the industrialized countries. This was clearly illustrated by Rachel Carson in the early 1960s, whose book *Silent Spring* described the disastrous effects of the wide scale use of pesticides on fish, birds and ecosystems.

> The need to establish legally binding frameworks for the control of chemicals was soon recognized and started in the 1960's. . . . [T]he focus was on the hazards of chemicals, i.e., the inherent or intrinsic properties of chemicals having the potential to cause adverse effects.

After citing the need for an EU chemicals policy that will "ensure a high level of protection of human health and the environment," the chapter continues:

> Fundamental to achieving these objectives is the precautionary principle. Whenever reliable scientific evidence is available that a substance may have an adverse impact

on human health and the environment but there is still scientific uncertainty about the precise nature or the magnitude of the potential damage, decision-making must be based on precaution in order to prevent damage to human health and the environment."[30]

Comparing the Book and the Principle

Of course, the best evidence of all that *Silent Spring* was mother to the precautionary principle comes from the many similarities between the beliefs expressed in *Silent Spring* and those espoused in the principle itself. The remainder of this chapter will examine several of the key similarities between the two.

Only Man-Made Risks are Important

The precautionary principle made its formal international debut in 1982.[31] That year, the United Nations World Charter for Nature declared that when "potential adverse effects [from activities likely to pose significant risks to nature] are not fully understood, the activities should not proceed."[32] In that UN world charter and in its later appearances, the precautionary principle has always been invoked for the purpose of curtailing man's activities or products made by man. Those wielding the principle clearly regard naturally occurring risks as undeserving of a precautionary approach and dismiss them as undeserving of consideration—for being inevitable, irrelevant, or, almost by definition, less important than man-made risks.

The precautionary principle's "blind spot" regarding natural risks may actually help to explain its allure, according to legal scholar Cass Sunstein, who currently is on leave from Harvard Law School while he directs the White House Office of Information and Regulatory Affairs. Sunstein, whose extensive writings on the precautionary principle include his 2005 book, *Laws of Fear: Beyond the Precautionary Principle*, described the principle's allure in a 2008 op-ed piece:

> [W]hy does the precautionary principle seem so appealing? Part of the answer is psychological. Particularly powerful is the belief that nature is benevolent and harmonious. Studies show that people overestimate the carcinogenic risk from pesticides and underestimate the risks of natural

carcinogens. People also believe that nature implies safety, so much that they will prefer natural water to processed water even if the two are chemically identical. Most people believe that natural chemicals are safer than man-made chemicals. Most toxicologists disagree.

The truth is that nature is often a realm of destruction, illness, killing, and death. Human activity is not necessarily or systematically more destructive than what nature does.[33]

The precautionary principle's willful disregard for naturally occurring risks springs right from the pages of *Silent Spring*. The book regales readers about risks posed by some 40 man-made hazards, from aldrin to urethane, yet says practically nothing about naturally occurring toxins. Naturally occurring toxins are mentioned primarily to contrast their apparent safety with the risks posed by synthetic chemicals:

In being man-made—by ingenious laboratory manipulation of the molecules, substituting atoms, altering their arrangement, [insecticides created in the laboratory during and after World War II] differ sharply from the simpler insecticides of prewar days. These were derived from naturally occurring minerals and plant products—compounds of arsenic, copper, lead, manganese, zinc, and other minerals, pyrethrum from the dried flowers of chrysanthemums, nicotine sulphate from some of the relatives of tobacco, and rotenone from leguminous plants of the East Indies.[34]

In their 1996 book, Bruce Ames and Lois Swirsky Gold, University of California at Berkeley toxicologists, commented on Carson's obsession with man-made risks. In words that echo Sunstein's critique of the precautionary principle and its underestimation of risks from natural carcinogens, Ames and Gold wrote:

Rachel Carson's fundamental misconception [in *Silent Spring*] was: "For the first time in the history of the world, every human being is now subjected to contact with dangerous chemicals, from the moment of conception until death." She was wrong. The vast bulk of the chemicals to which humans are exposed are natural, and for every chemical some amount is dangerous. Carson thus lacked perspective about the wide variety of naturally occurring chemicals to which all people are exposed and did not address the fact that, outside the workplace, exposures to synthetic pollutants are extremely low relative to the natural background. . . . Since the vast proportion of human exposures are to naturally occurring chemicals, while the vast proportion of chemicals tested for carcinogenicity are synthetic, there is an imbalance in data and perception about chemicals and cancer.[35]

Accentuate the Negative

One of the most remarkable things about *Silent Spring* is how few of its words are devoted to saying anything positive about the many pesticides, herbicides, and other chemicals it discusses—an omission acknowledged by one of Carson's biographers: "Carson was not always neutral in her use of sources and . . . she was sometimes driven by moral fervor more than by scientific evidence. Indeed, her use of evidence was selective, and she made no attempt to catalogue the benefits of pesticides. . . ."[36]

The precautionary principle is similarly characterized by refusal to recognize any benefits offered by the chemicals or technologies that it would restrict—one of the main reasons that Sunstein has dubbed it "The Paralyzing Principle." In his article by the same name, Sunstein wrote that "the most serious problem with the Precautionary Principle is that it offers no guidance" because "risks of one kind or another are on all sides of regulatory choices."[37]

In elaborating, Sunstein discusses five controversial topics that have attracted precautionary attention: strong controls on arsenic in drinking water, genetic engineering of food, global warming, threats to marine mammals posed by naval exercises, and nuclear power. Reflexively invoking the precautionary principle, he warns, could lead to "substitute risks in the form of hazards that materialize, or are increased, as a result of regulation." Nuclear power provides a good illustration of this conundrum, Sunstein notes:

> Many people fear nuclear power on the ground that nuclear power plants raise various health and safety issues, including some possibility of catastrophe. But if a nation does not rely on nuclear power, it is likely to rely on fossil fuels, and in particular on coal-power plants. Such plants create risks of their own, including risks associated with global warming.[38]

255

"What guidance does the Precautionary Principle provide [in dealing with those five controversies]?" Sunstein asks. "It is tempting to say that the principle calls for strong controls on [them]. In all of those cases, there is a possibility of serious harms, and no authoritative scientific evidence suggests that the possibility is close to zero."

He then suggests asking "a more fundamental question":

> Is more stringent regulation really compelled by the Precautionary Principle? The answer is that it is not. In most of the cases above, it should be easy to see that in its own way, stringent regulation would actually run afoul of the Precautionary Principle [and its goal of protecting people against risks to their safety and health]. The simplest reason is that such regulation might well deprive society of significant benefits, and for that reason produce risks and even deaths that would otherwise not occur.[39]

"Safe" Exposure is Impossible

In an apparent effort to portray Carson as having rationally assessed pesticides in *Silent Spring*, her biographers invariably emphasize that she did not favor outlawing them. For example, in the first nine pages of her 2005 book, Priscilla Coit Murphy states three times that *Silent Spring* did not call for a pesticide ban. The third iteration reads as follows:

> With respect to the conduct of the debate [over *Silent Spring*'s scientific validity], even more important [than her list of principal sources of information in an appendix] is the fact that Carson explicitly declined to prescribe total abstinence from pesticides. Early on, in the second chapter, she makes the following statement: *"It is not my contention that chemical insecticides must never be used.* I do contend that we have put poisonous and biologically potent chemicals indiscriminately into the hands of persons largely or wholly ignorant of their potentials for harm."* Many of her critics chose to ignore that disclaimer, however. . . .[40] [Emphasis added.]

True, Carson did say that she wasn't calling for a ban on pesticide use. But on other pages of her book, she makes a claim that, as a practical matter, would clearly require a ban: that no level of pesticide exposure can be considered safe. Carson articulated that belief in "One in Every Four," *Silent Spring's* "cancer" chapter. "One in every four" refers to the proportion of Americans who allegedly will develop cancer sometime during their lives.[41] She makes the case that "dangerous chemicals" have "entered the environment of everyone—even of children as yet unborn," and that it is "hardly surprising, therefore, that we are now aware of an alarming increase in malignant disease."[42]

Carson presented her "no safe dose" argument twice in this chapter. The first mention occurs in the context of man's exposure to many different chemicals at once: "Human exposures to cancer-producing chemicals (including pesticides) are uncontrolled and they are multiple," she writes and goes on to note, "It is quite possible that no one of these exposures alone would be sufficient to precipitate malignancy—yet any single supposedly 'safe dose' may be enough to tip the scales that are already loaded with other 'safe doses.'"[43]

In the next paragraph, she describes yet another malignant scenario, this one involving synergistic interactions among toxins:

> Or again the harm may be done by two or more different carcinogens acting together, so that there is a summation of their effects. The individual exposed to DDT, for example, is almost certain to be exposed to other liver-damaging hydrocarbons, which are so widely used as solvents, paint removers, degreasing agents, dry-cleaning fluids, and anesthetics. What then can be a "safe dose" of DDT?[44]

Carson's motive for putting "safe dose" in quotation marks was the subject of an interesting analysis by Randy Harris who writes that they were Carson's way of emphasizing that *any* exposure to DDT should be considered hazardous:

> If someone asks you what a "safe dose" of DDT is, as Carson just has, you know right away that the words in quotation marks are not hers. She is disavowing them. She has brought them in from elsewhere and bagged them in pairs of raised commas, one pair inverted, so you will know that someone else—someone without enough knowledge, or someone

with duplicitous intentions—has used them in a way that is misleading and dangerous. The words are not hers, but you have no trouble recognizing that she has a belief about them or that the belief concerns their veracity. The quotation marks deliver a truth judgment, a negative truth judgment, on the material they flank. There is no safe dose of DDT, Carson says with her quotation marks, and you shouldn't believe anyone who tells you there is.[45]

Then, on the following page, Carson expands on her "no exposure is safe" argument by raising the possibility that chemicals *not* known to cause cancer could possibly enhance the potency of carcinogens:

Water pollution experts throughout the United States are concerned by the fact that detergents are now a troublesome and practically universal contaminant of public water supplies. There is no practical way to remove them by treatment. Few detergents are known to be carcinogenic, but in an indirect way they may promote cancer by acting on the lining of the digestive tract, changing the tissues so that they may more easily absorb dangerous chemicals, thereby aggravating their effect. But who can foresee and control this action? In the kaleidoscope of shifting conditions, what dose of a carcinogen can be "safe" except a zero dose?[46]

The chemophobia spawned by *Silent Spring* is now inscribed in the precautionary principle, which calls for assurances of safety before new chemicals or technologies can be marketed. As Adler notes in his critique of the precautionary principle, proving safety requires proving a negative ("no harm")—something that is scientifically impossible to do:

The scientific process can test the robustness of a given hypothesis—substance X will cause cancer or substance Y disrupts amphibian production—but it cannot prove that a given substance is risk-free. Substance X might not cause rodent tumors, but it could always cause something else. For this reason, scientists fear that the Precautionary Principle could "block the development of any technology if there is the slightest theoretical possibility of harm."[47]

Meanwhile, environmental and consumer extremists who espouse the precautionary principle have fanned the public's *Silent Spring*-induced fear that we're in the midst of a chemical-induced cancer epidemic and that zero is the only safe dose of chemical exposure. As C. F. Wilkinson, writing in *Silent Spring Revisited*, noted:

> What society will not tolerate is the possibility, no matter how remote, that long-term, low-level exposure to pesticides and other chemicals might ultimately lead to sinister chronic effects such as cancer, mutagenesis, or birth defects, which are generally considered the ultimate insults to human health. Public fears in this area have been greatly heightened in recent years by a vocal group of toxicological apocalyptics who claim that up to 90% of current human cancers can be attributed directly to pesticides and other synthetic chemicals.[48]

These "toxicological apocalyptics"—Public Citizen, the Center for Science in the Public Interest, Greenpeace, and other environmental and consumer groups—whip up fear over cancer to attract media attention and scare up contributions. In their obsession with highlighting cancer risks, the apocalyptics make demands for adhering to the precautionary principle that can border on the ludicrous.

I encountered my favorite example of precautionary zealotry while researching my article on food irradiation for *American Health*. It involved an anti-nuclear group called Food & Water, which led the opposition to food irradiation during the 1980s and 1990s. Food & Water insisted that irradiating food creates dangerous "unique radio-lytic products," or URPs, capable of causing "cancer and birth defects." URPs, it turned out, were entirely hypothetical—as is often the case with the "risks" that precautionary proponents inveigh against. When I asked Michael Colby, Food & Water's national director, to name an URP, his reply was somewhat tortured: "No one has identified them," he said. "We know they exist; they just haven't been identified."[49]

Carson's concept of zero-dose exposure has become the rallying cry of precautionary advocates. For example, Dr. Samuel Epstein, a well-known adherent, has declared that "no safe level or thresholds are recognized for chemicals inducing carcinogenic, teratogenic, or mutagenic effects."[50] Equally important, the concept has been adopted by several of America's most important regulatory agencies.

In the realm of chemical regulation, zero-doze exposure now goes by the name "linear, no-threshold theory," which presumes that the dose-response curve extends linearly to the origin (at least for low-level exposures) and that there are no thresholds below which exposure to a given carcinogen can be considered safe. During the 1970s, the Consumer Product Safety Commission, EPA, FDA, and Occupational Safety and Health Administration "all adopted no-threshold models on the grounds that, given the uncertainties inherent in animal studies [which provide much of the data used in constructing dose-response curves], it was *prudent* to assume low-dose linearity."[51] (Emphasis added.)

In a 2000 op-ed piece, Kenneth Smith addressed the controversy over the proposed repository for spent nuclear fuel in Nevada, lamenting Carson's influence in foisting the no-threshold theory on EPA. Smith noted that industry, consistent with recommendations from the National Academy of Sciences, said it was sufficient to limit annual radiation exposure levels to "the dose one would receive on five coast-to-coast, round-trip plane trips across the United States." EPA, however, was "insisting on limiting exposure to the equivalent of three trips and possibly even lower." After noting that this contest between five and three coast-to-coast trips "is precisely the kind of regulatory regime with which Rachel Carson cursed the United States," Smith wrote:

> Ms. Carson based her influential "novel," *Silent Spring*, on the fiction that exposure to disappearingly small amounts of man-made chemicals and radiation might poison man and everything else on the globe. The author was a biologist, not an expert in cancer research, and almost four decades later there is still no scientific basis for her warnings. But in the name of protecting the public, regulators now rely on her theory that there is no threshold below which exposure to alleged carcinogens is safe.[52]

Despite what seems to be a growing scientific consensus that safe thresholds for carcinogens *do* exist, today's EPA seems even more closely wedded to Rachel Carson and the precautionary principle than it was 10 years ago, when Smith wrote his piece.

The Dioxin Saga

That message is clearly conveyed by Jon Hamilton's 2010 National Public Radio segment about what to do with the many sites around the country where soil is contaminated with low levels of dioxin, "considered one of the world's most dangerous chemicals." Hamilton recounts that in December 1982, the people of Times Beach, Missouri, were ordered to abandon their town forever because EPA had found high levels of dioxin in the soil—the result of dioxin-contaminated waste oil spread on roads years earlier to keep down the dust. Hamilton notes that in ordering the evacuation, federal officials "had taken a drastic step—one that was based more on a hunch than on definitive science":

> They knew the chemical came from industrial processes, including chlorine bleaching at paper mills, pesticide production, and waste incineration. And they knew high doses caused liver tumors in rodents. So federal officials took a cautious approach. They decided residential soil should contain less than one part per billion of dioxin. In some areas of Times Beach, levels were 100 times that high. As a result, the empty town became one of the nation's first Superfund sites.[53]

A few years later, EPA's attention shifted from the high dioxin levels of Times Beach to the very low levels that the agency was finding in many other places, from sources such as the burning of backyard trash—findings that created challenges for the agency. Hamilton quotes Joshua Cohen, deputy director of the Center for the Evaluation of Value and Risk in Health at Tufts University and a member of a committee assembled by the National Academy of Sciences to review EPA's assessment of risks from dioxin: "The problem," said Cohen, "is that there is no ideal study that directly answers the question: Does dioxin cause cancer at typical everyday exposure levels, and, if so, how big a risk does it pose?"[54] EPA scientists decided to extrapolate cancer risk from studies of workers who had been exposed to high levels of dioxin. So for exposure levels one-tenth as high as those experienced by workers, EPA would assume that the risk is one-tenth as large. As a result, says Hamilton, every bit of dioxin-contaminated soil in the country would pose a risk.[55]

Cohen and many other scientists outside EPA argue that this is the wrong approach for evaluating dioxin and some other chemicals. According to Hamilton, "They say that because of the way these chemicals behave in the body, there's a threshold below which the risk of cancer disappears. If that's true, and these scientists are

261

correct, there would be no reason to worry about exposure in most places." In 2006, Cohen and other members of the National Academy of Sciences committee supported experts who were asking EPA to reconsider its no-threshold position for dioxin risk. But in late 2009, the agency proposed making the acceptable level of dioxin in soil even lower. And in May of 2010, EPA scientists issued their latest rejection of the threshold approach to cancer risk.[56]

EPA's stance contrasts sharply with European regulators and the World Health Organization, who decided a decade ago that dioxin does have a safe threshold. As a result, they accept exposure levels that are much higher than EPA's proposed standard.

Most experts on the precautionary principle regard it as being more deeply entrenched in Europe than in the United States. They might be both surprised and distressed to see EPA regulators pursuing dioxin with far more zeal than even their European counterparts have shown.

A World of Unintended Consequences

If anything can be said to be the *raison d'etre* of the precautionary principle, it is the need to avoid the unintended consequences of new chemicals and technologies—a sentiment spelled out in the first sentence of the Wingspread Consensus Statement on the Precautionary Principle:

> The release and use of toxic substances, the exploitation of resources, and physical alterations of the environment have had substantial unintended consequences affecting human health and the environment.[57]

This basic premise—that tampering with nature can have unforeseen and tragic results—seems clearly to have been inspired by *Silent Spring*, a book whose working title was *Man against Nature*.[58] In the book's first few pages, Carson calls environmental pollution "the central problem of our age":

> Along with the possibility of the extinction of mankind by nuclear war, the central problem of our age has . . . become the contamination of man's total environment with such substances of incredible potential for harm—substances that accumulate in the tissues of plants and animals and even

penetrate the germ cells to shatter or alter the very material
of heredity upon which the shape of the future depends.

Some would-be architects of our future look toward a time
when it will be possible to alter the human germ plasma by
design. *But we may easily be doing so now by inadvertence,* for
many chemicals, like radiation, bring about gene mutations.
It is ironic to think that man might determine his own future
by something so seemingly trivial as the choice of an insect
spray.[59] [Emphasis added.]

The remainder of the nearly 300 pages in *Silent Spring* consists
largely of a litany of anecdotes—cases of environmental depreda-
tions trotted out one after the other to illustrate what Carson calls "a
new kind of havoc":

As man proceeds toward his announced goal of the conquest
of nature, he has written a depressing record of destruction,
directed not only against the earth he inhabits but against the
life that shares it with him. The history of the recent centuries
has its black passages—the slaughter of the buffalo on the
western plains, the massacre of the shorebirds by the market
gunners, the near-extermination of the egrets for their plum-
age. Now, to these and others like them, we are adding a new
chapter and a new kind of havoc—the direct killing of birds,
mammals, fishes, and indeed practically every form of wildlife
by chemical insecticides indiscriminately sprayed on the land.

Under the philosophy that now seems to guide our destinies, nothing must get in the way of the man with the spray
gun.[60]

And so, for example, readers of Chapter 6, "Earth's Green Mantle,"
are regaled with this vivid anecdote:

The spraying [to clear roadside brush] is not only improperly
planned but studded with abuses such as these. In a southern New England town one contractor finished his work
with some chemical remaining in his tank. He discharged
this along woodland roadsides where no spraying had been
authorized. As a result the community lost the blue and
golden beauty of its autumn roads where asters and golden-
rod would have made a display worth traveling far to see.[61]

Chapter 8, "And No Birds Sing," cites more than 40 cases in which birds allegedly succumbed to man-made poisons, including the following:

> During the winter of 1957–1958, Dr. Wallace saw no chickadees or nuthatches at his home feeding station for the first time in many years. Three nuthatches he found later provided a sorry little step-by-step lesson in cause and effect: one was feeding on an elm, another was found dying of typical DDT symptoms, the third was dead. The dying nuthatch was later found to have 226 parts per million of DDT in its tissues.[62]

Silent Spring's anecdotes, of course, are not limited to instances of environmental damage. In Chapter 14, "One in Every Four," Carson trots out numerous cases, such as the following, in which exposure to DDT and other toxic chemicals allegedly caused serious health problems:

> Such word-famous institutions as the Mayo Clinic admit hundreds of victims of these diseases of the blood-forming organs [that is, leukemia]. Dr. Malcolm Hargraves and his associates in the Hematology Department at the Mayo Clinic report that almost without exception these patients have had a history of exposure to various toxic chemicals, including sprays which contain DDT, chlordane, benzene, lindane, and petroleum distillates.[63]

When Unintended Consequences Undermine a Principle

The great irony, of course, is that deployment of the precautionary principle can itself lead to damaging consequences. Frank Cross has described this "dark side":

> The truly fatal flaw of the precautionary principle . . . is the unsupported presumption that an action [that is, a regulatory action] aimed at public health protection cannot possibly have negative effects on public health. Yet these unanticipated adverse effects are demonstrably common. . . . Because the precautionary principle counsels for action against even those uncertain hazards that might be nonexistent, the presence of real adverse health effects consequent to that action means that regulation will often cause more health harm than good.[64]

In arguing that the precautionary principle can backfire badly—endangering instead of safeguarding the environment and public health—Cross cites some instructive examples:

- The 1984 ban on the fumigant ethylene dibromide resulted in increased public exposure to aflatoxin, a mold-produced food contaminant estimated to be 1,000 times more carcinogenic than ethylene dibromide.

- Greenpeace campaigned in the early 1990s for a ban on all uses of chlorine, in part because chlorination of drinking water forms small amounts of carcinogenic trihalomethanes. Peru responded to the chlorine scare by halting the chlorination of many of the country's water supplies. That decision—made in an effort to prevent "a handful of purely speculative cancer cases"—caused one of Latin America's worst cholera epidemics, when more than 1.3 million people contracted cholera and at least 11,000 died from the infection.[65]

Most ironic of all, however, Cross cites the precautionary bungle whose unintended consequences may have caused more deaths than any other. That was the 1972 decision by EPA Administrator William Ruckleshaus to ban the use of DDT, the pesticide at the scientific and emotional center of *Silent Spring* itself:

> Countries around the globe had used DDT to eradicate or at least control insect-borne diseases, particularly malaria. These countries followed U.S. action in prohibiting or restricting the use of DDT. At the time of the ban, malaria was close to being eradicated. Malaria experienced a resurgence after DDT was banned and currently causes millions of deaths each year throughout the world. This mortal enormity is at least partially attributable to the decision to prohibit the use of DDT.[66]

The Tragedy of Eradicating DDT Instead of Mosquitoes

"There was once a town in the heart of America where all life seemed to live in harmony with its surroundings," *Silent Spring*'s first chapter famously begins. But by the next page, the idyllic had become the apocalyptic:

> Then a strange blight crept over the area and everything began to change. Some evil spell had settled on the community: mysterious maladies swept the flocks of chickens; the cattle and sheep sickened and died. Everywhere was a shadow of death. The farmers spoke of much illness among their families. In the town the doctors had become more and more puzzled by new kinds of sickness appearing among their patients. There had been several sudden and unexplained deaths, not only among adults but even among children, who would be stricken suddenly while at play and die within a few hours. . . . No witchcraft, no enemy action had silenced the rebirth of new life in this stricken world. The people had done it to themselves.[67]

Although, in succeeding chapters, Carson describes numerous chemicals that could be implicated in the health and environmental degradation that enveloped this fictional town—most notably a plethora of pesticides including dieldrin, endrin, heptachlor, lindane, and parathion—by the book's end there is little doubt that DDT is the prime suspect. DDT is discussed on 51 of *Silent Spring*'s 297 pages—far more than any other chemical in the book. Almost overnight, DDT went from being considered a public health savior—its mosquito-killing ability credited with preventing millions of malaria deaths worldwide since the end of World War II—to being public enemy number one.

Some 10 years after *Silent Spring's* publication, what may have been the first use of the precautionary principle in a legal setting in the United States came during the DDT cancellation hearings that preceded the pesticide's ban. After a federal court canceled all uses of DDT in the United States, a group of chemical manufacturers asked for a hearing to plead its case. Between August 1971 and March 1972, expert witnesses and lawyers representing chemical companies and their environmentalist opponents appeared before a hearing examiner, where they produced about 9,000 pages of testimony. Twenty-seven manufacturers, USDA, and several agricultural users defended DDT, while EPA, the Environmental Defense Fund, the Sierra Club, the National Audubon Society, and the Western Michigan Environmental

Action Council argued against the insecticide. Using money from a fund Carson had provided in her will, the Audubon Society helped finance the "prosecution's" case.

This "trial of DDT" is vividly described in *The Gentle Subversive: Rachel Carson,* Silent Spring, *and the Rise of the Environmental Movement,* a sympathetic book by Mark Hamilton Lytle about Rachel Carson's life and influence:

> Each side presented its evidence and then faced hostile cross-examination from opposing attorneys. *The burden of proof lay with the industry and its allies, who had to establish that DDT was not harmful to animals, to consumers, or to those who applied it.* Most contentious was the question of whether DDT caused cancer or other human health problems. A lesser issue arose about whether DDT was needed to control disease-bearing insects.[68] [Emphasis added.]

DDT's supporters managed to meet the high standard of proof required of them. As Ronald Bailey noted in *"Silent Spring* at 40":

> After listening to that testimony, the EPA's own administrative law judge declared, "DDT is not a carcinogenic hazard to man. . . . DDT is not a mutagenic or teratogenic hazard to man. . . . The use of DDT under the regulations involved here [does] not have a deleterious effect on freshwater fish, estuarine organisms, wild birds or other wildlife.[69]

In his decision to permit DDT's continued use in the United States, the judge noted that evidence suggesting possible risks from the use of DDT must be weighed against "the well documented proof of the benefits that DDT has bestowed on mankind."[70]

In June 1972, Ruckelshaus overruled EPA's administrative law judge and banned the use of DDT in the United States. His final order had "precautionary principle" written all over it: "The evidence of record showing storage [of DDT] in man and magnification in the food chain is a warning to the prudent that man may be exposing himself to a substance that may ultimately have a serious effect on his health."[71]

Ultimately, it was the judge—and not Ruckelshaus—who was correct about DDT and its alleged risks. Virtually everyone now agrees that DDT can harm certain bird species: its magnification up the food chain does cause thinning to occur in the eggs of raptors (including the bald eagle, the peregrine falcon, and the osprey), resulting in a decline in the numbers of those birds. But despite intensive research, little evidence has turned up to support Carson's contention that DDT poses dangers to people, as even her supporters have acknowledged: "Carson strongly believed that DDT would be proven harmful to human beings, but this has not yet been borne out by research."[72]

The ban on DDT's use in the United States fulfilled one of Rachel Carson's main goals in writing *Silent Spring*. It was "celebrated by many environmentalists as one of the twentieth century's greatest environmental victories."[73] But in retrospect, the DDT ban constitutes one of *Silent Spring*'s most unfortunate legacies, as Donald Roberts and Richard Tren vividly describe in this volume.

Not content with a ban on DDT's use in the United States, environmentalists mounted a campaign for a worldwide ban. And even though malaria had staged a comeback in many parts of the developing world, an international agreement aimed at phasing out DDT's use worldwide was reached in December 2000 under the auspices of the United Nations Environmental Programme. As Goklany notes, the rationale offered for a global DDT ban was that "the Precautionary Principle requires it."[74]

Thanks to a compromise with developing countries still using DDT to control malaria, the global DDT ban has not been implemented. But even in the absence of an "official" ban, *Silent Spring*'s success in demonizing DDT has sharply curtailed the pesticide's global use, allowing malaria cases to surge:

> We know that whatever harm DDT may have caused, ceasing its use in many countries was absolutely catastrophic. Well-documented is the case of Sri Lanka, in which 2.8 million malaria cases per year in 1948 dwindled to but 17 cases after fifteen years of DDT spraying. But after spraying was stopped in 1964, as a direct result of Carson's book, malaria cases quickly shot back up to almost their original level.[75]

About 250 million people now contract malaria each year and nearly one million people die from the disease. The vast majority of malaria cases and deaths occur in developing countries—mainly because use of DDT has helped in almost completely eliminating malaria from the developed world. As Goklany stresses in his book, a rational use of "precaution" in guiding a decision on a global DDT ban would involve balancing costs and benefits:

> [P]rohibiting DDT use worldwide would most likely lead to substantial net increases in death and disease because the net harm caused by such a ban in the developing countries far outweighs its net benefits in the developed world. The harms are greater in magnitude and more certain and are likely to occur more rapidly than the benefits. Thus, under the Precautionary Principle, there ought not to be a global ban on DDT use.[76]

Goklany goes on to note that an even better case can be made for banning DDT in developed countries while permitting its continued use as an indoor spray in countries where malaria remains a threat. "Specifically," he says, "the Precautionary Principle supports a two-tiered approach toward DDT; that is, the policy for countries where malaria has been eradicated is different from that for countries where malaria is still prevalent or threatens to make a comeback."[77]

Unfortunately, Goklany's vision of a wisely used precautionary principle is far removed from the principle defined in the Wingspread Consensus Statement. As was true of *Silent Spring*, the precautionary principle ignores the benefits inherent in the chemicals and technologies that it targets. DDT may be the most extreme example of damage from the precautionary principle. But unless its influence is curtailed, this principle that was created "to protect human health and the environment" can be expected to cost many more lives in the future.

Just as a parent and child share certain traits, *Silent Spring* and its offspring, the precautionary principle, are examples of the seductive—and ultimately destructive—power of seemingly reasonable proposals for minimizing harm and improving health. In the case of *Silent Spring*, an acclaimed author was making an argument that, on its surface, was logical in the extreme: Since herbicides and insecticides kill weeds and insects, those chemicals must also pose a threat to humans and other nontarget organisms inevitably exposed to them; therefore, banning those chemicals will serve the interests of people and their environment. But as we know, *Silent Spring*'s most notable "accomplishment"—the ban on DDT's use in the United

States and its pariah status in the rest of the world—may well have led to millions of deaths from malaria and other insect-borne diseases. The precautionary principle, with its patina of "better safe than sorry," is similarly appealing. After all, what could be the harm in preventing the use of a technology that could pose serious risks to public health and the environment? But, as this chapter has shown, regulations guided by the precautionary principle can actually backfire badly.

Silent Spring and the precautionary principle teach us that translating popular and appealing ideas into policy can lead to serious unintended consequences. This was illustrated most recently by the public-health debacle in which life-saving childhood vaccines were falsely linked to autism, causing vaccination rates to drop[78] and measles outbreaks to occur.[79] Clearly, this is a lesson that we ignore at our peril.

"Look before you leap," the precautionary principle urges. By the same token, society must constantly guard against the principle's siren song. Whenever the principle is invoked to justify regulatory action, we must examine such proposals scientifically and objectively so that unintended consequences can be avoided.

12. Risk Over-Simplified: The Enduring and Unfortunate Legacy of *Silent Spring*

Gary E. Marchant[1]

Rachel Carson's *Silent Spring* is often credited with creating a new precautionary approach for managing environmental risks. Yet that approach is premised on a simplistic risk paradigm about environmental toxicity that was predominant at that time. Over the past couple of decades, the paradigm underlying the perspective of Carson and her contemporaries has been outdated by new findings showing that toxicological risks are much more nuanced, complex, and ubiquitous. Unfortunately, many of our current environmental statutes were crafted and enacted in that earlier period. The result has been ineffective, inefficient, and often impossible regulatory goals. Just as these statutes' failure to account for the complexity of real-life risk has resulted in their failure to achieve their stated goals, so too applying this overly simplified risk paradigm in its current guise as the precautionary principle will lead to failure and disappointment.

This chapter proceeds in three parts. First, I will summarize the simplified, "all-or-none" risk paradigm that was predominant in the era of *Silent Spring* and its shortcomings. Next, I will discuss the failure of three prominent statutes from that era to achieve their stated zero-risk objectives: the Delaney Clause, the National Ambient Air Quality Standard provision of the Clean Air Act, and the zero-discharge objective of the Clean Water Act. And finally, I will discuss the inevitable failure of the precautionary principle, the current incarnation of the unrealistic worldview underlying *Silent Spring*.

The Outdated Risk Paradigm of *Silent Spring*

Silent Spring is premised on an outdated and simplistic view of environmental risk, albeit one that was both respectable and fashionable when it was published.[2] Under this paradigm, a relatively small set of man-made "poisons," such as pesticides and industrial chemicals, present unique and unacceptable risks, primarily carcinogenic risks. These "bad actors" are harmful in every possible context and dosage, provide no countervailing benefits, and can and should be eliminated altogether. In the view of many Americans in Carson's era, pollution can therefore be made obsolete.[3] As such, zero risk is a feasible and rational goal—if we can only eliminate those toxic outliers, we can return to our natural, healthy, and ecologically balanced preindustrial environment.

Rachel Carson put forward a pastoral vision that is consistent with one stream of American environmentalism discussed in Chapter 3 in this volume by Desrochers and Shimizu (although it is a vision in competition with other, more practical streams). It embraces a return to a (mythical or, as Nelson discusses in Chapter 4, religious) pristine and pure world in which humans live in harmony with nature, and to which modern society and industrialization are antithetical.[4] This strand of environmentalism, like Carson, emphasizes guilt and fear with dire warnings of the imminent destruction of nature and collapse of civilization caused by industrialization,[5] specters that have repeatedly and consistently turned out to be exaggerated.[6] Ted Nordhaus and Michael Shellenberger describe the tactic employed by Carson and many of her successors as follows: "wrap the latest scientific research about an ecological calamity in a tragic narrative that conjures nostalgia for Nature while prophesying ever worse disasters to come, unless human societies repent for their sins against Nature and work for a return to a harmonious relationship with the natural world."[7]

The pastoral vision of the world is portrayed in the opening chapter of *Silent Spring*, where Carson sets forth a dark vision of a world polluted and dying from industrial chemicals and pesticides.[8] The idyllic, pastoral world "where all life seemed to live in harmony" was transformed by the "grim specter" of chemicals that "has crept upon us almost unnoticed," into a dying, lifeless "stricken world." Although described by the author as a "fable," the book claims that

272

every one of the disasters imagined in the chapter actually happened somewhere, and that unless we take immediate action "this imagined tragedy may easily become a stark reality we all shall know."[9]

Synthetic chemicals such as pesticides are portrayed as an unnecessary scourge. To be sure, some of the pesticide applications that Carson addresses were indeed harmful to the environment or human health (e.g., widespread field applications of DDT and other organophosphate pesticides), and we are better off without them. To the extent that Carson's book contributed to the cessation of such blunderbuss practices, she deserves credit. But the benefits of industrial chemicals and pesticides more generally are not presented in the book—other than some passing references to a temporary positive effect that is quickly undone by the more lasting and serious negative consequences. For example, Carson avoids any significant discussion of the benefits of DDT in combating deadly diseases like malaria.[10] Neither does she try to recount the health benefits of avoiding insect and mold damage to foods.[11] Nor does she mention the improving health and longevity that has come with our synthetic age.[12] Rather, Carson gives only dire warnings and bleak predictions, such as this:

> [T]he central problem of our age has therefore become the contamination of man's total environment with such substances of incredible potential for harm—substances that accumulate in the tissues of plants and animals and even penetrate the germ cells to shatter or alter the very material of heredity upon which the shape of the future depends.[13]

While the risks of synthetic chemicals are played up, the harms of "natural risks" are discounted, purportedly because our bodies have adapted to such risks and are somehow now immune. Thus,

> The environment, rigorously shaping and directing the life it supported, contained elements that were hostile as well as supporting. Certain rocks gave out dangerous radiation; even within the light of the sun, from which all life draws its energy, there were short-wave radiations with power to injure. Given time—time not in years but in millennia—life adjusts, and a balance has been reached. For time is the essential ingredient; but in the modern world there is no time.[14]

273

Later in her book, Carson sounds the alarm against genotoxic chemical and physical agents, including the radioactive isotopes from atomic bomb testing. Still, she ignores her own concern about such agents when it comes to natural radiation in the environment, claiming that we somehow "adjust" to and come into "balance" with such exposures,[15] even though radiation works by the same genotoxic mechanism she later warns about. Similarly, Carson ignores that almost every food, environment, material, drink of water, and breath of air that humans are exposed to (even putting aside synthetic chemicals) have been modified by humans over a timescale far too short for our biological systems to have adapted evolutionarily. Thus, Carson engaged in what Gregg Easterbrook describes as "selective doomsaying: citing the arguments for trepidation but not the countervailing arguments for equanimity."[16]

Of course, we now know that the world is much more complex and nuanced than the simple "good versus bad" chemical worldview found in *Silent Spring* and widely accepted from the late 1950s through the mid-1970s. First, Carson's vision of an idyllic, pastoral past where humans were in perfect harmony with their natural environment is largely a myth. For example, Carson claims that "[u]nder primitive agricultural conditions the farmer had few insect problems,"[17] when in fact the lives and harvests of earlier farming societies were filled with pestilence, disease, and scarcity.[18] I'm reminded of the *New Yorker* cartoon by Alex Gregory in which two cavemen are sitting, talking pensively, with one stating: "Something's just not right—our air is clean, our water is pure, we all get plenty of exercise, everything we eat is organic and free-range, and yet nobody lives past thirty."[19]

Bruce Ames and his colleagues have refuted Carson's erroneous assumption that synthetic chemicals are inherently more dangerous than naturally occurring substances—approximately half of both synthetic and natural chemical substances have been found to induce tumors in rodent studies.[20] So Carson is mistaken when she claims that "[f]or the first time in the history of the world, every human being is now subjected to contact with dangerous chemicals, from the moment of conception until death."[21] In fact, as Aaron Wildavsky writes, "virtually everything human beings breathe or eat or drink brings them into contact with carcinogens. Poisons are an integral part of nature. So is chemical warfare among plants, animals and insects. To ban carcinogenic substances, therefore, is to ban life."[22] Our environment has always presented us with risks; indeed, life has always been full of risk, even if the nature, characteristics, and identity of those risks shift over time.[23] We have always been exposed to harmful chemical agents in our food, air, water, and soil—indeed, no "chemical" is more corrosive to our tissue than oxygen, which causes the oxidation process that creates dangerous free radicals.[24]

Thus, not surprisingly, Carson's crusade to restore the mythical natural harmony of the past by ridding the world of dangerous synthetic chemicals was doomed to failure. As *New York Times* writer Keith Schneider documented in a series of articles in the mid-1990s, the environmental movement and statutes from the 1960s and 1970s have made important progress in reducing pollution, but their ultimate objective of eliminating pollution has been (inevitably) frustrated: "Pollution has not ended, though, and more than that, it is more complicated, vexing and persistent than anybody knew."[25] Environmental risks are not limited to a handful of bad actors that can simply be eliminated; rather, they are a ubiquitous potentiality of almost any substance in the right (or more accurately, wrong) circumstances or exposure level. As recognized hundreds of years ago by Paracelsus, the founder of toxicology, the dose makes the poison, and any substance can be hazardous at high enough concentrations.

Given the ubiquity of risk, it is neither possible to eliminate all risk, nor prudent to try to reduce risks without considering the benefits of the risk-creating product or activity, or the costs of reducing those risks. Yet Carson advances an argument in favor of reducing exposure and risk to zero—as much as possible. She criticizes, for example, the recommendation of a Food and Drug Administration committee to reduce exposure to one (potentially hazardous chemical) part per million rather than zero, claiming that such a decision to manage rather than eliminate risks makes the public a "guinea pig."[26] At one point in her book, Carson recognizes that it "would be unrealistic to suppose that all chemical carcinogens can or will be eliminated from the modern world."[27] Yet on the very same page, she states that, unlike germs, which man did not put in the environment, "man *has* put the vast majority of carcinogens into the environment, and he can, if he wishes, eliminate many of them."[28] She then issues a call: "The most determined effort should be made to eliminate those carcinogens that now contaminate our food, our water supplies, and our atmosphere, because these provide the most dangerous type of contact—minute exposures, repeated over and over throughout the years."[29]

Carson's determination to achieve zero risk and zero carcinogens was both influential and emblematic of her times. In that era, widespread belief—reflected in and promoted by *Silent Spring*—held that we need not settle for managing risks to acceptable levels, that we could and should eliminate them altogether and return to that imagined more pristine and pure time before the contamination brought by modern industrialized society. Carson was not alone in this sentiment. As summarized by a National Academy of Sciences report, "Through the 1960s and early 1970s, toxicologists avoided the problem of identifying 'acceptable' intakes of carcinogens. Where it was possible, regulators simply prohibited introduction of carcinogens into commerce."[30] As a result of these unrealistic assumptions, regulatory decisions were increasingly "stalemated, postponed, [or] ignored."[31]

The environmental statutes adopted in that period, many of which remain in effect today (and some of which are discussed in the following sections of this chapter), followed and were no doubt influenced by the zero-risk paradigm espoused by Carson in *Silent Spring*. Cass Sunstein describes this mindset as follows:

> How might we explain the enactment of provisions that seem at once so vague, rigid, and artificial? Much of the answer lies in the distinctive political dynamic of environmental debates in the late 1960s and early 1970s, in which citizens wanted air to be "safe" and politicians who failed to respond were at great risk. We might even describe the result as "1970s environmentalism," a form of thinking that accomplished a great deal of good, by producing rapid decreases in pollution levels, but that also seems increasingly anachronistic, even counterproductive. In the 1970s in particular, politicians would proceed at their peril if they asserted that "safety" could be compromised by other goals. At the same time, politicians were affected by, and doubtless catered to, the pervasive psychological urge for certainty, as confirmed by evidence that people are willing to pay a great deal for "no risk" and much less for "substantially less risk."[32]

We better understand now why the quest for zero risk is quixotic and self-defeating. Actions to reduce one risk often have the unanticipated effect of increasing other risks through substitute products or offsetting behaviors. As Justice Stephen Breyer writes in his book, *Breaking the Vicious Circle*, the drive to try to eliminate rather than manage risk, a tendency he calls "tunnel vision," carries a "single-minded pursuit of a single goal too far, to the point where it brings about more harm than good."[33] In short, the ideal of simply banning a relatively discrete set of harmful industrial chemicals to restore the pastoral vision of natural harmony and zero risk is a myth. "As a practical matter, the idea that humans can be absolutely protected from chemical carcinogens died as a defensible concept."[34] Risks are complex and must be assessed and managed in their full context. Unfortunately, our statutory legacies from the *Silent Spring* era do not reflect this modern understanding.

Three Statutory Legacies

The legacy of the overly simplistic, zero-risk paradigm espoused by Rachel Carson remains with us today in the form of important statutes enacted in that era. While Carson does not shoulder sole responsibility for these statutes (indeed, one of them, the so-called Delaney Clause, was enacted before the publication of *Silent Spring*), she adopted and spread this perspective with her writings. Motivated by the same zero-risk take on life,[35] Congress adopted a series of zero-risk absolutist environmental statutes that have no real chance of being implemented as written. Describing the adoption of such statutes as the "pathology of symbolic legislation," Professor John Dwyer notes the difficulty in implementing zero-risk statutes:

> The programs mandated by such legislation are more symbolic than functional. Frequently, the legislature has failed to address the administrative and political constraints that will block implementation of the statute. By enacting this type of statute, legislators reap the political benefits of voting for "health and the environment" and against "trading lives for dollars," and successfully sidestep the difficult policy choices that must be made in regulating public health and the environment. Thus, while the statute, literally read, promises a risk-free environment, the hard issues involved in defining acceptable risk are passed on to the regulatory agency or to the courts.[36]

277

Dwyer concludes that the implementation of symbolic legislation has resulted in regulatory delays and undermines the integrity of the regulatory process.[37] John Mendeloff has written on how absolutist regulatory standards can ironically result in less rather than more regulation, as agencies resist taking action in order to avoid the unreasonable outcomes and procedural fights that inevitably result from such absolute standards.[38] Thus, over-regulation may cause under-regulation. Mandating zero risk may sound attractive in the abstract, but in practice it results in legal fictions, science charades, repeated litigation, and obfuscation as regulatory agencies attempt to implement statutory provisions that are inconsistent with scientific reality. Some examples of zero risk legislation are discussed below.

The Delaney Clause

No statutory provision better signifies the zero-risk paradigm of Rachel Carson's era, nor the mischief, dissembling, and obfuscation involved in trying to implement such an impossible proposition, than the so-called Delaney Clause. The Delaney Clause was an amendment to the Food, Drug, and Cosmetic Act authored by Rep. James J. Delaney (D-NY) and enacted in 1958, which provided that "no additive shall be deemed to be safe if it is found to induce cancer when ingested by man or animal, or if it is found, after tests which are appropriate for the evaluation of the safety of food additives, to induce cancer in man or animal."[39] Three identical clauses were actually inserted in different parts of the statute—the original for food additives in 1958,[40] a second for color additives added two years later in 1960,[41] and a third for animal drugs in 1968.[42] Although the original Delaney Clause preceded *Silent Spring*, it was based on many of the same concerns and the zero-risk paradigm for change that would be most eloquently expressed a few years later by Carson's book. Thus, the "Delaney Clause's skepticism about the marketplace's ability to insure safety against chemical exposures presaged the message of Rachel Carson's *Silent Spring*."[43]

The Delaney amendment was based on two assumptions: only a small number of carcinogens contaminated food, and these rare carcinogens posed a major public health threat that could be eliminated completely.[44] At the time of Congressman Delaney's amendment, and through the period in which Rachel Carson wrote *Silent Spring*, those assumptions received considerable, albeit not universal, support within the relevant scientific community.[45] Both premises would gradually, however, be shown to be flawed.[46] As David Kessler wrote, prior to assuming the role of FDA commissioner, at the time the Delaney Clause was adopted, "most experts believed that it was possible to eliminate from the food supply all substances that may increase the risk of cancer to humans or animals. . . . Today, . . . the goal of eliminating all such substances is viewed by many, including the FDA, as unattainable."[47]

The D.C. Circuit Court of Appeals, in a decision addressing the Delaney Clause, cited figures provided by an industry trade group that there were only four known human carcinogens in 1958 when the clause was enacted; but 20 years later, there were 37 known human carcinogens and more than 500 substances known to cause cancer in animals, all of which would be banned under the Delaney Clause.[48] Richard Merrill cites a paper by a leading National Cancer Institute scientist written at the time the clause was enacted; it notes that the number of carcinogens in food was in single-digits and that the discovery of many more in the future was thought to be unlikely: "It is unlikely . . . that many of the presently used additives and contaminants of foodstuffs, especially most of those of purely inorganic nature, unless they are radioactive or belong to the group of carcinogenic metals . . . introduce any carcinogenic hazard into the general food supply."[49]

Today, we know that the number of agents with possible carcinogenic activity at high doses is much higher. Ames and colleagues have found that approximately half of the synthetic chemicals tested, as well as the same proportion of naturally occurring substances tested, can cause cancer at high doses in animal studies.[50] Indeed, under the Delaney Clause, whether or not the dose and exposure route in animals is relevant to humans does not matter. That means virtually any substance could be shown to be a potential carcinogen in animals under certain conditions—and potentially banned. Specifically, if a large glob of almost any chemical were implanted or injected in pure form into the forestomach or lung lining of a rodent (an exposure route sometimes used in animal studies even though humans are not exposed this way), it would almost always cause irritation, which in turn would increase the rate of cell proliferation and hence result in an increase in tumor incidence.[51] Accordingly, it would be classified as an animal carcinogen under the Delaney Clause and banned.

The widespread prevalence of "potential" carcinogens, in conflict with the understanding of the Delaney Clause, is further documented by the International Agency for Research on Cancer (IARC), a scientific organization whose carcinogen evaluations are adopted by governments around the world, including the United States. IARC has evaluated in detail the carcinogenicity of almost 1,000 substances to date, and has found only one (caprolactam) that may "possibly" not be carcinogenic.[52] IARC does not even have a category for known noncarcinogens, to parallel its category of known carcinogens, because presumably no such substance exists. Virtually anything can cause cancer under some circumstances, even though those circumstances are usually not relevant to any realistic human exposure. Unfortunately, the authors of the Delaney Clause had a much less nuanced understanding of cancer and carcinogens. Thus, as Bruce Ames wrote in *Science* in 1984, "our current regulatory policies, which assume carcinogens are rare, are in trouble."[53]

The scientific plausibility of the Delaney Clause was further undermined by the rapidly increasing analytical capability to detect substances in foods at lower and lower concentrations. Many foods that present, at most, *de minimis* risks could be prohibited under the Delaney Clause because they contained minute quantities of a substance that had been found to cause cancer in animals (usually at many orders of magnitude higher doses). New analytical techniques permit detection of contaminants at levels at least one million times lower than was possible when the Delaney Clause was enacted.[54] As one scholar put it, "the refinement of detection technologies rendered Delaney applicable to an extent that seemed absurd and counterproductive."[55]

The absurdity of the Delaney Clause and the zero-risk paradigm promoted by Carson were demonstrated in a 1987 D.C. Circuit Court decision forcing the FDA to ban products containing low levels of a color additive (D&C Orange No. 17) that the agency had found to present a microscopically trivial cancer risk of 1 in 19 billion (i.e., 5.1×10^{-11}), on the grounds that the Delaney Clause was absolute and provided no exception for *de minimis* risks (or apparently common sense).[56] According to the congressional testimony of one expert, "our continued enforcement of the Delaney Clause represents a scientific embarrassment which perpetuates misinformation and

280

increases consumer anxiety rather than providing meaningful public health protection."[57]

In addition to its zero-risk emphasis, the Delaney Clause adopts the related pathologies of *Silent Spring*. Just as Carson assumes nature to be innocuous, the Delaney Clause gives a free pass to natural substances in foods that may be carcinogenic. Yet many naturally occurring compounds in food are equally or even more carcinogenic than substances prohibited by the Delaney Clause.[58] The clause also fails to give any consideration to the benefits of the substances it seeks to ban (see Desrochers and Shimizu in Chapter 5). It also does not consider the costs of compliance with harsh regulatory prohibitions. Finally, the Delaney Clause, like *Silent Spring*, fails to consider the risk-risk trade-offs of its proposed restrictions. The so-called "Delaney Paradox" is the finding by the National Academy of Sciences and others that the zero-risk mandate of the Delaney Clause actually increases risks by blocking the approval of new products—products which would have replaced more dangerous chemicals currently on the market and grandfathered under Delaney.[59]

Given all these problems with the Delaney Clause, it is not surprising that numerous congressional hearings, expert reports, and agency statements over the span of decades recommended reform or repeal of the Delaney Clause.[60] For example, then Secretary of the Department of Health, Education and Welfare Robert Finch declared way back in 1969 that "[i]f the Delaney Clause, as it is now written, were to be strongly enforced for pesticide residues, it would convert us to a nation of vegetarians. Much of our red meat, many dairy products, some eggs, fish and fowl—all parts of basic food groups deemed necessary to a balanced diet—would be outlawed because of very small pesticide residues from the ecological chain."[61] Yet the Delaney Clause remained resistant to repeal or softening, with legislators and regulators alike intimidated by the inevitable public and media outcry that would result if the government tried to climb down from its zero-risk pedestal. Meanwhile, regulatory agencies such as the FDA and the Environmental Protection Agency, subject to the Delaney Clause, never fully complied with its zero-risk mandate, nor could they, given that that would have required banning almost all processed foods in the United States. Instead, they engaged in a number of tactics and maneuvers to try to circumvent the harsh dictates of the statute.[62]

The Delaney Clause for food additives (but not color additives) was finally put into its long overdue rightful place in the dustbin of history when it was rescinded by the Food Quality Protection Act of 1996.[63] Congress finally acted after the Ninth Circuit Court of Appeals held that EPA must apply the Delaney Clause consistent with its absolute language, which would mean banning most food.[64] It took almost 30 years from the realization that the Delaney Clause was scientifically obsolete to remove it from the statute books—a testament to the rhetorical and symbolic power of the zero-risk paradigm espoused by Carson.

Clean Air Act

A second example of a statutory provision that adopts the zero-risk mindset of Rachel Carson is section 109 of the Clean Air Act, which directs EPA to set National Ambient Air Quality Standards (NAAQS). It is the nation's most important environmental statutory provision, with the ambient air quality standards saving the most lives, while also costing the most dollars, of any environmental provision.[65] Notwithstanding the importance of the NAAQS program, the statutory language governing this undertaking is scant, simply directing that NAAQS be set at a level "requisite to protect the public health" with an "adequate margin of safety."[66]

EPA and the courts have construed this brief statutory language to require that air quality standards "be set at a level at which there is 'an absence of adverse effect' on . . . sensitive individuals."[67] In setting these standards, EPA is not permitted to consider the cost or feasibility of achieving such protection.[68] The Supreme Court upheld long-standing D.C. Circuit precedent and EPA's position when it ruled unanimously in 2001 that EPA could not consider costs in setting NAAQS standards.[69] Beyond those stringent requirements, NAAQS must provide a "margin of safety" to ensure that "a reasonable degree of protection is to be provided against hazards which research has not yet identified."[70] In short, by requiring that the standards be set at a level which would protect against any adverse effects in the most susceptible individuals in the population, and then adding an extra margin of safety to protect against any yet undiscovered health effects, the NAAQS were apparently intended to provide zero risk from exposure to ambient air pollutants.

This statutory provision—adopted in 1970 when *Silent Spring* was still generating powerful ripple effects—was based on an assumption that pollutants such as ozone and particulate matter have thresholds below which no adverse effects occur, and thus it should be possible to set a "safe" level.[71] As William Reilly wrote in 1981, prior to becoming EPA administrator, the "Clean Air Act incorporates the notion of threshold values of pollutants, levels below which there are presumed to be no adverse health effects, and requires that standards be set on the basis of the threshold, with a margin of safety."[72]

Yet, at least by 1977 if not before, Congress realized that few, if any, of the ambient air pollutants regulated under section 109 exhibit a clear threshold, but rather can adversely affect some susceptible individuals down to the lowest measurable levels.[73] Sen. Edmund Muskie (D-ME), the leading proponent of the 1970 legislation and the 1977 amendments in the Senate, expressly acknowledged this erroneous assumption at a hearing in 1977, acknowledging that "[t]he Clean Air Act is based on the assumption, although we knew at the time it was inaccurate, that there is a threshold."[74] The House likewise acknowledged in 1977 that the "safe threshold" concept underlying section 109 was "at best, a necessary myth" since "no safe thresholds can be established."[75]

Thus, Congress adopted a zero-risk requirement for ambient air pollutants but quickly recognized that such a requirement was not feasible. As Senator Muskie stated in 1977:

> I wish it were possible for the Administrator to set national primary and secondary standards that fully implement the statutory language. . . . The fact is, as testimony and documents disclose, the standards do not fully protect in accordance with the statutory language which gives the Administrator authority to provide for additional protection. He has had to make a pragmatic judgment in the face of the fact that he found there is no threshold on health effects, which makes it very difficult then to apply absolute health protection, and he has not been able to do that.[76]

The House also recognized that the zero-risk approach adopted in 1970 was not feasible: "Some have suggested that since the standards are to protect against all known or anticipated effects and since no safe thresholds can be established, the ambient standards should [b]e set at zero or background levels. Obviously, this no-risk philosophy ignores all economic and social consequences and is impractical."[77]

Congress has adhered to the zero-risk paradigm written into section 109 by rejecting any statutory corrections in 1977 and up to the present, driven no doubt by the zero-risk mindset that has been widely adopted into popular opinion—even if it is no longer scientifically credible. And this mindset can be traced, in good measure, to the influence of Rachel Carson. Despite the recognition today that the zero-risk approach adopted in the 1970 Clean Air Act is not feasible, it remains on the books. Thus, while the legislation is often referred to as "symbolic" or "aspirational,"[78] EPA and the courts must still try to implement this impossible requirement. As the D.C. Circuit once noted, "as any student of the legislative process soon learns, it is one thing for Congress to announce a grand goal, and quite another for it to mandate full implementation of that goal."[79] Congress may have perceived the section 109 zero-risk requirement as a "necessary myth"; but EPA and the courts are forced to engage in science charades and legal fictions to set standards at non-zero-risk levels while presuming to adhere to the zero-risk statutory language.[80] This practice not only demeans and diminishes open and honest administrative practice, but also undercuts the effectiveness and efficiency of the Clean Air Act.[81] Commentators have suggested that air quality "could be improved more quickly and at less cost if the laws were more realistic, if the statutes set more feasible goals, for example."[82] The fact that the zero-risk language of section 109 has survived—despite the realization more than 30 years ago that the approach was scientifically implausible—further demonstrates the rhetorical and political power of the world-view Rachel Carson helped launch.

Clean Water Act

The modern Clean Water Act was enacted by Congress in the 1972 Federal Water Pollution Control Act, with the expressly stated objective in section 101 "to restore and maintain the chemical, physical, and biological integrity of the Nation's waters."[83] To achieve this objective, Congress adopted the zero-risk paradigm of the *Silent Spring* era and expressly called for zero discharge of pollutants, providing that "it is the national goal that the discharge of pollutants into the navigable waters be eliminated by 1985."[84] Furthermore, "it is the national policy that the discharge of toxic pollutants in toxic amounts be prohibited."[85] Of course, these unrealistic goals have not been achieved, either by the 1985 deadline or decades later, and their continued unfulfilled presence in the statute is an embarrassing legacy of an outdated mindset. As Mark Sagoff writes, "[t]hese directives have evaporated into vague aspirations which may attract less respect than scorn to the law."[86]

While other provisions of the statute reflect a more realistic approach to reducing, managing, and controlling pollutants rather than trying to eliminate them altogether, the objectives in section 101 were seen as the "guiding star" of the statute.[87] The zero-discharge (and hence zero-risk) goals in the 1972 act were not symbolic aspirations, but real goals that were viewed at the time as both feasible and necessary. As Senator Muskie emphasized, "[t]hese are not merely the pious declarations that Congress so often makes in passing laws; on the contrary, this is literally a life-or-death proposition for the nation."[88] Senator Muskie described water pollution as a "cancer" that needed to be eliminated: "The cancer of water pollution was engendered by our abuse of our lakes, streams, rivers, and oceans; it has thrived on our half-hearted attempts to control it; and like any other disease, it can kill us."[89] Eschewing the "half-hearted" attempts of the past, the 1972 statute sought to excise the cancer of water pollution, and any objective less than total elimination was seen as allowing the cancer to continue and ultimately grow.

What should have been clear at the time, and was certainly clear soon after enactment, was that the costs of achieving zero discharge would be astronomical and compliance would be both infeasible and imprudent.[90] Shortly after Congress adopted the zero-discharge goal, the congressionally mandated National Water Commission issued its report recommending rescission of the zero-discharge requirement on the grounds that it was infeasible.[91] EPA's deputy administrator testified at Senate hearings in 1982 that the zero-discharge requirement, if taken literally, was unrealistic:

> To limit those [discharges] is certainly a goal. To control these discharges so that we have fishable/swimmable streams is a goal that we would support. But zero discharge is not scientifically attainable in an absolute sense. . . . If you take it in a more literal sense, then in that narrowest definition of removing all materials out of water, it is an indefensible argument and one we can't support.[92]

Two scholars who have researched the history of these statutory provisions explain:

> In hindsight, the goal of eliminating all surface water pollution within thirteen years of the CWA's adoption appears to be wildly aspirational, and perhaps even to amount to foolhardy optimism. It is hard to escape the question of whether those who fashioned that goal operated under serious misconceptions about the nature of water pollution and an industrial society's ability to control it.[93]

These authors concluded that Congress must have known that its zero-discharge goal was unattainable, yet adopted it nevertheless, again showing the power of the zero-risk paradigm.[94]

The adoption of unrealistic goals based on the zero-risk paradigm of *Silent Spring* in the Clean Water Act, as in the Clean Air Act, has ongoing and continuing disruptive consequences. The clean water goal of zero risk skews both planning and regulation—as well as the discourse surrounding those programs—because the goal of zero risk is impossible. Not surprisingly, some organizations and individuals adopt and advocate that goal,[95] especially given that it remains the stated goal of the statute. Indeed, at least one eminent scholar extolled such "daredevil laws" for their "audacity" and "visionary mission."[96] But such unrealistic laws come with a price. Instead of focusing collectively on what nonzero levels of pollution we should strive to attain, and setting priorities for the limited resources we have available, the statutorily sanctified illusion of zero discharge and zero risk dominate and skew the discussion. Both regulators and stakeholders have difficulty focusing on more realistic goals under the shadow of the much more attractive and powerful zero-risk paradigm.

The Most Recent Incantation of *Silent Spring*: The Precautionary Principle

As elaborated in Chapter 11, *Silent Spring* is often portrayed as a precursor to the precautionary principle.[97] At least in its more extreme forms, the precautionary principle rejects any concept of "acceptable risk"; when it is applied (always selectively), it drives toward zero risk.[98] For example, in the European Union, where the precautionary principle has been most widely invoked, the courts have applied the principle (again, only selectively) to require the equivalent of zero risk.[99] Thus, one EU judicial opinion stated that the precautionary principle required withdrawing antibiotic products from the market once it determined that there was a possibility of a risk, "until it can be conclusively demonstrated that they pose no present or future risk to human health."[100] In another decision, the EU advocate general held that "[i]n accordance with the precautionary principle, any discharge should, broadly speaking . . . thus be avoided."[101] These are undisguised demands for zero risk.

The precautionary principle exhibits other characteristics of Rachel Carson's risk paradigm in addition to its push for zero risk. Like Carson's approach, the precautionary principle is applied selectively—or perhaps more accurately discriminatorily—by, for example, exempting "natural" products and exposures. Thus, on the one hand, the precautionary principle is often applied to genetically modified foods, which are already tested extensively for safety and have never been found to cause any harm to human health. On the other hand, the precautionary principle is never applied to organic foods, which receive no safety testing and have occasionally been shown to cause health problems.[102] Like Carson, the precautionary principle usually gives no weight to the benefits of a product or technology, and seems uninterested in the compliance and other costs of regulatory prohibitions and restrictions. Similarly, the precautionary principle ignores the risk-risk trade-offs inherent in restricting many products and technologies.[103] Finally, like Carson's zero-risk paradigm, the precautionary principle has great rhetorical appeal that makes it very popular with the general public, but is unworkable and problematic when applied in practice.[104] The 50-year record of programmatic failure, legal fictions, and regulatory gridlock that has resulted from the statutory legacy of Carson's zero-risk framework provides a compelling argument against going down that same road with the precautionary principle.

Conclusion

Rachel Carson's view of risk, chemicals, and nature in *Silent Spring* was fundamentally flawed. She, like many of her contemporaries, adhered to a world view that nature was benign and harmonious with healthy human existence, whereas many industrial chemicals were an abomination to the natural order and presented unique and unacceptable risks to human health. According to this view, cancer-causing chemicals could and should be identified and eliminated altogether, unmitigated evils that we would be better off without. The paradigm calls for the complete elimination of cancer-causing poisons, without considering the foregone benefits, costs of compliance, or risk-risk trade-offs that such prohibitions would inevitably impose. However, "[a]s the capability and sensitivity of analytical chemistry grew, insisting upon zero risk became more and more unrealistic. It has become apparent that . . . all substances, no matter how pure, can be shown to be contaminated with one or more carcinogens. Therefore, as a practical matter, the idea that humans can be absolutely protected from chemical carcinogens died as a defensible concept."[105] Yet the legal legacy of the zero-risk approach, to which Carson gravitated, remains with us today.

Rachel Carson might be excused for her well-meaning but now outdated views, since such views were widely held by many influential scientists and policymakers of her day. Today, we know better. Zero risk is an impossible dream. All substances, whether natural or synthetic, have the potential to impose risks in at least some scenarios. The goal cannot be to eliminate risk, but rather to try to minimize, control, and manage risk. This can only be achieved rationally by considering relevant factors such as the magnitude of risk, the costs and foregone benefits of reducing risks, and risk-risk trade-offs. The world and the risks inherent in it pose a much more complex and difficult challenge than the simple solutions of Carson's era imply.

While Carson's error might be excused or at least understood, what cannot be forgiven or fathomed is the continued influence of her outdated zero-risk paradigm today. The unfortunate legacy of *Silent Spring* is the series of statutes that incorporated her premise. The popular appeal of the zero-risk ideal, notwithstanding its practical infeasibility, makes it politically difficult to back down from any such zero-risk requirement adopted into law, as discussed with the Delaney Clause and the zero-risk elements of the Clean Air Act and Clean Water Act. These statutes continue to foster an illusion that is resurgent in the rise of the precautionary principle and the growing chemophobia among consumers who flock toward "natural" and "organic" products they mistakenly believe are purer and safer than anything man-made. As Martin Lewis has written, the time has come "to recognize such thinking for the fantasy that it is. We must first relinquish our hopes for utopia if we really wish to save the earth."[106]

Notes

Chapter 1

1. Rachel Carson, *Silent Spring* (Boston: Houghton Mifflin, 1994 [1st ed. 1962]), p. 297.

2. "Rachel Carson Sense of Wonder Contest," Environmental Protection Agency, accessed March 2012, http://www.epa.gov/agingepa/resources/thesenseofwonder/.

Chapter 2

1. Andrew Fletcher, *Selected Discourses and Speeches: A Discourse of Government with Relation to Militias* (Edinburgh, 1698); *Two Discourses concerning the Affairs of Scotland* (Edinburgh, 1698); *Speeches by a Member of the Parliament* (Edinburgh, 1703); and *A Conversation concerning a Right Regulation of Government* (Edinburgh, 1704), accessed July 2011, http://oll.libertyfund.org/?option=com_staticxt&staticfile=show.php%3F title=1222&chapter=83366&layout=html&Itemid=27.

2. Rachel Carson, Testimony before the Senate Committee on Government Operations, 88th Congress, 1st sess., June 4, 1963, http://www.itnsource.com/shotlist/ BHC_FoxMovietone/1963/06/05/X05066302. Reference: X05066302 Fox tape ref: UP (WA 9887) (WA NO #). Fox short list lib ref: 156243 Source: DAM. Rachel Carson, "Interagency Coordination in Environmental Hazards (Pesticides)," testimony before the Subcommittee on Reorganization and International Organizations of the Senate Committee on Government Operations, 88th Cong., 1st sess., June 4, 1963 (Washington, DC: Government Printing Office, 1964).

3. Herman Melville, 1819–1891. Moby-Dick, or, The Whale Electronic Text Center, University of Virginia Library, p. 3, http://etext.virginia.edu/etcbin/toccer-new2?id=Mel2Mob.sgm&images=images/modeng&data=/texts/english/modeng/ parsed&tag=public&part=1&division=div1.

4. Rachel Carson, *The Sea Around Us* (New York: Oxford University Press, 1951), p. 15.

5. Walt Whitman, "Out of the Cradle Endlessly Rocking," http://www.princeton. edu/~batke/logr/log_101.html.

6. Chris Cleave, "A Survey of the Seafaring Man Booker Prize," accessed July 2011, http://www.themanbookerprize.com/perspective/articles/106.

7. Linda J. Lear, *Rachel Carson: Witness for Nature* (New York: H. Holt, 1997), pp. 33–34.

8. Ibid., pp. 61–62.

9. Ibid., p. 75.

10. "A Roundtrip to Davy Jones's Locker," *National Geographic*, June 1931, p. 655.

11. Lear, *Witness for Nature*, p. 116.

12. Rachel Carson, "The Real World around Us." A talk to Theta Sigma Phi, Sorority of Women Journalists, 1954, in *Lost Woods: The Discovered Writing of Rachel Carson*, ed. Linda Lear (Boston: Beacon Press, 1998).

13. Lear, *Witness for Nature*, p. 81

14. Ibid., p. 86.

15. Ibid., p. 80.

16. Ibid., p. 88.

17. Ed Weeks, "Contributors' Column," *Atlantic Monthly*, September 1937, p. 160.

18. Rachel Carson, *Under the Sea-Wind, A Naturalist's Picture of Ocean Life* (New York: Simon and Schuster, 1941), p. xiii.

19. Linda J. Lear, ed., *Lost Woods: The Discovered Writing of Rachel Carson* (Boston: Beacon Press, 1998), p. 105.

20. Carson, "The Real World around Us," pp. 150–51.

21. "The Sea around Us," Wikipedia, accessed July 2011, http://en.wikipedia.org/wiki/The_Sea_Around_Us.

22. Charles Poore, "Books of the Times," *New York Times*, October 26, 1955, p. 17.

23. Carson, *The Sea Around Us*, p. 15.

24. Arlene Rodda Quaratiello, *Rachel Carson: A Biography* (Westport, CT: Greenwood Publishing Group, 2004), p. 59. This passage is sometimes cited from the National Book Award in 1963.

25. Rachel Carson, Speech accepting the John Burroughs Medal, April 1952, in *Lost Woods*, p. 94.

26. Leo Tolstoy, *What Is Art? And Essays on Art* (London: Oxford University Press, 1959), p. 56.

27. Rachel Carson, Speech accepting the National Book Award for Nonfiction, 1952, in *Lost Woods*, p. 91.

28. This idea is central to Tolstoy's essay, but see, for example, page 227: "There is one indubitable sign distinguishing real art from its counterfeit—namely, the infectiousness of art. If a man without exercising effort and without altering his standpoint, on reading, hearing, or seeing another man's work experiences a mental condition which unites him with that man and with others who are also affected by that work, then the object evoking that condition is a work of art." Tolstoy, *What Is Art?*.

29. Ibid., p. 51.

30. Ibid., p. 228.

31. Rachel Carson, *Silent Spring* (Boston: Houghton Mifflin, 1962).

32. Lear, *Witness for Nature*, p. 185.

33. Ibid., p. 367.

34. Ibid., p. 119.

35. Quaratiello, p. 89 and "Rachel Carson's Sense of Wonder," http://www.todayinliterature.com/print-today.asp?Event_Date=5/27/1907.

36. Ibid., p. 328.

37. Paul Brooks, "Introduction," *Always, Rachel: The Letters of Rachel Carson and Dorothy Freeman, 1952–1964*, ed. Martha E. Freeman (Boston: Beacon Press, 1994), p. xxix.

38. Lear, *Witness for Nature*, p. 327.

39. Carson, *Silent Spring*, p. 12.

40. Carson, Testimony before the Senate Committee on Government Operations, June 6, 1963.

41. Carson, *Silent Spring*, p. 127.

42. Ibid., p. 30.

43. Ibid., p. 41.

44. Ibid., p. 85.

45. Ibid., p. 184.

46. Ibid., p. 198.

47. Ibid., p. 277.

48. Rachel Carson, *Always, Rachel: The Letters of Rachel Carson and Dorothy Freeman, 1952–1964*, ed. Martha E. Freeman (Boston: Beacon Press, 1994), p. 231.

49. Carson, *Silent Spring*, p. 296.

50. Aldous Huxley, *The Doors of Perception* (New York: Harper and Brothers, 1954), p. 73.

51. Albert Gore, "Introduction," White House website, http://clinton4.nara.gov/WH/EOP/OVP/_24hours/carson.html (accessed February 16, 2011; website is no longer on line).

52. Rachel Carson, Excerpt from "Essay on the Biological Sciences," in *Good Reading*, 1958, accessed July 2011, http://www.fws.gov/northeast/rachelcarson/writings.html.

53. Paul Ehrlich, *The Population Bomb* (New York: Ballantine Books, 1968).

54. Carl Safina, "Introduction," *The Sea around Us* (New York: Oxford University Press, 2003), pp. xvi–xvii.

55. Jean-Baptiste Michel et al., "Quantitative Analysis of Culture Using Millions of Digitized Books," *Science* 331, no. 6014 (2011): 176–182. DOI:10.1126/science.1199644.

56. Google Labs Books Ngram Viewer, accessed July 21, 2011, http://ngrams.googlelabs.com/graph?content=Rachel+Carson&year_start=1935&year_end=2010&corpus=0&smoothing=3.

57. No one knows exactly what Lincoln said. The earliest record of something like this passage is "Is this the little woman who made the great war?" accessed July 21, 2011, http://wraabe.wordpress.com/_2008/06_/26/abraham-lincoln-to-harriet-beecher-stowe-the-author-of-this-great-war/.

58. *English Essays: Sidney to Macaulay*, The Harvard Classics, vol. 27, ed. Charles Eliot (New York: P. F. Collier & Son, 1909–14), accessed July 26, 2011, http://www.bartleby.com/27/.

Chapter 3

1. Paul R. Ehrlich and Anne H. Ehrlich, *The Population Bomb* (New York: Ballantine Books and Sierra Club, 1968).

2. Garrett Hardin, "The Tragedy of the Commons," *Science* 162 (1968): 1243–48.

3. Barry A. Commoner, *The Closing Circle: Nature, Man and Technology* (New York: Alfred A. Knopf, 1971).

4. Roderick F. Nash, *Wilderness and the American Mind* (New Haven: Yale University Press, 1967).

5. Ernst Friedrich Schumacher, *Small Is Beautiful: Economics as If People Mattered* (New York: Harper and Row, 1973).

6. Donella H. Meadows, Dennis L. Meadows, Jørgen Randers, and William W. Behrens III, *The Limits to Growth: A Report for the Club of Rome's Project on the Predicament of Mankind* (New York: Universe Books, 1972).

7. Joseph Edward de Steiguer, *The Origins of Modern Environmental Thought* (Tucson: University of Arizona Press, 2006), p. 1.

8. Steven Stoll, *U.S. Environmentalism since 1945: A History with Documents* (Boston: Bedford and St. Martin's, 2006), p. 13.

9. Some scholars take a more nuanced position on the issue. For example, environmental historian William Cronon observes that while "it may be an oversimplification to say that the modern environmental movement began with Rachel Carson's *Silent Spring* . . . it is hard to overstate the book's impact" because it was "a lightning rod like no other." See William Cronon, "Foreword: *Silent Spring* and the Birth of Modern Environmentalism," in *DDT, Silent Spring, and the Rise of Environmentalism: Classic Texts*, ed. Thomas H. Dunlap (Seattle: University of Washington Press, 2008), pp. ix–xii.

For a more detailed and nuanced discussion of the context and reception of Rachel Carson's work, see Charles T. Rubin, *The Green Crusade: Rethinking the Roots of Environmentalism* (Lanham, MD: Rowman & Littlefield Publishers, 1998).

10. John Bellamy Foster and Brett Clark, "Rachel Carson's Ecological Critique," *Monthly Review* 59, no. 9 (2008), http://monthlyreview.org/080201foster-clark.php.

11. Carson lists not only introduced predators and parasites, but also microbial and viral infection of insects, chemical attractants, repellent sounds, and juvenile hormones that seem likely, in our opinion, to have major impact beyond a targeted pest species. She also discusses other technological means, such as the X-ray sterilization of male insects, which are certainly less problematic in this respect, yet certainly "unnatural."

12. Marjory Stoneman Douglas, *The Everglades: River of Grass* (New York: Rinehart, 1947).

13. Aldo Leopold, *A Sand County Almanac* (New York: Oxford University Press, 1949).

14. Rachel Carson, *Under the Sea-Wind* (New York: Oxford University Press, 1952); and *The Sea around Us* (New York: Oxford University Press, 1951).

15. de Steiguer, *The Origins of Modern Environmental Thought*.

16. Rubin, *The Green Crusade*, p. 30.

17. Arthur Kallet and Frederick J. Schlink, *100,000,000 Guinea Pigs: Dangers in Everyday Foods, Drugs, and Cosmetics* (New York: Vanguard Press, 1933).

18. William Vogt, *Road to Survival* (New York: W. Sloane Associates, 1948).

19. Vaughan Bell, "Don't Touch That Dial! A History of Media Technology Scares, from the Printing Press to Facebook," *Slate.com*, February 15, 2010, http://www.slate.com/articles/health_and_science/science/2010/02/dont_touch_that_dial.html.

20. Steiner's take on life and agriculture came to be known as "anthroposophy," meaning literally "man-body knowledge." In short, it holds that, through relevant training, one can be taught to see and sense the nonphysical and spiritual world that surrounds us and affects our health and well-being. Anthroposophy eventually led to the development of "biodynamic" agriculture. In light of the hard evidence that demonstrates that organic food has no superior nutritional value, however, much of the rhetoric surrounding organic farming now revolves around its alleged—and in our opinion similarly implausible—claims that it is significantly less environmentally damaging that industrial farming.

For critical perspectives on Steiner and organic farming, see Alex Avery, *The Truth about Organic Food* (Chesterfield, MO: Henderson Communications LLC, 2006); and Thomas R. DeGregori, *Bountiful Harvest: Technology, Food Safety and the Environment* (Washington, DC: Cato Institute, 2002).

21. Although our discussion of pesticide history is limited to arsenic-based compounds, traditional pesticides also comprised substances whose main active ingredients were copper and sulfur, as well as pesticides produced by plants such as hellebores, larkspurs, chrysanthemums (pyrethrum), and tropical vines (rotenone) to protect themselves against pests. These old-fashioned products are still used by organic producers because they are mostly "manufactured" by nature rather than chemical industrial processes—even though they are demonstrably less efficient and more environmentally damaging than modern synthetic pesticides.

22. Technically speaking, the most common arsenical compound was arsenic trioxide. See James Whorton, *Before* Silent Spring: *Pesticides and Public Health in Pre-DDT America* (Princeton, NJ: Princeton University Press, 1974), chapter 1. See also the chapter by Meiners and Morriss, this volume.

23. Whorton, *Before* Silent Spring, p. 26.

24. Ibid.

25. Ibid.

26. Kallet and Schlink, *100,000,000 Guinea Pigs.*

27. Based on the copy used in the preparation of this essay.

28. Kallet and Schlink, *100,000,000 Guinea Pigs,* p. vi.

29. Ibid., p. viii.

30. Ibid., p. 4.

31. Ibid., p. ix.

32. Ibid., p. 47.

33. Ibid., p. 52.

34. Ibid., p. 56.

35. F. J. Schlink, *Eat, Drink, and Be Wary* (New York: Grosset and Dunlap, 1935).

36. Ruth de Forest Lamb, *American Chamber of Horrors: The Truth about Food and Drugs* (New York: Farrar and Rinehart, 1936).

37. While the names of these ladies might not be of direct interest to 21st-century readers, the organizations they headed might be. They included the American Association of University Women, the American Dietetic Association, the YWCA, the National Women's Christian Temperance Union, and the American Nurses' Association. See also Meiners and Morriss, this volume.

38. Lamb, *American Chamber of Horrors,* pp. vii and 3. Interestingly, a mention is made of one Dr. Wirt who was, according to his critics, the "Bolshevist in the Department of Agriculture" then trying "to make himself czar of the food and drug industries at the same time that he seeks to destroy them."

39. Ibid., p. 251.

40. Ibid., p. 229.

41. Lamb did not seem to detect much cynicism in these actions. We suspect that she probably viewed them as both good local politics and good economics.

42. Ibid., p. 238.

43. Ibid., p. 217.

44. For a more detailed list of such books along with more background, see, among others, Charles McGovern, *Sold American: Consumption and Citizenship, 1890–1945* (Chapel Hill, NC: UNC Press Books, 2006). Interestingly, *American Chamber of Horrors* was based on a U.S. Food and Drug Administration internal exhibit specifically designed to pressure politicians to expand the agency's regulatory authority.

45. John Grant Fuller, *200,000,000 Guinea Pigs: New Dangers in Everyday Foods, Drugs and Cosmetics* (New York: Putnam, 1972).

46. Edwin Diamond, "The Myth of the 'Pesticide Menace,'" *Saturday Evening Post*, September 28, 1963, p. 18ff, reprinted in *DDT, Silent Spring, and the Rise of Environmentalism*, ed. Dunlap, pp. 115–20.

47. Ibid., pp. 116 and 118. Because of her bad health and other engagements, Carson originally felt unable to write a significant book on pesticides by herself. The managers of Houghton Mifflin asked Diamond to be Carson's collaborator on what was tentatively titled *Control of Nature*. The collaboration was a fiasco. Carson's supporters typically blame this outcome on Diamond's arrogance and perception of being treated as nothing more than a research assistant, while Diamond's defenders often suggest he was uncomfortable with Carson's biased predispositions and lack of balance toward her subject.

For further discussion, see Linda Lear, *Rachel Carson: Witness for Nature* (New York: H. Holt, 1997); Arlene Rodda Quaratiello, *Rachel Carson: A Biography* (Westport, CT: Greenwood Publishing Group, 2004); Priscilla Coit Murphy, *What a Book Can Do: The Publication and Reception of Silent Spring* (Amherst: University of Massachusetts Press, 2007).

48. For concise, although somewhat technical overviews of the history of pesticides, fungicides, and rodenticides, see P. E. Russell, "Centenary Review: A Century of Fungicide Evolution," *Journal of Agricultural Science* 145, no. 1 (2005): 11–25; Erich Christian Oerke, "Centenary Review: Crop Losses to Pests," *Journal of Agricultural Science* 144, no. 1 (2006): 31–43; and Roberts and Tren, this volume.

49. For a more detailed list of early popular columns and articles critical of DDT, see Jesse Malkin, "Is DDT a Chemical of Ill Repute?" in *But Is It True? A Citizen's Guide to Environmental Health and Safety Issues*, ed. Aaron Widalsky (Cambridge: Harvard University Press, 1997), pp. 55–80.

50. The most problematic was the insecticide pyrethrum produced from chrysanthemum flowers whose main sources before the war were Kenya and Japan.

51. One of our mothers, then a child struggling with food shortages and a serious lice infestation problem, vividly remembers being sprayed with DDT once American troops landed in Japan.

52. James Stevens Simmons, "How Magic Is DDT?" *Saturday Evening Post* 217 (1945), reprinted in *DDT, Silent Spring, and the Rise of Environmentalism*, ed. Dunlap, p. 32.

53. Ibid., p. 38.

54. "Medicine: Worse Than Insects?" *Time*, January 11, 1949, http://www.time.com/time/_magazine/article/0,9171,800094,00.html.

55. Vincent Brian Wigglesworth, "DDT and the Balance of Nature," *The Atlantic Monthly* 176 (1945): 107–13. The magazine factually described Wigglesworth, then a Reader in Entomology in the University of Cambridge, as "Britain's foremost authority on insect physiology and tropical diseases." For a detailed biography of Wigglesworth, see Michael Locke, "Sir Vincent Brian Wigglesworth, C.B.E., 17 April 1899–12 February 1994," *Biographical Memoirs of Fellows of the Royal Society* 42 (1996): 541–53.

56. Wigglesworth, "DDT and the Balance of Nature," p. 109.

57. Ibid., p. 111.

58. Ibid., p. 112.

59. Ibid.

60. Ibid., p. 113. Wigglesworth describes beekeepers as a "vociferous race" that did not "take kindly to DDT" at the time. Of course, beekeepers had suffered from the use of other insecticides in the past.

61. Ibid.

62. Ibid.

63. Clarence Cottam and Elmer Higgins, "DDT and Its Effect on Fish and Wildlife," *Journal of Economic Entomology* 39, no. 1 (1946): 44–52. Although originally published in an academic journal, this piece was re-released as a 14 page stand-alone leaflet by the U.S. Fish and Wildlife Service in 1946, http://www.fws.gov/contaminants/pdf/historic/19460518.pdf.

64. The summary of a typical debate pitting Vogt and Cottam on the one hand and proponents of marshland drainage for malaria control on the other can be found in Science Services, "Aquatic Wildlife Refuges May Breed Malaria Mosquitos, Doctor Warns. Control Problem Subject of Lively Discussion at Third Annual North American Wildlife Conference," *The Niagara Falls Gazette*, March 17, 1938.

For a more detailed treatment of the issue, see Gordon Patterson, *The Mosquito Crusades: A History of the American Anti-Mosquito Movement from the Reed Commission to the First Earth Day* (New Brunswick, NJ: Rutgers University Press, 2009).

65. Byron Anderson, "Clarence Cottam (January 1, 1899–March 30, 1974)," in *Modern American Environmentalists: A Biographical Encyclopedia*, ed. George A. Cevasco, Richard P. Harmond, and Everett Mendelsohn (Baltimore: The Johns Hopkins University Press, 2009), pp. 112–16, http://books.google.ca/books?id=mTSIPaCr2D YC&source=gbs_navlinks_s.

66. For Cottam's influence on Carson's thinking and works, see, among others, Lear, *Rachel Carson: Witness for Nature*; and Paul Brooks, *Rachel Carson: The Writer at Work* (San Francisco: Sierra Club Books, 1989), first published as *The House of Life: Rachel Carson at Work* (Boston: Houghton Mifflin, 1972).

For biographies of Cottam, see Anderson, "Clarence Cottam (January 1, 1899–March 30, 1974)"; and Eric G. Bolen, "In Memoriam: Clarence Cottam," *The Auk* 92 (1975): 118–25, http://elibrary.unm.edu/sora/Auk/v092n01/p0118-p0125.pdf. Cottam's co-author, Elmer Higgins, had hired Rachel Carson a decade earlier and encouraged her to write for a broad audience. Carson was serving as the Fish and Wildlife Service's scientific editor when the department's early DDT work was being conducted and was in charge of checking it before publication. See Julie Dunlap, "Remembering Rachel Carson: The Woman Who Would Not Be Silent," *Audubon Naturalist News* 33, no. 3 (2007), http://audubonnaturalist.org/default.asp?page=669.

Commenting on the importance of the Audubon Society to Carson, Lear (*Rachel Carson: Witness for Nature*, p. 181), observes that what "little social life [she] had centered on [the Audubon Society]." Carson was first elected to the District of Columbia Audubon Society's board (now the Audubon Naturalist Society) in 1948. One of her colleagues there was William Vogt, whom Lear (ibid., p. 574) describes as "Carson's friend." (See also Julie Dunlap, "Remembering Rachel Carson.")

67. John K. Terres, "Dynamite in DDT," *The New Republic*, March 25, 1946, pp. 415–16.

68. It is possible that Cottam and Terres knew each other going back to the latter's time in government service.

69. To reemphasize the point, the dosage in this case was deliberately extreme in order to assess birds' tolerance levels to DDT. Other aerial spraying tests were simultaneously conducted in other locations with much lower doses.

70. Terres, "Dynamite in DDT," pp. 415–16.

71. Ibid.

72. "Medicine: Worse Than Insects?"

73. Coit Murphy, *What a Book Can Do*, p. 140.

74. Robert S. Strother, "Backfire in the War against Insects," *Reader's Digest* 74 (1959): 64–69, reprinted in *DDT, Silent Spring, and the Rise of Environmentalism*, ed. Dunlap, pp. 85–90.

75. Murray Bookchin (as Lewis Herber), *Our Synthetic Environment* (New York: Knopf, 1962), http://dwardmac.pitzer.edu/Anarchist_Archives/bookchin/syntheticenviron/osetoc.html.

76. In the acknowledgments to his book (not freely available online unlike the remaining content), Bookchin (ibid., p. viii) thanked F. J. Schlink for "offering many suggestions on portions of my book on food additives and food and drug control" and further regretted "that limitations of space made it impossible for [him] to provide the reader with the wealth of material that Consumers' Research has accumulated on these problems."

77. Ibid., not paginated.

78. Robert L. Rudd, "The Irresponsible Poisoners," *The Nation*, May 30, 1959, pp. 496–97; and "Pesticides: The Real Peril," *The Nation*, November 28, 1959, pp. 399, 401.

79. Robert Rudd, *Pesticides and the Living Landscape* (Madison, WI: University of Wisconsin Press, 1964).

80. Ibid., p. vii.

81. Osborn, *Our Plundered Planet* (Boston: Little Brown, 1948).

82. Ibid, p. 61. Our purpose in raising the issue is not to suggest that Osborn or any other Conservation Foundation officers telegraphed the desired results to Rudd, but rather to suggest that grave misgivings about synthetic pesticides were by then widespread and that funding was available for critical voices.

83. Ibid., p. ix. For an in-depth discussion of her collaborators in this endeavor, see Lear, *Rachel Carson: Witness for Nature*.

84. Rachel Carson, *Silent Spring: 40th Anniversary Edition* (Boston: Houghton Mifflin, 2002), p. 16. Yet Carson goes on writing about the serious problems associated with arsenic two paragraphs later. In *Rachel Carson: Witness for Nature*, Lear observes that Carson had thought of writing an article on the topic in 1938.

85. Ibid., p. 18.

86. For more on this issue, see, among others, John Bellamy Foster, "Malthus' *Essay on Population* at Age 200: A Marxian View," *Monthly Review* 50, no. 7 (1998), http://www.monthlyreview.org/1298jbf.htm; Pierre Desrochers and Christine Hoffbauer, "The Post War Intellectual Roots of the Population Bomb: Fairfield Osborn's *Our Plundered Planet* and William Vogt's *Road to Survival* in Retrospect," *Electronic Journal of Sustainable Development* 1, no. 3 (2009): 73–97, http://www.ejsd.org/public/journal_article/12#abstract; David Lowenthal, "Awareness of Human Impacts: Changing Attitudes and Emphasis," in *The Earth as Transformed by Human Action: Global and Regional Changes in the Biosphere over the Past 300 Years*, ed. B. L. Turner II, et al. (Cambridge, U.K.: Cambridge University Press, 1990), pp. 121–35; *The Economics of Population Growth: Classic Writings*, ed. Julian Simon (New Brunswick, NJ: Transaction Publishers, 1998); J. J. Spengler, "History of Population Theories," in *The Economics of Population: Classic Writings*, ed. J. L. Simon (New Brunswick, NJ: Transaction Publishers, 1998), pp. 3–15; J. A. Tainter, "Collapse, Sustainability and the Environment," *Reviews in Anthropology* 37, no. 4 (2008): 342–71; and J. A. Tainter, "Archeology of Overshoot and Collapse," *Annual Review of Anthropology* 35 (2006): 59–74.

87. Frederick Winslow Taylor, *The Principles of Scientific Management* (New York: Norton, 1911) From the nonpaginated version of the Project Gutenberg available at http://archive.org/details/theprinciplesofs06435gut

88. G. V. Jacks and R. O. Whyte, *The Rape of the Earth: A World Survey of Soil Erosion* (London: Faber and Faber Ltd., 1939). The title of the American edition was the more prudish *Vanishing Lands: A World Survey of Soil Erosion*.

89. Samuel P. Hays, "The Mythology of Conservation," in *Perspectives on Conservation*, ed. Henry Jarrett (Baltimore: The Johns Hopkins University Press for Resources for the Future, 1958), pp. 41–42.

90. B.-O. Linnér, *The Return of Malthus: Environmentalism and Post-War Population-Resource Crises* (Isle of Harris, Scotland: The White Horse Press, 2003), p. 37.

91. Alfred Sauvy, "La population du Monde et les ressources de la planète: Un projet de recherches," *Population* 27, no. 6 (1972): 967–77.

92. Sauvy (1898–1990) was not only the dean of French demographers but also the most well-known member of his profession in the French-speaking world because of his numerous short essays published over several decades in *Le Monde*. He first coined the term "Third World" in 1952 in reference to the French Third Estate in pre-revolutionary France. Sauvy discussed and rejected Vogt's core thesis in detail soon after the publication of *Road to Survival*. See Alfred Sauvy, "Alfred Sauvy on the World Population Problem: A View in 1949," *Population and Development Review* 16, no. 4 (1990): 759–74, trans. Paul Demeny; originally, Alfred Sauvy, "Le 'Faux Problème' de la Population Mondiale," *Population* 4, no. 3 (1949).

93. For example, Alston Chase, *The Legacy of Malthus: The Social Costs of the New Scientific Racism* (New York: Knopf, 1977); Desrochers and Hoffbauer, "The Post War Intellectual Roots of the Population Bomb"; Donald Gibson, *Environmentalism: Ideology and Power* (Huntington, NY: Nova Science Publishers, 2002); Linnér, *The Return of Malthus*; T. B. Robertson, "The Population Bomb: Population Growth, Globalization and American Environmentalism, 1945–1980," PhD diss., University of Wisconsin–Madison, 2005; and Kolson Schlosser, "Malthus at Mid-Century: Neo-Malthusianism as Bio-political Governance in the Post-WWII United States," *Cultural Geographies* 16, no. 4 (2009): 465–84.

94. David Cameron Duffy, "William Vogt: A Pilgrim on the Road to Survival," *American Birds* 43, no. 5 (1989): 1256–57, http://elibrary.unm.edu/sora/NAB/v043n05/p01256-p01257.pdf.

95. Patterson, *The Mosquito Crusades*.

96. Vogt reportedly tried to engineer an internal coup to oust and then replace the association's sitting president. He was unsuccessful.

97. Ibid.

98. Desrochers and Hoffbauer, "The Post War Intellectual Roots of the Population Bomb"; Duffy, "William Vogt: A Pilgrim on the Road to Survival"; and Gibson, *Environmentalism: Ideology and Power*.

99. Vogt, *Road to Survival*, p. 78.

100. Ibid., p. 285.

101. Ibid., p. 56.

102. Ibid., p. 86.

103. Ibid., p. 86.

104. Ibid., p. 87.

105. Ibid., p. 194.

106. Ibid., p. 110.

107. Ibid., p. 72.

108. Ibid., p. 63.

109. Ibid., p. 63.

110. Ibid., p. 68.

111. Ibid., p. 206.

112. Ibid., p. 77.

113. Ibid., p. 186.

114. Ibid., p. 33.

115. The case of rodents was viewed as more complex, inasmuch as their presence was more a consequence of man's maltreatment of the land.

116. Ibid., pp. 28 and 31.

117. In his only other significant comment on DDT, Vogt (p. 30) denounced its "widespread and unselective use that destroyed not only pests, but also valuable insects which "pollinate fruit trees and parasitize destructive insects."

118. Ibid., p. 257.

119. The "lifeboat ethics" was proposed in 1974 by the ecologist Garrett Hardin who described the case of a lifeboat bearing 50 people with room for a few more floating on an ocean surrounded by 100 swimmers. The dilemma stems from whether or not (and under what circumstances) swimmers should be taken aboard. The "economics of spaceship earth" is economist Kenneth E. Boulding's 1966 discussion of earth as a spaceship devoid of unlimited resources in which men must find their place in a cyclical ecological system. See Garrett Hardin, "Lifeboat Ethics: The Case against Helping the Poor," *Psychology Today* 8 (1974): 38–43; and K. E. Boulding, "The Economics of the Coming Spaceship Earth," in *Environmental Quality in a Growing Economy*, ed. H. Jarrett (Baltimore: Johns Hopkins University Press for Resources for the Future, 1966), pp. 3–14.

120. Vogt, *Road to Survival*, p. 13.

121. Ibid., p. 48.

122. Ibid., p. 59.

123. Ibid., p. 33.

124. Ibid., p. 147.

125. Ibid., pp. 43–44.

126. Ibid., pp. 34–37.

127. Ibid., p. 38.

128. Ibid., pp. 129–30.

129. Ibid., p. 262.

130. Ibid., p. 145.

131. Ibid., p. 67.

132. Ibid.

133. Ibid., p. 148.

134. Ibid.

135. Ibid., p. 28.

136. Rent-seeking occurs when an individual, organization, or firm seeks to earn money by manipulating the economic and/or legal environment rather than through trade and the creation of wealth. "Perverse subsidies" have both economic and environmentally negative impacts.

137. Ibid., p. 35.

138. Ibid., p. 43.

139. Ibid., p. 127.

140. Ibid., pp. 183–86. Although he occasionally stumbled upon some of the key insights of the perspective later known as "free-market environmentalism," Vogt failed to ask why polluting industries could not be sued for the damage they inflicted upon others—as was traditionally the custom in market economies until these rights were taken away or drastically curbed by politicians seeking to "balance" economic growth and environmental protection—or why agricultural producers had become so dependent on subsidies or were often taking a short-term perspective on the impact of their activities. While he was well aware that the "subsidized industrialist" and the farmer benefiting from subsidy payments were very keen "to protest any real attempt at free enterprise" (p. 43), he was nonetheless more inclined to favor greater (although obviously better) as opposed to lesser political management.

141. Ibid., p. 264.

142. Ibid., p. 265.

143. Chase, *The Legacy of Malthus*, p. 381.

144. Vogt, *Road to Survival*, p. 24.

145. H. von Storch and N. Stehr, "Anthropogenic Climate Change: A Reason for Concern since the 18th Century and Earlier," *Geografiska Annaler: Series A, Physical Geography* 88, no. 2 (2006): 107–13.

146. William Vogt, "On Man the Destroyer," *Natural History* 72, no. 1 (1963): 3–5.

147. Ibid., pp. 3, 5.

148. Ibid., p. 4.

149. Ibid.

150. Ibid., p. 5.

151. Ibid.

152. Coit Murphy, *What a Book Can Do*, p. 144.

153. Lear, *Rachel Carson: Witness for Nature*.

154. William J. Darby, "Silence, Miss Carson," *Chemical & Engineering News*, October 1, 1962, pp. 62–63.

155. Diamond, "The Myth of the 'Pesticide Menace,'" p. 18, reprinted in Dulap, *DDT, Silent Spring, and the Rise of Environmentalism: Classic Texts*, p. 115.

Chapter 4

1. See Robert H. Nelson, "The Office of Policy Analysis in the Department of the Interior," *Journal of Policy Analysis and Management* (Summer 1989), reprinted in Carol H. Weiss, *Organizations for Policy Analysis: Helping Government Think* (Newbury Park, CA: Sage Publications, 1992).

2. Robert H. Nelson, "Unoriginal Sin: The Judeo-Christian Roots of Ecotheology," *Policy Review* (Summer 1990).

3. Robert H. Nelson, *Reaching for Heaven on Earth: The Theological Meaning of Economics* (Lanham, MD: Rowman & Littlefield, 1991).

4. See most recently Robert H. Nelson, *The New Holy Wars: Economic Religion versus Environmental Religion in Contemporary America* (University Park, PA: Penn State University Press, 2010). See also Robert H. Nelson, *Economics as Religion: From Samuelson to Chicago and Beyond* (University Park, PA: Penn State University Press, 2001); Robert H. Nelson, "What Is 'Economic Theology,'" *The Princeton Seminary Bulletin*

(February 2004); and Robert H. Nelson, "Environmental Religion: A Theological Critique," *Case Western Reserve Law Review* (Fall 2004). A complete listing including electronic versions of many other past writings on economic religion and environmental religion can be found at my website at http://www.publicpolicy.umd.edu/faculty/nelson.

5. Paul Tillich, *Dynamics of Faith* (New York: HarperOne, 2001 [1st ed. 1957]), p. 5.

6. Karl Lowith, *Meaning in History* (Chicago: University of Chicago Press, 1949).

7. Ian Buruma, "Who Did Not Collaborate?" *New York Review of Books*, February 24, 2011, p. 16.

8. Igal Halfin, *From Darkness to Light: Class, Consciousness, and Salvation in Revolutionary Russia* (Pittsburgh: University of Pittsburgh Press, 2000), p. 39.

9. Ibid., p. 40.

10. Rachel Carson, *Silent Spring* (Boston: Houghton Mifflin, 1994 [1st ed. 1962]).

11. See Hal K. Rothman, *The Greening of a Nation: Environmentalism in the United States since 1945* (New York: Harcourt Brace, 1998); and Philip Shabecoff, *A Fierce Green Fire: The American Environmental Movement*, rev. ed. (Washington, DC: Island Press, 2003).

12. On environmentalism as a religion, see Thomas R. Dunlap, *Faith in Nature: Environmentalism as Religious Quest* (Seattle, WA: University of Washington Press, 2004); Andrew P. Morriss and Benjamin Cramer, "Disestablishing Environmentalism," *Environmental Law* 39 (2009); and Joel Garreau, "Environmentalism as Religion," *The New Atlantis* (Summer 2010).

13. See Wallace Kaufman, chapter 2, this volume. See also Linda J. Lear, *Rachel Carson: Witness for Nature* (New York: Henry Holt, 1997); and Mark Hamilton Lytle, *The Gentle Subversive: Rachel Carson, Silent Spring, and the Rise of the Environmental Movement* (New York: Oxford University Press, 2007).

14. See Robert Bellah, "Civil Religion in America," *Daedalus* (Winter 1967).

15. Text of State of the Union address available at http://www.washingtonpost.com/wp-dyn/content/article/2011/01/25/AR2011012506398.html

16. Sacvan Bercovitch, *The Puritan Origins of the American Self* (New Haven, CT: Yale University Press, 1975).

17. See Robert William Fogel, *The Fourth Great Awakening & the Future of Egalitarianism* (Chicago: University of Chicago Press, 2000).

18. See Emilio Gentile, *Politics as Religion*, trans. George Staunton (Princeton, NJ: Princeton University Press, 2006).

19. See Robert J. Samuelson, *The Good Life and Its Discontents: The American Dream in the Age of Entitlement, 1945–1995* (New York: Times Books, 1995).

20. Carson, *Silent Spring*, p. 113.

21. See Robert H. Nelson, *Public Lands and Private Rights: The Failure of Scientific Management* (Lanham, MD: Rowman & Littlefield, 1995); and Richard Wahl, *Markets for Federal Water: Subsidies, Property Rights and the Bureau of Reclamation* (Washington, DC: RFF Press, 1989). It might be noted that both Nelson and Wahl served in the Office of Policy Analysis in the Office of the Secretary of the Interior during the 1980s.

22. Carson, *Silent Spring*, pp. 66, 67.

23. Ibid., p. 277.

24. See Pierre Desrochers and Hiroko Shimizu, chapter 3, this volume.

25. Mark A. Noll, *A History of Christianity in the United States and Canada* (Grand Rapids, MI: Eerdmans, 1992).

26. See Nelson, "Calvinism Minus God," in *The New Holy Wars*, Part II.

27. Mark Stoll, *Protestantism, Capitalism and Nature in America* (Albuquerque: University of New Mexico Press, 1997), p. 49.

28. The contemporary philosopher Alasdair MacIntyre declares that "Marxism shares in good measure both the content and the functions of Christianity as an interpretation of human existence, and it does so because it is the historical successor of Christianity"—or at least so it appeared to many people for much of the 20th century. See Alasdair MacIntyre, *Marxism and Christianity* (Notre Dame, IN: University of Notre Dame Press, 1984), p. 6.

29. See Samuel P. Huntington, *Who Are We? The Challenges to America's National Identity* (New York: Simon and Schuster, 2005).

30. See Nelson, *Economics as Religion*.

31. Frank and Fritzie Manuel, *Utopian Thought in the Western World* (Cambridge, MA: Harvard University Press, 1979), pp. 723, 727, 728.

32. Quoted in Friedrich A. Hayek, *The Counter-revolution of Science: Studies on the Abuse of Reason* (Indianapolis: Liberty Fund, 1979 [1st ed. 1952]), p. 355.

33. Richard Ely, *Social Aspects of Christianity and Other Essays* (New York: Thomas Y. Crowell, 1899), p. 72.

34. Samuel Haber, *Efficiency and Uplift: Scientific Management in the Progressive Era, 1890–1920* (Chicago: University of Chicago Press, 1964), p. ix.

35. Dwight Waldo, *The Administrative State: A Study of the Political Theory of American Public Administration* (New York: Holmes and Meier, 1984 [1st ed. 1948]), pp. 19–20.

36. J. B. Bury, *The Idea of Progress* (Westport, CT: Greenwood Press, 1982 [1st ed. 1932]), p. 4.

37. Environmentalists such as Carson were not the only strong critics of American economic religion. John Cobb, a leading American Protestant theologian, writes that in the 20th century "neoclassical economics became the theology of those who saw economic growth as the savior of humankind." Although economic religion "does not dominate the spirituality of all peoples, it is the 'religion' that governs planetary affairs," based on an idolatrous "devotion" to the "increase of economic production." See John B. Cobb, Jr., *Sustaining the Common Good: A Christian Perspective on the Global Economy* (Cleveland: The Pilgrim Press, 1994), pp. 49, 28, 40.

38. See Robert H. Nelson, "Is 'Libertarian Environmentalist' an Oxymoron? The Crisis of Progressive Faith and the Environmental and Libertarian Search for a New Guiding Vision," in *The Next West: Public Lands, Community and Economy in the American West*, ed. John A. Baden and Donald Snow (Washington, DC: Island Press, 1997).

39. James C. Scott, *Seeing Like a State: How Certain Schemes to Improve the Human Condition Have Failed* (New Haven, CT: Yale University Press, 1998).

40. Ibid., pp. 89–90.

41. Fogel, *The Fourth Great Awakening & the Future of Egalitarianism*, p. 172.

42. Carson, *Silent Spring*, p. 267.

43. Ibid., p. 255.

44. Ibid., pp. 252, 253.

45. Ibid., pp. 92, 93, 96.

46. Ibid., p. 93.

47. See Desrochers and Shimizu, chapter 5, this volume.

48. Carson, *Silent Spring*, pp. 162–63.

49. Jane Jacobs, *The Death and Life of Great American Cities* (New York: Modern Library, 1993 [1st ed. 1961]).

50. Carson, *Silent Spring*, pp. 165–66, 167.

51. Ibid., pp. 165, 163.

52. See John McPhee, *Conversations with the Archdruid* (New York: Farrar, Straus and Giroux, 1971).

53. Ibid., p. 159.

54. Quotation in Steven F. Hayward, *Mere Environmentalism: A Biblical Perspective on Humans and the Natural World* (Washington, DC: AEI Press, 2011), p. 44.

55. Robert Royal, *The Virgin and the Dynamo: The Use and Abuse of Religion in Environmental Debates* (Grand Rapids, MI: William B. Eerdmans, 1999), p. 14.

56. William C. Dennis, "Wilderness Cathedrals and the Public Good," *The Freeman* 37, no. 5 (May 1987).

57. Robert H. Nelson, "Dick Cheney Was Right: The Energy Debate *Is* about Virtue," *The Weekly Standard*, June 11, 2001.

58. See Roger Meiners, chapter 6, this volume.

59. See also Roger Meiners and Andrew P. Morriss, chapter 9, this volume.

60. Carson, *Silent Spring*, pp. 173–74.

61. Ibid., p. 242.

62. See Nathan Gregory, chapter 7, this volume.

63. Carson, *Silent Spring*, p. 219.

64. Ibid., pp. 219, 220.

65. Ibid., p. 208.

66. R. Doll and R. Peto, "The Causes of Cancer: Quantitative Estimates of Avoidable Risks of Cancer in the United States Today," *Journal of the National Cancer Institute* (June 1981).

67. Bruce N. Ames and Lois Swirsky Gold, "Environmental Pollution and Cancer: Some Misconceptions," in *Phantom Risk: Scientific Inference and the Law*, ed. Kenneth R. Foster, David E. Bernstein, and Peter W. Huber (Cambridge, MA: MIT Press, 1993), pp. 153, 154.

68. Ibid., p. 157.

69. Ibid., p. 164.

70. Nelson, *The New Holy Wars*.

71. See Nathan Gregory, chapter 7, this volume.

72. Carson, *Silent Spring*, pp. 1, 2.

73. Ibid., pp. 2, 3.

74. Ibid., p. 6.

75. See Nathan Gregory, chapter 7, this volume.

76. Carson, *Silent Spring*, pp. 5–7.

77. Ibid., pp. 7, 8, 13.

78. Ibid., pp. 12, 13.

79. David R. Williams, *Searching for God in the Sixties* (Newark, DE: University of Delaware Press, 2010), pp. 45, 39.

80. See Donald Roberts and Richard Tren, chapter 8, this volume.

81. Daniel B. Botkin, *Discordant Harmonies: A New Ecology for the Twenty-First Century* (New York: Oxford University Press, 1990).

82. Ibid., pp. 9, 188–89, 191.

83. See also Wallace Kaufman, *No Turning Back: Dismantling the Fantasies of Environmental Thinking* (New York: Basic Books, 1994).

84. Botkin, pp. 6, 10, 193.

85. See Donald Worster, *Nature's Economy: A History of Ecological Ideas*, 2nd ed. (New York: Cambridge University Press, 1994).

86. Donald Worster, "The Ecology of Order and Chaos," in *The Wealth of Nature: Environmental History and the Ecological Imagination*, ed. Donald Worster (New York: Oxford University Press, 1994), p. 155.

87. Ibid., 158.

88. D. Foster and J. Aber, "Background and Framework for Long-Term Ecological Research," in *Forests in Time: The Environmental Consequences of 1,000 Years of Change in New England*, ed. David R. Foster and John D. Aber (New Haven, CT: Yale University Press, 2004), pp. 5–6.

89. See also Charles C. Mann, *1491: New Revelations of the Americas before Columbus* (New York: Knopf, 2005).

90. D. Foster, et al., "The Environmental and Human History of New England," in *Forests in Time: The Environmental Consequences of 1,000 Years of Change in New England*, ed. David R. Foster and John D. Aber (New Haven, CT: Yale University Press, 2004), pp. 64, 62.

91. Ibid., pp. 43–44.

92. See Robert Royal, *1492 and All That: Political Manipulations of History* (Washington, DC: Ethics and Public Policy Center, 1992).

93. See Charles T. Rubin, *The Green Crusade: Rethinking the Roots of Environmentalism* (New York: Free Press, 1994).

94. William Cronon, *Changes in the Land: Indians, Colonists, and the Ecology of New England* (New York: Hill and Wang, 1983).

95. William Cronon, "Getting Back to the Wrong Nature," *Utne Reader* (May–June 1996), pp. 76–78.

96. See Alan Weisman, *The World without Us* (New York: Thomas Dunne Books, 2007).

97. Bill McKibben, *The End of Nature* (New York: Random House, 1989), pp. 180, 186.

98. Quoted in "Bulletin Board," *High Country News*, September 23, 1991, p. 16.

99. See Tobias Lanz, "Calvinism without God," *Chronicles*, August 2011.

Chapter 5

1. Adam J. Lieberman and Simona C. Kwon, *Facts versus Fears: A Review of the Greatest Unfounded Health Scares of Recent Times*, 4th ed. (New York: American Council on Science and Health, 2004), p. 7, available at http://www.acsh.org/docLib/20040928_fvf2004.pdf

2. Clarence Dean, "Cranberry Sales Curbed; 45 Million Loss Feared Cranberry Crop Facing Huge Loss," *New York Times*, November 11, 1959, p. 1; Richard E. Mooney, "Color Additives to Stir New Feud; Debates Similar to Those of Cranberry Tiff Will Be Heard in Congress Questions: What's Safe? Delaney Readies a Clause to Prohibit Chemicals That Produce Cancer," *New York Times*, November 30, 1959, p. 39.

3. Lieberman and Kwon, *Facts versus Fears*, p. 7.

4. Thomas H. Jukes. "People and Pesticides," *American Scientist* 51 (3) (1963): 355–61; John A. Osmundsen, "Food Trade Waits Impacts on U.S. Law on Additives," *New York Times*, February 23, 1959, p. 1; Desrochers and Shimizu, chapter 3, this volume; Meiners and Morriss, chapter 9, this volume.

5. Gladwin Hill, "Atom Test Studies Show Area Is Safe: Radiation Is Found Well below Hazardous Level–Damage to Property Remains Small," *New York Times*, May 25, 1953, p. 21; Harry Schwartz, "Long-Deadly Part Found in Atom Ash; Japanese Doctors Concerned because of the Presence of Dangerous Strontium 90," *New York Times*, March 26, 1954, p. 5; *New York Times*, "Hot Ashes," June 24, 1954, p. E6; *New York Times*, "Stevenson Sees Cover-Up on Bomb; Says Administration Kept Secret Contamination of U.S. Milk by Strontium," *New York Times*, November 3, 1956, p. 20; Richard K. Plumb, "Fall-Out of Bomb a Defense Factor; Shower of Radioactive Dust after the Explosion Makes Wide Area Unsafe Experts Split on Text. A. E. C. Scientists Discount Genetic Dangers but Others Have Doubts," *New York Times*, June 10, 1955, p. 10; Waldemar Kaempffert, "Special International Body Is Proposed to Consider Danger of Atomic Fall-Out," *New York Times*, June 26, 1955, p.E9.

6. Indur M. Goklany, *Clearing the Air: The Real Story of the War on Air Pollution* (Washington, DC: Cato Institute, 1999); Edith Evans Asbury, "Smog Is Really Smaze; Rain May Rout It Tonight; Four-Day Concentration of Smoke and Haze Causes Optical Illusions and Discomfort—Two Airports Close as Fog Is Added Heavy, Heavy Hangs Over: Smaze, a Blend of Smoke and Haze, Smothers City Area With a Grayish Pall Rain May Wash Out 4-Day Smog Tonight," *New York Times*, November 21, 1953, p. 1; *New York Times*, "Smog and Ire Fill Los Angeles Air; City Has Worst Atmospheric Pall and Clamor for Action Reaches Insistent High," October 17, 1954, p. 34.

7. Lieberman and Kwon, *Facts versus Fears*, p. 7.

8. *New York Times*, "Rachel Carson's Warning," July 2, 1962, p. 28.

9. John W. Finney, "Curbs on 'Wonder Drugs' Urged to Avoid Harm to Unborn Babies," *New York Times*, May 11, 1962, p. 36.

10. National Toxicological Program, *Thalidomide*. Available at http://cerhr.niehs.nih.gov/common/thalidomide.html, visited April 15, 2011.

11. Wallace F. Janssen, "The Story of the Laws behind the Labels," FDA, June 1981, available at http://www.fda.gov/AboutFDA/WhatWeDo/History/Overviews/ucm056044.htm.

12. Ibid.

13. Ibid.

14. *New York Times*, "Transcript of the President's News Conference on Domestic and Foreign Matters," August 30, 1962, p. 10.

15. Marjorie Hunter, "U.S. Sets Up Panel to Review the Side Effects of Pesticides; Controls Studied—Kennedy Finds Work Spurred by Rachel Carson Book," *New York Times*, August 31, 1962, p. 9.

16. Rachel Carson, "What's the Reason Why: A Symposium by Best-Selling Authors," *New York Times Book Review*, December 2, 1962, p. 3.

17. For a broader critical discussion of the issue that is not limited to the years before the publication of *Silent Spring*, see J. Gordon Edwards. "DDT Effects on Bird Abundance and Reproduction" in Jay Lehr, ed., *Rational Readings on Environmental Concerns* (New York: Van Nostrand Reinhold, 1992) pp. 195–216. For a defense of Carson's stance written by an Audubon staffer, see Robert C. Clement, "The Pesticides Controversy," *Boston College Environmental Affairs Law Review* 2, no. 3 (1972): 445–68.

18. Rachel Carson, *Silent Spring* (Boston: Houghton Mifflin, 1962), p. 3.

19. Thomas H. Jukes. "People and Pesticides," *American Scientist* 51, no. 3 (1963): 355–61, p. 360.

20. Thomas H. Jukes, "The Tragedy of DDT," In *Rational Readings on Environmental Concerns*, ed. Jay Lehr (New York: Van Nostrand Reinhold, 1992), pp. 217–20.

21. Philip H. Marvin, "Birds on the Rise," *Bulletin of the ESA* 10, no. 3 (1964): 194–96.

22. Audubon Society, *History of the Christmas Bird Count*, available at http://birds.audubon.org/history-christmas-bird-count, visited February 22, 2011. For the specific claim of increases in the population of 26 different kinds of birds, see J. Gordon Edwards, "DDT Effects on Bird Abundance and Reproduction," In *Rational Readings on Environmental Concerns*, ed. Jay Lehr (New York: Van Nostrand Reinhold, 1992) pp. 195–216.

23. Eugene E. Kenaga, "Are Birds Increasing in Numbers?" *Bulletin of the ESA* 11, no. 2, (1965): 81–83. The Aubudon Society justifies its bird count on the grounds that "local trends in bird populations can indicate habitat fragmentation or signal an immediate environmental threat, such as . . . improper use of pesticides." Audubon Society website,"How CBC Helps Birds," http://web4.audubon.org/bird/cbc/howcbchelpsbirds.html, accessed May 2012.

24. Arlene Rodda Quaratiello, *Rachel Carson: A Biography* (Westport, CT: Greenwood Press, 2004), pp. 37 and 136.

25. Carson, *Silent Spring*, pp. 93, 103, 112, 118.

26. Ibid., pp. 93, 103.

27. Ibid., pp. 93, 166.

28. Ibid., pp. 103–04, 111.

29. Ibid., p. 17.

30. Ibid., p. 118.

31. Ibid., p. 119.

32. Christmas Bird Count, *Historical Results*, available at http://birds.audubon.org/historical-results, visited March 2012.

33. Carson, *Silent Spring*, pp. 118–19.

34. Mark V. Stalmaster, *The Bald Eagle* (New York: Universe, 1987), p. 135.

35. Thomas H. Jukes, 115 *Congressional Record*, 1969, pp. 11338–340.

36. J. C. Howell, "The 1966 Status of 24 Nest Sites of the Bald Eagle in East-Central Florida," *Auk* 85 (1968): 680–81.

37. Howell, ibid., p. 681; Stalmaster, *The Bald Eagle*, p. 136.

38. Carson, *Silent Spring*, pp. 91–92.

39. Ibid., p. 95.

40. Jennifer Price, "Hats Off to Audubon," *Audubon* (December 2004), http://archive.audubonmagazine.org/features0412/hats.html.

41. William T. Hornaday, *Our Vanishing Wild Life* (New York: Charles Scribner's Sons, 1913), nonpaginated version, chapter 11, retrieved August 1, 2008, from http://www.fullbooks.com/Our-Vanishing-Wild-Life.html.

42. For instance, in 1969, one commentator was "now convinced" that the decline of the peregrine falcon was "due to a climate change, with increasing annual temperatures, decreasing precipitation, and a shrinkage of the aquatic habitats on lake edges which peregrines probably use in that region." Quoted by J. Gordon Edwards, "DDT Effects," p. 202.

43. That these facts were well known is attested by their discussion to various degrees in Jukes, 115 *Congressional Record*, and a number of sources listed in Desrochers and Shimizu, chapter 3, this volume.

44. For more detailed overview on the subject and additional references, see P. E. Russell, "Centenary Review: A Century of Fungicide Evolution," *Journal of Agricultural Science* 145, no. 1 (2005): 11–25; Erich Christian Oerke, "Centenary Review: Crop Losses to Pests," *Journal of Agricultural Science* 144, no. 1 (2006): 31–43. For a broad

overview of plant diseases, see the website of the American Phytopathological Society at http://www.apsnet.org/Pages/default.aspx. For more detailed yet relatively concise cases on behalf of synthetic pesticides, see Leonard Gianessi, "The Quixotic Quest for Chemical-Free Farming," *Issues in Science and Technology* 10, no. 1 (1993): 29–37 and Alex Avery, *The Truth about Organic Foods* (Chesterfield, MO: Henderson Communications L.L.C., 2006).

45. International Institute of Tropical Agriculture, "Maize," http://www.iita.org/maize.

46. International Potato Center. "'Amarilis' – Late Blight Resistant Potato Improves Andean Smallholders' Production, press release, June 28, 2010," http://www.cipotato.org/pressroom/press_releases_detail.asp?cod=84.

47. For a book-length treatment of the issue, see John I. Pitt and Ailsa D. Hocking, *Fungi and Food Spoilage*, 3rd ed. (New York: Springer, 2009).

48. Dennis Normile, "Holding Back a Torrent of Rats," *Science* 327 (5967) (2010): 806.

49. See Avery, *The Truth about Organic Foods*, chapter 10; Nathan Gregory, chapter 7, this volume.

50. Avery, *The Truth about Organic Foods*, chapter 10.

51. Homer, *Odyssey* (8th century BC), Scroll 22, line 12 ff (from Samuel Butler's *Homer. The Odyssey. Rendered into English prose for the Use of Those who cannot Read the Original* (A. C. Fifield, 1900), http://www.perseus.tufts.edu/hopper/text?doc=Perseus%3Atext%3A1999.01.0218%3Abook%3D22%3Acard%3D12.

52. The background story of Bordeaux mixture is well known, but is worth retelling. Its inventor originally devised the mixture to keep small boys from stealing his grapes, telling them in no uncertain terms that it was as deadly a poison as it looked. It then turned out to be an excellent fungicide whose use spread rapidly all over the world.

53. Avery, *The Truth about Organic Foods*, p. 113. For a video short during World War II that illustrates how farmers of the time mixed themselves a few potent ingredients and how they sprayed them without any protection to themselves, see USDA's *Victory Gardens* (1942) available at http://archive.org/details/victory_garden.

54. Avery, *The Truth about Organic Foods*.

55. Carson, *Silent Spring.*, p. 74.

56. Oerke, "Centenary Review"; Indur M. Goklany, "Saving Habitat and Conserving Biodiversity on a Crowded Planet," *BioScience* 48 (1998): 941–53; Indur M. Goklany and Merritt W. Sprague, "Sustaining Development and Biodiversity: Productivity, Efficiency and Conservation," Policy Analysis No. 175, Cato Institute, Washington, DC, 1992.

57. Daniel Simberloff, "Introduced Species: The Threat to Biodiversity and What Can Be Done," *ActionBioscience*, American Institute of Biological Science, 2000, available at http://www.actionbioscience.org/biodiversity/simberloff.html.

58. National Agricultural Statistics Service, *QuickStats 1.0 (2010)*, available at http://www.nass.usda.gov/ Statistics_by_Subject/index.php?sector=CROPS.

59. Ibid.

60. Roger Meiners and Andrew P. Morriss, Chapter 9, this volume.

61. See, among others, William J. White, "Economic History of Tractors in the United States," *Eh.Net Encyclopedia of Economic and Business History*, 2008, http://eh.net/encyclopedia/article/white.tractors.history.us. At the peak of animal power,

American farms hosted 21 million horses and 5 million mules—about three or four animals per average farm, more than was theoretically needed because of causes ranging from peak work periods (such as plowing) to animal sickness.

62. Carson, *Silent Spring*, pp. 254–55.

63. David A. Pimentel, Lori McLaughlin, Andrew Zepp, et al., "Environmental and Economic Effects of Reducing Pesticide Use in Agriculture," *Agriculture, Ecosystems and Environment* 46 (1993): 273–88, table 2.

64. Oerke, "Centenary Review."

65. David Zilberman, Andrew Schmitz, Gary Casterline, Erik Lichtenberg, and Jerome B. Siebert, "The Economics of Pesticide Use and Regulation," *Science* 253 (1991): 518–22.

66. Carson, *Silent Spring*, p. 9.

67. *New York Times*, Search Engine, available at http://query.nytimes.com/search/alternate/query?query= &st=fromcse (requires payment).

68. *New York Times*, "Surplus Food and Progress," December 15, 1961, p. 36.

69. U.S. Bureau of the Census, *Historical Statistics of the United States from Colonial Times to 1970* (Washington, DC: Government Printing Office, 1975), p. 510.

70. Edward H. Faulkner, *Ploughman's Folly* (London: Michael Joseph, 1945), available at http://journeytoforever.org/farm_library/folly/follyToC.html.

71. Carson, *Silent Spring*, pp. 68–69.

72. David Pimentel, "Environmental and Economic Costs of the Application of Pesticides Primarily in the United States," *Environment, Development and Sustainability* 7 (2005): 229–52.

73. Carson, *Silent Spring*, p. 11.

74. Simberloff, "Introduced Species."

75. Carson, *Silent Spring*, pp. 289–90.

76. University of California, San Diego. *Bacillus thurengiensis: History of Bt*, available at http://www.bt.ucsd.edu/bt_history.html, undated, visited April 15, 2011.

77. Economic Research Service, http://www.ers.usda.gov/Data/BiotechCrops/ (2011).

78. Carson, *Silent Spring*, p. 12.

79. Ibid., p. 183.

80. See Donald R. Roberts and Richard Tren, chapter 8, this volume.

81. Donald R. Roberts and Richard Tren, "International Advocacy against DDT and Other Public Health Insecticides for Malaria Control," *Research and Reports in Tropical Medicine* 2011, available at http://www.dovepress.com/articles.php?article_id=6101.

82. *New York Times*, "Rachel Carson's Warning," July 2, 1962, p. 28.

Chapter 6

1. Rachel Carson, *Silent Spring* (Boston: Houghton Mifflin, 1962), p. 1.

2. Ibid., p. 3.

3. Ibid.

4. Central Intelligence Agency, "Life Expectancy at Birth," *World Factbook*, https://www.cia.gov/library/publications/the-world-factbook/rankorder/2102rank.html.

5. Laura B. Shrestha, *Life Expectancy in the United States*, Table 1 (Washington, DC: Congressional Research Service, 2006), p. CRS-3, http://aging.senate.gov/crs/aging1.pdf.

6. Carson, *Silent Spring*, p. 3.

7. Ibid., p. 15.

8. Ibid., p. 219.

9. Ibid., p. 221.

10. For statistics on the rise of cancer as we age, see Bruce N. Ames, *The Causes and Prevention of Cancer: Do Federal Regulations Help?* (Washington, DC: Marshall Institute, 2002), p. 2.

11. See Siddhartha Mukherjee, *The Emperor of All Maladies: A Biography of Cancer* (New York: Scribner, 2010) for a discussion of the rise of public awareness of cancer in the 1950s. While the disease had been known for centuries, the scientific knowledge was abysmal.

12. Carson, *Silent Spring*, p. 220.

13. Ibid., pp. 222–23; see also pp. 58–59.

14. "War on Smoking Asked in Britain," *New York Times*, March 8, 1962, p. 33.

15. "New Study Adds Data on Smoking; Confirms Cancer-Tobacco Link," *New York Times*, May 8, 1959, p. 17.

16. "Experts on Cancer Voice Differences on Heavy Smoking," *New York Times*, October 13, 1960, p. 48.

17. Hueper was noted for more than his science work. An early Nazi enthusiast, he ended his letters with "Heil Hitler" as he was much impressed by Hitler's environmental purity. Apparently his enthusiasm waned in the 1930s as the atrocities became more apparent. See Robert N. Proctor, *The Nazi War on Cancer* (Princeton, NJ: Princeton University Press, 1999).

18. Wilhelm Hueper, "Lung Cancers and Their Causes," *CA Cancer Journal for Clinicians* 5 (1955): 95–100. For a review of the role of the tobacco industry at that time, see Subcommittee on Health and the Environment, "The Hill and Knowlton Documents: How the Tobacco Industry Launched Its Disinformation Campaign," Staff Report, Majority Staff, Subcommittee on Health and the Environment, House Committee on Energy and Commerce, May 26, 1994, p. 7, http://tobaccodocuments.org/lor/95527328-7343.html.

19. Devra Davis, *The Secret History of the War on Cancer* (New York: Basic Books, 2007).

20. Hanspeter Witschi, "A Short History of Lung Cancer," *Toxicological Sciences* 64 (2001): 4–6.

21. Colin Talley, Howard J. Kushner, and Claire E. Sterk, "Lung Cancer, Chronic Disease Epidemiology, and Medicine, 1948–1964," *Journal of the History of Medicine and Allied Sciences* 59 (2004): 329–74.

22. Ibid., pp. 330–31. See also, Witschi, "A Short History of Lung Cancer," p. 6.

23. Carson, *Silent Spring*, p. 258–59.

24. Richard Doll and Richard Peto, "Causes of Cancer: Quantitative Estimates of Avoidable Risks of Cancer in the United States Today," *Journal of the National Cancer Institute* 66, no. 6 (1981): 1191–308.

25. Ames, *The Causes and Prevention of Cancer*, pp. 3–5.

26. Bruce N. Ames, Lois Swirsky Gold, and William C. Willett, "The Causes and Prevention of Cancer," *Proceedings of the National Academy of Sciences USA* 92 (1995): 5258.

27. Ibid.

28. Ibid.

29. Bureau of the Census, *Mortality Statistics—1936* (Washington, DC: GPO, 1938), p. 132.

30. Public Health Service, *Vital Statistics of the United States—1956,* (Washington, DC: GPO, 1958), Table 59. Carson knew of this data source—she cites it in the book when discussing leukemia.

31. Doll and Peto, "Causes of Cancer," Table 20.

32. Richard W. Clapp, Genevieve K. Howe, and Molly Jacobs, "Environmental and Occupational Causes of Cancer Re-visited," *Journal of Public Health Policy* 27 (2006): 63.

33. Julian Peto, "Cancer Epidemiology in the Last Century and the Next Decade," *Nature* 411 (2001): 390–95.

34. P. Boffetta et al., "The Causes of Cancer in France," *Annals of Oncology* 20 (2009): 550–55.

35. Carson, *Silent Spring,* p. 242.

36. Ibid., p. 219.

37. "With the advent of man the situation began to change, for man, alone of all forms of life, can create cancer-producing substances, which in medical terminology are called carcinogens. A few man-made carcinogens have been part of the environment for centuries. An example is soot, containing aromatic hydrocarbons. With the dawn of the industrial era the world became a place of continuous, ever-accelerating change. Instead of the natural environment there was rapidly substituted an artificial one composed of new chemical and physical agents, many of them possessing powerful capacities for inducing biologic change. Against these carcinogens which his own activities had created man had no protection, for even as his biological heritage has evolved slowly, so it adapts slowly to new conditions. As a result these powerful substances could easily penetrate the inadequate defenses of the body." Ibid., pp. 219–20.

38. Ames, Gold, and Willett, "The Causes and Prevention of Cancer," p. 5262.

39. Ibid., p. 5256.

40. "'It is scarcely possible . . . to handle arsenicals with more utter disregard of the general health than that which has been practiced in our country in recent years,' said Dr. W. C. Hueper, of the National Cancer Institute, an authority on environmental cancer. 'Anyone who has watched the dusters and sprayers of arsenical insecticides at work must have been impressed by the almost supreme carelessness with which the poisonous substances are dispensed.'" Carson, *Silent Spring,* p. 18.

41. Boffetta et al., "The Causes of Cancer in France," p. 554.

42. Carson, *Silent Spring,* pp. 226–27.

43. Alexander G. Gilliam and William A. Walter, "Trends in Mortality from Leukemia in the U.S., 1921–55," *Public Health Reports* 73, no. 9 (1958): 773–84. The authors were epidemiologists with the National Cancer Institute.

44. Ibid., p. 776.

45. Ibid., p. 784.

46. S. Milham and E. M. Ossiander, "Historical Evidence that Residential Electrification Caused the Emergence of the Childhood Leukemia Peak," *Medical Hypotheses* 56, no. 3 (2001): 290–95.

47. Carson, *Silent Spring,* p. 221.

48. Ibid., p. 226.

49. Arnold L. Aspelin, *Pesticide Usage in the United States: Trends during the 20th Century* (Raleigh, NC: Center for Integrated Pest Management, North Carolina State University, 2003), Part 1, p. 5; Part 4, pp. 4, 18.

50. Carson, *Silent Spring,* pp. 7–8.

51. Ibid., p. 222.

52. Ibid., p. 223.

53. Aspelin, *Pesticide Usage in the United States*, Table 2.1.

54. Carson, *Silent Spring*, pp. 222–24.

55. Nonetheless, as discussed by Roger Meiners and Andrew P. Morriss, chapter 9, this volume, the Fish and Wildlife Service where Carson worked publicly attacked DDT starting in 1945.

56. Carson, *Silent Spring*, p. 58.

57. Ibid., chapter 16.

58. See Agency for Toxic Substances and Disease Registry (ATSDR), *Toxicological Profile for DDT, DDE, and DDD* (Washington, DC: U.S. Department of Health and Human Services, Public Health Service, 2002), pp. 17–19; and AMAP, *Arctic Pollution 2009* (Oslo: Arctic Monitoring and Assessment Programme, 2009), pp. 26, 29, http://amap.no/documents/index.cfm?action=getfile&dirsub=&filename=SOAER %5F2009. pdf&sort=default.

59. "Rachel Carson's Warning," *New York Times*, July 2, 1962, p. 28.

60. Apparently, this should have been "confounders."

61. ATSDR, *Toxicological Profile*, p. 24.

62. Donald R. Roberts and Richard Tren, chapter 8, this volume.

63. Carson, *Silent Spring*, p. 12.

64. Ibid., p. 189.

65. Ibid., p. 183.

66. Donald R. Roberts and Richard Tren, chapter 8, this volume.

67. Carson, *Silent Spring*, p. 99.

68. Online Ethics Center for Engineering and Research, "Rachel Carson—Silent Springs" (National Academy of Engineering, Washington, DC, 2006), http://www.onlineethics.org/Topics/ ProfPractice/Exemplars/BehavingWell/carsonindex.aspx.

Chapter 7

1. Rachel Carson, *Silent Spring* (Boston: Houghton Mifflin, 1962), p. 297.

2. John Bellamy Foster and Brett Clark, "Rachel Carson's Ecological Critique," *Monthly Review* 59, no. 9 (2008), http://monthlyreview.org/080201foster-clark.php.

3. Linda J. Lear, "Bombshell in Beltsville: The USDA and the Challenge of 'Silent Spring,'"*Agricultural History* 66, no. 2 (1992): 151–70.

4. See chapters 8 through 12, this volume.

5. Simon A. Levin, "The Evolution of Ecology," in *The Chronicle of Higher Education*, August 8, 2010, http://chronicle.com/article/The-Evolution-of-Ecology/123762, accessed March 2, 2011. See also Desrochers and Shimizu, chapter 3, this volume.

6. Maril Hazlett, "'Woman vs. Man vs. Bugs': Gender and Popular Ecology in Early Reactions to Silent Spring," *Environmental History* 9, no. 4 (2004): 701–29.

7. Michael B. Smith, "'Silence, Miss Carson!' Science, Gender, and the Reception of *Silent Spring*," *Feminist Studies* 27, no. 3 (2001): 733–52.

8. See Meiners and Morriss, chapter 9, this volume.

9. Yaakov Garb, "Rachel Carson's *Silent Spring*," *Dissent* (Fall 1995): 539–46; and Smith, "'Silence Miss Carson!'"

10. Carson, *Silent Spring*, pp. 113–14.

11. Garb, "Rachel Carson's *Silent Spring*."

12. Ibid.

13. Mark Sagoff, "Biodiversity and the Culture of Ecology," *Bulletin of the Ecological Society of America* 74, no. 4 (1993): 374–81; D. E. Jelinski, "There Is No Mother Nature—There Is No Balance of Nature: Culture, Ecology and Conservation," *Human Ecology* 33, no. 2 (2005): 271–88; John Kricher, *The Balance of Nature: Ecology's Enduring Myth* (Princeton, NJ: Princeton University Press, 2009; and Jason Simus, "Metaphors and Metaphysics in Ecology," a submission to the Sixth Annual Joint Meeting of the International Association for Environmental Philosophy and the International Society for Environmental Ethics, Allenspark, CO, June 16–19, 2009), accessed February 28, 2011, http://www.environmentalphilosophy.org/ISEEIAEPpapers/2009/Simus.pdf.

14. Quoted in Simus, "Metaphors and Metaphysics in Ecology."

15. Sagoff, "Biodiversity and the Culture of Ecology."

16. See Nelson, chapter 4, this volume.

17. Carson, *Silent Spring*, chapter 15, pp. 245–61.

18. Carson, *Silent Spring*, p. 57.

19. Charles S. Elton, *The Ecology of Invasions by Plants and Animals* (Chicago: University of Chicago Press, 1958), p. 142.

20. Carson, *Silent Spring*, p. 246.

21. Smith, "'Silence, Miss Carson!'"

22. Tim Lambert, "The Unending War on Rachel Carson," *ScienceBlogs*, May 19, 2007, accessed March 6, 2011, http://scienceblogs.com/deltoid/2007/05/the_unending_war_on_rachel_car.php.

23. Ira L. Baldwin, "Chemicals and Pests: Man's Use, Misuse, and Abuse of the Products of Science Determine Whether These Valuable Assets Are Also Harmful," *Science* 137, no. 3535 (1962): 1042–43.

24. R. M. MacPherson, "A Modern Approach to Pest Control," *Canadian Journal of Comparative Medicine and Veterinary Science* 11, no. 4 (1947): 108–13.

25. Frank N. Egerton, "Changing Concepts of the Balance of Nature," *Quarterly Review of Biology* 48, no. 2 (1973): 322–50.

26. See Nelson, chapter 4, this volume.

27. Carson, *Silent Spring*, pp. 64–65.

28. Sewall Wright, "The Roles of Mutation, Inbreeding, Crossbreeding, and Selection in Evolution," *Proceedings of the Sixth International Congress on Genetics* 1 (1932): 355–66.

29. Henry A. Gleason, "The Individualistic Concept of the Plant Association," *Bulletin of the Torrey Botany Club* 53 (1926): 7–26.

30. Charles S. Elton, *Animal Ecology and Evolution* (New York: Oxford University Press, 1930), p. 17.

31. Herbert George Andrewartha and L. Charles Birch, *The Distribution and Abundance of Animals* (Chicago: University of Chicago Press, 1954).

32. Simon A. Levin and R. T. Paine, "Disturbance, Patch Formation, and Community Structure," *Proceedings of the National Academy of Sciences of the United States of America* 71, no. 7 (1974): 2744–47.

33. Simon A. Levin, "The Problem of Pattern and Scale in Ecology: The Robert H. MacArthur Award Lecture," *Ecology* 73, no. 6 (1992): 1943–67.

34. Jiangero Wu and Orie L. Loucks, "From Balance of Nature to Hierarchical Patch Dynamics: A Paradigm Shift in Ecology," *Quarterly Review of Biology* 70, no. 4 (1995): 439–66.

35. Simus, "Metaphors and Metaphysics in Ecology."

36. Wu and Loucks, "From Balance of Nature to Hierarchical Patch Dynamics."

37. Carson, "The Other Road," chapter 17 in *Silent Spring*.

38. Carson, *Silent Spring*, p. 10.

39. F. J. Simmons, J. M. Franz, and R. I. Sailer, "History of Biological Control," in *Theory and Practice of Biological Control*, ed. C. B. Huffaker and P. S. Messenger (New York: Academic, 1976), pp. 17–39.

40. See Meiners and Morriss, chapter 9, this volume.

41. J. Eilenberg, Ann Hajek, and C. Lomer, "Suggestions for Unifying the Terminology in Biological Control," *Biocontrol* 46, no. 4 (2001): 387–400.

42. See Desrochers and Shimizu, chapter 5, this volume.

43. Garb, "Rachel Carson's *Silent Spring*," p. 541.

44. David H. Jennings, William Threlfall, and Donald G. Dodds, "Metazoan Parasites and Food of Short Tailed Weasels and Mink in Newfoundland, Canada." *Canadian Journal of Zoology* 60, no. 2 (1982): 180–83.

45. Jeffrey A. Lockwood, "Competing Values and Moral Imperatives: An Overview of Ethical Issues in Biological Control," *Agriculture and Human Values* 14, no. 3 (1997): 205–10.

46. Ann E. Hajek, *Natural Enemies: An Introduction to Biological Control* (Cambridge, U.K.: Cambridge University Press, 2004).

47. L. E. Caltagirone and Richard L. Doutt, "The History of the Vedalia Beetle Importation to California and Its Impact on the Development of Biological Control," *Annual Review of Entomology* 34, no. 1 (1989): 1–16, p. 13.

48. Ibid.

49. Ibid.

50. Mark S. Hoddle, "Classical Biological Control of Arthropods in the 21st Century," *Proceedings of the 1st International Symposium on Biological Control of Arthropods* (2002): 3–16.

51. Simmons, Franz, and Sailer, "History of Biological Control."

52. Caltagirone and Doutt, "The History of the Vedalia Beetle Importation," p. 12.

53. Carson, *Silent Spring*, p. 292.

54. Hajek, *Natural Enemies*.

55. Jeff K. Waage et al., "Biological Control: Challenges and Opportunities [and Discussion]," *Philosophical Transactions of the Royal Society B: Biological Sciences* 318, no. 1189 (1998): 111–28.

56. Paul DeBach, *Biological Control by Natural Enemies* (London: Cambridge University Press, 1974); Richard L. Doutt, "Biological Control: Parasites and Predators," in *Pest Control Strategies for the Future* (Washington, DC: National Academy of Sciences Printing and Publishing, 1972), pp. 288–97; and F. J. Simmonds and F. D. Bennett, "Biological Control of Agricultural Pests," in *Proceedings of the 15th International Congress of Entomology*, ed. D. White (Washington, DC: Entomological Society of America, 1977), pp. 464–72.

57. Francis G. Howarth, "Classical Biocontrol: Panacea or Pandora's Box?" *Proceedings of the Hawaii Entomological Society* 24 (1983): 239–44.

58. Francis G. Howarth, "Environmental Impacts of Classical Biological Control," *Annual Review of Entomology* 36 (1991): 485–509.

59. René E. Honegger, "List of Amphibians and Reptiles Either Known or Thought to Have Become Extinct since 1600," *Biological Conservation* 19 (1981): 141–58.

60. See Katzenstein, chapter 11, this volume.

61. Jay A. Rosenheim, "Intraguild Predation of Orius Tristicolor by Geocoris spp. and the Paradox of Irruptive Spider Mite Dynamics in California Cotton," *Biological Control* 5 (2005): 303–35; Daniel Simberloff and Peter Stiling, "How Risky Is Biological Control?" *Ecology* 77, no. 7 (1996): 1965–74; and Svata M. Louda and Peter Stiling, "The Double-Edged Sword of Biological Control in Conservation and Restoration," *Conservation Biology* 18, no. 1 (2004): 50–53.

62. Mark Sagoff, "Do Non-Native Species Threaten the Natural Environment?" *Journal of Agricultural and Environmental Ethics* 18 (2005): 215–36; and Joop C. Van Lenteren et al., "Assessing Risks of Releasing Exotic Biological Control Agents of Arthropod Pests," *Annual Review of Entomology* 51 (2006): 609–34.

63. Svata M. Louda et al., "Nontarget Effects—The Achilles' Heel of Biological Control? Retrospective Analyses to Reduce Risk Associated with Biocontrol Introductions," *Annual Review of Entomology* 48 (2003): 365–96.

64. Mark S. Hoddle, "Restoring Balance: Using Exotic Species to Control Invasive Exotic Species," *Conservation Biology* 18, no. 1 (2004): 38–49.

65. Van Lenteren et al., "Assessing Risks of Releasing Exotic Biological Control Agents."

66. Dylan Parry, "Beyond Pandora's Box: Quantitatively Evaluating Non-Target Effects of Parasitoids in Classical Biological Control," *Biological Invasions* 11, no. 1 (2008): 47–58.

67. Diana N. Kimberling, "Lessons from History: Predicting Successes and Risks of Intentional Introductions for Arthropod Biological Control," *Biological Invasions* 6, no. 3 (2004): 301–18.

68. Louda et al., "Nontarget Effects—The Achilles' Heel of Biological Control?"

69. David Pimentel, Rodolfo Zuniga, and Doug Morrison, "Update on the Environmental and Economic Costs Associated with Alien-Invasive Species in the United States," *Ecological Economics* 52 (2004): 273–88.

70. Sagoff, "Do Non-Native Species Threaten the Natural Environment?"; and A. D. Rodewald, "Spreading Messages about Invasives," *Diversity and Distributions* (2011): 1–3.

71. David Tilman, "Biodiversity: Population versus Ecosystem Stability," *Ecology* 77, no. 2 (1996): 350–63; J. Loreau et al., "Biodiversity and Ecosystem Functioning: Current Knowledge and Future Challenges," *Science* 294, no. 5543 (2001): 804–8; and David Tilman et al., "Diversity and Productivity in a Long-term Grassland Experiment," *Science* 294, no. 5543 (2001): 843–45.

72. Daniel Simberloff, "Non-Native Species DO Threaten the Natural Environment!" *Journal of Agricultural and Environmental Ethics* 18, no. 6 (2005): 595–607.

73. Elton, *The Ecology of Invasions by Plants and Animals.*

74. Taylor H. Ricketts et al., "Economic Value of Tropical Forest to Coffee Production," *Proceedings of the National Academy of Sciences of the United States of America* 101, no. 34 (2004): 12579–82; and Rachael Winfree, "Wild Bee Pollinators Provide the Majority of Crop Visitation across Land-use Gradients in New Jersey and Pennsylvania, USA," *Journal of Applied Ecology* 45, no. 3 (2008): 793–802.

75. Kimberling, "Lessons from History"; and R. H. Messing, "Hawaii as a Role Model for Comprehensive U.S. Biocontrol Legislation: The Best and the Worst of It," in *Proceedings of the Second International Symposium on Biological Control of Arthropods*, Davos, Switzerland, September 12–16, 2005, USDA Forest Service, Publication FHTET-2005-08.

76. Lloyd Knutson and Jack R. Coulson, "Procedures and Policies in the USA regarding Precautions in the Introduction of Classical Biological Control Agents," *EPPO Bulletin* 27, no. 1 (1997): 133–42.

77. Peter G. Mason, Robert G. Flanders, and Hugo A. Arrendondo-Bernal, "How Can Legislation Facilitate the Use of Biological Control of Arthropods in North America?" in *Proceedings of the Second International Symposium on Biological Control of Arthropods*, Davos, Switzerland, September 12–16, 2005, USDA Forest Service, Publication FHTET-2005–08; and David M. Lodge et al., "Biological Invasions: Recommendations for U.S. Policy and Management," *Ecological Applications* 16, no. 6 (2006): 2035–54.

78. Jorge Hendrichs et al., "Medfly Area Wide Sterile Insect Technique Programmes for Prevention, Suppression or Eradication: The Importance of Mating Behavior Studies," *Florida Entomologist* 85, no. 1 (2002): 1–13.

79. Ibid.

80. Marc J. B. Vreysen et al., "Glossina austeni (Diptera: Glossinidae) Eradicated on the Island of Unguja, Zanzibar, Using the Sterile Insect Technique," *Journal of Economic Entomology* 93, no. 1 (2000): 123–35.

81. Waldenar Klassen, "Introduction: Development of the Sterile Insect Technique for African Malaria Vectors," *Malaria Journal* 8, suppl. 2 (2009): page II.

82. Carson, *Silent Spring*, "The Other Road," chapter 17.

83. Carson, *Silent Spring*, p. 163.

84. Marina S. Ascunce et al., "Global Invasion History of the Fire Ant Solenopsis invicta," *Science* 331, no. 6020 (2011): 1066–68.

85. Sanford Porter, "Host Specificity and Risk Assessment of Releasing the Decapitating Fly Pseudacteon curvatus as a Classical Biocontrol Agent for Imported Fire Ants," *Biological Control* 19, no. 1 (2000): 35–47.

86. Ibid.

87. Micky Eubanks, "Estimates of the Direct and Indirect Effects of Red Imported Fire Ants on Biological Control in Field Crops," *Biological Control* 21, no. 1 (2001): 35–43.

88. Mark Sagoff, "Why Exotic Species Are Not as Bad as We Fear," *The Chronicle of Higher Education*, June 23, 2000, B7.

89. Nicholas Gotelli and Aaron E. Arnett, "Biogeographic Effects of Red Fire Ant Invasion," *Ecology Letters* 3, no. 4 (2002): 257–61.

90. George H. Boettner, Joseph S. Elkinton, and Cynthia J. Boettner, "Effects of a Biological Control Introduction on Three Nontarget Native Species of Saturniid Moths," *Conservation Biology* 14, no. 6 (2000): 1798–1806; and Louda et al., "Nontarget Effects—The Achilles' Heel of Biological Control?"

91. Joseph S. Elkington et al., "Interactions among Gypsy Moths, White-Footed Mice, and Acorns," *Ecology* 77, no. 8 (1996): 2332–42.

92. Simus, "Metaphors and Metaphysics in Ecology"; Tasos Hovardas and Konstantinos Korfiatis, "Towards a Critical Re-Appraisal of Ecology Education: Scheduling an Educational Intervention to Revisit the 'Balance of Nature' Metaphor," *Science & Education* (November 2010). See also Nelson, chapter 4.

93. Simus, "Metaphors and Metaphysics in Ecology."

94. S. T. A. Pickett and J. N. Thompson, "Patch Dynamics and the Design of Nature Reserves," *Biological Conservation* 13, no. 1 (1978): 27–37.

95. Sian Sullivan, "Towards a Non-Equilibrium Ecology: Perspectives from an Arid Land," *Journal of Biogeography* 23 (1996): 1–5.

96. Peter Westbroek et al., "World Archaeology and Global Change—Did Our Ancestors Ignite the Ice-Age?" *World Archaeology* 25 (1993): 122–33.

97. Michael I. Bird and J. A. Cali, "A Million-Year Record of Fire in Sub-Saharan Africa," *Nature* 394 (1998): 767–69.

98. Hugh J. Christian et al., "Global Frequency and Distribution of Lightning as Observed from Space by the Optical Transient Detector," *Journal of Geophysical Research* 108 (2003): 1–15.

99. Caroline Grigson, "An African Origin for African Cattle?—Some Archaeological Evidence," *African Archaeological Review* 9 (1991): 119–44.

100. Katherine M. Homewood and W. A. Rodgers, *Maasailand Ecology: Pastoralist Development and Wildlife Conservation in Ngorongoro, Tanzania* (Cambridge, U.K.: Cambridge University Press, 1991), p. xiii.

101. C. A. D. M. Van de Vijver, P. Poot, and H. H. T. Prins, "Causes of Increased Nutrient Concentrations in Post-Fire Regrowth in an East African Savanna," *Plant and Soil* 214 (1999): 173–85; and K. G. Roques, T. G. O'Connor, and A. R. Watkinson, "Dynamics of Shrub Encroachment in an African Savanna: Relative Influences of Fire, Herbivory, Rainfall and Density Dependence," *Journal of Applied Ecology* 38 (2001): 268–80.

102. Joseph Thomson, *Through Masai Land* (London: Sampson Low, Marston and Co., 1895), p. 238.

103. Leslie H. Brown, "The Biology of Pastoral Man as a Factor in Conservation," *Biological Conservation* 3 (1971): 93–100.

104. Lotte Hughes, *Moving the Maasai: A Colonial Misadventure* (Basingstoke, England, and New York: Palgrave Macmillan with St. Antony's College, 2006), p. xvii.

105. Roy H. Behnke and Ian Scoones, "Rethinking Range Ecology: Implications for Rangeland Management in Africa," in *Range Ecology at Disequilibrium: New Models of Natural Variability and Pastoral Adaptation in African Savannas*, ed. Roy H. Behnke, Ian Scoones, and Carol Kerven (London: Overseas Development Institute, 1993), p. xi; James E. Ellis, Michael B. Coughenour, and D. M. Swift, "Climate Variability, Ecosystem Stability, and the Implications for Range and Livestock Development," in *Range Ecology at Disequilibrium: New Models of Natural Variability and Pastoral Adaptation in African Savannas*, ed. Roy H. Behnke, Ian Scoones, and Carol Kerven (London: Overseas Development Institute, 1993); Samuel D. Fuhlendorf and David M. Engle, "Restoring Heterogeneity on Rangelands: Ecosystem Management Based on Evolutionary Grazing Patterns," *Bioscience* 51 (2001): 625–32; and S. Vetter, "Rangelands at Equilibrium and Non-Equilibrium: Recent Developments in the Debate," *Journal of Arid Environments* 62 (2005): 321–41.

106. Katherine Homewood and W. A. Rogers, "Pastoralism, Conservation and the Overgrazing Controversy," in *Conservation in Africa: People, Policies, and Practice*, ed. David Anderson and Richard Grove (Cambridge, U.K.: Cambridge University Press, 1987).

107. Behnke and Scoones, "Rethinking Range Ecology"; Ellis, Coughenour, and Swift, "Climate Variability, Ecosystem Stability, and the Implications for Range and Livestock Development"; and Fuhlendorf and Engle, "Restoring Heterogeneity on Rangelands."

108. Elliot Fratkin, "East African Pastoralism in Transition: Masai, Boran, and Rendille Cases," *African Studies Review* 44 (2001): 1–25; and P. D. Little et al., "Avoiding Disaster: Diversification and Risk Management among East African Herders," *Development and Change* 32 (2001): 401–33.

109. David Western and Virginia Finch, "Cattle and Pastoralism—Survival and Production in Arid Lands," *Human Ecology* 14 (1986): 77–94.

110. Nathan C. Gregory, Ryan L. Sensenig, and David S. Wilcove, "Effects of Controlled Fire and Livestock Grazing on Bird Communities in East African Savannas," *Conservation Biology* 24, no. 6 (2010): 1606–16.

111. William Cronon, *Changes in the Land: Indians, Colonists, and the Ecology of New England* (New York: Hill and Wang, 1983), p. 241.

112. Behnke and Scoones, "Rethinking Range Ecology"; Fuhlendorf and Engle," Restoring Heterogeneity on Rangelands"; Alexis F. L. A. Powell, "Effects of Prescribed Burns and Bison (Bos Bison) Grazing on Breeding Bird Abundances in Tallgrass Prairie," *The Auk* 123 (2006): 183–97; and Charles Curtin and David Western, "Grasslands, People, and Conservation: Over-the-Horizon Learning Exchanges between African and American Pastoralists," *Conservation Biology* 22 (2008): 870–77.

113. For example, James E. Lovelock and Lynn Margulis, "Atmospheric Homeostasis by and for the Biosphere: The Gaia Hypothesis," *Tellus* 26, no. 1–2 (1974): 2–10.

114. Hovardas and Korfiatis, "Towards a Critical Re-Appraisal of Ecology Education."

115. Corinne Zimmerman and Kim Cuddington, "Ambiguous, Circular and Polysemous: Students' Definitions of the 'Balance of Nature' Metaphor," *Public Understanding of Science* 16, no. 4 (2007): 393–406.

116. Marida Ergazaki and Georgios Ampatzidis, "Students' Reasoning about the Future of Disturbed or Protected Ecosystems and the Idea of the 'Balance of Nature,'" *Research in Science Education* (February 2011).

117. Pickett and Thomson, "Patch Dynamics and the Design of Nature Reserves."

118. Roderick P. Neumann, *Imposing Wilderness: Struggles over Livelihood and Nature Preservation in Africa* (Berkeley, CA: University of California Press, 1988).

119. Beatrix E. Beisner, Daniel T. Haydon, and Kim Cuddington, 2003. "Alternative Stable States in Ecology," *Frontiers in Ecology and the Environment* 1, no. 7 (2003): 376.

Chapter 8

1. D. Roberts, et al. "A Probability Model of Vector Behavior: Effects of DDT Repellency, Irritancy, and Toxicity in Malaria Control," *J Vector Ecology* 25, no. 1 (2000): pp. 48–61.

2. Oswald. T. Zimmerman and Irvin Lavine, *DDT, Killer of Killers* (Dover, NH: Industrial Research Service, 1946), pp. 31–32.

3. David Tschanz, "Typhus Fever on the Eastern Front in World War I," http://entomology.montana.edu/_historybug/WWI/TEF.htm; and Epic Disasters, "The Worst Outbreaks of Disease," http://www.epicdisasters.com/index.php/site/comments/the_worst_outbreaks_of_disease/, accessed April 30, 2012.

4. Zimmerman and Lavine, *DDT, Killer of Killers*, pp. 31–32.

5. Trustham F. West and George A. Campbell, *DDT and Newer Persistent Insecticides* (New York: Chemical Publishing Co., Inc., 1952), p. 2.

6. Andrew Spielman and Michael D'Antonio, *Mosquito: A Natural History of Our Most Persistent & Deadly Foe* (New York: Hyperion, 2001), p. 143.

7. I. D. Hirschy, Memo for Director, Pre. Med. Div., *DDT Insecticide*, August 11, 1943.

8. Zimmerman and Lavine, *DDT, Killer of Killers*, p. 39; and West and Campbell, *DDT and Newer Persistent Insecticides*, p. 7.

9. Müller's Nobel lecture can be found at http://www.nobelprize.org/nobel_prizes/medicine/ laureates/1948/muller-lecture.html

10. West and Campbell, *DDT and Newer Persistent Insecticides*, p. 21.

11. Ibid., p. 8.

12. Robert Gottlieb, *Typhus FAQ*, January 9, 2002, http://homepage.mac.com/msb/163x/faqs/typhus.html.

13. Donald R. Roberts, *Impact of Anti-DDT Campaigns on Malaria Control: Outlooks on Pest Management* 21, no. 1 (2010): 4–11.

14. Naomi Baumslag, *Murderous Medicine: Nazi Doctors, Human Experimentation, and Typhus* (Westport, CT: Praeger Publishers, 2005), p. 27.

15. I (DR) have a small bottle of DDT powder, dated 1959, issued by the U.S. State Department with instructions for sprinkling in underclothing.

16. Fred C. Bishopp, "Present Position of DDT in the Control of Insects of Medical Importance," *American Journal of Public Health and the Nation's Health* 36, no. 6 (1946): 603–4.

17. Frederick L. Hoffman, *A Plea and a Plan for the Eradication of Malaria throughout the Western Hemisphere* (Newark, NJ: Prudential Press, 1917).

18. Ibid.

19. Ibid.

20. U.S. Public Health Service (PHS), *Malaria Control in War Areas: 1944–45* (Washington, DC: Federal Security Agency, 1945), p. 14.

21. U.S. PHS, "CDC Bulletin: Jul., Aug., Sept. 1946" (Atlanta: Communicable Disease Center [CDC], 1946), p. 1.

22. U.S. PHS, "CDC Bulletin: Jan., Feb., Mar. 1947" (Atlanta: CDC, 1947), pp. 2–3.

23. U.S. PHS, "CDC Bulletin: Nov., Dec. 1948" (Atlanta: CDC, 1948), p. 10.

24. U.S. PHS, "CDC Bulletin: Oct., Nov., Dec. 1946" (Atlanta: CDC, 1946), p. 19.

25. U.S. PHS, "CDC Bulletin: Oct., Nov., Dec. 1948" (Atlanta: CDC, 1948), p. 10.

26. U.S. PHS, "CDC Bulletin: Jul., Aug., Sept. 1946," p. 4.

27. U.S. PHS, "CDC Bulletin: Oct., Nov., Dec. 1946," p. 1.

28. Ibid.

29. U.S. PHS, "CDC Bulletin: 1946–1947" (Atlanta: CDC, 1947), p. 7.

30. U.S. PHS, "CDC Bulletin: Jan. 1950" (Atlanta: CDC, 1950), p. 11. Surveys were conducted in 13 southeastern states, and approximately 65,000 houses were inspected. Evaluations of effectiveness were based on inspections of randomly selected sprayed and unsprayed houses for presence or absence of the malaria mosquito.

31. U.S. PHS, *Malaria Control in War Areas*, p. 18.

32. Centers for Disease Control and Prevention, *The History of Malaria, an Ancient Disease* (Atlanta: Centers for Disease Control and Prevention, 2010), http://www.cdc.gov/malaria/history/.

33. Sonia Shah, *The Fever: How Malaria Has Ruled Humankind for 500,000 Years* (New York: Sarah Crichton Books, 2010), p. 191.

34. U.S. PHS, "CDC Activities, 1946–1947" (Atlanta: CDC, 1947), p. 11.

35. Ibid.

36. Ibid., p. 10.

37. Ibid., Jul., Aug., Sept. 1946, p. 35; and Oct., Nov., Dec. 1946, pp. 38–39.

38. Ibid., Apr., May, Jun. 1948, p. 28.

39. Ibid., Oct., Nov., Dec. 1949, p. 43.

40. Ibid., Jul., Aug., Sept. 1946, p. 32.

41. Russell E. Fontaine, John A. Mulrennan, and D. J. Schliessmann, "1964 Progress Report of the *Aedes Aegypti* Eradication Program," *American Journal of Tropical Medicine and Hygiene* 14, no. 6 (1964): 900–3.

42. U.S. PHS, "*Aedes Aegypti* Eradication Program," *CDC Operations Manual*, Operational Letters No. 7.1 and No. 7.2 (Atlanta: CDC, 1966).

43. U.S. PHS, "CDC Activities, 1946–1947," pp. 151–52.

44. Frederick L. Hoffman, "A Plea for a National Committee on the Eradication of Malaria," *Southern Medical Journal* 9, no. 5 (1916): 413–19.

45. Centers for Disease Control and Prevention, "Trends in Childhood Cancer Mortality—United States, 1990–2004" *Morbidity and Mortality Weekly Report* 56, no. 48 (2007): 1257–61, http://www.cdc.gov/MMWR/preview/mmwrhtml/mm5648a1.htm#tab.

46. Hoffman, "A Plea for a National Committee on the Eradication of Malaria."

46 Ernest C. Faust, "The Distribution of Malaria in North America, Mexico, Central America, and the West Indies," in *A Symposium on Human Malaria, with Special Reference to North America and the Caribbean*, ed. Forest R. Moulton, (Washington, DC: AAAS, 1941), p. 9.

47. Robert B. Watson and Redginal Hewitt, "Topographical and Related Factors in the Epidemiology of Malaria in North America, Central America, and the West Indies," in *A Symposium on Human Malaria, with Special Reference to North America and the Caribbean*, ed. Forest R. Moulton (Washington, DC: AAAS, 1941), p. 140.

48. Faust, "The Distribution of Malaria in North America, Mexico, Central America, and the West Indies," p. 11.

49. George W. Cox, *Report by the State Health Officer, Texas*, undated; and L. J. Trotti, Report from the Assistant State Director of Communicable Disease Control Activities to the State Health Director George W. Cox, M.D., for Fiscal Year 1947, Austin, Texas, August 15, 1947.

50. U.S. PHS, "CDC Activities, 1947–1948" (Atlanta: CDC, 1948), p. 126.

51. U.S. PHS, "CDC Bulletin: Jan. 1950," p. 20; and "CDC Bulletin: Oct., Nov., Dec. 1949" (Atlanta: CDC, 1949), p. 42.

52. U.S. PHS, "CDC Activities, 1949–1950" (Atlanta: CDC, 1950), p. 4.

53. U.S. PHS, "CDC Bulletin: Jul., Aug., Sept. 1952" (Atlanta: CDC, 1952), p. 40.

54. U.S. PHS, "CDC Activities, 1951–1952" (Atlanta: CDC, 1952), p. 28; and Monthly Narrative Report of Insect Vector Control Activities for the Texas State Department of Health, Nov. 1953.

55. U.S. PHS, "CDC Bulletin: Jul., Aug., Sept. 1952," p. 30.

56. U.S. PHS, "CDC Bulletin: Dec. 1951" (Atlanta: CDC, 1951), pp. 54 and 56.

57. L. J. Trotti, Report from the Assistant State Director of Communicable Disease Control Activities.

58. Ibid., Monthly Narrative Report of Insect Vector Control Activities for the Texas State Department of Health, Nov. 1953.

59. D. J. Schliessmann, "Initiation of the *Aedes aegypti* Eradication Programme of the USA," *Bulletin of the World Health Organization* 36 (1967): 604–9.

60. U.S. PHS, *Fiscal Year 1964 Annual Report*, Aedes aegypti *Eradication Branch* (Atlanta: CDC, 1964), p. 1.

61. Schliessmann, "Initiation of the *Aedes aegypti* Eradication Programme."

62. "Deaths from Dengue Fever in Brazil up 90% in 2010," *English.news.cn*, November 11, 2010, accessed April 18, 2011, http://news.xinhuanet.com/english2010/health/2010–11/12/c_13603142.htm.

63. National Research Council, *The Life Sciences: Recent Progress and Application to Human Affairs, The World of Biological Research Requirements for the Future* (Washington, DC: National Academies Press, 1970), p. 432, http://www.nap.edu/openbook.php?record_id=9575&page=432)

64. Arnoldo Gabaldon, "The Nation-wide Campaign against Malaria in Venezuela," *Transactions of the Royal Society of Tropical Medicine and Hygiene* 43, no. 2 (1949): 113–64; and World Health Organization (WHO), "Part II, Appendix 14: The Place of DDT in Operations against Malaria and Other Vector-Borne Diseases," in *Official Records* No. 190, Executive Board, Forty-Seventh Session (Geneva: WHO, 1971), p. 178.

65. Gabaldon, "The Nation-wide Campaign against Malaria in Venezuela."

66. George Giglioli, "Changes in the Pattern of Mortality following the Eradication of Hyperdemic Malaria from a Highly Susceptible Community," *Bulletin of the World Health Organization* 46, no. 2 (1972): 181–202.

67. Ibid.

68. Ibid.; and George Giglioli, *Demerara Doctor: An Early Success against Malaria: The Autobiography of a Self-taught Physician: George Giglioli 1897–1975*, ed. Chris Curtis (London: Smith-Gordon, 2006).

69. Gabaldon, "The Nation-wide Campaign against Malaria in Venezuela"; and Giglioli, "Changes in the Pattern of Mortality."

70. Fernando M. de Bustamante, "Distribuição Geográfica e Periodicidade Estacional da Maaria no Brasil e Sua Relação com o Fatores Climáticos. Situação Atual do Problema," *Revista Brasileira de Malariologia e Doenças Tropicais* (1957): 187.

71. Musawenkosi L. Mabaso, Brian Sharp, and Christian Lengeler, "Historical Review of Malarial Control in Southern African with Emphasis on the Use of Indoor Residual House-Spraying," *Tropical Medicine & International Health* 9, no. 8 (2004): 846–56.

72. WHO, "Part II, Appendix 14," p. 179.

73. Anthony W. Brown, J. Haworth, and A. R. Zahar, "Malaria Eradication and Control from a Global Standpoint," *Journal of Medical Entomology* 13, no. 1 (1976): 1–25.

74. Ibid.

75. *Malaria Eradication in Taiwan, May 1991*, Department of Health, The Executive Yuan, Republic of China.

76. Ibid.

77. WHO, "Part II, Appendix 14," Table 1, p. 177; and Brown, Haworth, and Zahar, "Malaria Eradication and Control from a Global Standpoint."

78. Christa A. Skerry, Kerry Moran, and Kay M. Calavan, *Four Decades of Development: The History of U.S. Assistance to Nepal 1951–1991*, (Kathmandu, Nepal: U.S. Agency for International Development, 1991), p. 141, http://pdf.usaid.gov/pdf_docs/PNABR755.pdf.

79. Ibid., pp. 128 and 130.

80. Ibid., p. 74.

81. Ibid., pp. 50–53, 141–50.

82. WHO, "Part II, Appendix 14," p. 177.

83. *Nepal: People and Society*, http://www.nepalhomepage.com/general/people.html.

84. For a full discussion, see Donald Roberts and Richard Tren, *The Excellent Powder, DDT's Political and Scientific History* (Indianapolis: DogEar Publishers, 2010).

85. Rachel Carson, *Silent Spring* (Boston: Houghton Mifflin, 1962), p. 29.

86. Ibid., p. 231.

87. Ibid.

88. Ibid., p. 192

89. Ibid.

90. For a full discussion, see Roberts and Tren, *The Excellent Powder, DDT's Political and Scientific History.*

91. Carson, *Silent Spring*, p. 238

92. Ibid, p. 25

93. World Health Assembly (WHA), Resolution 23.12 includes this statement: "The Twenty-third World Health Assembly . . . Realizing Further that Safe, Effective and Inexpensive Insecticides Are Essential for the Effective Control of Malaria." See WHA, Resolution 23.12 (Geneva: WHO, 1970).

94. Ibid.

95. WHO Executive Board, *Summary Records* (Geneva: WHO, 1970), p. 31.

96. Ibid. p. 154

97. WHO Expert Committee on Malaria, "Fifteenth Report," WHO Technical Report Series No. 467 (Geneva: WHO, 1971), p. 42.

98. WHO, "Official Records of the World Health Organization, No. 205," *The Work of WHO 1972, Annual Report of the Director-General to the World Health Assembly and to the United Nations* (Geneva: WHO, 1973), p. 171.

99. WHO, "Official Records of the World Health Organization, No. 229," *The Work of WHO 1975, Annual Report of the Director-General to the World Health Assembly and to the United Nations* (Geneva: WHO, 1976), p. 103.

100. Ibid.

101. WHO, "Official Records of the World Health Organization, No. 235," WHO Executive Board, Fifty-Eighth Session, May 24–25, 1976, p. 37.

102. WHO, "Official Records of the World Health Organization, No. 243," *The Work of WHO, 1976–1977, Biennial Report of the Director-General to the World Health Assembly and to the United Nations* (Geneva: WHO, 1978), p. 111.

103. WHO Executive Board, *Summary Records*, Seventy-Fifth Session, EB75/1985/REC/2 (Geneva: WHO, 1985), p. 264.

104. WHO Health and Environment Linkages Initiative (HELI), *Malaria Control: The Power of Integrated Action*, 2005, http://www.who.int/heli/risks/vectors/malariacontrol/en/index.html; WHO, "Countries Move toward More Sustainable Ways to Roll Back Malaria," News Release, May 2009, http://www.who.int/mediacentre/news/releases/2009/malaria_ddt_20090506/en/; WHO, *Vector Control: Methods for Use by Individuals and Communities*, 1997, http://www.who.int/malaria/publications/atoz/9241544945/en/index.html; WHO, *Malaria Vector Control and Personal Protection*, 2006, http://www.who.int/malaria/publications/atoz/who_trs_936/en/ index.html; WHO, *Manual on Environmental Management of Mosquito Control with Special Emphasis on Malaria Vectors*, 1982, http://whqlibdoc.who.int/publications/1982/9241700661_eng.pdf; V. P. Sharma, *South-East Asia Advisory Committee on Health Research Twenty-first Session: Research on Newer Strategies for Vector Control* (Geneva: WHO, 1995), http://www.searo.who.int/LinkFiles/Technical_Documents_achr-21–8.pdf; and WHO, *Regional Framework for an Integrated Vector Management Strategy for the South-East Asia Region*, 2005, http://www.searo.who. int/LinkFiles/Kala_azar_VBC-86.pdf.

105. WHO Executive Board, *Review of the Malaria Action Programme*, Sixty-Seventh Session, EB/67/WP/1, Annex EB67/PC/WP/7 (Geneva: WHO, 1980), Appendix 2, p. 3.

106. Roll Back Malaria, "Part II: The Global Strategy," *Global Malaria Action Plan for a Malaria-Free World*, http://rbm.who.int/gmap/2–2b.html.

107. Malaria R&D Alliance, *Malaria Research & Development: An Assessment of Global Investment*, 2005, http://www.malariavaccine.org/files/MalariaRD_Report_complete.pdf.

108. PATH, *Staying the Course? Malaria Research and Development in a Time of Economic Uncertainty* (Seattle: PATH, 2011).

109. Donald R. Roberts and Richard Tren, "International Advocacy against DDT and Other Public Health Insecticides for Malaria Control," *Research and Reports in Tropical Medicine* 2011, no. 2 (2011): 23–30, http://www.dovepress.com/articles.php?article_id=6101.

Chapter 9

1. Some ecologists argue that Carson embodied a "deeper, more spiritual approach to Nature." Bill Devall and George Sessions, *Deep Ecology: Living as if Nature Mattered* (Layton, UT: Gibbs M. Smith, 2001), p. 65. See generally Andrew P. Morriss and Benjamin Cramer, "Disestablishing Environmentalism," *Environmental Law* 39 (2009): 309; and Robert H. Nelson, *Economic vs. Environmental Religion: The New Holy Wars* (University Park, PA: Penn State University Press, 2010).

2. Ciba-Geigy held the original patent on DDT as an insecticide. As part of the negotiations over the production of DDT for use by the Army during World War II, DuPont secured the right to produce it after the war as well. See Edmund Russell, *War and Nature: Fighting Humans and Insects with Chemicals from World War I to* Silent Spring (Cambridge, U.K.: Cambridge University Press, 2001), p. 148.

3. Donald R. Roberts and Richard Tren, *The Excellent Powder: DDT's Political and Scientific History* (Indianapolis: Dog Ear Publishing, 2010), pp. 197–203.

4. Paul K. Conkin, *A Revolution Down on the Farm: The Transformation of American Agriculture since 1929* (Lexington, KY: University Press of Kentucky, 2008), p. 4.

5. Ibid., p. 100.

6. Hiram M. Drache, *History of U.S. Agriculture and Its Relevance Today* (Danville, IL: Interstate, 1996); and Conkin, *A Revolution Down on the Farm*.

7. Conkin, *A Revolution Down on the Farm*, p. 49.

8. Drache, *History of U.S. Agriculture and Its Relevance Today*, p. 267. Many farm women saw this as a positive development. Women who started farming in the pre–World War II era commented that getting rid of the chickens, hogs, and dairy cattle caused the greatest change and freed them from some of their most burdensome tasks. The little flock or herd could not compete with large-scale poultry, hog, or dairy enterprises. Women no longer had to make butter or cheese, collect eggs, wash the cream separator, or butcher. Commercialization of food production enabled the farm wife to work on the major enterprises or off the farm. Many women became the farm bookkeepers, "gofers," and marketeers. Ibid., pp. 285–86.

9. Ibid., p. 358.

10. Ibid., p. 361.

11. Ibid., p. 261.

12. Ibid., p. 98.

13. Sally H. Clarke, *Regulation and the Revolution in United States Farm Productivity* (Cambridge, U.K.: Cambridge University Press, 1994), p. 4.

14. This began during the war. R. Douglas Hurt, *American Agriculture: A Brief History* (Ames, IA: Iowa State University. Press, 1994), p. 317.

15. Clarke, *Regulation and the Revolution in United States Farm Productivity*, pp. 5–6.

16. Conkin, *A Revolution Down on the Farm*, p. 108.

17. Including the Department of War, which funded boll weevil extermination efforts in the 1920s. Russell, *War and Nature*, p. 64.

18. Clarke, *Regulation and the Revolution in United States Farm Productivity*, p. 44. See also Russell, *War and Nature*, p. 47, noting increased appropriations of $441,000 ($7.4 million in 2010 dollars) in 1917 and $811,300 ($11.6 million in 2010 dollars) to the federal Bureau of Entomology to develop and spread pest control methods to ensure production of crops for the war effort.

19. Russell, *War and Nature*, p. 148, noting Hercules "had spent large sums of money on fellowships and research" in pesticides.

20. Drache, *History of U.S. Agriculture and Its Relevance Today*, p. 330.

21. Conkin, *A Revolution Down on the Farm*, p. 112.

22. Noel D. Uri, "A Note on the Development and Use of Pesticides," *Science of the Total Environment* 204 (1977): 57, 58. ("The mechanization revolution of the 1930s and 1940s has been augmented since 1945 by a chemical revolution in terms of pesticides.")

23. Hurt, *American Agriculture*, p. 300.

24. Russell, *War and Nature*, pp. 20–21.

25. Clarke, *Regulation and the Revolution in United States Farm Productivity*, p. 44.

26. Conkin, *A Revolution Down on the Farm*, p. 115.

27. Drache, *History of U.S. Agriculture and Its Relevance Today*, p. 337. Aerial spraying was used in 1921 in an orchard in Troy, Ohio, and the technique quickly spread, with 125,485 acres of cotton dusted with calcium arsenate in Louisiana in 1922 and the first planes specifically designed for crop dusting appearing in 1924. Ibid., p. 337. The Army Air Service collaborated with the Bureau of Entomology to develop crop dusting in the 1920s. Russell, *War and Nature*, p. 79.

28. Drache, *History of U.S. Agriculture and Its Relevance Today*, p. 338.

29. Ibid., p. 339.

30. See Andrew P. Morriss, "Cattle vs. Retirees: Sun City and the Battle of Spur Industries v. Del E. Webb Development Co.," in *Property Stories*, ed. Gerald Korngold and Andrew P. Morriss (New York: Foundation Press, 2004).

31. Bruce L. Gardner, *American Agriculture in the Twentieth Century* (Cambridge, MA: Harvard University Press, 2002); and Conkin, *A Revolution Down on the Farm*, p. 28. Until 1930, "almost all prior agricultural policies had worked in the exact opposite direction—to increase production."

32. Conkin, *A Revolution Down on the Farm*.

33. Drache, *History of U.S. Agriculture and Its Relevance Today*, p. 308; and Hurt, *American Agriculture*, p. 266.

34. The proposal would have had the federal government purchase surplus farm products and then either store them or sell abroad at a loss. The cost of the program was to be paid by farmers through an equalization fee, which they would then pass on to consumers. See John Philip Gleason, "The Attitude of the Business Community toward Agriculture during the McNary-Haugen Period," *Agricultural History* 32, no. 2 (1958): 127–38; and C. Fred Williams, "William M. Jardine and the Foundations for Republican Farm Policy, 1925–1929," *Agricultural History* 70, no. 2 (1996): 216–32.

35. Drache, *History of U.S. Agriculture and Its Relevance Today*, p. 308.

36. Conkin, *A Revolution Down on the Farm*, p. 53.

37. Drache, *History of U.S. Agriculture and Its Relevance Today*, p. 302. USDA also organized an agricultural outlook conference in 1923.

38. Gardner, *American Agriculture in the Twentieth Century*, pp. 245–46.

39. Conkin, *A Revolution Down on the Farm*, p. 64.

40. Ibid., p. 51. "Over eight years, during two presidential administrations and four Congresses, the federal government, responding to a large array of interest groups and competing policy alternatives, matured a complex body of laws and administrative agencies to gain what everyone hoped would be fair and stable prices for almost all major agricultural products. Details have changed through the years, but aspects of every policy option undertaken in the 1930s have endured until the present, providing the political constraints and opportunities that allowed American agriculture to remain the most productive, and food prices to remain the lowest as a percentage of total spending, in the world."

41. Ibid., pp. 64–65.

42. Ibid., pp. 52, 76. Roosevelt was, "at one time or another, open to almost all strategies."

43. Drache, *History of U.S. Agriculture and Its Relevance Today*, p. 306. Fifteen thousand were in the USDA and 10,000 were in the cooperative groups.

44. Conkin, *A Revolution Down on the Farm*, pp. 75–76.

45. Ibid., p. 76. Tractors also encouraged consolidation. Hurt, *American Agriculture*, p. 358. "Tractors enabled farmers to plant and harvest more acres, but small-scale farmers often could not compete with farmers who could afford this implement and had sufficient land to make it profitable. And increased production, resulting from acres planted with a tractor, drove prices down. As a result, farm sizes continued to increase as small-scale farmers withdrew from agriculture."

46. Drache, *History of U.S. Agriculture and Its Relevance Today*, p. 266.

47. Hurt, *American Agriculture*, p. 321. "Congressional wartime agricultural policy proved highly favorable to farmers, and the major agricultural organizations such as the American Farm Bureau, Farmers' Union, and Grange lobbied effectively for it."

48. Conkin, *A Revolution Down on the Farm*, p. 131.

49. Clarke puts great emphasis on the role of farm credit in speeding adoption of new technology: "the FCA in refinancing farm loans created new conditions under which farmers borrowed money, conditions that made debt financing more profitable to a competitive farmer." Clarke, *Regulation and the Revolution in United States Farm Productivity*, p. 165. The government's participation changed loans' terms from "a year to a generation" in many instances. Ibid., p. 192 (quoting a banker).

50. Uri, "A Note on the Development and Use of Pesticides," p. 66.

51. Conkin, *A Revolution Down on the Farm*, pp. 80, 126 (describing struggles over level of parity).

52. Hurt, *American Agriculture*, p. 325.

53. Ibid., p. 327.

54. Ibid., pp. 352–53; and Conkin, *A Revolution Down on the Farm*, p. 67. "The 'capture' of food aid [for the poor] by the Department of Agriculture proved politically invaluable in future years. It created a second constituency for the department and its programs and often helped deflect criticism from its commodity programs, as it did during debates on a 2007 farm bill."

55. Roberts and Tren, *The Excellent Powder*, p. 13 (describing expansion of use).

56. James Whorton, *Before Silent Spring: Pesticides & Public Health in Pre-DDT America* (Princeton, NJ: Princeton University Press, 1974), p. 6.

57. Paris Green sold 500 tons a year in New York City alone in its first decade of use (1867–1877). Ibid., p. 22.

58. John Perkins, *Insects, Experts and the Insecticide Crisis: The Quest for New Pest Management Strategies* (New York: Plenum Press, 1982), pp. 3–4. "The commercialization of the insecticide industry was accompanied by substantial fraud including adulterating legitimate products and making extravagant claims for absolutely worthless junk."

59. Roger E. Meiners and Andrew P. Morriss, "Agricultural Commons Problems and Responses," in *Agricultural Policy and the Environment*, ed. Roger E. Meiners and Bruce Yandle (Lanham, MD: Rowman & Littlefield, 2003), pp. 19, 29–31. Whorton discusses the issue at length, noting that state "[e]ntomologists had urged such legislation for some time [by the end of the 19th century], on the grounds that farmers who did not spray imposed unfair financial hardship on their more conscientious neighbors. So long as just one farm in an area was left as an unsprayed refuge for insects, it was maintained, surrounding farmers would have to spray more frequently to prevent reinfestation of their fields." Whorton, *Before Silent Spring*, p. 72.

60. Andrew P. Morriss and Roger E. Meiners, "Property Rights, Pesticides and Public Health: Explaining the Paradox of Modern Pesticide Policy," *Fordham Environmental Law Journal* 14 (2002): 9.

61. Ibid., p. 5.

62. Maurice B. Green, "Energy in Pesticide Manufacture, Distribution and Use," in *Energy in Plant Nutrition and Pest Control*, ed. Zane R. Helsel (New York: Elsevier, 1987), pp. 165, 176–77.

63. Hearings before the House Select Committee to Investigate the Use of Chemicals in Food Products, U.S. House of Representatives, 82nd Cong., 1st Sess., 1951, at 161ff (hereafter "House Select Committee 1951").

64. Whorton, *Before Silent Spring*, p. 24.

65. Ibid., pp. 178–81.

66. Ibid., pp. 190–205.

67. Or organochlorides. DDT and other pesticides of that time, such as aldrin and dieldrin, were also popular and are classified in this group.

68. DDT "was the best insecticide ever developed—inexpensive, broad spectrum, and with no apparent threat to humans." Conkin, *A Revolution Down on the Farm*, p. 113.

69. Drache, *History of U.S. Agriculture and Its Relevance Today*, p. 373.

70. Russell, *War and Nature*, p. 149. Companies were allowed five-year write-offs of either 35 percent or 100 percent of the plant costs (theoretically depending on whether there was postwar value to the plant, but at least DuPont was able to use the 100 percent rate for its DDT plant), and the government built a plant in Parlin, New Jersey, operated by Hercules. Ibid.

71. House Select Committee 1951, pp. 9, 363. Gross domestic product in 1950 was just under $300 billion. See *Gross Domestic Product, 1947–2011*, Economic Research, Federal Reserve Bank of St. Louis, http://research.stlouisfed.org/fred2/series/GDP.

72. House Select Committee 1951, p. 9.

73. Ibid., p. 358.

74. Russell, *War and Nature*, p. 154.

75. Ibid., p. 155.

76. Department of the Interior, Information Service, Fish and Wildlife Service, *For Release to PM's, Friday, August 10, 1945*. The FWS had reported earlier that it was beginning tests of DDT, a substance about which there was concern. Ibid.; *For Advance Release to Sunday Papers, June 17, 1945*.

77. Ibid., *For Release to PM's of Wednesday, August 22, 1945*. FWS's location in Interior was the result of Ickes' "larger plan of turning Interior Department into a Department of Conservation," a plan that included the shift of FWS from Commerce during Carson's early years at FWS.

78. Russell, *War and Nature*, p. 159.

79. Rachel Carson, Letter to Harold Lynch, July 15, 1945, quoted in Mark Hamilton Lytle, *The Gentle Subversive: Rachel Carson, Silent Spring, and the Rise of the Environmental Movement* (New York: Oxford University Press, 2007), p. 60.

80. Quoted in Russell, *War and Nature*, p. 176.

81. Department of the Interior, Information Service, Fish and Wildlife Service, *For Release to AM's, Saturday, May 18, 1946*.

82. Lytle, *The Gentle Subversive*, p. 40.

83. Department of the Interior, Information Service, Fish and Wildlife Service, *FWS Releases Annual Report for Fiscal Year 1948*.

84. Ibid., *For Release June 21, 1959*, noting that the agency was seeking an 11 percent increase in authorization for such studies.

85. Ibid., *For Release September 7, 1965*.

86. For example, "More DDT Victories," *Science News Letter*, February 17, 1945, p. 102.

87. A Joint Statement of Policy by the United States Army and the United States Public Health Service, "Use of DDT for Mosquito Control in the United States," *Public Health Reports* 60 (April 27, 1945): 469.

88. Frederick L. and Clinton S. Smith, "DDT Residual House Spray—A Method of Malaria Control in Rural Areas," *Public Health Reports* 60 (October 26, 1945): 1274.

89. F. D. Mott and M. I. Roemer, "A Federal Program of Public Health and Medical Services for Migratory Farm Workers," *Public Health Reports* 60 (March 2, 1945): 229, 234.

90. Justin M. Andrews, "The United States Public Health Service Communicable Disease Center," *Public Health Reports* 61 (August 16, 1946): 1203, 1206.

91. J. J. Landers, "Bug Disinfestation in a Prison," *The Journal of Hygiene* 45 (August 1947): 354.

92. Arnold B. Erickson, "Effects of DDT Mosquito Larviciding on Wildlife: II," *Public Health Reports* 62 (August 29, 1947): 1254, 1257. This study continued over time. Later, it was reported that spraying reduced the population of assorted pests but did not impact bee or aphid populations. Harvey J. Scudder and Clarence M. Tarzwell, "Effects of DDT Mosquito Larviciding on Wildlife: IV," *Public Health Reports* 65 (January 20, 1950): 71. The key to not harming fish and wildlife, PHS concluded, was in the method of spraying and dosage. Properly done, there was "little or no significant harm to aquatic organisms." Clarence M. Tazwell, "Effects of DDT Mosquito Larviciding on Wildlife: V," *Public Health Reports* 65 (February 24, 1950): 231, 252.

93. Cornelius W. Kruse, "The Airplane Application of DDT for Emergency Control of Common Flies in the Urban Community," *Public Health Reports* 63 (November 26, 1948): 1535.

94. John W. Kirkpatrick and H. F. Schoof, "Fly Production in Treated and Untreated Privies," *Public Health Reports* 71 (August 1956): 787; and Frank J. Von

Zuben, George R. Hayes, and E. C. Anderson, "Public Health Disaster Air in the Rio Grande Flood of 1954," *Public Health Reports* 72 (November 1957): 1009.

95. For example, Samuel W. Simmons, "Insecticides and World Health," *Public Health Reports* 67 (May 1952): 451.

96. FDA, "Significant Dates in U.S. Food and Drug Law History," http://www.fda.gov/AboutFDA/WhatWeDo/History/Milestones/ucm128305.htm. Its location in USDA weakened the bureau's ability to act on food safety issues, given USDA's overall mission of promoting agriculture. Whorton, *Before Silent Spring*, p. 114. Even into the 1920s, the agency was more focused on educating farmers than punitive regulatory actions. Ibid., pp. 116, 120.

97. Philip J. Hilts, *Protecting America's Health: The FDA, Business, and One Hundred Years of Regulation* (New York: Knopf, 2003), p. xii.

98. Russell, *War and Nature*, p. 81.

99. Whorton, *Before Silent Spring*, p. 96.

100. Ibid., pp. 133–40.

101. Ibid., p. 140.

102. Ibid., pp. 160–64.

103. Ibid., p. 164.

104. Hilts, *Protecting America's Health*, pp. 77–78. Tugwell had to battle Agriculture Secretary Henry Wallace over a lead tolerance Tugwell established while Wallace was out of town. Wallace eventually forced Tugwell to loosen the standard. Whorton, *Before Silent Spring*, p. 222.

105. Samuel Fromartz, *Organic, Inc.* (Boston: Houghton Mifflin, 2006), pp. 20–21.

106. J. I. Rodale, *Pay Dirt: Farming & Gardening with Composts* (New York: Devin-Adair Co., 1948). Carson viewed Rodale as "an eccentric" and distanced herself from him. Fromartz, *Organic, Inc.*, p. 21.

107. Russell, *War and Nature*, p. 75.

108. See Pierre Desrochers and Christine Hoffbauer, "The Post War Intellectual Roots of the Population Bomb," *Electronic Journal of Sustainable Development* 1, no. 3 (2009): 37–61; and Frederick Buell, *From Apocalypse to Way of Life: Environmental Crisis in the American Century* (London: Taylor & Francis, 2003).

109. Russell, *War and Nature*, p. 151.

110. Professor Ruhl summarizes FIFRA's approach: "In short, so long as the label instructions are followed, the applicator is properly certified and the applicator follows worker safety and recordkeeping requirements, FIFRA imposes no direct restrictions or requirements on farms. While this does not amount to a complete safe harbor for farm use of pesticides, FIFRA's hands-off approach to farms—the primary users of pesticides—pales in comparison with the [later] regulatory approach to . . . targeted industries. Under FIFRA, with regard to farmers, no permits are required, no environmental or efficiency performance standards are imposed, no technology-based standards are applied, no regular public reporting of pesticide applications is required, and no monitoring of pesticide levels in soils, runoff, or groundwater is required. Although some states regulate pesticide applications more aggressively than does FIFRA, it is fair to say that the nation has no comprehensive regulatory framework governing farm use of pesticides." J. B. Ruhl, "The Environmental Law of Farms," *Environmental Law Reporter* 31 (2001): 10,203, 10,215.

111. A. Roger Greenway, *Environmental Permitting Handbook* (New York: McGraw-Hill Professional, 2000), p. 4.1.2.

112. Russell, *War and Nature*, p. 175.

113. 52 US Stat. 1040.

114. Greenway, *Environmental Permitting Handbook*, p. 4.1.3. The Delaney Amendment of 1958, which provided for zero risk, caused endless dancing around a standard that was not realistic. While not central to our concern here, the impact on pesticides was the same as for any food additive. The standard was impossible, giving FDA power to prohibit nearly any substance. Ibid., p. 4.1.5. USDA expanded its authority as well, adding authority in 1959 and 1964 to remove chemicals from the market.

115. Whorton, *Before Silent Spring*, pp. 228–30.

116. Hilts, *Protecting America's Health*, pp. 118–19.

117. House Select Committee 1951, pp. 1–2.

118. C. C. Alexander, *Notes on DDT Case* (1958) (unpublished manuscript on file with authors and available in the Cornell University Library). See also Robert J. Spear, *The Great Gypsy Moth* War (Amherst, MA: University of Massachusetts Press, 2005), pp. 257–58.

119. Lytle, *The Gentle Subversive*, pp. 126–27.

120. www.kkblaw.com/history/html, accessed Jan. 16, 2011.

121. "Public Warned on DDT," *New York Times*, March 10, 1951; and "Public Health Held Imperiled by Pesticides," *Los Angeles Times*, November 24, 1951.

122. In the discussion that follows, we focus on the 1951 hearings, cited in note 63. These were preceded by 20 days of hearings by the same committee in 1950, which covered much the same ground. Kleinfeld's first witness in 1950 was a retired professor of medicine who stated that you simply could not prevent agricultural chemicals from getting into the nation's food supply and not enough was known about the toxic effects, so the FDA needed the ability to regulate all such matters. Hearings before the House Select Committee to Investigate the Use of Chemicals in Food Products, U.S. House of Representatives, 81st Cong., 2nd Sess., 1950, p. 12.

123. House Select Committee 1951, p. 4f.

124. Ibid., p. 60f.

125. Ibid., p. 89f.

126. Ibid., p. 113. On the virus X scare, see Aaron Wildavsky, *But Is It True?* (Cambridge, MA: Harvard University Press 1995), p. 56. ("In 1949 New York physician Morton Biskind published a series of articles claiming that DDT caused the mysterious 'virus X' in humans—a disease that had been linked with polio. His claims were refuted a few months later, but the scare had nonetheless increased public concern about DDT.") The article Wildavsky cites as evidence that the link had been refuted was published in *Science Digest* in 1949, long before the hearings. See "DDT Danger Refuted," *Science Digest* 26 (July 1949): 47.

127. House Select Committee 1951, p. 149.

128. Ibid., p. 151.

129. Ibid., p. 154.

130. Ibid., p. 156.

131. Ibid., p. 162.

132. Ibid., p. 177f.

133. Ibid., p. 191.

134. Ibid., p. 183.

135. Ibid., p. 192.

136. Ibid., p. 194.

137. Ibid., p. 193.

138. Ibid., p. 195. Note that the elements of the so-called precautionary principal were present in the argument made by Kleinfeld and others supporting the FDA position.

139. Ibid.

140. Ibid., p. 249f. Rat studies do not settle matters, but they have been beneficial in understanding the potential consequences of many chemicals on humans. Nevertheless, when the results are contrary to one side or the other of an issue, the methodology will be disputed as not dispositive.

141. Ibid., p. 217f.

142. Ibid., p. 206.

143. Ibid., p. 237f.

144. Ibid., p. 295.

145. Apparently a false belief. At another session, a member of the committee from Washington state asserted that French grape growers pioneered the use of the previous generation of highly toxic sprays. Ibid., 162. That account is given credence in a Cornell University posting, *A Brief History of Pest Management,* which notes that Paris Green was sprayed on grapes beginning in the 1860s to deter theft but was found also to deter insects. See http://instruct1.cit.cornell.edu/courses/ipm444/test/01Intro/01 intro_2.html.

146. House Select Committee 1951, p. 305.

147. Ibid., p. 308.

148. Ibid., p. 314f.

149. Ibid., p. 321f.

150. These hearings were held before the widespread acknowledgment of the link between cigarette smoking and lung cancer, which first came to public attention in 1953. See Bruce Yandle, Joseph Rotondi, Andrew P. Morriss, and Andrew Dorchak, "Bootleggers, Baptists and Televangelists: Regulating Tobacco by Litigation," *University of Illinois Law Review* (2008): 1225, 1247.

151. House Select Committee 1951, p. 344f.

152. Ibid., p. 367f.

153. Ibid., p. 429f.

154. Ibid., pp. 917f, 924f.

155. Ibid., p. 931f.

156. Ibid., p. 948f.

157. A representative of Ortho Pharmaceutical; Ibid., p. 444f.

158. Ibid., p. 134. Apparently an ingredient improperly used in baking was mislabeled or not labeled at all. No one ever claimed the maker tried to pass off the product as suitable for consumption; the product simply ended up in the wrong place. But this was taken as evidence that there are dangerous chemicals in the food chain.

159. Ibid., p. 547f.

160. Ibid., pp. 562f, 695f.

161. Ibid., p. 585f.

162. Ibid., p. 603f.

163. Ibid., p. 833.

164. Ibid., p. 889f.

165. Ibid., p. 858f. The president of the company that made the product in question explained that the woman died of a heart attack, not instant poisoning by the

hair treatment product. The FDA had condemned the product based on hysteria, not science. Furthermore, if the product caused the death, he asked, why was the company not sued? Kleinfeld pressed the attack, noting that the company did not have evidence that its products would not cause any harm.

166. Ibid., p. 1047f.

167. James Delaney, "Peril on Your Food Shelf," *American Magazine* (July 1951): 1–4.

168. Whorton, *Before Silent Spring*, p. 252.

169. As seen in similar incidents, dubious quality research that does not meet the generally accepted standards of quality work is presented as a point of view that is equally valuable to the accepted wisdom. In recent years, a there was great concern over the safety of vaccines based on a claim of one physician, published in *The Lancet*, asserting that childhood vaccines were related to autism. The claim was complete bosh, but it took more than a decade to fully expose the fraud. For a brief summary, see "Journal Retracts 1998 Paper Linking Autism to Vaccines," *New York Times*, February 2, 2010, http://www.nytimes.com/2010/02/03/health/research/03lancet.html.

170. Morriss and Meiners, "Property Rights, Pesticides and Public Health," pp. 8–13.

171. See, for example, Alexander, *Notes on DDT Case*, on February 13, 1958, p. 1 ("During testimony, [Dr. Malcolm] Hargraves [witness for plaintiffs, physician at Mayo Clinic, and blood expert] indicated that the U.S. Public Health Service is a reputable organization. Kleinfeld tried to bring out that they could make mistakes—brought up the Salk vaccine trouble, but this line of questioning was ruled out."); on February 24, 1958, p. 1 ("Kleinfeld pressed [a defense witness who was a Public Health Service doctor] for an opinion as to the lowest level that could cause damage to the human body and the witness replied that he didn't know since the feeding experiments have been at levels too low to show damage."); and on February 24, 1958, p. 1 ("Kleinfeld asked Hayes if DDT is a poison like strychnine, lead arsenate.")

172. For example, in 1942 the Texas Supreme Court had held a sausage manufacturer liable on an implied warranty theory for contaminated sausages, even when the contamination was not the fault of the manufacturer. *Jacob E. Decker & Sons, Inc. v. Capps*, 164 S.W.2d 828 (Tex. 1942). That same day, it held a retailer liable for an "unwholesome" can of spinach, despite the retailer's defense that the can was sealed and so the retailer could not have been at fault. *Griggs Canning Co. v. Josey*, 164 S.W.2d 835 (Tex. 1942). In a large number of states, the Uniform Sales Act had been held to preclude such implied warranties. See, for example, *Rinaldi v. Mohican Co.*, 121 N.E. 471 (N.Y. 1918). However, food processors and retailers would have been concerned (correctly) about states such as Texas where the statute did not apply and about the direction of the law because the then-proposed Uniform Commercial Code provided for strict liability for food sellers without privity limitations.

173. See, for example, Reed Dickerson, *Products Liability and the Food Consumer* (Boston: Little, Brown and Company, 1951), a 300-page treatise that the *ABA Journal* praised in a review, saying it "could not have come at a better time" to help lawyers with its analysis of "more than 1,000 American cases as well as English cases." William Tucker Dean, Jr., "Products Liability and the Food Consumer," *ABA Journal* 38 (February 1952): 145.

174. "Food Man Depicts Fight on Pesticides," *New York Times*, February 1, 1952.

175. House Select Committee 1951, p. 296. The scientist from Swift explained that the company did extensive rat tests to assure the public of safety and that such tests

could take years. The representative of the American Bakers Association endorsed expanded FDA powers over any chemicals used in baking products. Ibid., p. 573. The technical director of Pet Milk, a major producer of processed milk used in commercial food products, endorsed extensive FDA controls of chemicals that entered the food system and stated that DDT is not safe; the company used no pesticides but could not stop farmers from using them. Ibid., p. 596. The manager of the central laboratories of General Foods stated that the company's 150 to 175 research chemists frequently consulted with the FDA and that there was concern about the cumulative effects of chemicals that entered into processed foods one way or another. Ibid., pp.762–69.

176. Hilts, *Protecting America's Health*, p. 120 (quoting Winton Rankin on George Larrick).

177. Lytle, *The Gentle Subversive*, p. 145.

178. A few years later, cranberry sales collapsed amid talk of poisoning from cranberries. William H. Rodgers, Jr., "The Persistent Problem of the Persistent Pesticides: A Lesson in Environmental Law," *Columbia Law Review* 70 (1970): 567, 593–94.

179. House Select Committee, p. 760f. California public health officials testified that fly-by-night companies are hard to monitor with respect to food safety; the big ones are not the problem; they advocated stronger FDA controls.

180. Roberts and Tren, *The Excellent Powder*, p. 13.

181. Department of Agriculture Appropriations fiscal year 1971, Subcommittee on Agriculture of the House Committee on Appropriations, 91st Cong., February 18, 1970, p. 28.

182. Russell, *War and Nature*, p. 147.

183. Geigy, Allied Chemical, Olin Corp., Diamond Shamrock, and Lebanon Chemicals. EPA, *DDT: A Review of Scientific and Economic Aspects of the Decision to Ban Its Use as a Pesticide* (Washington, DC: National Technical Information Service, 1975), p. 148.

184. Agriculture Appropriations FY1971, pp. 29–30.

185. EPA, *DDT: A Review*, p. 16.

186. Ibid., pp. 168, 184.

187. Ibid., pp. 184, 189.

188. Agriculture Appropriations FY1971, p. 28.

189. Ibid., p. 29. Delaney and Kleinfeld won that battle.

190. Ibid.

191. Desrochers and Hoffbauer, "The Post War Intellectual Roots of the Population Bomb." Moreover, as the debate developed over a domestic ban, some pointed out that if U.S. agriculturalists were forced to use higher-priced substitutes, foreign producers would gain a small cost advantage by using pesticides banned in the United States. Hence, a world ban on DDT was in order. If foreign farmers wanted to use pesticides, they should have to do so on a level playing field—that is, using higher-priced proprietary products dominated by U.S. manufacturers.

192. Bruce Yandle, "Baptists and Bootleggers: The Education of a Regulatory Economist," *Regulation* (1983): 12–16.

193. Stewart Udall, *The Quiet Crisis* (New York: Avon Books, 1964).

194. Lytle, *The Gentle Subversive*, p. 164.

195. See Walter B. Shurden, *Turning Points in Baptist History* (Macon, GA: Center for Baptist Studies, Mercer University, 2001), http://www.centerforbaptiststudies.org/pamphlets/style/turningpoints.htm.

Chapter 10

1. The author would like to thank Daniel Smith and Lisa Peters for their research assistance.

2. William Cronon, "Foreword: *Silent Spring* and the Birth of Modern Environmentalism," in *DDT, Silent Spring, and the Rise of Environmentalism*, ed. Thomas R. Dunlap (Seattle: University of Washington Press, 2008), p. x.

3. Andrew P. Morriss, "Pesticides and Environmental Federalism: An Empirical and Qualitative Analysis of §24(c) Registrations," in *Environmental Federalism*, ed. Terry L. Anderson and Peter J. Hill (Lanham, MD: Rowman & Littlefield Publishers, 1997), p. 136.

4. Angus A. MacIntyre, "Why Pesticides Received Extensive Use in America: A Political Economy of Agricultural Pest Management to 1970," *Natural Resources Journal* 27 (1987): 546.

5. Ibid.; and National Research Council, *Regulating Pesticides* (Washington, DC: National Academies Press, 1980), p. 20. (Congress passed the Insecticide Act "in response to pressure from the U.S. Department of Agriculture and farm organizations.")

6. Christopher J. Bosso, *Pesticides and Politics: The Life Cycle of a Public Issue* (Pittsburgh, PA: University of Pittsburg Press, 1987), p. 48.

7. Insecticide Act, ch. 191, 36 Stat. 331 (1910).

8. Benjamin Ross and Steven Amter, *The Polluters: The Making of Our Chemically Altered Environment* (New York: Oxford University Press, 2010), p. 46. ("Environmental protection and public health were not the concerns of the Insecticide Act of 1910, which remained in effect until 1947.")

9. John T. Coyne, "Pesticide Regulation in the Department of Agriculture," *Food, Drug & Cosmetic Law Journal* 12 (1957): 632.

10. James Whorton, *Before* Silent Spring: *Pesticides and Public Health in Pre-DDT America* (Princeton, NJ: Princeton University Press, 1974), p. 99.

11. Bosso, *Pesticides and Politics*, p. 48.

12. Ibid., p. 50.

13. Thomas R. Dunlap, *DDT: Scientists, Citizens, and Public Policy* (Princeton, NJ: Princeton University Press, 1981), p. 41.

14. Ibid.

15. Douglass F. Rohrman, "Pesticide Laws and Legal Implications of Pesticide Use—Part I," *Food, Drug & Cosmetic Law Journal* 23 (1968): 142, 146, n. 11. After enactment of the 1910 Insecticide Act, several more states adopted laws similar to the federal law.

16. Jeffrey D. Huffaker, "The Regulation of Pesticide Use in California," *U.C. Davis Law Review* 11, no. 2 (1978): 273, 275.

17. Morriss, "Pesticides and Environmental Federalism," p. 138; and Whorton, *Before* Silent Spring, p. 72.

18. Morriss, "Pesticides and Environmental Federalism," p. 138.

19. Whorton, *Before* Silent Spring, p. 122. ("The states essentially merely understudied, and often without much enthusiasm, the federal role in residue control.")

20. California Environmental Protection Agency, "The History of the California Environmental Protection Agency," January 19, 2006, http://www.calepa.ca.gov/about/history01/.

21. Huffaker, "The Regulation of Pesticide Use in California," p. 276.

22. Ibid.

23. CalEPA, "The History."

24. Huffaker, "The Regulation of Pesticide Use in California," p. 277.

25. Harrison C. Dunning, "Pests, Poisons, and the Living Law: The Control of Pesticides in California's Imperial Valley," *Ecology Law Quarterly* 2 (1972): 642–43.

26. John Wargo, *Our Children's Toxic Legacy: How Science and Law Fail to Protect Us from Pesticides* (New Haven, CT: Yale University Press, 1998), p. 69.

27. Gerald Malkan, "Pesticide Residues: A Study in Federal Law," *UCLA Law Review* 2 (1954–55): 515, 516; and Bosso, *Pesticides and Politics*, p. 63.

28. Ross and Amter, *The Polluters*, pp. 57–58.

29. Morriss, "Pesticides and Environmental Federalism," p. 138.

30. Ibid. (citing industry testimony from a 1946 congressional hearing).

31. Bosso, *Pesticides and Politics*, p. 54.

32. Ibid., pp. 10–11. FIFRA "essentially was the product of close cooperation among members of the House Committee on Agriculture, mid-level personnel within the U.S. Department of Agriculture (USDA), and those representing the major agricultural pesticide makers—a classic 'iron triangle.'"

33. Ibid., p. 35.

34. Wargo, *Our Children's Toxic Legacy*, p. 73.

35. MacIntyre, "Why Pesticides Received Extensive Use in America," p. 569.

36. Rohrman, "Pesticide Laws—Part I," p. 147, n. 16 (quoting Harris and Cummings, "Enforcement of the Federal Insecticide, Fungicide and Rodenticide Act in the United States," *Residue Reviews* 6 (1964): 104, 106.

37. Coyne, "Pesticide Regulation," p. 632.

38. Bosso, *Pesticides and Politics*, p. 11.

39. Morriss, "Pesticides and Environmental Federalism," p. 140.

40. MacIntyre, "Why Pesticides Received Extensive Use in America," p. 259.

41. NRC, *Regulating Pesticides*, p. 21.

42. Bosso, *Pesticides and Politics*, p. 21.

43. Donald T. Hornstein, "Lessons from Federal Pesticide Regulation on the Paradigms and Politics of Environmental Law Reform," *Yale Journal of Regulation* 10 (1993): 369, 424.

44. Bosso, *Pesticides and Politics*, p. 31.

45. NRC, *Regulating Pesticides*, p. 21.

46. Dunlap, *DDT: Scientists, Citizens, and Public Policy*, p. 129.

47. Morriss, "Pesticides and Environmental Federalism," p. 142.

48. MacIntyre, "Why Pesticides Received Extensive Use in America," p. 259.

49. Ibid., p. 254.

50. Dunlap, *DDT: Scientists, Citizens, and Public Policy*, p. 200.

51. Rachel Carson, *Silent Spring*, 40th anniversary edition (Boston: Houghton Mifflin, 2002), pp. 115, 165.

52. Ibid., p. 172.

53. Rachel Carson, "Interagency Coordination in Environmental Hazards (Pesticides)," testimony before the Subcommittee on Reorganization and International Organizations of the Senate Committee on Government Operations, 88th Cong., 1st sess., June 4, 1963 (Washington, DC: Government Printing Office, 1964), pp. 210–11, 232.

54. Dunlap, *DDT: Scientists, Citizens, and Public Policy*, p. 87.

55. Mrak Commission, *Report of the Secretary's Commission on Pesticides and Their Relationship to Environmental Health* (Washington, DC: U.S. Department of Health, Education, and Welfare, 1969), p. 80.

56. Brian P. Baker, "Pest Control in the Public Interest: Crop Protection in California," *UCLA Journal of Environmental Law & Policy* 8 (1988–89): 31, 49–50.

57. Dunning, "Pests, Poisons, and the Living Law," p. 668; and Robert van den Bosch, "Insecticides and the Law," *Hastings Law Journal* 22 (1971): 615, 621.

58. Douglass F. Rohrman, "The Law of Pesticides: Present and Future," *Journal of Public Law* 17 (1968): 351, 363–64. The three exceptions were Indiana, Delaware, and Alaska, though Indiana and Alaska did have some other regulations of pesticides in place.

59. Huffaker, "The Regulation of Pesticide Use in California," p. 283.

60. van den Bosch, "Insecticides and the Law," pp. 621–22.

61. Rohrman, "Pesticide Laws—Part I," p. 396–401.

62. Bosso, *Pesticides and Politics*, p. 138.

63. Dunlap, *DDT: Scientists, Citizens, and Public Policy*, p. 152.

64. Ibid., p. 171.

65. Ibid., p. 177.

66. Ibid., pp. 178–79. The cancellation order made exceptions for control of mice, bats, and body lice.

67. Ibid., p. 205.

68. Council on Environmental Quality, *Environmental Quality: The Third Annual Report of the Council on Environmental Quality* (Washington, DC: Government Printing Office, 1972), pp. 178–79.

69. Rohrman, "Pesticide Laws—Part I," p. 154.

70. Ibid., p. 155.

71. Morriss, "Pesticides and Environmental Federalism," p. 148 (quoting testimony by Florida officials).

72. Douglass F. Rohrman, "Pesticide Laws and Legal Implications of Pesticide Use—Part II," *Food, Drug & Cosmetic Law Journal* 23 (1968): 172, 180.

73. Ibid., p. 181. The aerial sprayer was generally considered the "agent" and the farm owner the "principal," so the property owner would be liable for the improper application by the sprayer.

74. Ibid., p. 180–81.

75. Ibid., p. 184.

76. Richard J. Gross, "Pesticide Use and Liability in North Dakota," *North Dakota Law Review* 47 (1970–71): 35, 345.

77. Carson, *Silent Spring*, pp. 158–59

78. 439 F.2d 584 (D.C. Cir. 1971).

79. MacIntyre, "Why Pesticides Received Extensive Use in America," p. 257.

80. 439 F.2d 584, p. 594.

81. Ibid., p. 593.

82. Dunlap, *DDT: Scientists, Citizens, and Public Policy*, p. 236.

83. Mary Jane Large, "The Federal Environmental Pesticide Control Act of 1972: A Compromise Approach," *Ecology Law Quarterly* 3 (1973): 290.

84. NRC, *Regulating Pesticides*, p. 22. ("The courts adopted a conservative strategy by giving USDA and, subsequently, EPA the discretion to ban pesticides on the basis of a comparison of benefits and risks that took a very conservative view of socially

acceptable risk. Congress accepted the necessity of basing decisions based upon risk as opposed to proof of harm, but attempted to ensure that risk would be only one of the relevant factors considered by EPA. To this end, Congress posed a process that based all decisions on a balanced benefit-cost analysis derived from neoclassical welfare economics.")

85. William E. Reukauf, "Regulation of Agricultural Pesticides," *Iowa Law Review* 62 (1976–77): 909.

86. Ibid., pp. 915–16.

87. Ibid., p. 918.

88. See Jonathan H. Adler, "The Fable of Federal Environmental Regulation," *Case Western Reserve Law Review* 55 (2004): 93.

89. See Malkan, "Pesticide Residues," p. 517. ("Since foods containing pesticide residue are frequently marketed on a nationwide basis, uniform control seems best suited to give certainty or protection and ease of compliance.")

90. Dunlap, *DDT: Scientists, Citizens, and Public Policy*, p. 68.

91. See Malkan, "Pesticide Residues," pp. 519–21.

92. Morriss, "Pesticides and Environmental Federalism," p. 134.

93. See Jonathan H. Adler, "When Is Two a Crowd: The Impact of Federal Action on State Environmental Regulation," *Harvard Environmental Law Review* 31 (2007): 67.

94. Dunlap, *DDT: Scientists, Citizens, and Public Policy*, p. 235.

Chapter 11

1. Ellen Levine, *Rachel Carson: A Twentieth-Century Life* (New York: Viking, 2007), p. 191.

2. Gregory Conko, "The Precautionary Principle: Protectionism and Environmental Extremism by Other Means," paper presented at the International Society of Regulatory Toxicology and Pharmacology Workshop on the Precautionary Principle, Arlington, Virginia, June 20, 2002, http://cei.org/outreach-regulatory-comments-and-testimony/precautionary-principle-protectionism-and-environmental-e.

3. World Commission on the Ethics of Scientific Knowledge and Technology, *The Precautionary Principle* (Paris: United Nations Educational, Scientific and Cultural Organization, 2005).

4. Jonathan Adler, "The Precautionary Principle's Challenge to Progress," in *Global Warming and Other Eco-Myths*, ed. Ronald Bailey (New York: Crown Publishing Group, 2002), http://earthlink.net/~jhadler/prec.html.

5. Ragnar E. Löfstedt, "The Swing of the Regulatory Pendulum in Europe: From Precautionary Principle to (Regulatory) Impact Analysis," Working Paper 04–07, AEI–Brookings Joint Center for Regulatory Studies, Washington, DC, March 22, 2004.

6. John Graham, "Risk and Precaution," paper presented at the AEI–Brookings Conference on Risk, Science, and Public Policy, Washington, DC, October 12, 2004, citing David Vogel, "Risk Regulation in Europe and the United States," in *The Yearbook of European Environmental Law*, vol. 3, ed. H. Somsen (New York: Oxford University Press, 2003).

7. John Graham, "The Perils of the Precautionary Principle: Lessons from the American and European Experience," paper presented at the Heritage Foundation Regulatory Forum, Washington, DC, October 20, 2003.

8. Indur M. Goklany, *The Precautionary Principle: A Critical Appraisal of Environmental Risk Assessment* (Washington, DC: Cato Institute, 2001), p. 2.

9. The Wingspread Conference on the Precautionary Principle has some interesting connections to Rachel Carson. One of the conference participants was Peter Montague, Ph.D., cofounder and director of the Environmental Research Foundation, which used the URLs www.rachel.org and www.precaution.org. Montague edited *Rachel's Precaution Reporter*, which billed itself as "the only publication dedicated to tracking the spread of precaution and prevention worldwide." Among the stated goals of *Rachel's Precaution Reporter* were the following: "expand[ing] the application of the precautionary principle from chemicals-and-health to land-use, waste, energy, food-policy and local economic development" and "continu[ing] to develop the precautionary approach into an overarching philosophy for community decision-making." Since February 2009, *Rachel's Precaution Reporter* has been published by the Science and Environmental Health Network, the organization that convened the Wingspread Conference on the Precautionary Principle.

10. Wingspread Conference on the Precautionary Principle, Racine, Wisconsin, January 26, 1998, http://www.sehn.org/wing.html.

11. Ronald Bailey, "Precautionary Tale," *Reason*, April 1999, http://reason.com/archives/1999/04/01/precautionary-tale.

12. "Are Hair Dyes Safe?" *Consumer Reports*, August 1979.

13. Larry Katzenstein, "Food Irradiation: The Story behind the Scare," *American Health* (December 1992): 62–68.

14. Ibid.

15. Larry Katzenstein, "Good Food You Can't Get," *Reader's Digest*, July 1993.

16. "The Truth about Irradiated Meat," *Consumer Reports*, August 2003.

17. Löfstedt, "The Swing of the Regulatory Pendulum."

18. Robert Percival, "Who's Afraid of the Precautionary Principle?" *Pace Environmental Law Review* 23, no. 1 (Winter 2005–2006): 21–81.

19. Löfstedt, "The Swing of the Regulatory Pendulum."

20. Al Gore, "Introduction," in *Silent Spring*, by Rachel Carson (Boston: Houghton Mifflin, 1994), p. i.

21. John Henricksson, *Rachel Carson: The Environmental Movement* (Brookfield, CT: The Millbrook Press, 1991), p. 85.

22. Ibid., p. 86.

23. Levine, *Rachel Carson*, pp. 182–83, 190.

24. Patricia Coit Murphy, *What a Book Can Do: The Publication and Reception of Silent Spring* (Amherst, MA: University of Massachusetts Press, 2005), p. 18.

25. Rachel Carson, *Silent Spring* (Boston: Houghton Mifflin, 1962).

26. Mark Hamilton Lytle, *The Gentle Subversive: Rachel Carson, Silent Spring, and the Rise of the Environmental Movement* (New York: Oxford University Press, 2007), p. 186.

27. Levine, *Rachel Carson*, p. 190.

28. Edwin O. Wilson, "On *Silent Spring*," in *Courage for the Earth: Writers, Scientists, and Activists Celebrate the Life and Writing of Rachel Carson*, ed. Peter Matthiessen (Boston: Houghton Mifflin, 2007).

29. C. J. Van Leeuwen, B. G. Hansen, and J. H. M. deBruijn, "The Management of Industrial Chemicals in the EU," in *Risk Assessment of Chemicals: An Introduction*, 2nd edition, ed. C. J. van Leeuwen and T. G. Vermeire (Dordrecht, Netherlands: Springer, 2007).

30. Ibid, p. 514.

31. Goklany, *The Precautionary Principle*, p. 4.

32. United Nations General Assembly, World Charter for Nature, October 28, 1982, Section 11(b), http://www.un.org/documents/ga/res/37/a37r007.htm.

33. Cass Sunstein, "Throwing Precaution to the Wind: Why the 'Safe' Choice Can Be Dangerous," *Boston Globe*, July 13, 2008.

34. Carson, *Silent Spring*, p. 16.

35. Bruce N. Ames and Lois Swirsky Gold, "The Causes and Prevention of Cancer," in *Risks, Costs and Lives Saved: Getting Better Results from Regulation*, ed. Robert W. Hahn (New York: Oxford University Press, 1996), pp. 22–23.

36. Lytle, *The Gentle Subversive*, p. 220.

37. Cass Sunstein, "The Paralyzing Principle," *Regulation* (Winter 2002–2003): pp. 33, 37.

38. Ibid., p. 34.

39. Ibid.

40. Murphy, *What a Book Can Do*, p. 9.

41. See Roger Meiners, chapter 6, this volume.

42. Carson, *Silent Spring*, p. 221.

43. Ibid., p. 237.

44. Ibid., p. 238.

45. Randy Harris, "Other-Words in *Silent Spring*," in *And No Birds Sing: Rhetorical Analyses of Rachel Carson's* Silent Spring, ed. Craig Waddell (Carbondale, IL: Southern Illinois University Press, 2000), p. 150.

46. Carson, *Silent Spring*, pp. 238–39.

47. Adler, "The Precautionary Principle's Challenge to Progress," p. 202, quoting Soren Holm and John Harris, "Precautionary Principle Stifles Discovery," *Nature* 400 (1999).

48. Charles F. Wilkinson, "The Science and Politics of Pesticides," in *Silent Spring Revisited*, ed. Gino J. Marco, Robert M. Hollingworth, and William Durham (Washington, DC: American Chemical Society, 1987), p. 34.

49. Katzenstein, "Food Irradiation," p. 23.

50. Robert N. Proctor, *Cancer Wars: How Politics Shapes What We Know and Don't Know About Cancer* (New York: Basic Books, 1995), p. 160.

51. Ibid.

52. Kenneth Smith, "Rachel Carson's Curse: How Safety Got So Dangerous," *Washington Times*, February 10, 2000.

53. Jon Hamilton, "A Chemical Conundrum: How Dangerous Is Dioxin?" National Public Radio, December 28, 2010, transcript.

54. Ibid.

55. Ibid.

56. Ibid.

57. Wingspread Conference 1998.

58. Lytle, *The Gentle Subversive*, p. 146.

59. Carson, *Silent Spring*, p. 8.

60. Ibid., p. 85.

61. Ibid., p. 70.

62. Ibid., p. 112.

63. Ibid., p. 227.

64. The article by Cross is the only other reference I encountered that makes a connection between *Silent Spring* and creation of the precautionary principle. But Cross's

discussion of that link is limited to the following sentence: "The [precautionary principle] can be traced back to Rachel Carson's *Silent Spring*, the environmentalist bible that warned against human tampering with nature with particular reference to pesticides."

65. Conko, "The Precautionary Principle."

66. Frank B. Cross, "Paradoxical Perils of the Precautionary Principle," *Washington & Lee Law Review* 53 (1996): 851.

67. Carson, *Silent Spring*, pp. 2–3.

68. Lytle, *The Gentle Subversive*, p. 214.

69. Ronald Bailey, "Silent Spring at 40: Rachel Carson's Classic Is Not Aging Well," *Reason*, June 12, 2002, http://reason.com/archives/2002/06/12/silent-spring-at-40/print.

70. Lytle, *The Gentle Subversive*, p. 216.

71. Michelle Malkin and Michael Fumento, *Rachel's Folly: The End of Chlorine* (Washington, DC: Competitive Enterprise Institute, 1996).

72. Carol Gartner, "When Science Writing Becomes Literary Art," in *And No Birds Sing: Rhetorical Analyses of Rachel Carson's* Silent Spring, ed. Craig Waddell (Carbondale, IL: Southern Illinois University Press, 2000), p. 110.

73. Goklany, *The Precautionary Principle*, p. 14.

74. Ibid.

75. Malkin and Fumento, *Rachel's Folly*.

76. Goklany, *The Precautionary Principle*, p. 25.

77. Ibid., p. 27.

78. "NCQA Report: Autism Fears Suspected as Children's Vaccinations Decrease in Private Plans," National Committee for Quality Assurance news release, October 13, 2010, http://www.ncqa.org/tabid/1259/Default.aspx.

79. Will Dunham, "Measles Outbreak Hits 127 People in 15 States," Associated Press, July 9, 2008. See also Steve Karnowski, "Autism/Vaccine Fears Cause Measles Outbreak in Minn. Somalis," Associated Press, April 3, 2011.

Chapter 12

1. The author appreciates the valuable research assistance of Cason Schmit.

2. See, generally, Edith Efron, *The Apocalyptics: Cancer and the Big Lie* (New York: Simon and Shuster, 1984).

3. Mark Sagoff, "The Principles of Federal Pollution Control Law," *Minnesota Law Review* 71 (1986): 19, 20, n. 5.

4. See, for example, Michael S. Pak, "Environmentalism Then and Now: From Fears to Opportunities, 1970–2010," *Environmental Science and Technology* 45 (2011): 5–9.

5. Ibid.

6. Julian Simon, *The State of Humanity* (Boston: Basil Blackwell, 1995).

7. Ted Nordhaus and Michael Shellenger, *Break Through: From the Death of Environmentalism to the Politics of Possibility* (Boston: Houghton Mifflin, 2007), p. 130.

8. Rachel Carson, *Silent Spring* (Boston: Houghton Mifflin, 1962), pp. 1–3.

9. Ibid., p. 3.

10. See Donald R. Roberts and Richard Tren, chapter 8, this volume.

11. Ira L. Baldwin, "Chemicals and Pests," *Science* 137 (1962): 1042–43.

12. See Roger Meiners, chapter 6, this volume.

13. Carson, *Silent Spring*, p. 8.

14. Ibid., p. 6.

15. Ibid.

16. Gregg Easterbrook, *A Moment on the Earth: The Coming Age of Environmental Optimism* (New York: Penguin Books, 1995), p. 85.

17. Carson, *Silent Spring*, p. 10.

18. See, for example, Frances Gies and Joseph Gies, *Life in a Medieval Village* (New York: Harper and Row, 1990).

19. Alex Gregory, cartoon published in the *New Yorker*, May 22, 2006, http://www.condenaststore.com/-sp/Something-s-just-not-right-our-air-is-clean-our-water-is-pure-we-all-ge-Prints_i8545559_.htm.

20. Bruce N. Ames, Renae Magaw, and Lois Swirsky Gold, "Ranking Carcinogenic Hazards," *Science* 236 (1987): 271; and Lois Swirsky Gold, Thomas H. Slone, Bonnie R. Stern, Neela B. Manley, and Bruce N. Annes, "Rodent Carcinogens: Setting Priorities," *Science* 258 (1992): 261.

21. Carson, *Silent Spring*, p. 16.

22. Aaron Wildavsky, *Searching for Safety* (New Brunswick, NJ: Transaction Publishers, 1988), p. 25.

23. Peter L. Bernstein, *Against the Gods: The Remarkable Story of Risk* (New York: John Wiley and Sons, 1996).

24. See H. W. Lewis, *Technological Risk* (New York: W. H. Norton, 1990), pp. 22–23.

25. Keith Schneider, "As Earth Day Turns 25, Life Gets Complicated," *New York Times*, April 16, 1995.

26. Carson, *Silent Spring*, p. 224.

27. Ibid., p. 242.

28. Ibid.

29. Ibid.

30. National Research Council, *Science and Judgment in Risk Assessment* (Washington, DC: National Academy Press, 1994), p. 31.

31. Gary Flamm, "Critical Assessment of Carcinogenic Risk Policy," *Regulatory Toxicology and Pharmacology* 9, no. 3 (1989): 218.

32. Cass R. Sunstein, "Is the Clean Air Act Unconstitutional?" *Michigan Law Review* 98 (1999): 315.

33. Stephen Breyer, *Breaking the Vicious Circle: Toward Effective Risk Regulation* (Cambridge, MA: Harvard University Press, 1993), p. 11.

34. Flamm, "Critical Assessment," p. 218.

35. See, for example, Jerry M. Melillo and Ellis B. Cowling, "Reactive Nitrogen and Public Policies for Environmental Protection," *Ambio* 31 (2002): 150; and Gary Kroll, "The 'Silent Springs' of Rachel Carson: Mass Media and the Origins of Modern Environmentalism," *Public Understanding of Science* 10 (2001): 403.

36. John P. Dwyer, "The Pathology of Symbolic Legislation," *Ecology Law Quarterly* 17 (1990): 233.

37. Ibid., pp. 277–82.

38. John M. Mendeloff, *The Dilemma of Toxic Substance Regulation: How Overregulation Causes Underregulation* (Cambridge, MA: MIT Press, 1988).

39. As shown by Meiners and Morriss, chapter 9 this volume, the groundwork for the Delaney Clause was laid in hearings held earlier in the decade, which raised the specter of rampant dangers in our foods from agricultural chemicals.

40. *Food Additive Amendments of 1958*, Public Law 85–929 § 4, 72 Stat. 1784, 1786 (1958), codified at *U.S. Code* § 341 (repealed in 1996).

41. *Color Additive Amendments of 1960*, Public Law 86–618, 74 Stat. 397 (1960), codified at *U.S. Code* § 376.

42. *Animal Drug Amendments of 1968*, Public Law 90–399, 82 Stat. 342 (1968), codified at *U.S. Code* § 360b.

43. Zygmunt J. B. Plater, "Environmental Law and Three Economies: Navigating a Sprawling Field of Study, Practice, and Societal Governance in Which Everything Is Connected to Everything Else," *Harvard Environmental Law Review* 23 (1999): 384.

44. Richard A. Merrill, "FDA's Implementation of the Delaney Clause: Repudiation of Congressional Choice or Reasoned Adaptation to Scientific Progress?" *Yale Journal on Regulation* 5 (1988): 13.

45. Nicholas Wade, "Delaney Anti-Cancer Clause: Scientists Debate an Article of Faith," *Science* 177 (1972): 588–91.

46. Merrill, "FDA's Implementation of the Delaney Clause," p. 13.

47. David A. Kessler, "Food Safety: Revising the Statute," *Science* 223 (1984): 1034.

48. *Public Citizen v. Young*, 831 F.2d 1108, 1119 (D.C. Cir. 1987).

49. Merrill, "FDA's Implementation of the Delaney Clause," p. 15–16 (citing Hueper, "Potential Role of Non-Nutritive Food Additives and Contaminants as Environmental Carcinogens," *A.M.A. Archives Pathology* 62 [1957]: 222–24).

50. Gold et al., "Rodent Carcinogens," p. 261.

51. Philip H. Abelson, "Testing for Carcinogens with Rodents," *Science* 249 (1990): 1357.

52. International Agency for Research on Cancer, *Agents Classified by the IARC Monographs,* Volumes 1–101, accessed April 13, 2011, http://monographs.iarc.fr/ENG/Classification/index.php.

53. Bruce Ames, "Cancer and Diet (Letter)," *Science* 224 (1984): 668.

54. Andrew J. Miller, "The Food Quality Protection Act of 1996: Science and Law at a Crossroads," *Duke Environmental Law & Policy Forum* 7 (1997): 400.

55. James Smart, "All the Stars in the Heavens Were in the Right Places: The Passage of the Food Quality Protection Act of 1996," *Stanford Environmental Law Journal* 17 (1998): 285.

56. *Public Citizen v. Young*, 1109.

57. Carl Winter, director, Foodsafe Program of the University of California, Testimony on the Food Quality Protection Act of 1995 before the Subcommittee on Health and Environment of the House Energy and Commerce Committee, 104th Cong., June 7, 1995, 34–35.

58. Gold et al., "Rodent Carcinogens," p. 262.

59. National Research Council, *Regulating Pesticides in Food: The Delaney Paradox* (Washington, DC: National Academy Press, 1986).

60. Samuel M. Cohen et al., "Delaney Reform (Letter)," *Science* 268 (1995): 1829–30.

61. Quoted in John Walsh, "Environment: Focus on DDT, the 'Uninvited Additive,'" *Science* 166 (1969): 977.

62. Smart, "All the Stars in the Heavens," pp. 283–84.

63. Ibid., p. 283.

64. *Les v. Reilly*, 968 F.2d 985 (9th Cir. 1992).

65. Environmental Protection Agency, *The Benefits and Costs of the Clean Air Act from 1990 to 2020* (Washington, DC: EPA Office of Air and Radiation, 2011), http://www.epa.gov/air/sect812/feb11/fullreport.pdf.

66. *Clean Air Act* §109(b)(1), codified at *U.S. Code* 42 §7409(b)(1).

67. *Lead Indus. v. EPA*, 647 F.2d 1130, 1153 (D.C. Cir. 1980).

68. *Whitman v. American Trucking Associations*, 531 U.S. 457, 464–70 (2001).

69. Ibid., p. 457.

70. *Lead Indus v. EPA*, p. 1150, quoting S. Rep. 91–1196, 1970, pp. 2–3.

71. See Sen. Edmund Muskie, member, Statement on Clean Air Act Amendments of 1977 at hearing of the Subcommittee on Environmental Pollution of the Senate Committee on the Environment and Public Works, 95th Cong., 1st sess., pt. 3, p. 8 (1977).

72. William K. Reilly, "foreword," in *Sensitive Populations and Environmental Standards*, by Robert D. Friedman (Washington, DC: Conservation Foundation, 1981), p. vii.

73. Cary Coglianese and Gary E. Marchant, "Shifting Sands: The Limits of Science in Setting Risk Standards," *Pennsylvania Law Review* 152 (2004): 1283–90.

74. See Muskie, Statement on Clean Air Act Amendments of 1977.

75. See Clean Air Act Amendments of 1977: Hearings before the Subcommittee on Environmental Pollution of the Senate Committee on Environment and Public Works, 95th Cong., 1st sess., (1977), H. Rep. 95–294, pp. 111, 127.

76. Senator Muskie, *Congressional Record* 123 (1977): 18,463.

77. H. Rep. 95–294, p. 127.

78. Christopher T. Giovinazzo, "Defending Overstatement: the Symbolic Clean Air Act and Carbon Dioxide," *Harvard Environmental Law Review* 30 (2006): 99; and James A. Henderson, Jr., and Richard N. Pearson, "Implementing Federal Environmental Policies: The Limits of Aspirational Commands," *Columbia Law Review* 78 (1978): 1429.

79. *National Wildlife Federation v. Gorsuch*, 683 F.2d 156, 178 (D.C. Cir. 1982).

80. Coglianese and Marchant, "Shifting Sands."

81. Ibid.

82. See, for example, Sagoff, "The Principles of Federal Pollution Control Law," p. 86 (collecting examples).

83. *Clean Water Act*, §101(a).

84. Id. §101(a)(1).

85. Id. §101(a)(3).

86. Sagoff, "The Principles of Federal Pollution Control Law," p. 87.

87. *American Petroleum Institute v. EPA*, 540 F.2d 1023, 1028 (10th Cir. 1976).

88. Congressional Research Service, "History of the Water Pollution Control Act Amendments of 1972," ser. 1, 93rd Cong., 1st sess. (1972), p. 164.

89. Ibid., pp. 161–62.

90. Aaron Wildavsky, "Economy and Environment/Rationality and Ritual," 29 *Stanford Law Review* 183, 191 (1976).

91. National Commission on Water Quality, Report to Congress by the National Commission on Water Quality, Washington, DC (1976), pp. 29–30.

92. John Hernandez, deputy administrator, EPA, Testimony on the Clean Water Act Amendments of 1982, S. 777 and S. 2652, before the Subcommittee on Environmental Protection of the Senate Committee on the Environment and Public Works, 97th Cong., 2d sess., 1982, pp. 9–10.

93. Robert L. Glicksman and Matthew R. Batzel, "Science, Politics, Law, and the Arc of the Clean Water Act: The Role of Assumptions in the Adoption of a Pollution Control Landmark," *Washington University Journal of Law and Policy* 32 (2010): 105.

94. Ibid., pp. 105–109.

95. See, for example, Robert W. Adler, Jessica C. Landman, and Diane M. Cameron, *The Clean Water Act: 20 Years Later* (Washington, DC: Island Press, 1993).

96. William H. Rodgers, Jr., "The Seven Statutory Wonders of U.S. Environmental Law: Origins and Morphology," *Loyola of Los Angeles Law Review* 27 (1994): 1016.

97. Miguel A. Receurda, "Dangerous Interpretations of the Precautionary Principle and the Foundational Values of European Food Law: Risk Versus Risk," *Journal of Food Law and Policy* 4 (2008): 5.

98. See, for example, David Santillo and Paul Johnston, "Is There a Role for Risk Assessment within Precautionary Legislation?" *Human and Ecological Risk Assessment* 5 (1999): 930–31.

99. Gary E. Marchant and Kenneth L. Mossman, *Arbitrary and Capricious: The Precautionary Principle in the European Union Courts* (Washington, DC: AEI Press, 2004).

100. *Pfizer Animal Health SA v. Council of the European Union,* Case T-13/99, 1999 E.C.R. II-1961 (Celex No. 699B00113) (President of Court of First Instance), p. 76.

101. *Commission v. Germany,* Case C-184/97, 1999 E.C.R. I-7837, ¶27 (opinion of Advocate General).

102. Gary E. Marchant, "From General Policy to Legal Rule: The Aspirations and Limitations of the Precautionary Principle," *Environmental Health Perspectives* 111 (2003): 1802.

103. Frank B. Cross, "Paradoxical Perils of the Precautionary Principle," *Washington and Lee Law Review* 53 (1996): 851.

104. See Marchant and Mossman, *Arbitrary and Capricious,* p. 101.

105. Flamm, "Critical Assessment of Carcinogenic Risk Policy," p. 218.

106. Martin W. Lewis, *Green Delusions: An Environmentalist Critique of Radical Environmentalism* (Durham, NC: Duke University Press, 1992), p. 250.

Index

Page references followed by t or f indicate tables and figures, respectively.

Adams, Douglas, 39
adaptation, 144
Adler, Jonathan H., 4–5, 6, 229, 246, 343
Aedes aegypti control, 177, 181–82
aerial crop dusting, 204, 235, 239
aflatoxin, 265
Africa, 169, 184
Agency for Toxic Substances and Disease Registry, 134
Agricultural Adjustment Act of 1933, 206
agricultural prices, 205–8
agricultural use of pesticides, 188
　Carson's awareness, 210–12
　DDT as primary target of critics, 223–27
　DDT battle in context, 225–27
　federal government's role in agriculture, 205–8
　growth of pesticide use, 208–10
　House Select Committee hearings, 202, 215–23
　second agricultural revolution and, 202–5
　struggle for regulatory authority, 4, 201–2, 212–23, 225–27
Agriculture, U.S. Department of (USDA), 4, 201–2, 206–8, 212–15, 225, 230–31, 233
　defense of DDT, 266–67
　FIFRA and, 214
Aiden, Erez Lieberman, 34
Alfred Knopf, 25
alien invasive species, 154
American Cancer Society, 125
American Ornithologists' Union, 107

American political thought and action, 16
American politics, corruption of, 64
American religious history, 63–65
the Americas
　DDT and malaria control, 182–83
Ames, Bruce, 83, 84, 254–55, 274, 279
　Science article, 280
aminotriazole, 97
Andrewartha, Herbert, 145
animal drugs, 278
Arctic National Wildlife Refuge, Alaska, 79
Arizona, 238
Arkansas
　malaria cases, 176
Army, U.S.
　joint statement of policy on DDT use, 211–12
arsenic-based pesticides, 30, 38, 41, 50, 109–10, 131–32, 209, 213. *see also* lead arsenate
　apples and, 42, 209, 213, 231
　in tobacco farming, 122, 219
Asia, 185
Audubon Society, 3, 16, 107
　Christmas Bird Census, 101–8, 117
　DDT conference, 211
Audubon Society, National, 38, 101

baby food, 218, 222
Bacillus thuringiensis, 116, 147, 157
Bailey, Ronald
　Silent Spring at 40, 267
balance of nature, 3, 6, 86–88, 91–92
　concerns, 50–51, 217
　"DDT and the Balance of Nature," 44–45
　Linnaeus and economy of nature, 141
　metaphor, 140–43, 163–65
　paradigm, 143–46, 158–59

Contributors

Jonathan H. Adler is Johan Verheij Memorial Professor of Law at Case Western Reserve University School of Law and Director of the Center for Business Law & Regulation at the Case Western Reserve University School of Law, where he teaches courses in environmental, administrative, and constitutional law. He is the author or editor of four books on environmental policy, and his articles have appeared in publications ranging from the *Harvard Environmental Law Review* and *Supreme Court Economic Review* to the *Wall Street Journal* and *Washington Post*. Adler is a contributing editor to National Review Online and a regular contributor to the popular legal blog, "The Volokh Conspiracy."

In 2004, Adler received the Paul M. Bator Award, given annually by the Federalist Society for Law and Policy Studies to an academic under age 40 for excellence in teaching, scholarship, and commitment to students; in 2007, the Case Western Reserve University Law Alumni Association awarded Professor Adler its annual "Distinguished Teacher Award." He has appeared on numerous radio and television programs, ranging from Public Broadcasting System's *News Hour with Jim Lehrer* and National Public Radio's *Talk of the Nation* to the Fox News Channel's *O'Reilly Factor* and *Entertainment Tonight*. Prior to joining the faculty at Case Western, Adler clerked for the Honorable David B. Sentelle on the U.S. Court of Appeals for the District of Columbia Circuit and directed environmental studies at the Competitive Enterprise Institute. He holds a BA magna cum laude from Yale University and a JD summa cum laude from the George Mason University School of Law.

Pierre Desrochers holds a PhD in geography from the University of Montreal and is an associate professor of geography at the University of Toronto. His main research interests are economic development, technical innovation, business-environment interactions, and energy and food policy. He has authored several peer-reviewed pieces on these and other topics published in various disciplinary and interdisciplinary journals such as *The Journal of Economic Behavior and Organization, Environmental and Resource Economics, Business History Review, Journal of Economic Geography, Geographical Journal, Industrial and Corporate Change, Environmental Politics,* the *Journal of Industrial Ecology,* and the *Journal of Cleaner Production.* He is affiliated with several policy institutes and is a frequent contributor to both the English and French-Canadian media.

Nathan Gregory is currently a research ecologist with the Institute for Wildlife Studies, a nonprofit conservation organization in Arcata, California. He earned his PhD in ecology and evolutionary biology from Princeton University in 2009 and was a Princeton Environmental Institute/Science, Technology, and Environmental Policy Fellow. Gregory's research examined how traditional pastoralism—specifically anthropogenic fire and livestock grazing—shapes bird communities in East African savannas. After completing his degree, Gregory continued at Princeton through 2010 as a postdoctoral research fellow and lecturer in ecology and conservation biology. Prior to starting his graduate work, Gregory worked for local and federal management agencies on invasive species and wildlife issues in Colorado, Hawaii, and Alaska. He was raised in Denver, Colorado, and earned his bachelor's degree in environmental biology at the University of Colorado at Boulder.

Lawrence Katzenstein is a science writer and editor who has worked on staff at *Consumer Reports* and *American Health* magazines. He has master's degrees in biology and journalism and is currently the science and publications editor at Albert Einstein College of Medicine in New York City. He has written articles for *Smithsonian* and the *New York Times* and published opinion pieces in the *Wall Street Journal* and the *Washington Times.* Among his books are *Living With Heart Disease: An AARP Guide* (2007) and *Taking Charge of Arthritis,* a Reader's Digest book published in 2001.

Wallace Kaufman's hands-on environmental work includes serving as president of three statewide environmental nonprofits, developing and applying environmental covenants to several thousand acres of land, mediating property disputes, consulting on ecotourism and land development, and serving on the boards of land trusts. He has also taught, lectured, and written about environmental history. He is a former resident adviser for housing and land reform to the government of Kazakhstan and has taught property valuation and journalism throughout Central Asia. In *No Turning Back* (Basic Books, 1995), he traced the history of environmental thinking. In *Coming Out of the Woods* (Perseus Books, 2000), he tells the story of building his own home in a forest and living there for more than two decades. His latest book is *Invasive Plants* (Stackpole, 2007), coauthored with his ecologist daughter, Dr. Sylvan Ramsey Kaufman.

Gary Marchant is the Lincoln Professor of Emerging Technologies, Law and Ethics at the Sandra Day O'Connor College of Law at Arizona State University. He is also a professor of life sciences; executive director of the ASU Center for Law, Science and Innovation; and associate director of the Origins Project, all at ASU. Marchant has a PhD in genetics from the University of British Columbia, a master's in public policy from the Kennedy School of Government, and a JD from Harvard Law School. Prior to joining the ASU faculty in 1999, he was a partner in the Washington, D.C., office of the law firm Kirkland & Ellis, where his practice focused on regulatory issues. Marchant teaches and researches in the subject areas of environmental law, risk assessment and risk management, genetics and the law, biotechnology law, food and drug law, legal aspects of nanotechnology, and science and technology.

Roger E. Meiners is the Goolsby Distinguished Professor of economics and law at the University of Texas at Arlington and a senior fellow at the Property and Environment Research Center in Bozeman, Montana. His PhD in economics is from Virginia Tech; his law degree is from the University of Miami. Meiners has also been a faculty member at Texas A&M University, Emory University, and Clemson University and was a regional director for the Federal Trade Commission. His research focuses on common law and market solutions to environmental issues. Meiners has published numerous books, including *Taking the Environment Seriously* (Rowman & Littlefield, 1993), with Bruce Yandle, and *Government v. the Environment* (Rowman & Littlefield, 2002), with Don Leal, and articles in various popular and scholarly economics and law journals.

Andrew P. Morriss is D. Paul Jones, Jr. & Charlene A. Jones Chairholder in Law and Professor of Business at the University of Alabama, Tuscaloosa. He has authored or coauthored more than 50 book chapters, scholarly articles, and books. These include *The False Promise of Green Energy* (Cato, 2011), with Roger Meiners, William T. Bogart, and Andrew Dorchak, and *Regulation by Litigation* (Yale,

2008), with Bruce Yandle and Andrew Dorchak. In addition, he is editorial board chair of the *Cayman Financial Review*. He serves as a research fellow at the New York University Center for Labor and Employment Law; a research scholar at the Regulatory Studies Center, George Washington University; a senior fellow at the Property and Environment Research Center; a senior scholar at the Mercatus Center at George Mason University; and a senior fellow for the Houston-based Institute for Energy Research.

Morriss received his AB from Princeton University, a JD and master's in public affairs from the University of Texas at Austin, and a PhD in economics from the Massachusetts Institute of Technology. After law school, Morriss clerked for U.S. District Judge Barefoot Sanders Jr. in the Northern District of Texas and worked for two years at Texas Rural Legal Aid in Hereford and Plainview, Texas. He has also taught at Case Western Reserve University, Cleveland, Ohio; the University of Illinois at Urbana-Champaign; and Universidad Francisco Marroquin in Guatemala, as well as in the Asia Institute for Political Economy in Hong Kong.

Robert H. Nelson is the author of many book chapters and journal articles and of eight books: *The New Holy Wars: Economic Religion versus Environmental Religion in Contemporary America* (Penn State University Press, 2010); *Private Neighborhoods and the Transformation of Local Government* (Urban Institute Press, 2005); *Economics as Religion: From Samuelson to Chicago and Beyond* (Penn State University Press, 2001); *A Burning Issue: A Case for Abolishing the U.S. Forest Service* (Rowman & Littlefield, 2000); *Public Lands and Private Rights: The Failure of Scientific Management* (Rowman & Littlefield, 1995); *Reaching for Heaven on Earth: The Theological Meaning of Economics* (Rowman & Littlefield, 1991); *The Making of Federal Coal Policy* (Duke University Press, 1983); and *Zoning and Property Rights* (MIT Press, 1977). *The New Holy Wars* was the 2010 Winner of the Grand Prize of the Eric Hoffer Book Award for the best book of the year by an independent publisher; and also silver medal winner for "Finance, Investment, Economics" at the 2010 Independent Publisher Book Awards.

Nelson has written widely in publications for broad audiences. He worked in the Office of Policy Analysis of the Office of the Secretary of the Interior from 1975 to 1993. He has been a visiting scholar at the Brookings Institution, visiting senior fellow at the Woods Hole Oceanographic Institution, research associate at the

Center for Applied Social Sciences of The University of Zimbabwe, visiting professor at Keio University in Tokyo, visiting professor at the Universidad Torcuato Di Tella in Buenos Aires, and visiting professor at the School of Economics of the University of the Philippines in Manila. He holds a PhD in economics from Princeton University.

Donald R. Roberts has had two careers. He received his doctoral degree in 1973 from the University of Texas School of Public Health. For years, he conducted research on malaria and arbovirus vectors in the Amazon Basin of Brazil. Focal points of research were the epidemiology and dynamics of malaria transmission and methods of malaria control with special emphasis on how DDT functioned to control indoor malaria transmission.

In 1980, Roberts became chief of the Department of Entomology at the Walter Reed Army Institute of Research in Washington, D.C. There he directed pioneering research that produced an assay for detecting malaria parasites in mosquitoes. He later moved to the Uniformed Services University of the Health Sciences (USUHS) in Bethesda, Maryland, where he served as a uniformed member of the faculty until his retirement from the Army at the end of 1987. He continued as a civilian member of the faculty there until his retirement as a professor of tropical public health in 2007.

As an academician, Roberts specialized in research on applications of remote sensing and geographic information systems (GIS) technologies to the study of malaria in many countries. He created and directed a center for applications of remote sensing and GIS to public health. He also continued to study how DDT functions as a spatial repellent to keep mosquitoes from entering houses and transmitting disease. This research was the topic of a major National Institutes of Health grant to screen compounds as potential replacements for DDT in malaria control programs. After retiring, he was awarded U.S. Medicine's Frank Brown Berry Prize for exceptional contributions to healthcare by a federal healthcare professional.

In recent years, he became intensely involved in advocacy for indoor residual spraying of DDT and other insecticides for malaria control. Roberts, with many others, campaigned to prevent a DDT ban through negotiations for the international persistent organic pollutants (the Stockholm Convention) treaty. DDT was not banned and is presently being used for control of malaria.

Roberts has published more than 120 peer-reviewed papers. He continues his work as an advocate for public health insecticides to include DDT for control of malaria and other important human disease and for increased investment of public funds to find a fully adequate replacement for DDT.

Hiroko Shimizu is a policy consultant who holds a master's in public policy from the University of Osaka and a BA in ancient Chinese history from Gakushuin University. She has studied and worked at several academic institutions and private companies in Canada, Japan, China, and the United States, where she was, among others things, an international fellow at the Johns Hopkins University Institute for Policy Studies and a research fellow at the Property and Environment Research Center. Fluent in four languages (Japanese, Mandarin, French, and English), Shimizu is the author of several policy reports on the nonprofit sector, food policy, and corporate social responsibility. She is currently working on a book on the "food miles" and locavorism controversies.

Richard Tren is a cofounder and chairman of Africa Fighting Malaria, a malaria policy and advocacy group with offices in South Africa and Washington, D.C. He works closely with malaria control programs, scientists, and researchers in sub-Saharan African countries, assisting in advocacy efforts and defending the use of insecticides in public health programs.

Tren has been widely published in the print media in the United States, Europe, and Africa with pieces in *Investor's Business Daily*, *New York Post*, *Washington Times*, *Wall Street Journal Europe*, *USA Today*, and *Business Day*. He has been published in the peer-reviewed scientific literature, including *PLoS One*, *Malaria Journal*, *Research and Reports in Tropical Medicine*, and *Environmental Health Perspectives* and has written many scholarly reports for think tanks and policy institutes in the United States, Europe, and South Africa. In 2010, he coauthored with Donald Roberts, *The Excellent Powder, DDT's Political and Scientific History*. Tren was the recipient of the Competitive Enterprise Institute's 2009 Julian Simon Memorial Award in recognition for his work on DDT and public health. He received his BS (Honors) in economics from the University of St. Andrews in Scotland and a master's in environmental and resource economics from University College London.

Cato Institute

Founded in 1977, the Cato Institute is a public policy research foundation dedicated to broadening the parameters of policy debate to allow consideration of more options that are consistent with the traditional American principles of limited government, individual liberty, and peace. To that end, the Institute strives to achieve greater involvement of the intelligent, concerned lay public in questions of policy and the proper role of government.

The Institute is named for *Cato's Letters*, libertarian pamphlets that were widely read in the American Colonies in the early 18th century and played a major role in laying the philosophical foundation for the American Revolution.

Despite the achievement of the nation's Founders, today virtually no aspect of life is free from government encroachment. A pervasive intolerance for individual rights is shown by government's arbitrary intrusions into private economic transactions and its disregard for civil liberties.

To counter that trend, the Cato Institute undertakes an extensive publications program that addresses the complete spectrum of policy issues. Books, monographs, and shorter studies are commissioned to examine the federal budget, Social Security, regulation, military spending, international trade, and myriad other issues. Major policy conferences are held throughout the year, from which papers are published thrice yearly in the *Cato Journal*. The Institute also publishes the quarterly magazine *Regulation*.

In order to maintain its independence, the Cato Institute accepts no government funding. Contributions are received from foundations, corporations, and individuals, and other revenue is generated from the sale of publications. The Institute is a nonprofit, tax-exempt, educational foundation under Section 501(c)3 of the Internal Revenue Code.

CATO INSTITUTE
1000 Massachusetts Ave., N.W.
Washington, D.C. 20001
www.cato.org